W9-AEI-097

03062956

Title Withdrawn

BIOGRAPHICAL ENCYCLOPEDIA OF
20th-Century
World Leaders

BIOGRAPHICAL ENCYCLOPEDIA OF
20th-Century
World Leaders

Volume 2

Clinton – Henderson

Editor
John Powell
Pennsylvania State University, Erie

Marshall Cavendish
New York • London • Toronto • Sydney

Marshall Cavendish Corporation
99 White Plains Road
Tarrytown, New York 10591-9001

© 2000 Marshall Cavendish Corporation
Printed in the United States of America
09 08 07 06 05 04 03 02 01 00   5 4 3 2 1

Library of Congress Cataloging-in-Publication Data

Biographical encyclopedia of 20th-century world leaders / John Powell
p. cm.
   v. cm.
   Includes bibliographical references and index.
   1. Heads of state Biography Encyclopedias.   2. Statesmen Biography Encyclopedias.   3. Biography 20th century Encyclopedias.   I. Powell, John, 1954-   . II. Title:
Biographical encyclopedia of twentieth-century world leaders
   ISBN 0-7614-7129-4 (set)
   ISBN 0-7614-7131-6 (vol. 2)
   D412.B56   1999
   920'.009'04—dc21

                           99-34462
                           CIP

∞ This paper meets the requirements of ANSI/NISO Z39.48-1992 (R1997)
Permanence of Paper for Publications and Documents in Libraries and Archives

CONTENTS

Key to Pronunciation

As an aid to users of the *Biographical Encyclopedia of 20th-Century World Leaders*, guides to pronunciation for all profiled leaders have been provided with the first mention of the name in each entry. These guides are rendered in an easy-to-use phonetic manner. Stressed syllables are indicated by capital letters.

Letters of the English language, particularly vowels, are pronounced in different ways depending on the context. Below are letters and combinations of letters used in the phonetic guides to represent various sounds, along with examples of words in which those sounds appear and corresponding guides for their pronunciation.

Symbols	Pronounced As In	Spelled Phonetically
a	answer, laugh	AN-sihr, laf
ah	father, hospital	FAH-thur, HAHS-pih-tul
aw	awful, caught	AW-ful, kawt
ay	blaze, fade, waiter	blayz, fayd, WAYT-ur
ch	beach, chimp	beech, chihmp
eh	bed, head, said	behd, hehd, sehd
ee	believe, leader	bee-LEEV, LEED-ur
ew	boot, loose	bewt, lews
g	beg, disguise, get	behg, dihs-GIZ, geht
i	buy, height, surprise	bi, hit, sur-PRIZ
ih	bitter, pill	bih-TUR, pihl
j	digit, edge, jet	DIH-jiht, ehj, jeht
k	cat, kitten, hex	kat, KIH-tehn, hehks
o	cotton, hot	CO-tuhn, hot
oh	below, coat, note	bee-LOH, coht, noht
oo	good, look	good, look
ow	couch, how	kowch, how
oy	boy, coin	boy, koyn
s	cellar, save, scent	SEL-ur, sayv, sehnt
sh	issue, shop	IH-shew, shop
uh	about, enough	uh-BOWT, ee-NUHF
ur	earth, letter	urth, LEH-tur
y	useful, young	YEWS-ful, yuhng
z	business, zest	BIHZ-ness, zest
zh	vision	VIH-zhuhn

BIOGRAPHICAL ENCYCLOPEDIA OF
20th-Century
World Leaders

Bill Clinton

Born: August 19, 1946; Hope, Arkansas

President of the United States (took office 1993)

William Jefferson Clinton (WIHL-yuhm JEH-fur-suhn KLIHN-tuhn) was born William Jefferson Blythe III. His father died in an automobile accident before he was born. His mother later remarried to Roger Clinton, and in high school Clinton took his stepfather's last name. After graduating from high school in Hot Springs, Arkansas, Clinton attended college at Georgetown University in Washington, D.C. He graduated with a degree in international affairs in 1968 and went to Oxford University as a Rhodes Scholar for two years. He attended Yale Law School, graduating in 1973. Upon graduation, he took a position as a professor of law at the University of Arkansas. In 1975, he married Hillary Rodham, a Wellesley College graduate, whom he had met while both were in law school. They had one daughter, Chelsea, born in 1980.

Arkansas Politics

In 1974 Clinton unsuccessfully ran for a seat in the U.S. House of Representatives. In 1976, he was elected attorney general of Arkansas, and he used that position as a springboard for his first election as governor two years later. After losing his bid for reelection in 1980, he regained the office in 1982 and was reelected three more times. He left the office to assume the U.S. presidency in 1993. During his terms as governor, Clinton led the reform of the public education system in Arkansas and encouraged a policy of industrial growth through favorable tax policies. He became a leader among centrists in the Democratic Party and earned a reputation for being pragmatic.

Ascent to the Presidency

In 1992, Clinton won the nomination of the Democrats for the U.S. presidency. Together, he and running mate Al Gore waged a strong campaign. Clinton used his ability to communicate with audiences in an informal, conversational style to great advantage. When he won the election, he became, at the age of forty-six, the youngest man elected president since John F. Kennedy.

Clinton's first term as president included a combination of success, failure, and scandal. He pushed through Congress the Family and Medical Leave Act, the North American Free Trade Agreement (NAFTA), and the General Agreement on Trade and Tariffs (GATT). He signed a major welfare reform package and minor reforms

Bill Clinton *(Library of Congress)*

333

Bill Clinton being sworn in as U.S. president in January of 1993. *(Library of Congress)*

gress in 1994. The drafting of the reform package had been spearheaded by his wife, Hillary. Then, later in 1994, the Republican Party won control of both houses of Congress from the president's Democratic Party.

Clinton's political fortunes began to look especially bleak because of personal problems. He and his wife were the subjects of an official investigation by an independent counsel into their investments in a failed real estate deal in Arkansas—the Whitewater case. More negative attention was focused on the president concerning his 1993 firing of employees in the

in health insurance legislation. He negotiated with Congress a program to reduce federal budget deficits through modest increases in taxes and spending reductions. His primary legislative failure came when a proposal for major reform of the American health care system—a cornerstone of his campaign in 1992—was defeated in Con-

White House Travel Office. In January, 1996, a lawsuit by former Arkansas state employee Paula Jones alleging that Clinton had harassed her sexually was allowed to move forward; ultimately, Clinton would agree to a settlement. As Clinton's first term came to a close, he seemed vulnerable to defeat in his bid for reelection.

The Presidential Election of 1992

The election of Bill Clinton as president in 1992 marked the end of an unusual campaign. At the beginning of the year, incumbent President George Bush appeared to have a commanding position for reelection, especially because of the recent American victory in the 1991 Persian Gulf War. His lead was so commanding that a number of leading Democrats, most notably Texas senator Lloyd Bentsen and New York governor Mario Cuomo, decided not to run, and Clinton won the nomination. An independent

candidate, billionaire H. Ross Perot, entered the election campaign. By spring, Perot's campaign had gained momentum—momentum that was lost when Perot unexpectedly dropped out of, then rejoined, the campaign. The U.S. economy went into a slump, and Bush's popularity fell. In the fall, Clinton and running mate Al Gore, ran a strong campaign that appealed especially to young voters. Their victory signaled the passing of political power to a new generation of leaders.

Second Term

The election in the fall of 1996 was proof of Clinton's resilience as a politician. He defeated Republican candidate Bob Dole, becoming the first Democrat to win reelection since Franklin D. Roosevelt. The Clinton campaign theme was "building a bridge to the twenty-first century." His second term was marked by continued economic prosperity and continued progress in balancing the federal budget. He announced on September 30, 1998, that the U.S. budget had been balanced for the first time since 1969. Indeed, there was a $70 billion surplus.

International affairs came to the fore in March of 1999, when the United States and its allies in the North Atlantic Treaty Organization (NATO) launched sustained air strikes against Yugoslavia. The attacks were an attempt to forestall widespread deaths in Yugoslavia's Kosovo province as a result of Yugoslavian Serbs' ethnic cleansing policies against Kosovo's Albanian population.

Impeachment

On the personal and legal fronts, Clinton had severe problems in 1998. The investigation of Clinton by Independent Counsel Kenneth Starr, which had been launched to probe the Whitewater real estate dealings, revealed that Clinton had had a sexual relationship with a young White House intern named Monica Lewinsky. At first, Clinton denied the relationship. However, after Lewinsky admitted the relationship before a grand jury, he admitted that his denial, while "legally accurate," had been "misleading." The furor that followed this revelation threatened Clinton's presidency. Clinton's detractors argued that he should resign or be impeached for lying. His supporters argued that his actions were not of the type that justify impeachment under the terms established by the U.S. Constitution.

The House Judiciary Committee, in October, 1998, recommended that the House of Representatives vote to impeach President Clinton for lying under oath (perjury) and for possible obstruction of justice. The House sent articles of impeachment to the Senate in December.

U.S. president Bill Clinton talking with Republican leaders Bob Dole (left) and Newt Gingrich (right) after the 1992 election. *(Library of Congress)*

Private Morality and the Presidency

The presidency of Bill Clinton was marked by extensive investigation of his personal life, first with regard to investments he made in the Whitewater Development Company while he was governor of Arkansas and then regarding sexual matters. Never before had a president's private behavior been examined so closely, and the investigation and subsequent impeachment hearings brought new urgency to long-standing questions: When is a public figure's private life a matter of public concern? How much does the public have a right to know about an elected official's private life? At what point do private morality and behavior become grounds for removal from office?

Paula Jones, an Arkansas state employee, alleged that Clinton had once sexually harassed her. The lawsuit was eventually settled out of court, but in the investigation of the charges, it was learned that Clinton had engaged in a sexual relationship with a White House intern named Monica Lewinsky. Clinton's misleading statements about his relationship with Lewinsky led critics to call for his removal from office. Some argued that, private behavior notwithstanding, Clinton's misleading statements before a grand jury and his alleged attempts to obstruct justice were public behavior. Others in Washington went further, arguing that character is important in evaluating a president and that President Clinton's private behavior showed a lack of the character requisite to the high office of the presidency. In the spring of 1999, an Arkansas judge found Clinton to be in civil contempt for lying under oath in his testimony in the Paula Jones lawsuit.

The Constitution requires that, for an impeached official to be convicted and removed from office, two-thirds of the Senate (not merely a majority) must vote for conviction. Ultimately, at the Senate trial, support for conviction fell significantly short of the votes needed. On February 12, 1999, the Senate voted to acquit Clinton of both articles of impeachment. In the spring of 1999, however, an Arkansas judge found Clinton to be in civil contempt of court for lying under oath in his testimony in the Paula Jones lawsuit.

Bill Clinton represented a new generation of American leaders when he was elected in 1992, and his administration oversaw a growing and healthy economy. He had modest success in the legislative arena, and the American people generally approved of his presidency and disapproved of the 1998-1999 impeachment proceedings. However, Clinton will always be viewed as a president with profound flaws in his private life.

Bibliography
Campbell, Colin, and Bert Rockman, eds. *The Clinton Presidency: First Appraisals*. Chatham, N.J.: Chatham House, 1996.
Drew, Elizabeth. *On the Edge: The Clinton Presidency*. New York: Touchstone, 1995.
Maraniss, David. *First in His Class*. New York: Touchstone, 1996.
Woodward, Bob. *The Choice: How Clinton Won*. New York: Touchstone, 1997.

James W. Riddlesperger, Jr.

Hillary Rodham Clinton

Born: October 26, 1947; Chicago, Illinois

First Lady of the United States (from 1993)

Hillary Rodham Clinton (HIH-lah-ree RO-duhm KLIHN-tuhn), born Hillary Rodham, grew up in the Chicago suburb of Park Ridge. Her father owned a small store, and her mother was a homemaker. Hillary participated in athletics and a Methodist church youth group, and she was student government vice president. After graduating in the top five percent of her class and being selected "most likely to succeed," Hillary attended Wellesley College. At Wellesley she served as student government president, graduated with honors, and even attracted national attention for her impressive commencement address to the class of 1969. After college Hillary attended Yale Law School, where she served on the board of editors of the *Yale Review of Law and Social Action* and graduated in 1973. At Yale, Hillary met fellow law student Bill Clinton. They were married in 1975. Their daughter Chelsea was born in 1980.

Law and Politics

Hillary Clinton has distinguished herself in law and politics. Her legal career started in 1974, when she served on the staff of the U.S. House of Representatives Judiciary Committee, working on the impeachment inquiry of President Richard Nixon. Moving to Arkansas to support Bill Clinton's budding political career, she taught at the state law school and accepted a position with the Rose Law firm, the state's most powerful law firm. By 1988 she was named by *National Law Journal* as one of America's one hundred most influential attorneys and was sitting on the boards of major corporations.

Since her youth, Clinton participated in politics and campaigns. While at Yale, both Hillary and Bill worked in Texas for Senator George McGovern's 1972 presidential campaign. Hillary helped manage each of her husband's campaigns, from his failed congressional bid in 1974 to his election as Arkansas attorney general in 1976 to his election as governor in 1978. She worked on each subsequent gubernatorial reelection campaign. During the 1992 presidential race, Hillary Clinton gained worldwide recognition for her key role in the campaign. She weathered unprecedented attacks on her by Republicans and media commentators, and she publicly defended her husband against rumors of marital infidelities—and she was at his side when he publicly admitted one infidelity.

Hillary Rodham Clinton is a leading advocate for children. Her affiliation with this issue

Hillary Rodham Clinton *(Library of Congress)*

Hillary Rodham Clinton at the United Nations in 1997, speaking at its observance of the fiftieth anniversary of the Universal Declaration of Human Rights. *(AP/Wide World Photos)*

of children. As First Lady, she authored the book *It Takes a Village* (1996), calling for all sectors of society to assume responsibility for children, and she hosted two White House conferences on children.

Activist First Lady

As Arkansas's First Lady, Clinton was named "Arkansas Woman of the Year" in 1983. Her activities included educational reform, and she developed the state's "Home Instruction Program for Preschool Youngsters," a model program for underprivileged children. She also founded Arkansas Advocates for Children and Families and was appointed by President Jimmy Carter to the board of the Legal Services Corporation. In the White House, the First Lady gained international

began in law school while she was interning with Marian Wright Edelman, long-time head of the Children's Defense Fund. As a law student, Clinton published what has since become a well-known and controversial article in the *Harvard Educational Review* on the legal rights

attention as one of the president's top advisers. Traveling to Africa, Asia, Europe, and Latin America, the First Lady advocated human rights, the rights of children, family planning, accessible health care, and the empowerment of women. She spoke to global audiences at several women's

Health Care Reform

The major political task of Hillary Rodham Clinton's first ladyship was heading the President's Task Force on National Health Care Reform. During the 1992 campaign, Bill Clinton made reforming the nation's costly and heavily burdened health-care system one of his top priorities. Stating that his wife was the best organizer he knew, the president selected her to lead this massive undertaking. The assignment caused immediate controversy, and the charge of nepotism was raised.

The First Lady made numerous appearances before the public, health-care experts, and Congress, generally impressing people with her knowledge of the issue. Six cabinet members and a sizeable staff reported to her. The final reform plan was very large and complex, and it died in Congress. Republicans strongly opposed the plan, offering other competing ideas of their own.

American first lady Hillary Rodham Clinton greeting local residents and U.S. military relief workers in hurricane-ravaged Honduras in 1998. *(Reuters/Jim Bourg/Archive Photos)*

conferences, including the U.N. Fourth World Conference of Women, held in 1995 in China. In 1995 she began writing "Talking It Over," a weekly syndicated newspaper column.

In 1998 the Clintons faced a political and personal crisis when President Clinton was forced to admit that he had had sexual relations with a young White House intern. He was impeached by the House of Representatives but was not convicted by the Senate. Clinton's presidency survived; through the troubled period Hillary Clinton said little publicly, but she maintained a dignified demeanor and earned considerable respect. In early 1999, strong support emerged for her own political future; she was considered a possible contender for a U.S. Senate seat from New York.

Bibliography

Burrell, Barbara. *Public Opinion, the First Ladyship, and Hillary Rodham Clinton*. New York: Garland, 1997.

Osborne, Claire. *The Unique Voice of Hillary Rodham Clinton: A Portrait in Her Own Words*. New York: Avon, 1997.

Warner, Judith. *Hillary Clinton: The Inside Story*. New York: Signet, 1993.

Robert P. Watson

Michael Collins

Born: October 16, 1890; Clonakilky, County Cork, Ireland
Died: August 22, 1922; Bael-na-Blath, County Cork, Ireland

Irish revolutionary and negotiator of 1921 treaty creating the Irish Free State

Michael Collins (MI-kuhl KO-lihnz) was the youngest of eight children born to an aged farmer and his much younger wife in an Ireland that had been under English rule for more than seven hundred years. Collins's formal education was limited, but he was a voracious reader in literature, technology, science, government, and military theory. In addition, he immersed himself in Irish history, from which he drew the lesson that independence from Great Britain could be won only by force, not through debates in the British

Michael Collins *(Library of Congress)*

Parliament. At the age of sixteen Collins moved to London to work as a banker and stockbroker. There he became a leader in Irish nationalist circles.

The War for Irish Independence

Collins remained in London until 1916, when he returned to Ireland to take part in the Easter Rebellion. Although the rebellion was crushed by the British military, the rebels sparked the War for Irish Independence. Collins assumed responsibility for establishing newspapers, smuggling arms, and manufacturing bombs. He also financed the independence movement through national loan programs. For centuries the British had relied on an elaborate system of spies and informers to subvert Irish independence movements. Collins turned the tables and infiltrated every arm of the British government in Ireland. The intelligence available to the nationalists allowed them to tighten security in their own ranks and to escape British traps. It became a deadly tool in Collins's terrorist campaign.

Collins was a realist; he knew that Irish independence would never be won by a frontal military assault on British forces. Instead he developed a form of guerrilla warfare in which columns attacked small government outposts. Each attack pinned down a much larger, less mobile force and allowed the guerrillas to control the countryside. One element of the military strategy was the assassination of leading British officials and those who protected them. That tactic demoralized both the British government and the British public. On November 21, 1920, eight of the most feared members of the British Secret Service were assassinated in what became known as Bloody Sunday.

In response to these attacks, the British sent reinforcements to the demoralized Royal Irish Constabulary. The new police forces consisted of two groups, the Black and Tans and the Auxiliaries, both of which engaged in brutal reprisals for the actions of Collins's forces. The reprisals had the effect of creating further support for the Irish revolutionaries, who by now had held their first meeting of the Dáil Éireann (the Irish parliament), had declared independence from England, had formed a government, and had created a military force—the Irish Republican Army (IRA). Collins was both minister of finance in the cabinet of President Eamon de Valera and director of intelligence for the IRA.

Michael Collins passionately advocating the Anglo-Irish Treaty in Cork in March, 1922. He was murdered less than six months later. *(Library of Congress)*

Treaty Negotiations

In July, 1921, President de Valera negotiated a truce with British prime minister David Lloyd George. De Valera appointed Michael Collins head of the delegation that was charged with negotiating a full settlement. Those negotiations produced the Anglo-Irish Treaty of December 6, 1921. The treaty created the Irish Free State, a semi-independent government for the southern part of Ireland. Six northern counties in the province of Ulster were to have their fate determined later. Collins hoped that the treaty would be a stepping-stone to full independence. The terms of the treaty were not acceptable to de Valera, however, and he led a bitter fight against its

---

The Easter Rebellion of 1916

The British Parliament debated home rule for Ireland for decades and was probably on the verge of approving it when World War I broke out in 1914. The war caused consideration of the measure to be postponed indefinitely. Frustrated by the delay, a nationalist group called the Irish Volunteers seized much of central Dublin, including the general post office, on Easter Monday, April 24, 1916. They declared Ireland a re-public and held out for a week before surrendering to British firepower. More than three hundred people were killed and more than two thousand wounded during the week. Initial local reaction to the rebellion was hostile, but British executions of its leaders fanned the flames of Irish nationalism and led to the beginning of the War for Irish Independence.

The Irish Free State

The Anglo-Irish Treaty of 1921 ended the union between Ireland and Great Britain and created the Irish Free State. The Free State comprised the twenty-six counties of Southern Ireland. The six counties of Northern Ireland declined to join the Free State. The Irish Free State became a member of the British Commonwealth of Nations. England reserved the right to use Irish harbors, fuel facilities, and airfields for military purposes, and Irish officials were obliged to take an oath of loyalty to the British King.

The government of the Free State consisted of a bicameral Parliament, an Executive Council that ran the day-to-day affairs of the country, and an independent judiciary. The constitution of the Free State protected freedom of expression and assembly, the right to privacy, freedom of religion, the right to vote, the right to trial by jury, and the right to a free elementary public education. The government of the Irish Free State gradually chipped away at the ties to England. In 1932 it abolished the oath of loyalty to the king. In 1937 it changed the name of the state to Eire and declared itself a sovereign democratic state. In 1948 it declared itself a republic and withdrew from the British Commonwealth of Nations.

---

ratification. The protreaty side prevailed in the Dáil by a slim margin.

Civil War

Unwilling to accept anything short of a completely independent Irish Republic, the de Valera faction walked out of the Dail. Collins became chairman of the executive council of the provisional government. Opposition to the treaty manifested itself in a number of antigovernment demonstrations and then by the seizure of the Four Courts in Dublin by antitreaty forces. Threatened by England's Winston Churchill with a military invasion if he failed to suppress the rebels, Collins ordered his artillery to shell the Four Courts. This action led to vicious engagements all over Ireland.

Collins spoke at rallies around the country, but he was frustrated by the continuing and bitter opposition to the treaty. He began drinking heavily and became reckless about his own safety. On August 21, 1922, disregarding warnings of assassination plans, he set off on a tour of County Cork—his home territory, but also a bastion of republicanism. On the first day he stopped at pubs and challenged old friends to impromptu wrestling matches. On the evening of August 22, his party was ambushed on a back road. Collins was the lone casualty in the half-hour gun battle.

The Collins Legacy

Michael Collins invented the modern form of guerrilla warfare in which infiltration of the government, assassination of high officials, and control of the countryside are used to defeat a superior military force. A realist, he accepted a treaty that did not give Ireland complete independence but that, he believed, provided a stepping stone to it. His willingness to tolerate the treaty's ambiguity on the final status of Northern Ireland led to the partitioning of Ireland and to decades of often-violent struggle.

Bibliography

Caulfield, Max. *The Easter Rebellion.* Boulder, Colo.: Roberts Rinehart, 1995.

Coogan, Tim Pat. *The Man Who Made Ireland: The Life and Death of Michael Collins.* Boulder, Colo.: Roberts Rinehart, 1992.

Flanagan, Thomas. *The End of the Hunt.* New York: Dutton, 1994.

William H. Coogan

Joseph Cook

Born: December 7, 1860; Silverdale, Staffordshire, England
Died: July 30, 1947; Sydney, New South Wales, Australia

Prime minister of Australia (1913-1914)

Joseph Cooke (JOH-sehf KOOK) grew up in a poor coal-mining family in England, leaving school at about nine to work in the mines. As a teenager, Joseph dropped the *e* from the end of his surname when he became a convert to the Primitive Methodists. He also became involved in the trade union movement. In 1885, he married Mary Turner, a schoolteacher, and they emigrated from England to the prosperous colony of New South Wales. They settled in the mining district of Lithgow, where Cook continued his union involvement.

Labor and the Pledge

From 1891 to 1901, Cook was a member of the Legislative Assembly of New South Wales. In October, 1893, he became leader of the Labor Party in the colonial Parliament. During the 1890's, the Labor movement was divided over "the pledge." The issue at hand was whether the Labor Party should require all its members of the Australian colonial parliaments to vote a certain way regarding the imposition of tariffs. Party members disagreed about the issue of tariffs, and many did not want to be bound by party discipline on the matter. Others believed that Labor parliamentarians should be required to take a pledge to vote in Parliament in accordance with the decision of the party majority. In 1894, a Labor conference resolved that members had to sign the solidarity pledge. Cook refused, and he stood thereafter as an Independent Labor candidate. In the election of 1894, George Reid formed a government in New South Wales with the help of antipledge Labor representatives.

Federal Career

With the creation of the Commonwealth of Australia in 1901 by the federation of the Australian colonies, Cook stood for the federal seat of Parramatta. He was successful, and he remained in the House of Representatives from 1901 to 1921. He became deputy leader of the Free Traders in 1905 and their leader in 1908. In 1908, the federal government adopted a national policy in favor of industry protection by means of customs tariffs. Some Free Traders had already accepted a degree of industry protection, and they had governed in coalition with the Protectionists in 1904-

Joseph Cook *(Library of Congress)*

Mining and the Australian Economy

As the Australian continent was settled by Europeans during the nineteenth century, mining became an important industry. Gold rushes were triggered in 1851 when gold was discovered in Bathurst and in rural Victoria. Prospectors later discovered gold in Queensland, the Northern Territory, and Western Australia. Great deposits of silver, lead, zinc, coal, and copper were also found, including the major fields of black coal in New South Wales near Newcastle, Wollongong, and Lithgow. In the second half of the 1800's, and until the depression of the 1890's, the boom in mining contributed to Australia's enormous social and economic development. High living standards were attained, and many new immigrants arrived. However, mining was also one of the primary industries affected by the depression, a situation that led to nationwide labor disputes, the virtual cessation of immigration, and the development of the labor movement and Labor Party.

1905. The Free Traders decided to join with the Protectionists and the Tariff Reformers to provide a united front against the Labor Party. In 1909, Cook became deputy leader and minister for defense in the Fusion Party government of Alfred Deakin.

In 1910, the Labor Party won a landslide electoral victory. By 1913, the remaining Fusonists in the Parliament came to be known as the Liberal Party. Cook became leader of the Liberals and won the May, 1913, election, but his party still had a minority of seats in the upper house. Cook was prime minister from 1913 to 1914, but he was able to accomplish little except announce support for Britain in World War I. In 1914, Labor regained power in the government following a double dissolution of the houses of Parliament. In 1917, the Australian Nationalist Federation, or Nationalist Party, was formed, and Cook became deputy leader to William Morris Hughes.

After Politics

Cook left politics in 1921 but served as Australian high commissioner in London from 1921 to 1927. He was a successful politician and a man of humble origins who achieved a position of national leadership. Cook was widely criticized, however, for moving from his roots in the Labor movement to a conservative political position. For much of the time he was an opposition leader, and as prime minister he was able to accomplish little because he lacked control of the upper house of Parliament.

Bibliography

Bebbington, G. *Pit Boy to Prime Minister: The Story of Rt. Hon. Sir Joseph Cooke, P.C., G.C.M.G.* Newcastle-under-Lyme, England: University of Keele, n.d.

Clark, C. H. M. *The People Make Laws, 1888-1915.* Vol. 5 of *A History of Australia.* Melbourne, Australia: Melbourne University Press, 1981.

Rickard, John. *Class and Politics: New South Wales, Victoria, and the Early Commonwealth, 1890-1910.* Canberra: Australian National University Press, 1976.

Russell Blackford

Calvin Coolidge

Born: July 4, 1872; Plymouth, Vermont
Died: January 5, 1933; Northampton, Massachusetts

President of the United States (1923-1929)

John Calvin Coolidge (JON KAL-vihn KEW-lihj) was the only son of a storekeeper and versatile mechanic, and a farmer's daughter. In 1895 he graduated cum laude from Amherst College, in Northampton, Massachusetts, where he had studied Greek, Latin, rhetoric, mathematics, philosophy, and public speaking. There he also solidified his celebrated traits of frugality, clipped expressiveness, and chilly wit. He clerked and studied law under two politically well-connected Northampton lawyers, was admitted to the Massachusetts bar in 1897, served on the Northampton city committee, and in 1898 opened his own law office. In 1905 he married Grace Anna Goodhue, a Vermont schoolteacher. They had two sons.

Emerging Politician

For several years Coolidge practiced law, served the Republican Party, and accomplished official political work at both city and state levels. Coolidge served as the mayor of Northampton (1910-1912) and then as state senator (1912-1916). He soon let his partner manage their law practice. Being senate president beginning in 1914 led to his nomination, election, and reelection to the lieutenant governorship (1916-1918), after which he was elected governor.

Widely regarded as merely competent as governor, Coolidge nevertheless helped reduce state bureaucracy, lower taxes, and resolve a textile strike in Lawrence. Chance, however, soon made him nationally known. In 1919 the Boston police illegally, if understandably, struck over low wages and dreadful working conditions. When rioting, looting, and property destruction followed, Coolidge summoned the state militia to restore civil order and issued his famous statement that no one ever has the right to strike against the public safety. Running on the terse slogan, "Have Faith in Massachusetts," he was returned as governor. In the summer of 1920 he ran for the U.S. vice presidency on the ticket of Warren G. Harding, who became president in 1921.

Coolidge and Harding

A quiet, cautious man of unquestioned integrity, Coolidge contrasted with President Harding—a handsome, gullible, generous gladhander

Calvin Coolidge *(Library of Congress)*

345

soon victimized by corrupt friends. Coolidge, though allowed to sit at cabinet meetings, necessarily was a nonentity as vice president until Harding died in San Francisco on August 2, 1923. One day later, Coolidge, while vacationing in Plymouth, was administered the oath of office as president by his father, then a local notary public.

President Coolidge

Coolidge retained the best members of Harding's cabinet, including Charles Evans Hughes, Andrew Mellon, and Herbert Hoover. However, he also kept Edwin Denby and Attorney General Harry Daugherty, both of whom were disgraced when congressional hearings in 1923 and 1924 exposed illegal private leasing of naval oil lands on Teapot Dome, Wyoming, and in California. Resignations, imprisonment, and suicides followed these and other investigations. Through it all Coolidge remained above reproach.

During his administration, which included his election to a full term in 1924, Coolidge sup-

ported big business by favoring high tariffs, by encouraging foreign loans which resulted in increased exports, and by suppressing antitrust investigations. He reduced taxes, denied aid to farmers through any stabilizing of prices or purchasing of surpluses, and pocket-vetoed a bill permitting government operation of the Muscle Shoals hydroelectric facility.

Coolidge looked with disfavor on the League of Nations and with near-indifference on the World Court. He restricted immigration. When it was proposed that the United States reduce the war debts owed by the European allies in World War I, he said, "They hired the money, didn't they?" On the other hand, his representatives were at least temporarily successful in quieting anti-American unrest in Mexico and Nicaragua. Frank B. Kellogg, his secretary of state from 1925, negotiated the idealistic antiwar Kellogg-Briand Pact of 1929.

It was only continued national prosperity, however, that made Coolidge's administration

The Boston Police Strike

In 1919 the Boston police were underpaid, worked eighty- to ninety-hour weeks, and were poorly quartered. When they disobeyed their commissioner's legal order not to unionize, he put nineteen union leaders on trial. A mayoral committee recommended arbitration, but the commissioner suspended the nineteen leaders instead. When the mayor appealed to Calvin Coolidge, then governor of Massachusetts, Coolidge merely urged all governmental agencies to follow the law. The commissioner stood firm, and the mayor took no steps to improve police wages or working conditions. In the afternoon of September 9, 1,117 patrolmen of the 1,544-man police force went on strike. A wave of looting and robbery began that night. The mayor called available state guardsmen to duty and

requested three thousand troops from Coolidge, who dispatched three regiments. Violence increased, and firemen, telephone operators, and other essential workers threatened to join the strike. On September 11 Coolidge therefore drafted the state militia, appealed for citizens' cooperation, and officially commanded the police to obey their commissioner. This action cost the jobs of all policemen who remained on strike. To American Federation of Labor President Samuel Gompers, who sought their reinstatement, Coolidge telegraphed his famous message: "There is no right to strike against the public safety, by anybody, anywhere, anytime." This message electrified the nation and indirectly led Coolidge to the White House.

Silent Cal

Calvin Coolidge, long known as a dry, terse speaker, was nicknamed Silent Cal. A 1918 cartoon in the *Boston Post* shows him sitting with his mouth closed during a debate. Opponents joked that he was often silent because he had little to say. According to one anecdote, when a young woman told Coolidge that she had bet she could make him say more than two words, he replied, "You lose." In truth, however, he spoke often—softly, for the most part—and always kept his word. In 1923 he was the first president to speak from the White House over the radio, and in 1924 he campaigned effectively over the radio. He evidently endorsed "Keep Cool with Coolidge" as his presidential campaign slogan. In 1925 alone he delivered 28 speeches as well as 61 official and 175 unofficial statements. In August, 1927, he addressed ten thousand Sioux Indians and was adopted into their tribe—hardly evidence of taciturnity.

appear effective. In reality, wealth was unevenly distributed, wages were often low, unemployment in some cities was above 10 percent, and international animosities were quietly growing. In August, 1927, Coolidge stated in writing, "I do not choose to run for President in nineteen twenty-eight." He, and the country at large, regarded Herbert Hoover's nomination and election as president as an endorsement of his own policies. The blame, however, fell on Hoover for the 1929 stock-market crash and the ensuing Great Depression.

Coolidge is remembered as a status-quo president, more interested in being an efficient administrator than in attempting progressive leadership. He reductively said that "the business of the United States is business." He presided thriftily over part of the tumultuous Roaring Twenties as a superficially steadying influence, un-aware of the fragility of the American economy, the need for a more creative foreign policy, and the many root causes of monumental problems lying just ahead. On the other hand, it now seems likely that no one could have done much to solve them.

Calvin Coolidge (left) as governor of Massachusetts in 1920, reviewing a police parade with Boston's chief of police a year after they quelled the Boston police strike. *(Library of Congress)*

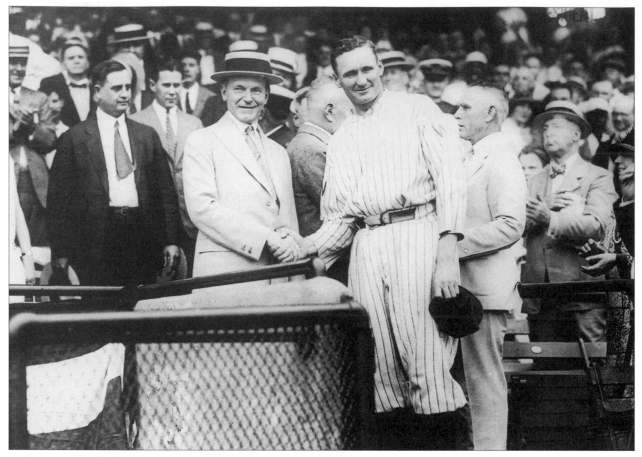

U.S. president Calvin Coolidge shakes hands with Washington Senators pitcher Walter Johnson at Griffith Stadium. *(CNP/Archive Photos)*

Bibliography

Allen, Frederick Lewis. *Only Yesterday: An Informal History of the Nineteen-Twenties.* New York: Harper & Brothers, 1931.

Ferrell, Robert H. *The Presidency of Calvin Coolidge.* Lawrence: University Press of Kansas, 1998.

McCoy, Donald R. *Calvin Coolidge: The Quiet President.* New York: Macmillan, 1967.

Moran, Philip R., ed. *Calvin Coolidge, 1872-1933: Chronology, Documents, Bibliographical Aids.* Dobbs Ferry, N.Y.: Oceana Publications, 1970.

Silver, Thomas B. *Coolidge and the Historians.* Durham, N.C.: Carolina Academic Press, 1982.

Robert L. Gale

Sheila Copps

Born: November 27, 1952; Hamilton, Ontario, Canada

Deputy prime minister (1933-1997) and heritage minister (from 1997) of Canada

Sheila Maureen Copps (SHEE-lah moh-REEN KOPZ) was born to a prominent family in Hamilton, Ontario. She grew up in Hamilton and went to college at the University of Western Ontario in London, from which she graduated in 1974. She also did postgraduate study at the University of Rouen in France and McMaster University, sharpening the fluency in French that would aid her national political rise. After working as a journalist in Hamilton and Ottawa for three years, Copps became involved in political activity on behalf of the Liberal Party. In 1981, she was elected to the Ontario provincial parliament as a Liberal. Ontario politics had been dominated for decades by the Conservatives, and it was ironic that the Liberals were finally able to gain power a year after Copps left the Ontario legislature at Queen's Park in order to enter federal politics. Her Ontario experience gave Copps valuable experience in acting constructively as a member of the opposition.

Rising Through the Ranks

At the time of the September, 1984, general election, Copps ran for and won the riding (district) of Hamilton East. Her party was not so fortunate, losing to the Conservatives under Brian Mulroney. The party's loss of power was actually beneficial for Copps's personal advancement, however, as the Liberal leadership looked away from tried-and-true veterans tarred by defeat and toward new faces that could be viewed as signals of fresh leadership. The fact that Copps was a woman at a time when all Canadian parties were seeking to elevate women certainly helped her prospects. Copps became the official opposition spokesperson for housing and labor. She had good communication skills and was telegenic and media-friendly. She was seen as one of the few bright spots in the decade of the 1980's for the Liberal Party. By the time the Liberals rallied for the next campaign in 1993, Copps was considered a viable leadership candidate, and indeed she ran for the leadership. Though she lost to Jean Chrétien, she appeared to be poised for a high position, as the party was sure to gain power because of the overwhelming unpopularity of the incumbent Conservatives.

A Force in Government

When the Liberals took power in 1993, Copps was named deputy prime minister as well as

Sheila Copps *(AP/Wide World Photos)*

349

minister for the environment. Although the position of deputy prime minister sounds powerful, its duties mostly entail maintaining consensus in the prime minister's cabinet and ensuring harmony among party parliamentarians. Nonetheless, the position gave Copps high visibility. As environment minister, she wrote legislation for the protection of endangered species and instituted environmental standards for governmental operations. The storm over the goods and services tax (GST) dimmed her luster somewhat, and Chrétien decided in July, 1997, to remove her as deputy prime minister.

In January, 1996, she had shifted from environment to become heritage minister. As heritage minister, Copps was entrusted with the task of preserving a distinctly Canadian culture and tradition in a world dominated by global, particularly American, media. She participated in international conferences, added large amounts of land to the Canadian national park system, and gave support to Canadian recording artists and television producers on intellectual property issues. In the late 1990's, Sheila Copps remained one of the most recognizable and popular of Canada's politicians.

Canadian deputy prime minister Sheila Copps being applauded by Prime Minister Jean Chrétien in 1996. *(Reuters/Peter Jones/Archive Photos)*

Politics and the GST

Canada's goods and services tax (GST) is similar to the value-added tax of some European countries. It is a blanket surcharge imposed on most categories of purchased goods. Since it is a burden on the consumer more than the producer, and because it affects people with all levels of income equally, it is often favored by Conservative parties.

The GST was introduced in Canada by the Conservative government of 1984-1993. When running in the 1993 election, Sheila Copps pledged to repeal the GST. Once in power, however, the Liberal Party was more cautious. Party leaders judged it inadvisable to make such a drastic change in the tax system while Canada was going through a difficult recession in the 1990's, a decade in which Canada's economic growth and currency value lagged behind other advanced democracies.

Accused of hypocrisy by her opponents, Copps, in February, 1997, resigned from office because she had not kept her promise about the GST. Since her seat of Hamilton East was now open, a by-election was held in which Copps was easily reelected. Although Copps manifested good political survival skills, the episode displayed the danger of making extravagant promises in times of limited economic options.

Bibliography

Copps, Sheila. *Nobody's Baby: A Survival Guide to Politics*. Toronto: Deneau, 1986.

Gingras, François-Piérre. *Gender and Politics in Contemporary Canada*. New York: Oxford University Press, 1995.

Greenspan, Edward, and Anthony Wilson-Smith. *Double Vision: The Inside Story of the Liberals in Power*. Toronto: Doubleday Canada, 1996.

Simpson, Jeffrey. *The Anxious Years: Politics in the Age of Mulroney and Chrétien*. Toronto: Lester, 1996.

Nicholas Birns

William T. Cosgrave

Born: June 5, 1880; Dublin, Ireland
Died: November 16, 1965; Dublin, Ireland

Irish nationalist, president of Ireland (1922-1932)

William Thomas Cosgrave (WIHL-yuhm TO-muhs KOZ-grayv) was born into a Dublin vintner's family, was educated in Roman Catholic schools, and joined the family business. Politically active, at age twenty-five he helped Arthur Griffith and others form the party Sinn Féin. In 1909 he was elected as a member of the party to the Dublin corporation (the city council). He served there in various capacities for thirteen years. In the Easter Rebellion of 1916 Cosgrave fought as a lieutenant in the Irish Volunteers at

William T. Cosgrave *(Library of Congress)*

the South Dublin Union and was condemned to be executed. His sentence was commuted to life imprisonment, however, and he was released in the general amnesty of 1917. He married Louise Flanagan in 1919, and the couple had two sons.

Early Responsibilities

Cosgrave entered national politics in 1917 and became the second Sinn Féin member of Parliament (for Kilkenny). Along with other party members, he refused to take his seat in Westminster. In 1919 the Dáil Éireann—the presumptive government of Ireland led by Eamon de Valera—named him its minister for local governments. In this position he coordinated Sinn Féin-led local bodies throughout Ireland, an important contribution to the armed resistance in the Black and Tan War of 1919-1921. Hunted by the British military, he spent much of this time on the run.

The treaty with Britain that was negotiated by Michael Collins and Griffith brought the war to a close, but it did not provide the level of independence desired by de Valera and hard-line republicans. In the cabinet, Cosgrave's vote was the swing, and he strongly favored the agreement. He reasoned that it offered enough of a foundation on which to build a future republic. The issue of ratification divided the Dáil and caused de Valera and other antitreaty members to walk out. They formed an abstentionist (refusing to sit) opposition party and a military force—the Irish Republican Army (IRA).

In the provisional government, Cosgrave served again as minister for local governments and rose to chair the government in July, 1922. After both Griffith and Collins died in August, he took over as acting president of the Dáil. He was officially elected Dáil president on September 9,

British soldiers behind a makeshift barricade during the Easter Rebellion of 1916; William T. Cosgrave fought with the Irish Volunteers during the uprising. *(Popperfoto/Archive Photos)*

merging the provisional government and Dáil Éireann. He introduced the new constitution to the Dáil on September 18, and it was confirmed three days later. On December 6, 1922, in the midst of a civil war over the treaty, he was elected the first president of the Executive Council of the Irish Free State. The following day IRA gunmen killed two Dáil members, and Cosgrave oversaw

Fine Gael

The dispute over the Anglo-Irish Treaty of 1921 led to a major split in Irish politics, with those supporting the treaty forming the party Cumann na nGaedheal in 1923. This party governed in Ireland from 1923 until 1932, when Eamon de Valera's party, Fianna Fáil, which had opposed the treaty and government, won the national elections. In September, 1933, William T. Cosgrave organized Fine Gael, including large elements of Cumann na nGaedheal, the Centre Party, and the quasi-fascist Blueshirts. Eoin O'Duffy of the Blueshirts served as first party leader, but he soon resigned because of lack of support. Cosgrave was chosen as O'Duffy's re-

placement in 1935. The party's fortunes waned in the late 1930's and early 1940's, with its representation in the Dáil falling from 34.8 percent in 1937 to 20.5 percent in 1944. In that year Cosgrave was replaced by Richard Mulcahy. Fine Gael, with 19.8 percent, led Ireland's first interparty government, which defeated Fianna Fáil in 1948. De Valera's party governed again from 1951 to 1954, and a Fine Gael coalition was in power from 1954 to 1957. In the 1960's Fine Gael moved toward social action and an alliance with the Labour Party, forming the National Coalition Party in 1973.

the retaliatory execution of four of their jailed colleagues. It was an effective response, but it cost him his home, which was destroyed by arsonists.

National Leadership

As president (essentially prime minister), Cosgrave laid important foundations for Ireland's future. Sinn Féin's abstentionist policy assured Cosgrave of an unopposed state-building program. Institutions were modeled on British forms, and national credit was established. He held the portfolio for finance, overseeing the establishment of important state-sponsored companies and the large-scale Shannon River hydroelectric system. He helped usher the Irish Free State into the League of Nations and shape the Statute of Westminster, which gave the dominions—including the Free State—political equality with Britain within the British Commonwealth. The statute was a major step toward national sovereignty. However, Cosgrave failed to unite the Protestant northeast (Northern Ireland) with the Catholic south, and the attempt to create fair boundaries through a commission was scandalous in effect. He was also quite willing to allow the heavy hand of the Catholic hierarchy to guide social legislation, as in the 1923 prohibition of divorce. On the whole, however, his guidance was judicious, even-handed, and determined, while he remained personally rather unassuming and even modest.

De Valera's party, Fianna Fáil, won the national election in 1932. From 1934 until his retirement in 1944, Cosgrave remained his party's leader. Ineffective in challenging de Valera, he nonetheless remained a popular figure. Cosgrave chaired the Irish Racing Board from 1946 to 1956 and again after 1957.

Bibliography

Collins, Stephen. *The Cosgrave Legacy*. Dublin: Blackwater Press, 1996.

Curran, Joseph M. *The Birth of the Irish Free State, 1921-1923*. Tuscaloosa: University of Alabama Press, 1981.

Harkness, D. W. *The Restless Dominion: The Irish Free State and the British Commonwealth of Nations, 1921-1931*. London: Macmillan, 1969.

O'Sullivan, Donal Joseph. *The Irish Free State and Its Senate: A Study in Contemporary Politics*. New York: Arno Press, 1972.

Joseph P. Byrne

Pierre de Coubertin

Born: January 1, 1863; Paris, France
Died: September 2, 1937; Geneva, Switzerland

French educator, founder of the International Olympic Committee (1894) and the modern Olympic Games

Pierre, Baron de Coubertin (pee-AYR bah-RO deh kew-behr-TA), son of a diplomat descended from an aristocratic line of spice merchants and a mother from Norman nobility, was educated by Jesuits at the Lycée Saint Ignace in Paris, a prestigious school. Its program of rigorous physical exercise shaped some of the goals of Coubertin's long career in educational reform. He graduated in 1880 and studied social science at the Free School of Political Science in Paris. He left in 1883 to continue schooling in England. His book *Education in England* (1888) records his enthusiasm for English instruction and its emphasis on sports.

Rebuilding French Confidence

In *Memories of Youth* (1936), Coubertin recalled his childhood excitement when France declared war with Prussia in 1870 and his profound despair over France's humiliating defeat a year later. His life could be said to have been a search for the cause of that loss, which he found in French education's rote instruction and lack of physical training. He believed that it produced a passive, unresponsive citizen. English schools rewarded independent thinking and inspired competition through sports, he wrote. Later, his interest in sports shifted from preparing France for future wars to creating international peace through the Olympic Games.

Convinced that France suffered from cultural isolation, Coubertin's many books on education and society in England, Germany, and, later, the United States and Canada, were aimed at opening French minds and introducing needed innovations into the French curriculum. After taking a law degree, Coubertin entered public life as a consultant to the Ministry of Education and other cabinet departments. In 1889 the French government commissioned him to make a four-year survey of American and Canadian schools in preparation for reforming the French education system. At the end of his tour, he declared at the Chicago World's Fair in 1893 his belief that the United States' ethnically diverse population had been united largely through the strengths of its public school system.

Pierre de Coubertin *(Archive Photos/Camera Press)*

The Battle of Sedan, Septernber, 1870. In later years Pierre de Coubertin recalled his childhood excitement when France declared war on Prussia in 1870. *(American Stock/Archive Photos)*

The International Olympic Committee

The Olympic Games are organized by the International Olympic Committee (IOC), formed in 1894 by Pierre de Coubertin and headquartered in Lausanne, Switzerland. Members are drawn from the National Olympic Committees (NOCs) and may serve until the age of eighty. The IOC selects the sites for the winter and summer games, which occur every two years in a four-year cycle. It sets policy for the NOCs and works closely with the International Amateur Athletic Federation and other groups that set standards and rules for Olympic sports.

The IOC's executive branch consists of a president, elected by the other members, an executive board, several vice presidents, and various commissioners. The membership of the committee represents a broad array of sponsoring nations but is chiefly composed of delegates from Europe and America. Begun as a Western organization of international sports, the Olympic Games reflected its growing international scope when IOC members were elected from Asia in 1908 and Africa in 1910.

For most of the twentieth century, the committee performed its functions without major problems. In early 1999 the IOC's reputation suffered a severe blow. A number of its officials were charged with unethical behavior, including accepting bribes, primarily in relation to the decision to hold the 2002 Winter Olympics in Salt Lake City, Utah. Some IOC officials resigned and others were expelled. An ethics panel created by the U.S. Olympic Committee recommended major changes in the organization of the IOC, calling its organization antiquated and autocratic.

The Olympic Games

By 1886 Coubertin had declared his intention to *rebronzer la France*—to darken French skin by outdoor activities. Asked how long it would take to reform French life, Coubertin responded, "Twenty years." He was drawn to the ideas of the social philosopher Frédéric le Play, founder of the Union for Social Peace (1871), who argued for the decentralization of power and for a "culture of peace." Putting the two interests together gave Coubertin the idea of reviving the Olympic Games to encourage national fitness and international peace.

In 1875 the German archaeologist Ernst Curtius had begun uncovering the original site of the Olympic Games, inspiring widespread interest in their revival. Greece had staged small versions of the games for its own citizens from 1829, after separation from Turkey, but had ended them by 1889. Coubertin announced his intention to revive the games on an international basis at an athletic conference convened in 1894. Delegates from nine nations unanimously endorsed the plan, and two years later, in Athens, the first Summer Olympic Games were held with 295 athletes and sixty thousand spectators.

The first Winter Olympics were held in 1924.

Though the public was slow to take an interest in the Olympics, Coubertin shepherded the Olympic Games through wars, depressions, and the attacks of critics who accused him of paganism and endangering youth. He procured additional support from sponsoring members and used his prodigious powers of persuasion to involve other nations. From 1896 to 1925, Coubertin was president of the International Olympic Committee (IOC); his dream of international peace through sports was not achieved, but the Olympic Games are recognized throughout the world as the pinnacle of athletic competition.

Bibliography
Lucas, John. "Baron Pierre de Coubertin and the Formative Years of the Modern International Olympic Movement: 1883-1896." Thesis, University of Maryland, 1962.

MacAloon, John J. *This Great Symbol*. Chicago: Chicago University Press, 1981.

Young, David. *The Modern Olympics*. Baltimore: Johns Hopkins University Press, 1996.

Paul Christensen

William Randal Cremer

Born: March 18, 1838; Fareham, Wiltshire, England
Died: July 22, 1908; London, England

British union activist and peace advocate, winner of 1903 Nobel Peace Prize

William Randal Cremer (WIHL-yuhm RAN-duhl KREE-mur) was born into a working-class family in a small town in the west of England. In spite of the extreme poverty of his childhood, he was able to obtain some education at a church school. When he was twelve he went to work in a shipyard. Three years later he was apprenticed to a carpenter. Cremer eventually became a carpenter himself and found work in London in 1852.

Early Labor Activism

In London Cremer became involved in trade-union activities. A natural leader and persuasive speaker, he was elected to a council that promoted a nine-hour workday. When that campaign resulted in a lock-out of seventy thousand workers in 1859 and 1860, Cremer was one of seven committee leaders who directed labor activities. These events sparked the formation of a single union for the carpentry trade, the Amalgamated Society of Carpenters and Joiners, which Cremer helped found in June of 1860.

Cremer also participated in the founding of the International Working Men's Association in London in 1864. Karl Marx, in his inaugural address to the organization, urged workers to gain political power for themselves in order to redress the problems they experienced in industrial society. As secretary of the organization's British chapter, Cremer led the British delegation to its conference in Geneva in 1866. The British delegates found that they sharply disagreed with the revolutionary program advocated by many European delegates, and Cremer soon severed ties with the group.

Peace Through Arbitration

Believing that labor interests should be represented in government, Cremer first ran for a seat in Parliament in 1868 as a Liberal Party candidate. He was resoundingly defeated then, and again in 1874. In 1886 and 1892, however, he was elected to represent a working-class London constituency. He lost his seat in 1895 but was reelected in 1900 and held office until his death in 1908.

Cremer used his position as a labor leader and member of Parliament to pursue international peace through arbitration. In 1870 he formed the Workmen's Peace Association. In 1887 he spearheaded a resolution in Parliament addressed to the U.S. Congress and president. It proposed that Britain and the United States agree by treaty that all disputes between the two countries that could not be solved through diplomacy would be sub-

William Randal Cremer *(The Nobel Foundation)*

Workmen's Peace Association

With the outbreak of war between France and Germany in 1870, Cremer formed a committee of British working men that advocated that Britain remain neutral in that conflict. This committee eventually developed into the Workmen's Peace Association, an organization of workers dedicated to resolving international disputes through arbitration rather than through military means. Cremer remained secretary of the association until his death in 1908, and he traveled extensively on its behalf, presenting petitions and appeals for peace through arbitration, both on the Continent and in the United States. These activities established him as an international figure and as a voice for working people on the issue of international peace. The Workmen's Peace Association was key in the formation of another peace organization, the International Arbitration League, which Cremer also helped found and for which he served as secretary. He donated the entire proceeds of his Nobel Prize winnings to the league in 1903.

mitted to arbitration. This resolution captured the attention of French deputy and peace advocate Frédéric Passy, who invited Cremer to Paris for talks in 1888. In 1889 Cremer and Passy cofounded the Interparliamentary Union, an international organization of parliamentary bodies that promoted peace through arbitration. The union was influential in establishing the International Court of Arbitration at The Hague.

Advocate for Labor and International Peace

He was always an advocate for working people, but it was Cremer's work for peace through arbitration that brought him recognition and acclaim. He received the Nobel Peace Prize in 1903 and was honored with a knighthood in 1907. He was secretary of the International Arbitration Society and active in many other peace organizations at the time of his death in July, 1908. Cremer remains one of the early twentieth century's important figures in the arenas of labor rights and international peace. His extensive travels in Europe and the United States on behalf of peace organizations caused him to be well known internationally, especially among workers.

Frédéric Passy, who cofounded the Interparliamentary Union with Cremer in 1889. Passy was awarded the 1901 Nobel Peace Prize. *(The Nobel Foundation)*

Bibliography

Evans, Howard. *Sir Randal Cremer: His Life and Work.* London: T. Fisher Unwin, 1909.

Ralston, Jackson H. *International Arbitration: From Athens to Locarno.* Stanford, Calif.: Stanford University Press, 1929.

Catherine Udall Turley

John Curtin

Born: January 8, 1885; Creswick, Victoria, Australia
Died: July 5, 1945; Canberra, Australia

Prime minister of Australia (1941-1945)

John Joseph Curtin (JON JOH-sehf KUR-tihn) was born the son of lower-middle-class parents of mainly Irish origins. Educated in public schools, he finished his formal schooling at age fifteen and went to work as a clerk in an industrial concern. There he developed the interest in workers' rights that led him to become secretary of the Timber Workers Union in 1911.

Youthful Radicalism

Curtin flirted with independent socialist movements before becoming a member of the Labor Party. He was opposed to World War I, but he shrewdly soft-pedaled this position in favor of an emphasis on Australian self-defense. Curtin decided to move to Western Australia and help unify the Labor Party there. In 1917, he became editor of the Westralian Worker, a radical newspaper in Perth. He also married Elsie Needham in that year. In 1928 he ran for and entered the federal Parliament from the seat of Fremantle. Curtin's strong convictions and eloquent manner of speaking gradually won for him a wide following among Labor supporters.

Leader of the Party

In 1937, Curtin became leader of the Australian Labor Party. His rapid rise to political prominence can be explained only by noting the disunity of the Australian Labor Party in the 1930's. A fresh face from the West, untainted by previous infighting, Curtin was able to unite its various geographical and ideological factions. As war clouds started to gather in 1938, Curtin was one of the first Australians to point out the dangers presented by Nazi Germany.

With the outbreak of World War II in 1939, Curtin reassured the Australian people that La-

bor's general principles of nonaggression and worker solidarity did not mean that the party did not fully support the war against Nazism. Curtin presented himself to the electorate as a basically centrist political figure. Thus he was poised to capitalize on events when friction within the government of Robert Menzies caused it to collapse; similar friction also undermined a short-lived successor administration under Arthur Fadden. Curtin became prime minister on October 7, 1941.

John Curtin *(Library of Congress)*

Wartime Prime Minister

Two months after Curtin took office, the Japanese declared war on Britain and its dominions, including Australia, as well as on the United States. British incapacity in the Far East, as demonstrated by the fall of Singapore, had left Australia with no choice but to turn to the United States as its primary ally. Curtin dramatically appealed to the United States, "free from any pangs as to our traditional links with the United Kingdom," to come to Australia's defense.

A strong commitment from American general Douglas MacArthur helped Australian troops stave off the Japanese assault on New Guinea. Although some Australian cities were briefly shelled by the Japanese, no serious assault ever occurred. Soon the tide of the war had turned to render Australia sufficiently safe from enemy attack. Since Curtin had become prime minister so soon before the Japanese attack, he had none of the onus for the years of unpreparedness and indecisiveness, which fell upon Menzies. Curtin profited by the glamour associated with being wartime prime minister,

Australian prime minister John Curtin (right) with U.S. general Douglas MacArthur in 1943. *(Library of Congress)*

Australia's Labor Party

The Australian Labor movement originally spelled its name "labour" but changed the spelling to "labor" about 1915. The Labor Party had been damaged throughout the 1920's and 1930's by internal squabbling and had almost fallen apart during the leadership of John Scullin (1929-1931). John Curtin's leadership reunited the party, focusing it once more on its heritage of championing workers' rights and mounting a social-democratic approach to government's role in the public sphere. In World War II, as during World War I, the issue of conscription (the drafting of men into the military) split the party, with those who favored no Australian involvement in any overseas quarrel ranged against those whose sympathy with communism led them to propose actively countering Nazi aggression. Curtin's emphasis on the defense of Australia itself defused these tensions. By 1941, the Labor Party was a cohesive political entity. Curtin, on becoming prime minister, did not need to establish a nationwide coalition as had been done in the previous war. The Labor Party spent most of World War II as the governing party of Australia. It thereby proved its ability to govern as a broad, inclusive party.

Australia and New Guinea

In 1906, the British portion of the island of New Guinea was put under Australian authority and renamed Papua. Australia, once a colony, had now itself become a colonizer. This status was fortified after World War I, when the former German portion was amalgamated with Papua as a League of Nations mandate under a single Australian administration. This mandate envisioned the eventual independence of New Guinea, though not in the foreseeable future. Australian rule was not oppressive. Under the long administration of John H. P. Murray, the welfare of the native Papuans was given high priority. In 1942, during World War II, New Guinea was all that lay between Australia and a Japanese invasion, and Australian troops defended the island fiercely. Japanese troops attempted to move down the Kokoda Trail from the north of New Guinea to the capital of Port Moresby. They made it most of the way before American air strikes helped the Australians to gain the upper hand and stop the Japanese advance. Australia continued to control New Guinea under the auspices of the United Nations until 1975, when the nation became independent as Papua New Guinea. Papua New Guinea remained a member of the commonwealth, as did Australia.

even though his own natural tendencies were pacifist ones.

Australia held an election during the war, in 1943. Curtin's opponents were divided and were led by the ineffective Fadden. Curtin's strong victory in the elections was also a testimony to his own political strength and to the voters' recognition of the fact that he had managed the war to the maximum benefit of Australia. Curtin was additionally helped by moderating his economic policies, promising that the government would not take over any industry during the course of the war.

Victory over Japan

Curtin had to struggle for visibility as part of the Allied coalition. Visibility was sometimes difficult in the light of the greater power of Britain and the United States and their relative inattention to Australian concerns. Curtin fell into a sharp dispute with British prime minister Winston Churchill when Churchill wanted an Australian regiment redeployed to Burma. Curtin felt, with the Japanese having penetrated as far as New Guinea, that the troops were better used for Australia's own defense. Curtin eventually prevailed, demonstrating that Australia had overcome the colonial mentality and could put its own needs above those of the British Empire. Curtin's diplomacy, in which he was assisted ably by his foreign minister, Herbert Vere Evatt, gave Australia a role in determining the future of the Asia-Pacific region after the war. Curtin's deteriorating health prevented him from being as vigorous a leader in 1944 and 1945 than he had been previously. By 1945, Germany was defeated, and the way to victory over Japan was clear. Curtin died before the final victory could be proclaimed. He had been under severe physical and psychological strain during the war.

An Australian Legend

As happened with U.S. president Franklin D. Roosevelt, Curtin's death in office cemented his reputation as one of Australia's great statesmen. His legend was continually appealed to by generation after generation of Australians, particularly Labor Party prime ministers. Curtin was one of Australia's foremost leaders of the twentieth century.

Bibliography

Lee, Norman E. *John Curtin, Saviour of Australia.* Melbourne: Longman, 1983.

Rickard, John. *Australia: A Cultural History.* New York: Longman, 1988.

Ross, Lloyd Maxwell. *John Curtin: A Biography.* South Melbourne: Macmillan, 1977.

Thorne, Christopher. *Allies of a Kind: The United States, Britain, and the War Against Japan, 1941-1945.* New York: Oxford University Press, 1978.

Nicholas Birns

George Nathaniel Curzon

Born: January 11, 1859; Kedleston Hall, Derbyshire, England
Died: March 20, 1925; London, England

British political figure, foreign secretary (1919-1924)

George Nathaniel Curzon (JOHRJ na-THAN-yehl KUR-zuhn) (the first marquis Curzon of Kedleston, also known as Lord Curzon) was born into the British aristocracy. He was the oldest son of the baron of Scarsdale. Curzon attended prestigious Eton, where, in spite of difficulties with teachers, he displayed academic brilliance and won many prizes. He entered Oxford University in 1878. He was elected president of the Oxford Union in 1880 and a fellow of All Souls College in 1883. Curzon married Victoria Leiter, a wealthy American woman from Chicago, in 1895. They had three daughters. After her death, he

George Nathaniel Curzon *(Library of Congress)*

married Mrs. Alfred (Grace) Duggan, a widow and the daughter of American diplomat J. Monroe Hinds.

Political Career

Curzon's brilliance brought him to the attention of prominent Conservative Party politicians, and they engineered his election to Parliament in 1886. His mentor, Lord Salisbury, was the Conservative leader of the House of Lords and encouraged him to undertake a world tour. Curzon's research while on this tour allowed him to write three well-received books on central and east Asia and prepared him for a career as an administrator in the British Empire.

In 1891 Salisbury, by this time foreign secretary, appointed Curzon undersecretary of state for India, and four years later he assumed the full role of undersecretary of state for foreign affairs with an additional title of privy councillor, which gave him cabinet-level rank. In 1898, at the age of thirty-nine, he won appointment as the viceroy of India, the youngest man ever to hold that post. Under Curzon, Indian education, police, commercial, and fiscal affairs were reorganized and modernized. He recognized and feared the rise of Indian nationalism and tried to deflate it by partitioning Bengal.

Although Curzon's work was recognized by reappointment as viceroy, he soon found himself embroiled in a fierce political struggle with Lord Kitchener, the commander in chief of the Indian army. This dispute led to Curzon's resignation in 1905. He held several important positions during his retirement, most notably chancellor of Oxford University. He became an earl in 1911 and became active in the House of Lords. In 1915 he entered the cabinet as lord privy seal. The following year

The Yalta Conference of February, 1945, convened to discuss the final phase of World War II, officially reaffirmed the Polish-Russian boundary that George Nathaniel Curzon's diplomatic efforts had established after World War I. Shown at Yalta are (seated from left to right) British prime minister Winston Churchill, U.S. president Franklin D. Roosevelt, and Soviet leader Joseph Stalin. *(AP/Wide World Photos)*

The War Cabinet

When World War I began in 1914, the Liberal H. H. Asquith was prime minister. George Nathaniel Curzon joined the cabinet when it was enlarged to include the Conservatives in the summer of 1915. Asquith did not have the temperament to be a wartime leader, and power gradually passed to David Lloyd George, the leader of the Labour Party. Lloyd George became prime minister in December, 1916. Curzon was the leader of the House of Lords, holding the office of lord president. From then on Curzon was one of the members of the inner cabinet responsible for shaping war policies. Although Lloyd George came from the Labour Party, all the leading figures in the war cabinet were Conservatives. Lloyd George dropped his earlier radicalism and singlemindedly devoted himself to winning the war by working closely with men he once would have vilified.

he became a member of the inner war cabinet under new prime minister David Lloyd George. Curzon remained in the cabinet after World War I and was appointed foreign secretary by Lloyd George. Lloyd George, however, had a deep distrust of professional diplomats and preferred to conduct foreign policy alone through his own private channels. Curzon was constantly ignored and found this time one of deep frustration.

Although Lloyd George's coalition government remained intact until 1922, economic depression and political and diplomatic disputes led to its collapse. Bonar Law replaced Lloyd George as prime minister. Ill health forced Law to leave office after six months. The most able and seasoned candidate for the position of prime minister was Curzon, but the political realities of postwar Britain destroyed his candidacy. Partly as recognition of the growing power of the militant Labor Party, the Conservative leadership decided that the prime minister should come from the House of Commons. They rejected Curzon in favor of Stanley Baldwin. That decision set a precedent that remained in force throughout the twentieth century.

Diplomacy

After World War I, the Allied Supreme Council established a temporary dividing line between Poland and Russia. Curzon's diplomacy had much to do with the creation of this border, and it came to be known as the Curzon Line. It later was recognized as the official border between Poland and Russia at the February, 1945, Yalta Conference.

Bibliography

Bennett, G. H. *British Foreign Policy During the Curzon Period*. New York: St. Martin's Press, 1995.

Goradia, Nayana. *Lord Curzon: The Last of the British Moghuls*. New York: Oxford University Press, 1993.

Mosley, Leonard. *The Glorious Fault: The Life of Lord Curzon*. New York: Harcourt, Brace, 1960.

Rose, Kenneth. *Superior Person: A Portrait of Curzon and His Circle in Late Victorian England*. London: Weidenfeld and Nicolson, 1969.

Zetland, Lawrence John Lumley Dundas, Marquis of. *The Life of Lord Curzon*. 3 vols. London: Ernest Benn, 1928.

C. James Haug

The Dalai Lama

Born: July 6, 1935; Taktser, Amdo, Tibet

Traditional leader of Tibet, winner of 1989 Nobel Peace Prize

"Dalai Lama" (DAH-li LAH-mah) is not a person's name but the title of the traditional religious and political leader of Tibet. Tenzin Gyatso (TEHN-zihn GYAHT-zoh), born Lhamo Dhondrub (LAH-moh DON-droob), was installed as the fourteenth Dalai Lama in 1940. According to Tibetan Buddhist tradition, each Dalai Lama is a successive incarnation of the bodhisattva Chenre-zi (or Avalokiteshvara), the personification of divine compassion. Thus, a deceased Dalai Lama's successor is not chosen, but rather discovered. The monks searching for the new Dalai Lama use various religious and astrological techniques to guide them.

The fourteenth Dalai Lama was found among a family of ethnic Tibetan farmers living under the jurisdiction of the Muslim Chinese governor of Qinghai. He proved his identity by penetrating the disguises of his searchers and by unerringly identifying objects that had belonged to the former Dalai Lama as being his own. When the Chinese authorities discovered that the monks had found the new Dalai Lama, they tried to use him as a bargaining chip to manipulate Tibet's leaders. Only by paying a substantial amount of money was Tibet able to bring the Dalai Lama out of China.

Training of a Leader

The young child was brought to the Tibetan capital of Lhasa in 1940, where he was renamed Tenzin Gyatso and installed as the new Dalai Lama. He was a very mature young man from the beginning and inspired the love and devotion of his flock. Even Western visitors were impressed by the intellectual capacities he exhibited at an exceedingly young age.

Normally the Dalai Lama would not have taken full authority until the age of eighteen. However, events forced him into an active leadership role several years early. In 1950 the Chinese communists (who had taken over China the year before) invaded Tibet. The necessities of a wartime situation led the monks to decide to give the young Dalai Lama the reins of government immediately. He appealed to the United Nations for aid, or at least for a censure of China, but he received no reply. Unable to maintain an active resistance against the Chinese, he had little choice but to submit to the occupation, with the condition that Tibet was to retain cultural and religious autonomy.

The Dalai Lama Under Siege

As the leader of occupied Tibet, the Dalai Lama

Tenzin Gyatso, the fourteenth Dalai Lama *(The Nobel Foundation)*

The Dalai Lama in India shortly after fleeing Tibet in 1959. *(National Archives)*

faced new challenges. China, as a communist nation, was dedicated to collectivism and atheism, practices diametrically opposed to the Buddhist traditions of Tibet. The Dalai Lama struggled tirelessly to preserve his people's religion and way of life in the face of constant pressure to adopt communistic practices. In this he showed substantial skills as a diplomat. In 1955 the Dalai Lama met Mao Zedong, the leader of China at that time, and was impressed by his acumen. The Dalai Lama did not regard Mao personally as the author of the oppression the Tibetan people had suffered and held no bitterness for him.

Tension increased in 1956, when ethnic Tibetans in Chinese border provinces rebelled against the Chinese government. These revolts were put down with such brutal force that the Dalai Lama made a visit to India, where he talked to Jawaharlal Nehru, Indian prime minister, about the possibility of receiving political asylum there. However, the Dalai Lama subsequently returned to Lhasa, as tensions were reduced.

The Communist Invasion of Tibet

Throughout most of the nineteenth century, Tibet had been a Chinese protectorate. However, this relationship ended in the early decades of the twentieth century, when the Qing (Manchu) dynasty gave way to a republic. Later, in 1949, the new communist government of China announced its intention to "liberate" (in other words, to take over) Tibet. In October of 1950, the Chinese army attacked a garrison in eastern Tibet. In the succeeding months, Chinese forces took the entirety of Tibet. The rest of the world ignored the invasion. In May of 1951, the Tibetan government was forced to sign an agreement recognizing Chinese sovereignty over Tibet but

granting a guarantee of autonomy for the Tibetan people. At first the Chinese left the Dalai Lama's government intact, but mounting tensions ultimately led to a full-scale revolt in 1959, in which many thousands of Tibetans were killed, and to the flight of the Dalai Lama to India. Through the years, Chinese occupation forces waged a campaign against Tibetan Buddhism, destroying temples and monasteries. Monks were harassed, and many were killed. The Chinese also created severe environmental problems, ravaging Tibet with harmful mining and forestry practices.

The Dalai Lama and the Movies

In 1997 Hollywood released two major motion pictures dealing with the life of Tibet's exiled leader, the fourteenth Dalai Lama. *Kundun*, directed by Martin Scorsese, was a historical drama dealing with the Chinese invasion of Tibet. It was unusual in that only actual Tibetans, rather than professional actors, appeared in the film. The film was heavily criticized as lacking a compelling story line to match its depiction of the fighting between the Chinese and Tibetan forces.

Jean-Jacques Arnaud's *Seven Years in Tibet*

starred Brad Pitt as Heinrich Harrer, an Austrian explorer who befriended the young Dalai Lama in the 1940's. The film was partly based on Harrer's book of the same title. Sony Pictures was careful to downplay the political element of this story and promoted it primarily as an adventure film. While there were few complaints about political content in regard to China, a number of critics raised concerns about the historical Harrer's alleged Nazi links, particularly because the film portrayed him as a hero.

In 1959 the ongoing resistance activities of Tibetan refugees from the Chinese border provinces led to a new crisis with the Chinese government in Beijing. The Dalai Lama refused to use the Tibetan militia to crush the refugees, as China demanded. In response, the Chinese army sought to take him hostage as a lever to force action against the rebellion. The Dalai Lama was warned of this danger by the faithful, who refused to permit him to fall for the trap of an invitation to visit a Chinese installation without his usual entourage. Finally he was left with no recourse save to flee Tibet. A dust storm, regarded by the faithful as a miracle, covered his escape from Lhasa. In a harrowing two-week journey through the snow-covered passes of the high Himalayas, he fled to India, where he was immediately granted political asylum.

Exile

Upon arrival in India, the Dalai Lama wasted neither time nor energy in bitterness toward the Chinese government for driving him from his beloved Tibet. He concentrated his efforts on settling the constant stream of refugees who were

The Dalai Lama in Washington, D.C., 1997, for the World Parliamentarians Convention on Tibet. At left is U.S. congressman Benjamin Gilman. *(Reuters/Robert Giroux/Archive Photos)*

following the trail he had blazed. Many of them arrived with nothing but the clothes on their backs and had suffered extreme privation to escape the growing repressions of the Chinese government and the puppet regime the Chinese had installed in Lhasa in the Dalai Lama's absence.

The Dalai Lama also gave attention to political and diplomatic matters. In his haven in Dharamsala, India, he established a government-in-exile for Tibet. Although he strove to preserve Tibet's traditional culture, he also recognized that changing times made it impossible to preserve all the old ways unchanged, particularly direct ecclesiastical (religious) rule of the secular society. Thus he helped to draft a modern democratic constitution for Tibet, hoping for the eventual restoration of Tibetan independence. The Dalai Lama also traveled the world to increase the world's awareness of the devastation visited on Tibet and its people by the Chinese. In recognition of his work, he was awarded the Nobel Peace Prize in 1989.

Bibliography

Avedon, John F. *In Exile from the Land of the Snows: The Definitive Account of the Dalai Lama and Tibet Since the Chinese Conquest.* New York: Harper-Collins, 1998.

Craig, Mary. *Kundun: A Biography of the Family of the Dalai Lama.* Washington, D.C.: Counterpoint Press, 1997.

Dalai Lama. *Freedom in Exile: The Autobiography of the Dalai Lama.* San Francisco: Harper San Francisco, 1991.

Leigh Husband Kimmel

Charles G. Dawes

Born: August 27, 1865; Marietta, Ohio
Died: April 23, 1951; Evanston, Illinois

U.S. public official, cocreator of the Dawes Plan and winner of 1925 Nobel Peace Prize

Charles Gates Dawes (CHAHRLZ GAYTZ DAWZ) was born into a prominent American family. His great-great grandfather rode with Paul Revere on that famous night in 1775, and his father, who operated a successful lumber company, had served as a Civil War general and as a U.S. congressman. Charles received his education in Ohio, first attending Marietta Academy and Marietta College, and then graduating from the Cincinnati Law School in 1886. Three years later he married Carol D. Blymer. They raised four children, including two that were adopted.

Businessman and Soldier

Less than two decades after finishing college, Dawes had established himself as a prominent businessman in the Midwest. In 1887 he opened a law practice in booming Lincoln, Nebraska, but his financial success stemmed more from lucrative investments in real estate, meat packing, and banking. After the economic panic of 1893, Dawes relocated to Chicago, where he prospered in the gas and electric utility industry. In 1902 he also organized the Central Trust Company, and he served as its president for twenty years.

The outbreak of World War I in 1914 enabled Dawes to apply his business skills in the military. At the age of fifty-two he joined the U.S. Army. Shipped to France, he worked on General John J. Pershing's staff and masterfully coordinated the army's purchase and distribution of supplies. He provided similar services as the United States' representative on the Military Board of Allied Supply. By war's end in 1918 he had earned the Distinguished Service Medal and had been promoted to brigadier general, a rank he maintained in the Officers Reserve Corps until 1926.

National and International Public Servant

After the war Dawes became an increasingly recognizable national figure. In 1921 President Warren G. Harding appointed him the first director of the Bureau of the Budget. Under his efficient management the government reportedly saved millions of dollars. Not surprisingly, Dawes was asked to head a commission investigating Germany's ability to pay war penalties in 1923. The committee's report, known as the Dawes Plan, proposed new terms and conditions under which Germany should pay reparations to the Allies.

Charles G. Dawes *(The Nobel Foundation)*

Charles G. Dawes in 1921 (second from right in front), at the White House with the Allied Supply Control Commission. *(Library of Congress)*

In the summer of 1924, the Republicans made Dawes the party's vice presidential nominee under Calvin Coolidge. With Dawes doing most of the campaigning, the Republicans won a landslide victory over the Democratic and Progressive Parties. The new vice president's outspoken and aggressive approach to political issues did not always please the more cautious Coolidge. Dawes, for example, actively supported giving bonuses to war veterans and granting government aid to struggling farmers. Both were controversial positions opposed by the ultra-conservative Coo-

The Dawes Plan

For several years after World War I, which ended in 1918, Europe remained politically and economically unstable. At the center of the problem was Germany's reluctance and growing inability to pay huge war penalties to the victorious Allies. An international commission of financial experts, led by Charles G. Dawes, proposed a compromise solution. The committee's report in April, 1924, called for a rescheduling of reparation payments, a new German currency and system of taxation, the end of foreign military occupation, and new loans to Germany. The plan was successfully implemented by 1925. The Dawes Plan may have been the United States' most important contribution to world peace and order in the 1920's. For his work Dawes won the Nobel Peace Prize in 1925.

lidge. After Herbert Hoover became president in 1928, he appointed Dawes to several important posts, including U.S. ambassador to Great Britain and, later, chairman of the Reconstruction Finance Corporation.

Charles Dawes enjoyed remarkably successful and diverse careers. In many ways his life typified the path also taken by other rich and influential Americans in the early twentieth century. Many leaders, including Hoover, Andrew W. Mellon, Charles E. Hughes, and Owen D. Young were accomplished business executives who chose to apply skills honed in the private sector to postwar public service. Their sincerity and dedication in the 1920's is reflected in pivotal achievements such as the Dawes Plan for international stabilization.

Bibliography

Cohen, Warren I. *Empire Without Tears: American Foreign Relations, 1921-1933*. New York: Alfred A. Knopf, 1987.

Dawes, Charles G. *A Journal of Reparations*. London: Macmillan, 1939.

Leach, Paul Roscoe. *That Man Dawes*. Chicago: Reilly and Lee, 1930.

Schuker, Stephen A. *The End of French Predominance in Europe: The Financial Crisis of 1924 and the Adoption of the Dawes Plan*. Chapel Hill: University of North Carolina Press, 1976.

Timmons, Bascom T. *Portrait of an American: Charles G. Dawes*. New York: Henry Holt, 1953.

Jeffrey J. Matthews

Moshe Dayan

Born: May 4, 1915; Deganiah, Palestine
Died: October 16, 1981; Tel Aviv, Israel

Israeli military and political leader, minister of defense during Six-Day War (1967)

Moshe Dayan (MOH-sheh dah-YAHN) was born into a Hasidic family that had emigrated from Ukraine to Palestine early in the twentieth century. Both Dayan's grandfather and great-grandfather had been rabbinical judges (*dayan* in Hebrew) in Ukraine, while his father, Shmuel, went to Palestine to be a farmer. Dayan's mother, Dvorah, came from a relatively well-to-do family, and she emigrated to Palestine following her engagement to Shmuel. They were married in 1914 in the kibbutz (communal farm settlement) of Deganiah. Moshe Dayan grew up during the turbulent years of World War I, traveling from

Moshe Dayan *(Library of Congress)*

place to place as his father attempted to establish stable roots. Eventually they became part of a *moshav*, a land cooperative in which each family is responsible for its own property, outside Nazareth. It was here that Dayan spent most of his childhood. In 1935 Dayan married Ruth Schwartz, and eventually they had three children, Yael, Assaf, and Ehud. In 1971 Moshe and Ruth divorced.

Member of Haganah

Following World War I, which ended in 1918, the British became responsible for administration of Palestine. As part of the British mandate, they were responsible for maintaining civil order, including the protection of Jewish settlers. For a number of reasons, including the small number of troops patrolling a largely unoccupied country, the British were often unable to come to the aid of small settlements subjected to terrorist attacks. In response, a self-defense force called the Haganah was illegally established to protect such isolated settlements. In 1929, at the age of fourteen, Dayan became a member.

Initially Dayan found himself allied with the British, some of whom sympathized with the Haganah. Dayan became a *ghaffir*, a member of the supernumerary police whose job it was to guide British troops. As the British proved ineffective, Dayan found himself increasingly involved in Haganah activities. He exhibited a strong knowledge of tactics, particularly an ability to exploit the use of terrain in military activity. His manual, "Fieldcraft," became required reading for other Haganah leaders. Among the British willing to work with Dayan was a British captain, Orde Wingate. Wingate's Zionist sympathies eventually led to his recall.

In 1939 Dayan was arrested by the British for his illegal activities with the Haganah. He was initially sentenced to ten years in prison, but the sentence was later reduced. In 1941 he was released to join the British in fighting against the Vichy French forces in the region. During the fighting in northern Palestine, a bullet smashed into Dayan's binoculars while he was using them, resulting in the loss of his left eye. After his face healed, Dayan donned the eye patch that was identified with him for the remainder of his life.

Israeli defense minister Moshe Dayan observing army positions along Israel's border with Syria. *(Camera Press/Archive Photos)*

Political Life

At midnight on May 14, 1948, the British mandate over Palestine terminated, and the state of Israel came into existence. The new state immediately came under attack from its Arab neighbors. Dayan was placed in charge of units defending the Jordan valley, shortly becoming commander of a mechanized assault battalion. His daring and ability eventually led to Dayan's appointment as commander of the Jerusalem region.

The Haganah

The Haganah was an underground military organization formed to provide self-defense for Jewish settlers in Palestine. The Haganah operated from 1920 to 1948, at which time it became part of the Israel Defense Forces. The British had a mandate to maintain civil order in Palestine after World War I, which they proved unable to do. This lack of protection resulted in an increased role of the Haganah in preventing terrorist acts. Nevertheless, the organization was outlawed by the British. Following the massacre of sixty-seven Jews during rioting in Hebron in 1929, Moshe Dayan joined the organization. During his years in the Haganah, Dayan frequently led forays against terrorist targets. He was noted for his knowledge of tactics, and his manual, "Fieldcraft," became the instruction manual for other field commanders. In 1939 Dayan was captured by the British, spending two years in prison for his illegal activities with the Haganah.

The Yom Kippur War

On October 6, 1973, during the Jewish holiday of Yom Kippur, Syria and Egypt launched a surprise attack on Israel. The brunt of the attack was along the Suez Canal, where eighty thousand Egyptian soldiers overran fewer than one thousand Israeli defenders. On the Golan Heights in northern Israel, Syrian tanks and a division of Iraqi troops also attacked. Despite repeated threats during the previous year by Egyptian president Anwar Sadat, the Israelis were caught by surprise.

Israel responded by mobilizing its reserves and regained the initiative. Eventually Israeli forces pushed the Arab troops back, even crossing the Suez Canal into Egypt. On October 22, the Israeli army completed an encirclement of the Egyptian army and was in position to destroy it. That day the U.N. Security Council adopted Resolution 338, which called for a cease-fire.

Nearly twenty-seven hundred Israeli soldiers died during the war. The lack of preparedness resulted in a number of changes within the Israeli army and government, including the eventual resignation of Prime Minister Golda Meir. As minister of defense, Moshe Dayan suffered significant criticism for not being more cognizant of the threat. Nevertheless, Dayan realized the futility of constant war with the Arab states, and as foreign minister in 1977 he played a significant role in establishing a peace treaty with Egypt.

Moshe Dayan (center) in Jerusalem's Old City after the Six-Day War in June, 1967. At left is Brigadier Uzi Narkiss; at right is future prime minister Yitzhak Rabin, then the Israeli military's chief of staff. *(AP/Wide World Photos)*

Following the war of independence, Dayan continued to move higher in rank. In 1949 he was promoted to major general and placed in charge of the southern command. In 1953 he became chief of staff, a position he held for four years. Israel continued to be subject to terrorist attacks; when Egypt nationalized the Suez Canal in 1956, Dayan directed the Israeli retaliation into the Suez and Gaza regions. The United Nations directed a cease-fire and established a force which maintained peace for another ten years.

In 1959 Dayan was elected to the Knesset, the Israeli parliament, as a member of the Mapai (Labor Party). Prime Minister David Ben-Gurion appointed Dayan minister of agriculture. His experience in farming served Dayan well, as he attempted to bring a sense of order to what had evolved into a chaotic economic crisis among the kibbutzim. Dayan established a planning authority to guide the farmers and to allow for better allocation of land and water resources. He also established a foreign aid program, attempting to aid the emerging African nations in their own land development. Following a change in government in 1964, Dayan resigned his position.

Military Hero and Peacemaker

Dayan continued to remain active in the role of military adviser. His position was formalized in 1967 with an appointment as minister of defense. Dayan reached his peak in popularity that year following the Six-Day War. On June 5, after continuing provocation from neighboring Arab states, the Israelis launched an attack against Egypt, Syria, and Jordan. The lightning victory of the Israelis came to be symbolized by Dayan and his characteristic eye patch. Dayan remained defense minister through the Yom Kippur War in 1973. The surprise attack and ensuing casualties in that war resulted in severe criticism of the government's handling of the crisis. In 1974 a new government took office, and Dayan was replaced by Shimon Peres.

In 1977 Dayan was appointed foreign minister in the government of Menachem Begin, where he played a major role in the peace agreement established by Israel and Egypt. Dayan felt, however, that the government was moving too slowly, and he resigned in 1979. Two years later, he launched a new center party, but he died of cancer shortly afterward.

Bibliography

Dayan, Moshe. *Moshe Dayan: Story of My Life.* New York: William Morrow, 1976.

Gilbert, Martin. *Israel: A History.* New York: William Morrow, 1998.

Sachar, Howard A. *History of Israel from the Rise of Zionism to Our Time.* 2d ed. New York: Alfred A. Knopf, 1996.

Richard Adler

Alfred Deakin

Born: August 3, 1856; Melbourne, Victoria, Australia
Died: October 7, 1919; Melbourne, Victoria, Australia

Three-time prime minister of Australia (1903-1904, 1905-1908, 1909-1910)

Alfred Deakin (AL-frehd DEE-kihn) was educated at Melbourne Grammar School and subsequently studied law at the University of Melbourne. In 1878 his early career as a lawyer was not proving a great success, so he began exploiting his literary talents by writing newspaper articles. A year later his publisher persuaded him to stand for a seat in Victoria's state parliament, which he won. Deakin was an active member in the state government until he entered federal politics.

Alfred Deakin *(Library of Congress)*

Toward a New Australia

The Australian states united to form a federal government in 1901. When Edmund Barton resigned as Australia's first prime minister in 1903, he proposed Deakin as his successor. Deakin faced many challenges as the new government attempted to build a foundation on which the framework of the nation could grow. In the early days of federation, most politicians belonged to one of three political groups: the Protectionists, the Free Traders, or the Labour Party. This inherently unstable three-party system made governing the country somewhat difficult, as illustrated by the fact that Deakin was prime minister on three separate occasions over a seven-year period. In the 1903 election, Deakin's Protectionists won more seats than either of the other two parties. With support from some Labour members, he was able to govern for seven months until Labour's support evaporated and he resigned.

Second Term

In July, 1905, Deakin became prime minister for a second time but continued to rely on Labour for support. Initially during this second term the economy was healthy and the effects of a recent depression and lengthy drought were waning. With increasing prosperity, however, came rising prices and a series of strikes in 1906 and 1907. The Excise Tariff Act and Customs Tariff Act on Australian-made agricultural machinery created much debate during Deakin's second term. Once again, in 1908, the Labor Party (the party's spelling changed from "Labour" around 1907) withdrew support for the Deakin government and it collapsed. During Deakin's three-and-a-half year second term, pensions were provided for the elderly and for incapacitated people, the long-

Tariff Legislation in 1906

In Australia's 1906 parliamentary session, two acts were introduced to ensure protection for farmers and the manufacturers of agricultural equipment. The Customs Tariff Act proposed introducing an import duty on certain agricultural machinery and fixing a maximum selling price. The Excise Tariff Act proposed an excise duty on Australian-made agricultural machinery but stated that the duty would be exempt if workers who made the equipment were paid a fair and reasonable wage. Prime Minister Alfred Deakin believed that the acts would encounter constitutional problems, and he avoided debating the issues. As Deakin suspected, the Excise Tariff Act was eventually declared unconstitutional by the High Court. However, the idea of a fair and reasonable wage gained support and gave rise to the concept of workers receiving a minimum or basic wage. Wage boards and arbitration courts were soon basing their decisions on the needs of the workers rather than on how much they earned and hence on their ability to pay.

debated future site of the permanent federal capital (Canberra) was settled, and the concept of a minimum (basic) wage for workers was widely discussed.

In 1909 Deakin formed an alliance between his Protectionists and the Free Traders and created the Fusion Party. Toward the end of May, the Fusion Party failed to support the Labor government, which resigned: Deakin became prime minister for a third time. The most notable legislation passed by the Fusion government was the introduction of compulsory military training for healthy males. For the first time the 1910 election gave Australians only two main political choices: Deakin's Fusion government or the Labor opposition. The voters chose Labor. Deakin remained in Parliament until 1913, when he retired.

Sir Robert Menzies, one of Australia's greatest statesmen (himself prime minister for eighteen years), called Deakin "the great builder." Despite the difficult times, Deakin contributed to the establishment of many national policies and practices that later generations of Australians accepted as commonplace.

Bibliography

Carroll, Brian. *From Barton to Fraser: Every Australian Prime Minister*. North Melbourne, Australia: Cassell, 1978.

Gabay, Al. *The Mystic Life of Alfred Deakin*. Cambridge, England: Cambridge University Press, 1992.

La Nauze, John A. *Alfred Deakin: A Biography*. Carlton, Australia: Melbourne University Press, 1985.

Nicholas C. Thomas

Alcide De Gasperi

Born: April 3, 1881; Pieve Tesino, near Trento, Tyrol, Austro-Hungarian Empire (now in Italy)
Died: August 19, 1954; Sella di Valsugana, Italy

Prime minister of Italy (1945-1953)

Alcide De Gasperi (ahl-SEE-day day GAHS-pay-ray) began developing his political views in his mid-twenties, as evidenced by his numerous writings defending Italian economic interests and culture. They were published in the journal he edited, entitled *Il Nuovo Trentino*. His political career began with his 1911 election as an Italian representative to the Austrian Parliament. De Gasperi joined other Italian deputies supporting the 1919 post-World War I annexation of the Trentino region by Italy. De Gasperi served as a

Alcide De Gasperi *(Library of Congress)*

Catholic deputy in the Italian Parliament from 1921 to 1924, adopting strong anti-Fascist views for which he was sentenced to four years' imprisonment and fined sixteen thousand lire on April 10, 1927. Released after serving only sixteen months through intervention by Pope Pius XI, De Gasperi began working as a librarian in the Vatican in 1929. He was visibly active in the Italian Resistance movement beginning in 1939.

Italian Political Turmoil

Following the 1922 appointment of Fascist leader Benito Mussolini as prime minister, the Italian government gradually evolved into a dictatorship. Although the 1929 creation of a politically separate Vatican City in Rome settled questions regarding papal political power, the economic depression that enveloped the rest of the world began influencing Italian economic policy. This policy became increasingly controlled by Mussolini, who made agreements with Adolf Hitler, chancellor of Germany beginning in 1933, providing for joint military expansion.

World War II (1939-1945) was a military disaster for Italy, creating economic hardships and anti-Fascist sentiment. In 1943, King Victor Emmanuel replaced Mussolini with Marshal Pietro Badoglio, who formed a new ministry. Following the 1943 Italian surrender to the Allies, De Gasperi held several cabinet positions. He was secretary of the Christian Democratic Party and minister of foreign affairs before his appointment as minister without portfolio in June, 1944, in Ivanoe Bonomi's first cabinet. The winter months of 1944 and 1945 caused widespread misery for most Italians, with large-scale unemployment, escalating inflation, and industrial stagnation. De Gasperi succeeded Ferruccio Parri as prime minister on December 10, 1945, and formed his own cabinet.

Restructuring After World War II

From 1945 to 1953, De Gasperi served as prime minister of eight successive coalition cabinets led by his center-right Christian Democratic Party. Italy voted to become a republic in 1946, and in the Constituent Assembly, De Gasperi's Christian Democrats emerged as the country's leading political party. During his years in office, De Gasperi oversaw the material and moral reconstruction of Italy following World War II and the fall of Mussolini's Fascist regime. De Gasperi signed the postwar peace treaty with the Allies and persuaded the Italian Parliament to ratify it in September, 1947. Also in 1947, De Gasperi excluded the Communists and left-wing Socialists from the government. This move caused political instability in Italy to continue.

During the postwar period there was a much-needed flow of supplies and financial credits into Italy, made available under the Marshall Plan. The materials and credits created favorable conditions

Livorno, Italy, in 1944. Many Italian towns had been reduced to rubble by the end of World War II. *(Archive Photos)*

The Italian Popular Party

The Italian Popular Party was founded by Sicilian priest Luigi Sturzo in 1919. It was banned by the Fascists in 1926 and driven underground along with all other non-Fascist political organizations. Following Italy's 1943 surrender during World War II, old Popular Party leaders organized the moderately conservative Christian Democratic Party, which was to dominate Italian politics for the next fifty years. Christian Democratic Party leader Alcide De Gasperi became prime minister of Italy in December, 1945.

His eight years in office were marked by social reform, economic planning, free enterprise, and the nationalization of some industries. Following the end of the Cold War between the Western democracies and the Soviet bloc, the Christian Democratic Party struggled as a consequence of its toleration of political corruption and financial scandals. In 1993, the party reverted to its older name, the Italian Popular Party. Its power decreased following defeats in the 1994 parliamentary elections.

The 1947 Communist Purge

In early 1947, six anti-Fascist socialist parties united in a coalition government called the Socialist Party of Italian Workers. The party stood in opposition to the cooperative relationship developing between the Italian Socialist Party and the Italian Communist Party. The Communists promoted a widespread strike for higher wages, which escalated into a national crisis requiring the Italian military and police forces to restore peace. Anticipating resistance to his Christian Democratic Party, Prime Minister Alcide De Gasperi excluded all parties considered socialist or communist from his new government in May, 1947. This move marked a significant change in Italian politics. The growing Cold War motivated De Gasperi to purge leftists from important public positions as well. The precarious balance that developed between Christian Democrats on one hand and the extreme Left on the other led Pope Pius XII to encourage the political involvement of Catholic Action leader Luigi Gedda. De Gasperi successfully protested this involvement, earning him the public disfavor of the Vatican in 1949.

for restructuring the national economy. De Gasperi's government enacted a new Italian constitution in January, 1948. In the 1948 elections, the Christian Democratic Party enjoyed overwhelming victories; they were maintained during the 1953 parliamentary elections. De Gasperi retained the prime ministership until August 2, 1953, when he was succeeded by Giuseppe Pella. De Gasperi then became secretary-general of the Christian Democratic Party, being named its president in May, 1954.

Major Accomplishments

Other major accomplishments during De Gasperi's era as an Italian statesman were the strengthening of ties with the United States, Britain, and France and Italy's 1951 joining of the North Atlantic Treaty Organization (NATO). Shortly thereafter, Italy began to rearm. As a leading proponent of the formation of a federation of democratic European states, De Gasperi helped organize the Council of Europe and the European Coal and Steel Community—a forerunner of the European Economic Community, or Common Market—in 1951. De Gasperi increased utilization of Italy's natural resources by constructing new power plants fueled by natural gas and steam of volcanic origin. He also inaugurated long-term land reform programs in central and southern Italy, led Italy into the European Recovery Program, and restored an influential role for Italy in foreign affairs and international politics.

Bibliography

Carrillo, Elisa A. *Alcide De Gasperi: The Long Apprenticeship*. Notre Dame, Ind.: University of Notre Dame Press, 1965.

Donatella, Della Porta. *Social Movements, Political Violence, and the State: A Comparative Analysis of Italy and Germany*. New York: Cambridge University Press, 1995.

Ferraresi, Franco. *Threats to Democracy: The Radical Right in Italy After the War*. Princeton, N.J.: Princeton University Press, 1996.

Mack Smith, Denis. *Modern Italy: A Political History*. Ann Arbor: University of Michigan Press, 1997.

McCarthy, Patrick. *The Crisis of the Italian State: From the Origins of the Cold War to the Fall of Berlusconi*. New York: St. Martin's Press, 1995.

Daniel G. Graetzer

F. W. de Klerk

Born: March 18, 1936; Johannesburg, Transvaaal, South Africa

President of South Africa (1989-1994) who oversaw the dismantling of apartheid

Frederik Willem de Klerk (FRAY-deh-rihk VIH-lehm deh KLAYRK), usually known as F. W. de Klerk, was the son of a school headmaster active in Afrikaner politics who rose to be the secretary of the National Party in the Transvaal province. An uncle, J. G. Strijdom, a major proponent of apartheid, served as prime minister of South Africa in the 1950's. De Klerk received a law degree from Potchefstroom University in 1958 and started an extremely successful law practice in Vereeniging. He married Marike Villemse in 1959 and is the father of two sons, Jan and Willem, and a daughter, Susan. Marike was a major force in building the National Party's woman's movement and was a main source of strength for de Klerk until their separation in 1998. The Afrikaner society that produced de Klerk was marked by a sense of cultural uniqueness and a fierce spirit of independence. These were coupled with distrust of English-oriented whites and contempt for blacks. For most of his life, de Klerk shared these values.

Rise to the Presidency

In 1972 de Klerk received an appointment to teach law at Potchefstroom University. At the same time, the National Party, which had dominated South African politics since 1948, asked him to run for the House of Assembly. He was elected to the House of Assembly on November 29, 1972, and rapidly rose to hold leadership positions in the National Party. He received his first ministerial portfolio in 1978 as minister of social welfare and pensions. He later held the portfolios of minister of sport: post and telecommunications; mining; interior; and national education. In 1986 he was elected leader of the House of Assembly. As a young politician he spent time in both the United Kingdom and the United States, which he visited in 1976 as part of an Agency for International Development (AID)-sponsored program for emerging leaders.

In January, 1989, P. W. Botha, leader of the National Party and president of South Africa, suffered a stroke and resigned his position as leader of the National Party. Botha kept his position as state president. De Klerk became head of the National Party. Although Botha attempted to regain his post following his recovery, de Klerk outmaneuvered him and forced him to resign as state president in August, 1989. De Klerk took his

F. W. de Klerk *(Reuters/Mike Hutchings/Archive Photos)*

South African president F. W. de Klerk and African National Congress leader Nelson Mandela giving a joint statement in 1990. *(Reuters/Ulli Michel/Archive Photos)*

place and was sworn in as state president of the Republic of South Africa on September 20, 1989. In his initial speech as president, he told his nation that he was looking forward to a "totally changed South Africa."

Breaking with the Past

Although South African society in 1989 was still dominated by the strict system of racial segregation known as apartheid, political leaders were under tremendous internal and external pressure to end it. An international boycott organized by the United Nations had increasingly isolated South Africa

The 1976 Soweto Uprising

Soweto is South Africa's largest black urban complex, located in Gauteng Province in the area formerly known as the Transvaal. It is a large area (called a township) with mostly shanties and cabins, although it does contain some substantial housing. Soweto is populated mainly by laborers employed in gold mines. In 1976 it had a population of about one million, with 52 percent being under the age of twenty-five. In 1974 the regional government issued an order requiring all education in the region to be conducted in Afrikaans. Afrikaans is the language of the descendants of the early Dutch settlers of the region. This policy was detested by the black population of Soweto, who wanted their children to be educated in their own languages. The government began to enforce the policy in 1976.

On June 16, 1976, organized demonstrations took place as Soweto residents protested the teaching of students in the Afrikaans language and the poor state of black education in general. Thousands of students took to the streets. The demonstrations rapidly degenerated into widespread destruction and looting. The prime minister of South Africa, B. J. Vorster, refused to compromise: He ordered the police to keep order at any cost. The result was a massacre of demonstrators: Sixty-two were shot by police. Black leaders used the situation to highlight the injustices of apartheid. As the white administration withdrew from Soweto, students took effective control of the towns away from the government. From this point, the black townships of South Africa became increasingly difficult to govern, and the unrest there played a key role in the ending of apartheid.

The Release of Nelson Mandela

Nelson Mandela, the leader of the African National Congress (ANC), an organization dedicated to ending apartheid—through violence if necessary—was imprisoned in 1962 for his political activities. In 1985 the South African government, under increasing international and internal pressure to end apartheid, began to discuss the conditions for his release. Kobie Coetsee, the minister of justice, led the negotiations. They largely involved trying to persuade Mandela to renounce violence as a condition for his release. Mandela refused, arguing that it was the state which was responsible for the violent struggle in South Africa. The negotiations resulted in a meeting with South African president P. W. Botha at his official residence. Mandela asked Botha to release all political prisoners unconditionally, but Botha refused, fearing a backlash from his National Party. When F. W. de Klerk became president in August, 1989, he quickly moved to meet with Mandela. Mandela told him that he wanted to be free but would not promise a renunciation of violence in return for his freedom. Nevertheless, de Klerk realized that dramatic change was necessary, and on February 9, 1990, he announced to Parliament that apartheid was coming to an end. On the following day, he brought Mandela to his residence and told him that he was about to become a free man.

politically and economically, and internal unrest, dating from the Soweto uprising of 1976, was becoming more violent and unmanageable. South African leaders had come to realize that apartheid had to end eventually. The main question was no longer whether it would end, but how and when.

Dismantling Apartheid

On February 9, 1990, in a major speech to Parliament, de Klerk announced that he was taking the first steps toward ending apartheid. De Klerk personally informed the jailed black leader Nelson Mandela that he would be a free man. In short order the apartheid laws were repealed, the state of emergency was ended, and work began on a new constitution. In 1992 de Klerk called a referendum on a new constitution that would give political and civil rights to the black majority. Although only whites could vote in the referendum, more than two-thirds of the electorate approved it. In 1993 F. W. de Klerk and Nelson Mandela jointly received the Nobel Peace Prize for peacefully engineering South Africa's move to democracy. A year later, in May, 1994, de Klerk passed the presidency to Mandela, who had won in the country's first democratic election. De Klerk remained in government by assuming the post of second deputy president under Mandela. He served in that position until 1996. He remained active in the National Party until his resignation from politics on August 26, 1997.

Bibliography

De Klerk, Willem. *The Man in His Time.* Johannesburg, South Africa: Jonathan Ball, 1991.
Mandela, Nelson. *Long Walk to Freedom: The Autobiography of Nelson Mandela.* Randburg, South Africa: MacDonald Purnell, 1994.
Waldmeir, Patti. *Anatomy of a Miracle: The End of Apartheid and the Birth of the New South Africa.* New York: W. W. Norton, 1997.

C. James Haug

Jacques Delors

Born: July 20, 1925; Paris, France

French statesman who played a central role in European economic integration in the 1980's and early 1990's

Jacques Lucien Jean Delors (ZHOK lew-see-EH ZHO deh-LOHR) was the son of Louis Delors, a bank employee, and Jeanne Delors. He began his working life in 1945 with the Banque de France. At the time, Delors, who came from a working-class background, had only a high school diploma, but he studied at night and graduated from the University of Paris with a degree in economics. Delors married Marie Lephaille in 1948. They had one daughter, Martine, and a son, Jean-Paul; Jean-Paul died of cancer.

Jacques Delors *(Archive France/Archive Photos)*

Climbing the Ladder

After leaving his executive position at the bank in 1962, Delors taught economics at the prestigious L'École nationale d'administration. During the 1960's he also worked in a high-level civil service position, and in 1969, he became chief adviser on social and cultural affairs to Jacques Chaban-Delmas, the French prime minister. He remained in this position until 1972, when he returned to academic life, teaching business management.

In 1974 Delors joined the French Socialist Party and quickly attained leadership positions. Six years later, in 1980, he was elected to the European Parliament, the legislative body of the European Community (EC). The following year he became chairman of the parliament's Committee on Economic and Monetary Affairs. He was also rising rapidly in French politics, becoming minister of economics and finance. On two occasions, in 1983 and 1984, he came close to being named French prime minister.

President of the European Commission

In January, 1985, Delors became president of the European Commission. He was convinced that Europe had to become a strong and unified economic unit in order to compete with the United States and Japan, and he worked furiously to accomplish his visionary goal. One of his first achievements was to reduce the EC's large budget deficit. By his skillful cultivation of business leaders, he also helped to promote a massive increase in private investment within the EC and to double the amount of EC financial aid to developing regions of Europe. In 1989, for example, the commission was authorized to provide aid to the countries of eastern Europe that had just thrown off communist rule. Delors also ex-

Former European Commission president Jacques Delors (right) meeting with French president Jacques Chirac in 1995. *(AP/Wide World Photos)*

The European Commission

The European Commission is the executive branch of the European Union (EU), formerly the European Community (EC). Based in Brussels, Belgium, the commission has seventeen members. Members are nominated by their governments and appointed by the European Council to four-year terms. (The European Council is an executive body composed of the heads of member governments.) The president and five vice presidents are officially appointed for two years, but in practice their terms are almost always extended to the full four years. The main responsibility of the European Commission is to propose policy and legislation for the European Union. It is also responsible for implementing decisions made by the European Council and for overseeing the day-to-day operation of EU affairs. The commission has about twelve thousand employees, grouped into twenty-three divisions, each with its own area of responsibility. However, the main decision-making power of the European Union rests not with the commission but with the European Council.

panded the scope of the European Commission into areas such as environmental regulation, transportation, employer-worker relations, security, and foreign policy.

Delors's principal achievement was to develop and execute a master plan that called for the removal of barriers to the free flow of trade, goods, services, and people among the member countries of the European Community. In December, 1985, the plan was incorporated into the Act of European Unity, with the reforms to be implemented by January, 1993. They were to make the EC, with 340 million consumers, the largest trading bloc in the world. After 1993 the EC became known as the European Union (EU).

In 1989, Delors went further, issuing a report calling for a unified EC monetary system and a European central bank. Member states accepted his recommendations that year. The central bank came into existence in 1998. During the period between January, 1999, and 2002, eleven members of the fifteen-member EU planned to adopt a single currency, the euro. So large was Delors's contribution to creating a united Europe that, by the time he left office in 1994, he was known simply as "Monsieur Europe."

Bibliography

Endo, Ken. *The Presidency of the European Commission Under Jacques Delors*. New York: St. Martin's Press, 1998.

Krause, Axel. *Inside the New Europe*. New York: HarperCollins, 1991.

Ross, George. *Jacques Delors and European Integration*. New York: Oxford University Press, 1995.

Bryan Aubrey

Deng Xiaoping

Born: August 22, 1904; Xiexing, Sichuan Province, China
Died: February 19, 1997; Beijing, China

Dominant political figure in China from 1977 into the 1990's

An ardent nationalist and lifelong communist, Deng Xiaoping (DUHNG CHOW-PIHNG) was a consummate political survivor. He withstood three purges by the Chinese Communist Party (CCP) to become China's paramount leader in the last two decades of the twentieth century. He was born Deng Xiansheng, the eldest son of a landlord and his second wife. In 1920, sixteen-year-old Deng left China to study in France. There he worked as a factory worker and joined the European branch of the CCP. In 1926, he left Paris for the Soviet Union to undertake a year's political study in Moscow.

Early Career

In 1927, Deng returned to China and changed his given name to Xiaoping. After holding a series of offices, including as political commissar of the Seventh Red Army, he was purged in 1933 for supporting Mao Zedong's unorthodox strategy of guerrilla warfare, rural bases, and peasant mobilization. (The CCP center followed a Moscow-directed policy of inciting a revolution among urban workers.) Three months later, however, Deng was rehabilitated, becoming in 1934 the editor of the Red Army's paper, *Red Star*.

From the Long March to 1949

In 1934, the Communists were decisively defeated by Chiang Kai-shek's Nationalist troops and retreated northward in the Long March across thousands of miles until they settled in remote Yan'an a year later. During the march, in January, 1935, the CCP ceded its leadership to Mao.

Deng's profile in the party and the military continued to rise. In 1935, he became secretary-general of the CCP Central Committee and head of the First Army Corps's Propaganda Department. He became director of the Corps' Political Department in 1936, political commissar of the Eighth Route Army's 129th Division in 1938 and comissar of the Central Plains Military Region in 1949. Deng also assumed administrative responsibilities in Communist base areas in northern, central, and eastern China. In 1946, civil war erupted between the Nationalists and the Communists. It ended with the CCP's victory and establishment of the People's Republic of China (PRC) on October 1, 1949.

Deng Xiaoping *(Archive Photos/AGIP)*

389

Chinese leader Deng Xiaoping meeting with former U.S. president Richard M. Nixon in 1989. *(Reuters/Richard Ellis/Archive Photos)*

The Four Modernizations

In December, 1978, the Communist Party initiated an economic reform program aimed at modernizing China's agriculture, industry, science and technology, and the military—the Four Modernizations. Agriculture was decollectivized through the introduction of a new land-rights system called the contract responsibility system. Private, collective, and foreign-owned businesses and enterprises sprouted. "Special economic zones" along the coast were established to attract foreign investment. Authority was delegated to enterprise managers and local and regional governments. Wage incentives to spur production were introduced. China's doors were opened to trade, investment, diplomatic,

and cultural linkages with the West. The army's personnel was downsized; its capabilities were upgraded through purchases of advanced weaponry and the expansion of the navy.

As a result of the reforms, China's average annual per-capita gross national product (GNP) increased 2,100 percent—from $139 in 1976 to $2,935 by 1996. Private and collective businesses became engines of growth, bringing prosperity especially to the coastal regions. By 1995, China had become the world's sixth-largest trading nation and its fastest-growing economy. In 1998, China ranked second in the world with $128 billion in foreign-exchange reserves.

The Tiananmen Square Demonstrations

One unintended consequence of the liberalizing reforms under Deng Xiaoping was the export to China of Western values of democracy and freedom. In April, 1989, Chinese university students began demonstrating in Beijing's Tiananmen Square for government accountability, freedom of the press, and the right to organize independent student unions. The students quickly attracted the support of tens of thousands of demonstrators from cities across China, whose ranks included urban workers, CCP members, and government functionaries. The ineffectiveness of the government's imposition of martial law on May 20 prompted party leaders, including Deng, to decide to use the military to suppress the democracy movement. In the predawn hours of June 4, troops in armored tanks entered the square to disperse the demonstrators, killing hundreds of people (estimates of fatalities range widely; some have put the toll as high as twenty-five hundred).

National Prominence

From 1949 to 1952, Deng helped to consolidate and stabilize southwestern China by serving as the region's party secretary and political commissar as well as mayor of Qongqing. In 1952, he was transferred to Beijing to assume national offices. He was vice premier of the Political Consultative Council and a senior member of the State Plan-

Deng Xiaoping, China's vice premier in 1974, meeting in Beijing with a U.S. congressional delegation; Senator James W. Fulbright is in the center, and Representative Peter H. B. Frelinghuysen is at left. *(AP/Wide World Photos)*

ning Commission in 1952, minister of finance and a drafter of the state constitution and electoral laws in 1953, secretary of the CCP Central Committee and head of its Organization Department, vice chairman of the National Defense Council, and vice premier of the State Council in 1954. He was elected to the all-important CCP Politburo in 1955.

By that time, the first stages of the Great Leap Forward into communism had begun. Almost immediately after land was confiscated from landowners and redistributed to peasants in the early years of the PRC, a process of agricultural collectivization began with the introduction of peasant cooperatives. In 1957, the cooperatives were amalgamated into gargantuan communes in which all property was publicly owned. The Great Leap ended in a disastrous famine in 1959-1961 that took 15 to 30 million lives.

The Third Purge and Rise

In 1959, in recognition of the Great Leap's failure, Mao retired from active governance. Head of state Liu Shaoqi, with Deng as his assistant, instituted liberalizing reforms in an attempt to revitalize the economy. To Mao, the reforms were a restoration of capitalism. To purge the party and country of "traitors" and "capitalist roaders," he used his personal charisma to mobilize the Chinese masses, especially the youth who formed the Red Guard, to launch the Great Proletarian Cultural Revolution (1966-1969). Party and government officials were subjected to mass humiliation, torture, and abuse. Many, including Liu, did not survive. Deng was stripped of his official posts and sent to perform manual labor in Jiangxi Province until his rehabilitation in 1973. In 1974, he became first vice premier of the State Council and chief of staff of the People's Liberation Army (PLA); he was also elected to the CCP Central Committee and its Politburo.

In 1976, Deng was purged for a third time by the radical Maoist faction—the Gang of Four, led by Mao's wife, Jiang Qing—for being a "capitalist revisionist." Mao's death in September, 1976, followed by the arrest of the Gang of Four, paved the way for Deng's reinstatement in July, 1977. In December, 1978, at the historic Third Plenum of the CCP's eleventh Central Committee, Deng became China's new leader when his party eschewed Maoism in favor of a reform program—the Four Modernizations.

Deng's Impact

Deng's reforms transformed both the Chinese economy and Chinese society. From 1979 to 1997, China's economy grew by an average annual rate of 9 percent, a rate that doubled the country's gross national product (GNP) every eight years. The CCP loosened its iron grip on society, allowing the Chinese people greater freedom. Unlike Mao, Deng groomed a younger generation to take over. By the end of 1989, he had retired from all public offices, although he remained as China's unofficial supreme leader until his death in 1997, at age ninety-two, from Parkinson's disease.

For all his achievements, Deng did not reform the political system or the inefficient state-owned enterprises. His economic reforms also spawned unintended consequences, such as the Tiananmen Square demonstrations in 1989, increased local and regional autonomy, rising crime rates, pandemic political corruption, and environmental degradation.

Bibliography

Chang, Maria Hsia. *The Labors of Sisyphus: The Economic Development of Communist China*. New Brunswick, N.J.: Transaction, 1998.

Goodman, David S. G. *Deng Xiaoping and the Chinese Revolution: A Political Biography*. New York: Routledge, 1994.

Salisbury, Harrison E. *Tiananmen Diary: Thirteen Days in June*. Boston: Little, Brown, 1989.

Maria Hsia Chang

Eamon de Valera

Born: October 14, 1882; New York, New York
Died: August 29, 1975; Blackrock, near Dublin, Ireland

Prime minister (1932-1948, 1951-1954, 1957-1959) and president (1959-1973) of Ireland

Eamon de Valera (AY-muhn deh veh-LEH-ruh) was born to an Irish immigrant mother, Kate Coll, and a Spanish-American father, Juan Vivion de Valera. Losing his father and abandoned by his mother, Eamon spent most of his youth with relatives in rural Bruree, County Limerick, Ireland. At age sixteen he enrolled in Blackrock College near Dublin. He earned a bachelor of arts degree and taught mathematics at various schools.

In 1908 de Valera began studying the Irish language, which he mastered, and he married his teacher, Sinéad Flanagan, in 1910. He also joined the Gaelic League, which advocated and organized Irish cultural and sports activities as a revival of native Irish life in the British province. His enthusiasm led him in 1913 to join the Irish Volunteers, a paramilitary organization dedicated to attaining Irish freedom from British rule. In 1916 he commanded a company of Irish rebels at Boland's Mill during the Easter Rebellion in Dublin. Because of his American birth he avoided execution but was jailed in England until June, 1917. He gained a reputation as a leader among the prisoners.

Political Rise and Fall

Shortly after his release de Valera won a seat in Parliament as a candidate from East Clare of the party Sinn Féin. Both the party and the reorganized Volunteers (soon the Irish Republican Army, or IRA) elected him president in 1917, establishing his leadership of the nationalist movement. He and other leaders were rounded up and imprisoned in England in May, 1918, but he escaped in February, 1919, and was elected first minister of the newly formed Irish Assembly (the Dáil Éireann). Seeking international recognition of an Irish Republic in the aftermath of World War I, he traveled to New York and gathered needed political funds during a sweep across the United States in 1920.

He returned to Ireland in the latter stages of the Black and Tan War (1919-1921) and began peace negotiations with British prime minister David Lloyd George. Refusing to continue, he sent a delegation led by Michael Collins and Arthur Griffith. They returned with a treaty that granted neither republic status nor a united Ireland. When the Dáil ratified the treaty, de Valera led a

Eamon de Valera *(Library of Congress)*

walkout and established a new party, Cumann na Poblacht (the Republican Party). Ensuing violence initiated a civil war for control of the new Irish Free State. De Valera served as an adjutant to the director of operations for the IRA and was arrested by victorious Free State forces near the war's end in August of 1923.

De Valera's Comeback

Released a year later, de Valera remained head of Sinn Féin until he left to found the party Fianna Fáil (warriors of destiny) in 1926. Setting a new political course, he decided to work from within the system. When elected to the Dáil in 1927 he took the hated oath of fidelity to Britain required of members and took his seat. Between 1927 and 1929 he again toured the United States seeking funds, this time in large part for his political newspaper venture, the *Irish Press*. When the government of William Cosgrave fell in 1932, de Valera formed a new one. He established a political machine that he would command for forty years by controlling the party, its press, and, for twenty-three years, the government.

International stature came in the form of his election to the presidency of the League of Nations Assembly in 1932, but his main efforts were aimed at eliminating British influence and power in Ireland. In 1932 he succeeded in removing the British governor-general and the oath of fidelity for Dáil members. Despite the international depression, he waged an economic war with Britain from 1932 until 1938, during which England placed hefty tariffs on Irish imports. The early 1930's also saw threats to the government from the outlawed (since 1931) IRA and the fascist Blueshirt movement. De Valera dealt with both successfully. Most important, he redesigned the constitution of the Free State in 1937. Establishing a de facto republic with minimal ties to Britain,

Sinn Féin

In 1905, journalist Arthur Griffith began Sinn Féin (ourselves) as a nationalistic umbrella group for several Irish cultural and economic organizations. Popular interest increased after the Easter Rebellion in 1916. Sinn Féin's first political candidate, Count George Plunkett, won a parliamentary seat for County Roscommon in February, 1917. Politically dedicated to Irish independence from British rule and economic prosperity, the party soundly defeated the traditional Irish Parliamentary Party in the December, 1918, elections, gaining 72 percent of the open seats in Ireland.

Forty-five of these seventy-six new members were in jail or prison, and the remaining twenty-one refused to take their seats in Parliament. Instead they founded the Irish Assembly (Dáil Éireann) and declared the Irish Republic on January 21, 1919. During the Black and Tan War (1919-1921), Sinn Féin dominated Irish politics, but at war's end they split (64-57) over the treaty. Protreaty members founded the conservative party Cumann na nGaedheal, while the anti-treaty elements (including Eamon de Valera) formed Cumann na Poblacht.

After de Valera departed in 1926, Sinn Féin and the Irish Republican Army (IRA) remained dedicated to ending the partition of Ireland (its division into Ireland and Northern Ireland) but were politically inactive. As the political wing of the paramilitary IRA, Sinn Féin reemerged as a force in the 1960's and 1970's in British-controlled northern Ireland as the Catholic civil rights movement attracted a violent reaction. After several splits Sinn Féin remained an influential nationalist political party at the end of the twentieth century and retained ties to the IRA.

The Republic of Ireland (Eire)

Though proclaimed during the Easter Rebellion of 1916, the Irish Republic remained unrecognized internationally until 1948. Initially established by treaty with Britain in 1922, the Irish Free State was a British imperial dominion whose twenty-six counties were partitioned from the six that formed most of traditional Ulster Province and remained part of Great Britain. Eamon de Valera hastened the evolution from Free State to Irish Republic with his 1937 constitution, which only tacitly admitted dominion status and allowed the de facto republic of Eire to remain neutral during World War II. The Republic of Ireland Act of 1948 severed all ties with Britain. Eire is governed by a popularly elected president as head of state (for a seven-year term), and a two-house legislature—Dáil (assembly) and Seanad (senate). From the Dáil the president appoints the taoiseach (pronounced "tee-shock," the prime minister), who acts as head of government.

de Valera became taoiseach (pronounced "tee-shock"; leader or prime minister) of the state. He introduced social strictures that reflected conservative Catholicism and alienated many Protestants and liberals, both north and south.

World War II and After

Negotiations led to the end of the economic war in 1938 and to Britain's relinquishing of naval ports in Ireland over which it had retained control. During the six years of World War II, de Valera managed to keep Ireland neutral despite strong pressure from Britain and, later, the United States to join the Allies. Neutrality kept the Allies from using Irish air-bases and ports, and it ensured that Ireland would not suffer the bombings, invasion threats, and manpower loss that a declaration of war would have brought. Nonetheless, de Valera readily aided the Allies to the extent that he could, returning downed flyers and keeping the activities of the IRA and German intelligence to a minimum. Though he was nearly blind, his iron constitution, self-assuredness, work ethic, and

Eamon de Valera reviewing Irish Republican Army troops in 1922. *(Popperfoto/ Archive Photos)*

vision of Ireland's place in the world all contributed to de Valera's successes.

Economic stagnation after the war led to de Valera's replacement by John Costello in 1948. After another international tour, de Valera returned as taoiseach from 1951 to 1954. He served again from 1957 to 1959, at which time he retired to act as president, a largely ceremonial position. He held the presidency until 1973, when he was ninety-one.

De Valera's stamp on Irish history is both undeniable and controversial. Critics condemn his role in starting the civil war, his imposition of a conservative Catholic ethos on the Irish state, his failure to participate in the war against fascism, and the cult of personality he fostered. Supporters praise his utter dedication, continuity of vision and political flexibility, and the relative stability he brought to Irish politics and civil life.

Bibliography

Coogan, Tim Pat. *Eamon de Valera: The Man Who Was Ireland*. New York: HarperCollins, 1993.

Dwyer, T. Ryle. *De Valera: The Man and the Myths*. Dublin: Poolbeg, 1991.

Fisk, Robert. *In Time of War*. Philadelphia: University of Pennsylvania Press, 1983.

Longford, Earl of, and T. P. O'Neill. *Éamon de Valera*. Boston: Houghton Mifflin, 1971.

Moynihan, Maurice, ed. *Speeches and Statements by Eamon de Valera, 1917-1973*. New York: St. Martin's Press, 1990.

Joseph P. Byrne

Diana, Princess of Wales

Born: July 1, 1961; Park House, near Sandringham, Norfolk, England
Died: August 31, 1997; Paris, France

British humanitarian, active in movement to ban land mines

Diana Frances Spencer (di-A-nah FRAN-sehs SPEHN-sur) was the daughter of the eighth earl of Spencer. Diana had two older sisters and a younger brother. She was educated at West Heath School, where her main interests were ballet and swimming. She then attended finishing school in Switzerland. She moved to London in 1979.

A Royal Wedding

In 1981 Diana married Charles, Prince of Wales, at St. Paul's Cathedral. The ceremony drew attention worldwide. It marked the first time in three hundred years that an Englishwoman had married an heir to the throne. Diana assumed the heavy responsibilities that accompany membership in the British royal family. In the early years of their marriage, the couple seemed quite happy. They had two sons, William (born in 1982) and Harry (1984). Diana accompanied Charles on a tour of Australia and New Zealand in 1983 and of Italy in 1985. They traveled to many other countries as well, including Brazil, India, Nigeria, and Japan. Diana also traveled on her own. Her first official solo visit was to Monaco, for the funeral of Princess Grace.

Diana broke with royal tradition in that she was personally involved with the daily upbringing of her sons. She actively participated in the education of Prince William for his future role as king and trained his younger brother to provide William with the support he would need. Coming as she did from a broken home (her parents divorced when she was six years old), Diana was deter-mined to provide a nurturing environment for her sons.

By the late 1980's, however, it had become apparent that Charles and Diana were spending less time together. Diana, agonized by the troubles in her marriage, suffered from bulimia. Charles spent much of his time with Camilla Parker Bowles, a married woman and a longtime friend. It was rumored that he had long been infatuated with Bowles. Charles and Diana announced their separation in 1992. The endless

Diana, Princess of Wales *(AP/Wide World Photos)*

Prince Charles and Princess Diana returning to Buckingham Palace after the royal wedding at St. Paul's Cathedral in 1981. *(AP/Wide World Photos)*

media scrutiny of the royal couple, and particularly the public adoration of the princess, undoubtedly strained the marriage. Diana was photogenic and charming, and it often seemed as though the world were watching her every move. No other member of the royal family, including the prince of Wales, enjoyed this type of frenzied public enthusiasm. After four years of separation, the prince and princess of Wales were divorced in 1996.

The People's Princess

During and after her marriage, Diana was admired for her compassion and love for the sick,

The Crusade Against Land Mines

In 1996 and 1997 Diana was involved in the international crusade against land mines. Land mines are pressure-sensitive explosive devices planted in the ground during wartime. They continue to maim and cripple thousands of civilians long after wars have formally ended. Although many volunteers had worked for this crusade, Diana's involvement immediately focused world attention on the issue. Her walk across an Angolan minefield was publicized around the world, as was her journey to Bosnia to console war victims. The efforts of countless individuals, including the princess, resulted in the signing by approximately one hundred countries on September 17, 1997, of the Treaty to Ban Antipersonnel Land Mines.

the elderly, the disabled, the homeless, and other victims of society. She gave freely of her time and energy. Diana hugged patients with acquired immunodeficiency syndrome (AIDS), touched lepers, and guided society toward greater tolerance. She developed friendships with ordinary people, people not in high places of government or members of royal families. They knew her simply as Diana. Her own private pain enabled her to understand the suffering of others. Diana was actively involved with more than one hundred charities and raised millions of dollars.

Death of Diana

Following her divorce from Prince Charles, Diana fell in love with Dodi al-Fayed, the son of Mohammad al-Fayed, the billionaire Egyptian owner of Harrods Department Store in London. The romance set off a media frenzy. Photographers ("paparazzi") stalked the couple to earn the huge amounts of money being paid by tabloid newspapers for photographs of the couple. Late on the night of August 30, 1997, in Paris, Diana and Fayed were chased by photographers

Diana, Princess of Wales, touring a land-mine field in central Angola in 1997. She spoke with mine victims and observed a mine-clearing demonstration. *(AP/Wide World Photos)*

on motorcycles. Their driver was driving extremely fast, and he lost control of the Mercedes while driving through the Alma Tunnel. The automobile crashed into a pillar, killing the driver and Fayed instantly and seriously injuring Diana and bodyguard Trevor Rees Jones. Diana died some hours later in a Paris hospital. Jones eventually recovered but suffered memory lapses about the accident.

People around the world mourned the loss of Diana. Her funeral, in Westminster Abbey, brought together members of the royal family, celebrities, and members of Diana's charities. El-

ton John, a friend of Diana, sang a funeral tribute, a new version of "Candle in the Wind." Diana's sons accompanied the casket in the funeral procession while huge crowds lined the streets.

Bibliography

Davies, Nicholas. *Diana: The People's Princess*. Secaucus, N.J.: Carol, 1997.

Morton, Andrew. *Diana: Her New Life*. New York: Pocket Star, 1995.

_____. *Diana: Her True Story*. London: Michael O'Mara Books, 1992.

R. K. L. Panjabi

Porfirio Díaz

Born: September 15, 1830; Oaxaca, Mexico
Died: July 2, 1915; Paris, France

Dictatorial president of Mexico (1876-1911)

José de la Cruz Porfirio Díaz (hoh-ZAY day lah KREWZ pohr-FEE-ree-oh DEE-ahs) was born into a poor, mestizo, peasant family. At age fifteen he entered the seminary and later studied law under Benito Juárez, the great liberal leader and president of Mexico. It was in the military, however, that Díaz achieved success. He won recognition in the Mexican-American War (1847-1848) and in Mexico's War of the Reform (*La Reforma*, 1858-1861), supporting Juárez. He became one of the most famous military leaders fighting the French in Mexico (1862-1867). After the wars he returned to civilian life.

Porfirio Díaz *(Institute of Texan Cultures, San Antonio, Texas)*

Entrance into Politics

In 1871 Benito Juárez decided to seek a fourth term as president. Díaz attacked constant reelection as a violation of republican principles and became a candidate for president. When he lost, Díaz led a revolt that was quickly defeated. Upon the death of Juárez in 1872, Sebastian Lerdo de Tejada became acting president. Díaz and Lerdo de Tejada ran for the presidency, and Lerdo de Tejada won easily. Díaz accepted the result of this election. When Lerdo de Tejada sought reelection, however, Díaz decided to rebel again, and this time he was successful. In November of 1876, he overthrew Lerdo de Tejada and assumed power.

The Juárez and Lerdo de Tejada administrations had been periods of transition, marking major political and economic changes. Both administrations pulled the country together rather than dividing it, as previous governments had done. Tax and tariff reforms were begun, and public security, especially in the rural areas, was increased. Their governments recognized the need to attract foreign capital and initiated improvements in transportation and communications. Improvements in relations between church and state began, and centralization of the government, disguised as federalism, increased. Díaz, exercising dictatorial power from 1876 to 1911, continued these developments.

Establishing Order

The first task facing Díaz was establishing public security. He knew that potential foreign investors would provide the capital and technology necessary for modernization and economic development only if they had confidence in the safety of their investments. When rebels were

The Mexican Revolution

The military phase of the Mexican Revolution began in November, 1910, when long-time Díaz opponent Francisco Madero declared an uprising. The uprising did not begin in earnest until a few months later, in early 1911. It extended to May, 1915. In 1911 Porfirio Díaz went into exile and Madero became president. Madero was unable to control the country, however, and an array of revolutionary leaders continued fighting to establish their own government: In the north were Pancho Villa, Álvaro Obregón, and Venustiano Carranza, and in the south was Emiliano Zapata. By the fall of 1915, Carranza, allied with Obregón, had defeated his opponents and assumed power. A new collectivist constitution that included many of the objectives of the revolution was adopted in 1917. It placed curbs on the Roman Catholic Church and foreign capital, provided for labor and land reform, and reasserted state ownership of all subsoil mineral rights.

The second stage of the revolution began in 1920. In this stage, presidents of Mexico began to implement the constitution through such measures as land redistribution and reduction of the economic and political power of the Roman Catholic Church. According to some historians, the revolution was over by 1940. Others say that at that point it entered a third stage in which economic rather than social considerations became the basis for determining policies.

captured, Díaz had them summarily shot without trials. Rural bandits were given the same treatment. Díaz used the policy of "bread or stick": Cooperation brought rewards, and antagonism brought punishment or execution. The masses had no voice in government.

Economic Development

During his first administration, Díaz addressed Mexico's economic problems. He reduced government expenditures and began a new, tough policy toward smuggling. It decreased the illegal trade but did not increase revenues as expected. In his second term, beginning in 1884, Díaz instituted economic reforms that brought modernization to Mexico. Electrical, telephone, and telegraph systems were built.

Railroads were constructed to connect Mexico City with the United States and with the Mexican state capitals. Increased transportation led to improvements in agriculture and industry. New lands were farmed, and specialized production became profitable. Harbor and dock improvements opened Mexico to world commerce. Mining was greatly stimulated; industry also grew, especially the production of consumer goods such as beer, glassware, soap, furniture, tobacco, bricks, and flour. However, the continuing poverty of the large majority of the Mexican people limited demand.

Dictatorship

The Díaz regime was based upon a combination of political maneuvering, intimidation, and, when necessary, brute force. Díaz did not hesitate to use imprisonment, exile, and assassination to silence opposition. He developed a powerful political machine that extended to the local level.

Society and Culture

The societal and cultural changes that occurred during the Díaz dictatorship were as profound as those in politics and the economy. The population grew, particularly in urban areas—Mexico City, state capitals, and industrial centers. Improvements in public order were noticeable. Mexican

Paris Exile

After Porfirio Díaz sent his resignation as president of Mexico to Congress on May 25, 1911, he boarded a train for Veracruz. From there he took a ship to Europe, where he lived in exile. He looked back with pride at the material progress made during his rule. He completely ignored the high price that Mexico and its people had paid. Díaz never showed any concern for the masses. He predicted that the country would degenerate into chaos after he left. In Paris he lived a quiet life, convinced that his prediction of disaster for Mexico had come true. Before he died on July 2, 1915, he saw the stability he had achieved destroyed in the first stage of the Mexican Revolution.

Mexican president Porfirio Díaz in full army uniform. *(Library of Congress)*

cultural and intellectual life flourished to a point, but as soon as artists or writers ran afoul of the government they found themselves in trouble. The government subsidized works it deemed acceptable but discouraged the use of native themes. If artists produced works that did not conflict with the image projected by the regime, the government supported and subsidized them. Those who did not accept these limitations were harassed, intimidated, or jailed. After the beginning of the twentieth century, young intellectuals began to examine the darker side of the regime and contributed to the outbreak of the Mexican Revolution in late 1910.

The Growth of Opposition

By the beginning of the twentieth century, some younger Mexican thinkers were beginning to balance the benefits and costs of the Díaz regime. Constitutional guarantees were repeatedly violated. Elections were a sham, and the administration of justice in rural areas followed the whims of local officials. Restrictions on the clergy were not enforced, and freedom of the press did not exist. Moreover, the economic benefits of progress accrued to only a few Mexicans and foreigners. Díaz granted lucrative concessions to foreigners and used the powers of government to protect foreign capitalists against strikes or other disturbances. Opposition leaders began to advocate political and social reforms. Rural laborers, miners, and factory workers began to agitate for improvement. When mine and factory workers went on strike, they were suppressed with violence.

After Díaz announced that he would not run in 1910 and that he would accept an opposition political party, political activity increased. However, Díaz did not truly plan on leaving the presidency, and he soon suppressed all opposition that developed after his announcement. He arranged his own reelection in 1910. However, Díaz did not realize the extent of the discontent. Political leaders and the army's generals no longer gave him unquestioned support. Riots broke out in cities and rural areas. Newspapers became ever more critical. By the time Díaz recognized the extent of his unpopularity and offered concessions, it was too late to save his regime. He was forced to resign and left the country in May of 1911.

Bibliography

Gil, Carol B., ed. *The Age of Porfirio Díaz: Selected Readings*. Albuquerque: University of New Mexico Press, 1977.

Meyer, Michael C., and William L. Sherman. *The Course of Mexican History*. New York: Oxford University Press, 1995.

Turner, John K. *Barbarous Mexico*. Austin: University of Texas Press, 1969.

Robert D. Talbott

John G. Diefenbaker

Born: September 18, 1895; Neustadt, Ontario, Canada
Died: August 16, 1979; Ottawa, Ontario, Canada

Prime minister of Canada (1957-1963)

The German and Scottish ancestors of John George Diefenbaker (JON JOHRJ DEE-fehn-BAY-kur) arrived in Canada in the early nineteenth century and settled in Ontario. In 1903 the Diefenbaker family moved to Saskatchewan and purchased a homestead. John's father taught school. Diefenbaker graduated with a B.A. from the University of Saskatchewan in 1915, and an M.A. in political science the following year. In 1919, he obtained his LL.B. and quickly established himself as a brilliant criminal defense lawyer, successfully defending eighteen men against the death penalty. Throughout his political career, Diefenbaker was a steadfast opponent of capital punishment and ardent advocate of individual rights.

The Long Road to Power

It has been said that the secret to success is going from one defeat to the next without losing heart, and Diefenbaker's career is certainly proof of this adage. Diefenbaker sought elective office in national, provincial, and even municipal elections without success no fewer than five separate times. He was finally elected leader of the provincial Conservative Party in Saskatchewan in 1936, but the party failed to win a single seat in the 1938 provincial election. In 1940 he won a seat in Parliament. Diefenbaker sought the leadership of the Conservative Party in 1942 and 1948, and he finally attained it in 1956. Under his leadership, the party won the election in 1957 but lacked a majority in the House of Commons. The following year, Diefenbaker led the Conservative Party to a landslide victory, thus crowning thirty years of unrelenting effort to attain the office of prime minister.

Fall from Grace

Diefenbaker's fall from grace was almost as quick as his struggle to power had been long. His popularity was short-lived, for he promised too much and governed too little. He was a brilliant orator and political campaigner. The Liberal Party had run the government for twenty-three years, and Canadians believed that it was time for a change. Diefenbaker's oratory promised

John G. Diefenbaker *(London Times/Archive Photos)*

great change. Having come from a rural background in the prairie provinces, he stood as a champion of the "little guy"—the worker and farmer. He distrusted corporate business and intellectuals. Diefenbaker was proud not to be a member of the Canadian elite class of central Canada, and they would later prove instrumental in his downfall.

His government's policy was nationalistic and pragmatic. He increased old-age pensions and other forms of government assistance, particularly price supports for western farm products. Under his leadership the government finances slipped into debt, and an untimely recession that began just as Diefenbaker assumed office made the government's position that much worse.

Diefenbaker had also campaigned on the theme of a new vision for Canada, one based upon what he called a "new frontier policy." It called for the extensive development of northern Canada by building a vast system of roadways that would facilitate eco-

Canadian prime minister John G. Diefenbaker (right) in India in 1958, being welcomed by Indian prime minister Jawaharlal Nehru. *(Archive Photos)*

The Prairie Provinces

Canada has a federal system of government in which power is constitutionally divided between a national government and ten provinces. Geographically, the country is divided into five regions: the Atlantic seaboard, the Great Lakes, the prairies, the Pacific coastal area, and the North. The provinces of Alberta, Saskatchewan, and Manitoba sit on the Great Prairie plain in the heartland of North America. Immigration into the prairie region in the early twentieth century was largely European and eastern European, and the prairie provinces have a political culture that is far less tied to British tradition than are those of Ontario and the Atlantic provinces. As a result, the "prairie provinces" share a common political economy and are often united by common interests that override the different outlooks of political parties. The provinces thus typically stand united in disputes with the national government over economic and social policy such as price supports for farm goods, free trade, and federal funds for health services.

The Atomic Weapons Dispute

John G. Diefenbaker was profoundly hostile to communism and thus was determined to remain a good partner in the North Atlantic Treaty Organization (NATO) and with the United States in defending North America. Canada agreed to position American-made Bomarc missiles, designed to use nuclear warheads, in Canada. At the same time, Canada refused to produce its own nuclear weapons or to have nuclear warheads stored on Canadian soil. Instead it was agreed that in the event of a crisis, Canada would arm the missiles with American warheads.

This approach created a difficult problem, however: Who would maintain and control the missiles? When President Kennedy imposed a naval blockade on Cuba in October, 1962, and put American forces on high-level alert, it was expected that Canada would do likewise and that the missiles would be armed immediately. Diefenbaker insisted on making his own assessment of the situation. Two days later, he agreed to move Canadian forces to the same alert status but refused to arm the missiles with nuclear weapons. This crisis undermined Canadians' confidence in their government and was probably the single most important event leading to Diefenbaker's political defeat the following year.

---

nomic development. However, the government's financial situation undercut these plans. Under Diefenbaker, the government was forced to devalue the Canadian dollar, and it faced a showdown with the independent governor of the Bank of Canada. The government forced him out of office in 1963. Symbolic of Diefenbaker's failure in office was his cancellation of the Avro Arrow jet-fighter project. Based on advice that the attempt to design and produce a made-in-Canada fighter plane would ultimately prove too costly, he cancelled the project, thereby putting fourteen thousand people out of work. This decision remains controversial among historians, but it was certainly a costly political mistake for a leader who had campaigned as a nationalist.

Without question Diefenbaker's greatest failure was his inability to manage Canada's foreign relations effectively. He became a bitter personal enemy of U.S. president John F. Kennedy, and his government's positions regarding both the British Commonwealth and the United States were confusing. Diefenbaker tried to maintain strong ties to Great Britain as a way to counterbalance the powerful influence of the United States on the Canadian economy and culture. At times he simply refused to take any position. His indecisiveness in the atomic weapons dispute, which became a crucial issue during the 1962 Cuban Missile Crisis, was a crushing blow to his government. The Conservative Party was reduced to a minority government in 1962, and the Liberal Party was back in power following the 1963 election.

Diefenbaker's Political Legacy

Diefenbaker was as stubborn in leaving office as he had been in pursuing it. He was forced out of the Conservative leadership in 1967 but remained a backbencher in Parliament until his death. Remembered as Dief the Chief, he continued through these twilight years to champion his causes of "one nation" and individual rights. His years in office were short, but his achievements were considerable. In 1960 his government brought in the Canadian Bill of Rights, moving Canada away from the British tradition of parliamentary sovereignty and toward the U.S. tradition of limited government based on individual rights. He also brought to Canadian politics a powerful nationalistic outlook—that Canada is one nation in which every individual should have equal rights as a citizen. This view remains predominant in the prairie provinces but runs counter to the view of French Canadians, who understand the country as a compact between two founding peoples. As a result, the Conservative Party continued to find it difficult to sustain political support in Quebec.

Bibliography
Bliss, Michael. *Right Honourable Men: The Descent of Canadian Politics from Macdonald to Mulroney*. Toronto: HarperCollins, 1994.

Grant, George. *Lament for a Nation: The Defeat of Canadian Nationalism*. Ottawa: Carleton University Press, 1965.

Nash, Knowlton. *Kennedy and Diefenbaker: The Feud That Helped Topple a Government*. Toronto: McClelland and Stewart, 1990.

Smith, Denis. *Rogue Tory: The Life and Legend of John G. Diefenbaker*. Toronto: Macfarlane Walter and Ross, 1995.

Patrick Malcolmson

Milovan Djilas

Born: June 12, 1911; Podbiće, Montenegro
Died: April 20, 1995; Belgrade, Serbia

Yugoslavian political leader and writer

Milovan Djilas (MEE-loh-vahn JEE-lahs) was the son of a poor soldier and farmer. When he was seven, his birthplace was incorporated into the kingdom later called Yugoslavia. He studied law and philosophy in Belgrade and joined the illegal Communist Party in 1932, which led to his arrest and a three-year imprisonment by the royalist government. In 1937 he married his first wife, Mitra; they had one daughter, Vukica, and divorced in 1948. He had one son, Aleksa, by his second wife, Stefanija, whom he married in 1952; she died in 1993.

Communist Leader

In 1938 Djilas was appointed to both the Central Committee and the Politburo of the Yugoslav Communist Party. During World War II (1939-1945), Yugoslavia was invaded by Germany and its allies. Djilas joined a partisan army led by the head of the Communist Party, Marshal Josip Broz Tito, and rose to the rank of general. By 1944 the Germans had been driven from Yugoslavia, and the next year Tito became head of the government and established a communist dictatorship closely allied with Soviet Russia. In this government Djilas was, successively, a minister, the head of the parliament, and vice president, which made him President Tito's heir apparent.

In 1948 Tito, with Djilas's help, ended his alliance with the Soviet leader, Joseph Stalin, and developed a national communism, proclaiming an independent course in foreign policy and ending some controls over the economy by the central government. However, he continued the police state, under which individual freedoms were severely limited.

Communist Critic

Although Djilas had supported his friend Tito in Yugoslavia's clash with Stalin, he began to oppose Tito's Communist Party policies publicly and to call for more democracy. For this stand he was removed from his official positions in 1951 and jailed. In jail he wrote the first attack on communism from the inside, *The New Class* (smuggled abroad and published in 1957). The book charged that communism only pretended to seek an end to all inequality, while party mem-

Milovan Djilas *(Library of Congress)*

Liberal Socialism

A political ideology also known as democratic socialism, liberal socialism joins liberalism's emphasis on legal and political equality with socialism's goal of greater economic equality to benefit the underprivileged. Milovan Djilas favored liberal socialism, which seeks to achieve its economic goals by political means that are democratic, legal, peaceful, and gradual. Therefore, it agrees with liberalism's support for individual rights, a free press, government under law, and competitive elections to determine who governs.

However, liberal socialists reject the limited role for government in the economy that liberalism favors. Rather, they believe that the government's role should be stronger in order to secure a more just distribution of wealth. Even so, many liberal socialists now oppose government planning as well as nationalization of major businesses, which would turn private companies into government-owned firms. Instead, they favor market socialism, in which businesses are owned and managed by their employees and government's role is to moderate the effects of severe economic swings and to manage growth.

bers were really a new elite class, hypocrites dedicated to enjoying their own privileges and power at the expense of the masses.

The book earned him an additional prison term, after which he was shunned by his former comrades and was kept under constant watch by the secret police. He continued to write: essays, novels, plays, and poetry. The government tried to block publication of his books, but they were smuggled out and printed abroad. He became very popular outside Yugoslavia, not only because of *The New Class* but also for *Conversations with Stalin* (1962), which gave an account critical of the Soviet leader and his henchmen. The book cost Djilas even more jail time. He also wrote twenty other works, including *The Unperfect Society: Beyond the New Class* (1969), a two-volume autobiography (*Land Without Justice*, 1958; *Memoir of a Revolutionary*, 1973) and *Tito* (1980).

Milovan Djilas was a central figure in the modern history of Yugoslavia as well as in the rise and fall of European communism. Revolutionary, soldier, political leader, and writer, he became the best known critic of the regime he helped to create and one of the most celebrated critics of communism. He earned fame and respect in the West, both for his political activity and as a major author of the twentieth century. He died still declaring that only democracy could save Yugoslavia.

Bibliography

Djilas, Milovan. *Fall of the New Class: A History of Communism's Self-Destruction.* New York: Knopf, 1998.

Lustig, Michael M. *Trotsky and Djilas: Critics of Communist Bureaucracy.* New York: Greenwood, 1989.

Sulzberger, C. L. *Paradise Regained: Memoir of a Rebel.* New York: Praeger, 1989.

Donald G. Tannenbaum

Samuel K. Doe

Born: May 6, 1950; Tuzon, Grand Gedeh, Liberia
Died: September 9, 1990; Monrovia, Liberia

President of Liberia (1980-1990)

Samuel Kanyon Doe's (SAM-yew-ehl KAN-yuhn DOH) parents were members of the Krahn tribe, living in the remote Grand Gedeh region of Liberia. His father was at one time a private in the Liberian army. Doe received a good, though provincial, education in the local grammar school, and he was deemed of sufficient promise to be sent to the town of Zwedru to attend the Richardson Baptist Junior High School. However, he left to join the army before he completed his secondary education. He was assigned to basic training in Montserrado County in 1970. By 1973 he was stationed near the Liberian capital of Monrovia and had achieved the rank of acting first sergeant. Doe made intermittent attempts to continue his education but spent most of his efforts cementing his fledgling military career. He was promoted to corporal in 1975.

From Sergeant to President

In January, 1979, Doe was transferred back to Tubman Military Camp, where he had trained. During the next year, the level of political unrest in Liberia noticeably increased. The rice riots in

Liberian president Samuel K. Doe with leaders of his security forces in 1986. *(Reuters/Iluc Novovitch/Archive Photos)*

410

the capital in April, 1979, were nominally about increases in the price of food, but more broadly they represented a widespread dissatisfaction with the regime of President William Tolbert, which was dominated by Americo-Liberians. Promoted to the rank of master sergeant in December (the highest level achievable by an enlisted man in the Liberian army), Doe rapidly became regarded as a leader by a group of enlisted men resenting their exploitation by officers and unhappy with the general inequality in Liberian society. On April 11, 1980, in the early morning hours, Doe and a select group of fellow soldiers assassinated President Tolbert and seized power in the capital.

Cementing the Regime

Many observers expected resistance in other areas of Liberia, but this did not prove forthcoming. Despite the brutal manner of its coming to power, the Doe regime was welcomed by many Liberians, who hoped that the native peoples would finally have their say in government. Foreign, especially American, opinion was at first nervous about the political complexion of the

Samuel K. Doe in the Liberian executive mansion in 1990, shortly before his government was overthrown in a civil war. *(Reuters/Jim Hollander/Archive Photos)*

Americo-Liberians

The Americo-Liberians are the descendants of American slaves who returned to Africa beginning in the 1820's. In 1865 they were joined by Barbadians from the West Indies. Ironically, despite their experience of discrimination in the United States, the Americo-Liberians regarded themselves as the elite of Liberia and permitted native tribal groups little say in governance. There were differences between those Americo-Liberians whose ancestors had spent a long time in the United States and those, usually known as "Congoes," who had been recently captured from other parts of Africa. These differences were minor, however, compared with the gap between

Americo-Liberians and the native peoples. By the time William Tolbert became president of Liberia in 1971, Americo-Liberian rule had become widely resented among the populace. Attempts by the Tolbert administration to diversify the cabinet by adding more people of native descent did not succeed. Americo-Liberian rule ended with the Doe takeover. Though Americo-Liberians such as Ellen Sirleaf-Johnson were prominent in the resistance to Doe, the prominence of the group waned, and the violence of the 1980's and 1990's did much to erode ethnic distinctions among Liberians.

U.S. Aid to Liberia

Although Liberia had received moral and material inspiration from the United States at its founding, American aid was of only intermittent significance through most of Liberian history. From about 1870 to 1935, Germany and then Britain took the lead in giving aid to Liberia. Only with the presidency of Franklin D. Roosevelt did the United States become Liberia's primary aid donor. When Doe took power in 1980, American aid was still very important. Despite the despotic nature of Doe's rule, American aid increased rather than decreased because of American fears of communist expansionism in Africa: The United States was willing to shore up a despotic regime if it professed a pro-Western stance. American aid rose from $20 billion in 1979 to more than $90 billion in the mid-1980's. In order to secure American largesse, Doe would periodically flirt with countries perceived as American opponents. For example, he sent his foreign minister, T. Ernest Eastman, to Libya less in order to gain aid from that country than to prompt the U.S. administration of President Ronald Reagan to provide more aid. The U.S. administration generally soft-pedaled human rights abuses in Liberia, although these were noticed by various American nongovernmental organizations and monitoring groups. After 1985 Congress began to cut aid to Liberia after seeing clear evidence of the problems of the Doe regime.

Doe regime, but Doe eased their worries by saying that, by nature, his beliefs were neither socialist nor capitalist. This statement sheltered him from charges of being procommunist. Doe also quickly obtained recognition from most neighboring African governments. He ruled through the seventeen-member People's Redemption Council (PRC), which vaguely promised a future transition to democracy.

At first Doe did not seem particularly to favor his own Krahn tribe, thereby protecting his government from accusations of tribalism. In 1984 a constitution was drafted that retained the democratic mechanisms present in the earlier Liberian constitution. Political parties were permitted to reemerge, and many different parties sought to gain leverage in the political arena. The biases that had previously favored Americo-Liberians were eliminated. Elections were held in 1985, and Doe's National Democratic Party of Liberia won an overwhelming majority. Most internal and external observers viewed the elections as unfair.

The real struggle for power, though, was between Doe and his former chief general, Thomas Quiwonkpa. Quiwonkpa, who was fired by Doe in 1983, fled the country, as did many of his Mano and Gio supporters. In November, 1985, Quiwonkpa suddenly returned to Liberia and attempted to seize power. The effort failed, mostly because Quiwonkpa neglected to mobilize his support in time.

Facing Unrest

Doe's forces brutally murdered Quiwonkpa, casting a shadow over Doe's formal installation as elected Liberian president in January, 1986. Moral leadership of the opposition at this point fell to Ellen Johnson-Sirleaf, a well-known international development official who was intermittently jailed and harassed during 1986 and 1987 because she had made a speech critical of the Doe government to a group of Liberian émigrés in the United States. This high-profile case, as well as many smaller instances of suppression of dissent, lost Doe credibility not only among his American benefactors but also among the neighboring African countries that had supported him up to this point. Doe reacted by trying to corral as many Liberian parties as possible into a coalition that would give the impression that the government was rising above sectarian interest. By the late 1980's, though, Doe was losing effective control of rural areas of the country. This situation was increasingly exploited by the guerrilla leader Charles Taylor, a former ally of Doe who had served time in the U.S. prison system. Taylor's challenge to Doe was the most serious so far, primarily because this time the rebels had a number of circumstances in their favor.

Rebellion and Overthrow

On December 24, 1989, Taylor's forces crossed into northern Liberia and began a seven-month invasion that in August was to lead them to the outskirts of Monrovia. Concurrently, another group of rebels led by Prince Yormie Johnson advanced upon the capital. The perceived brutality of Doe's regime was the prime motivator for these rebellions. Yet many observers also saw elements of tribalism. The Gio and Mande troops that largely composed the rebel armies sharply resented the domination of Doe's own Krahn tribe. Doe rapidly began to lose his remaining popular support as his effective authority became constricted to certain sections of Monrovia. A Nigerian-led peacekeeping force arrived in July, welcomed both by Doe and Johnson. By this point, twenty thousand people had died in the civil war and many more Liberians had fled the country as refugees.

Aftermath of the Regime

In a wave of anarchic street fighting in Monrovia, the Johnson and Taylor forces battled Doe and each other, knowing that as long as Doe survived he could make a claim to authority. Johnson finally apprehended Doe and tortured him to death in September, 1990. In July, 1997, Taylor, who had cemented his authority as president of Liberia, authorized the burial of Doe's remains as a gesture of national reconciliation. Despite the tyranny of Doe's government, it did have a particular accomplishment in achieving the end of Americo-Liberian control.

Bibliography

Boley, G. E. Saigbe. *Liberia: The Rise and Fall of the First Republic*. New York: Macmillan, 1983.

Dolo, Emmanuel. *Democracy Versus Dictatorship: The Quest for Freedom and Justice in Africa's Oldest Republic, Liberia*. Lanham, Md.: University Press of America, 1996.

Liebenow, J. Gus. *Liberia: The Quest for Democracy*. Bloomington: Indiana University Press, 1987.

Nicholas Birns

Robert Dole

Born: July 22, 1923; Russell, Kansas

U.S. senator (1968-1992)

The son of a small businessman, Robert "Bob" Joseph Dole (RO-burt "BOB" JOH-sehf DOHL) dropped out of college and volunteered for the U.S. Army in World War II. Three weeks before the end of the war in Europe, Second Lieutenant Dole was severely wounded while leading his troops in the Italian campaign and was paralyzed from the neck down. Following four years of surgery and intensive physical therapy he regained the ability to walk but had only limited sensation in his left hand. He was permanently

Robert Dole *(Library of Congress)*

unable to use his withered right arm. In 1948 he married his physical therapist, Phyllis Holden; they had one daughter. He divorced his first wife in 1972 and married Elizabeth Hanford in 1975.

Political Career

After earning both a B.A. and a law degree in 1952, Dole served as Russell County attorney from 1953 to 1961. In 1960 he was elected to the first of his four terms in the U.S. House of Representatives, where he supported legislation favorable to farmers and championed the rights of the disabled. He opposed most of President Lyndon B. Johnson's Great Society programs but voted for the Civil Rights Act of 1964 and the Voting Rights Act of 1965. He won election to the U.S. Senate in 1968 with 60 percent of the vote.

Dole chaired the Republican National Committee during the election of 1972, traveling around the country raising money and attacking Democrats. Resigning from the chairmanship shortly after the election, Dole escaped the stigma of the Watergate scandals and was able, narrowly, to win reelection to the Senate in 1974.

President Gerald R. Ford chose Dole as his vice presidential candidate in 1976. Ford generally remained in Washington while Dole campaigned aggressively throughout the country. His sarcastic attacks on the Democratic ticket of Jimmy Carter and Walter Mondale helped energize Republican voters. Starting some thirty points behind in the polls, the Republicans ended with 49 percent of the vote. On the other hand, some analysts have argued that Dole's slashing partisan tactics, especially in the nationally televised debate with Mondale, may have done more harm than good. They suggest that negative voter reactions to his attacks may have cost the Republicans enough votes to lose the election.

Presidential Campaigns

Dole ran for the Republican nomination for president in 1980 but dropped out after his poor showing in the New Hampshire primary. That year Ronald Reagan's landslide presidential victory also produced a Republican majority in the Senate. As chairman of the Senate Finance Committee, 1981-1984, and as Senate majority leader, 1984-1987, Dole attracted national attention for his support of Reagan's programs. Although the Republican loss of a Senate majority in the 1986 election demoted Dole to minority leader, his national prominence enabled him to run a competitive campaign for the 1988 presidential nomination. Dole easily won the first primary in Iowa, but in New Hampshire he fell behind Vice President George Bush (whom he accused of lying about Dole's record), and was never able to catch up. As Senate minority leader, Dole loyally acted as spokesman for the Bush administration during the next four years.

Robert Dole (right) and Walter Mondale during the 1976 vice-presidential debate televised from Houston, Texas. *(AP/Wide World Photos)*

After Bush lost the election to Governor Bill Clinton in 1992, Dole's position as Republican leader in the Senate made him the national Republican spokesman and the leading candidate for the presidency. Despite his advanced age he was able to hold off challenges from younger candidates and win the Republican nomination in 1996. However, his subsequent campaign lacked focus and, despite personal attacks on

---

The Dole-Mondale Debate

On October 15, 1976, Bob Dole faced Senator Walter Mondale in the first televised debate between vice presidential candidates. Dole's aggressive attacks on the Democratic Party pleased Republican listeners but risked antagonizing independent voters. When one reporter asked if the Watergate scandal was still a legitimate issue in 1976, Dole answered with a combative comment that all listeners would remember. "It's not a very good issue any more than the war in Vietnam would be or World War II. . . . I figured up the other day, if we added up the killed and wounded in Democrat wars in this century, it'd be about 1.6 million Americans—enough to fill the city of Detroit." Mondale responded that the war with Nazi Germany was not a partisan affair, and he scathingly remarked that "Senator Dole has richly earned his reputation as a hatchet man tonight."

Robert Dole leaving the Capitol after resigning from the U.S. Senate to run for president full-time in June, 1996. Elizabeth Dole is at left. *(AP/Wide World Photos)*

Clinton's character late in the race, he never overcame Clinton's early lead.

Bibliography

Hilton, Stanley G. *Senator for Sale: An Unauthorized Biography of Senator Bob Dole*. New York: St. Martin's Press, 1995.

Thompson, Jake H. *Bob Dole: The Republican's Man for All Seasons*. New York: Donald A. Fine, 1994.

Wertime, Marcia. *Bob Dole: Politician*. Philadelphia: Chelsea, 1997.

Milton Berman

Karl Dönitz

Born: September 16, 1891; Grünau, near Berlin, Germany
Died: December 24, 1980; Aumühle-Bilenkamp, near Hamburg, West Germany

German admiral, commander of the German navy (1943-1945)

Karl Dönitz (KAHRL DOO-nihtz) came from modest origins—his father was an engineer with the Zeiss optical firm—and became a naval cadet in 1910 in the Imperial Germany Navy. During World War I, Dönitz served on the light cruiser *Breslau* and later commanded a small submarine that was sunk by the British; Dönitz was captured. Following the German defeat, Dönitz was retained in the *Reichmarine*, the new German navy. He was appointed chief of the *Reichmarine's* submarine force in 1935.

Blitzkrieg at Sea

Promoted to rear admiral on October 1, 1939, shortly after the outbreak of World War II, Dönitz was named commander of the German submarine fleet. At the beginning of the war, he had fifty-seven U-boats (submarines), of which only twenty-six were large enough for operations in the Atlantic. However, Dönitz soon inflicted considerable damage to the British merchant marine and warships—the U-29, for example, sank the battleship *Royal Oak* in Scapa Flow, the British navy's home base. After the fall of France in May, 1940, Dönitz used his U-boats in the "wolf pack" tactics that concentrated German submarines on Allied convoys.

Dönitz's strategy was to cut off Britain's vital maritime supply line. To accomplish this, his U-boats undertook the Battle of the Atlantic, a concentrated assault on all naval shipping bound for Great Britain, especially ships from the United States. Dönitz's demands for ever greater resources brought him into conflict with the *Reichmarine's* commander, Erich Raeder, who favored traditional surface vessels. When German dictator Adolf Hiter approved the U-boat strategy, Raeder was replaced by Dönitz, who retained personal control of the U-boat campaign.

The Tide Turns

When the United States entered the war in late 1941, the Battle of the Atlantic intensified. The Germans constructed bomb-proof bases along the French coast and produced increasingly sophisticated and powerful submarines. Under Dönitz, the German navy pioneered the snorkel, or breathing tube, which allowed U-boats to re-

German admiral Karl Dönitz (far right), commander of the German navy from 1943 to 1945. *(Library of Congress)*

417

main underwater longer, and the acoustic homing torpedo, which targeted a ship's propellers. Early in 1945, innovative designs such as the Type XXI and Type XXII submarines were introduced, but these were too late and too limited to affect the course of the war.

Dönitz had been an early recruit to the Nazi Party and was steadfast in his commitment to Hitler. In January, 1944, he was awarded the Golden Party Badge, the highest Nazi honor. In April, 1945, as Germany's defeat appeared certain, Hitler named Dönitz as his successor. On May 1, 1945, Dönitz learned that Hitler had committed suicide in Berlin; he briefly became the Third Reich's second, and last, führer. On May 4, Dönitz

A new German submarine being launched for action in World War II. *(Archive Photos)*

ordered the surrender of German troops. He was captured and arrested by British forces on May 23.

Along with other surviving Nazi leaders, Dönitz was tried for war crimes at Nuremberg.

He was convicted and sentenced to ten years, the lightest punishment given to any defendant. He was incarcerated in Spandau Prison until his release in 1956. He lived the rest of his life in Hamburg, where he died in 1980.

The Battle of the Atlantic

"The only thing that ever really frightened me during the war was the U-boat peril," Winston Churchill wrote in his memoirs. This peril peaked during the Battle of the Atlantic in the spring of 1943, when German U-boat commander Karl Dönitz nearly succeeded in sinking enough ships to defeat Britain. In March, 1943, Dönitz had 114 U-boats in the Atlantic. His "wolf pack" tactics concentrated large numbers of submarines against individual convoys. In a series of major convoy battles, German submarines were destroying Allied ships faster than they could be replaced.

By May, 1943, however, the Battle of the Atlantic had turned in favor of the Allies. Their radar, submarine spotting, attack by long-range bombers, and escort carriers forced the U-boats to retreat. Dönitz hoped in vain that improved technology would allow him to retake the offensive. The naval Battle of the Atlantic, like the Battle of Britain, fought in the air, was a crucial Allied victory.

A Narrow Moral Vision

A gifted naval strategist, Dönitz refused to consider the moral implications of the regime he served. He believed the German military owed unquestioning obedience to their superiors, especially to Adolf Hitler, their führer. He ordered his U-boat captains to inflict the greatest possible damage, including the killing of Allied sailors and merchant seamen. Such acts were the basis of many of the charges against him at Nuremberg. In his defense, it could be argued that Dönitz merely accepted the dictum that "war is hell" and that he also felt its sting: Both of his sons died in World War II, one on a torpedo boat and the other in a submarine.

Bibliography

Blair, Clay. *Hitler's U-Boat War*. New York: Random House, 1996.

Keegan, John. *The Price of Admiralty: The Evolution of Naval Warfare*. New York: Viking, 1988.

_____. *The Second World War*. New York: Viking, 1989.

Padfield, Peter. *Dönitz: The Last Führer*. New York: Harper and Row, 1984.

Polmar, Norman, and Thomas B. Allen. *World War II: The Encyclopedia of the War Years, 1941-1945*. New York: Random House, 1996.

Michael Witkoski

Tommy Douglas

Born: October 20, 1904; Falkirk, Scotland
Died: February 24, 1986; Ottawa, Canada

Canadian political leader, long-time premier of Saskatchewan (1944-1961)

Thomas "Tommy" Clement Douglas (TO-muhs "TO-mee" KLEH-mehnt DUHG-luhs) immigrated to western Canada with his family in 1911. His father joined the Canadian army in World War I. The family went back to Scotland for the duration of the war, returning to Winnipeg in 1919. In his childhood Douglas was strongly influenced by experiences with working-class labor movements in Scotland and in Winnipeg. His family was living in Winnipeg at the time of the Winnipeg general strike of 1919. Douglas left school at fourteen to apprentice as a printer and the entered Brandon College to become a Baptist minister at the age of twenty. During his college years he came into close contact with the social gospel movement and the unique brand of Christian socialism it embodied.

Premier of Saskatchewan

In 1930, Douglas took up his first parish in Weyburn, Saskatchewan. Nowhere in the country were the combined effects of drought and the Great Depression more devastating. Already convinced that Christianity was a social movement that was as concerned with improving life in this world as in the next, Douglas was actively involved in the local Independent Labour Party. He also took part in the founding convention of a new political party, the Co-operative Commonwealth Federation (CCF). In 1934, he stood as a CCF candidate in the provincial election and lost. Douglas proved to be a skilful campaigner, however, and he quickly showed signs of becoming one of Canada's greatest political orators. The following year he won a seat in Parliament.

Having established a reputation in national politics as a man of courage who defended the rights of the everyday working person, Douglas became the logical choice to lead the Saskatchewan CCF. In 1944, he became the first elected social democratic premier in Canada. His Saskatchewan government remained in office through the next seventeen years and introduced major reforms in social policy and workers' rights. The CCF government pioneered public automobile insurance, the development of public

Tommy Douglas *(Library of Congress)*

utilities and crown corporations, and improvements in mass education. Most important, it instituted publicly financed universal medical care. The establishment of the health-care system was the great battle of Douglas's political career, ending in a showdown with the province's medical establishment and a strike by doctors. The CCF government carried the day, and Douglas's achievement in Saskatchewan led to the eventual establishment of a public health-care system throughout Canada.

Leader of the NDP

In 1961, Douglas stepped down as premier of Saskatchewan to become the first leader of a new national party, the New Democratic Party (NDP)—an alliance of the CCF and the trade-union movement. He served as its leader for the next ten years. Despite Douglas's abilities as a leader and brilliant parliamentary debater, the NDP remained

Tommy Douglas being hoisted aloft by supporters after winning the leadership of the New Democratic Party at its 1961 Ottawa convention. *(Library of Congress)*

The Great Depression in Canada

The international economic collapse known as the Great Depression, combined with drought in western Canada, devastated the country in the early 1930's. In 1928, western farmers had brought in their largest crop ever; the following year, grain prices completely collapsed. Between 1929 and 1933, the country's gross national expenditure declined by 42 percent. Almost one in three workers was unemployed. The western Canadian provinces were hardest hit because of their relatively undiversified economies. Canada's national government was forced to take on new responsibilities for providing employment in the form of work camps, setting monetary policy, and establishing a government entity to regulate wheat prices. Ultimately, the Depression led to massive changes in the way Canadians viewed the role of government, and it marked the beginning of Canada's establishment of a modern welfare state.

a distant third in popularity. Nonetheless, the party had substantial influence in bringing about progressive reforms. The party also actively opposed the United States' military involvement in Vietnam and became increasingly nationalistic in the late 1960's. In 1971, Douglas stepped down from the leadership but remained in Parliament as the party's energy critic until his retirement in 1979.

Douglas stands as one of Canada's most successful political leaders. He is remembered as a model of political integrity and progressive leadership. The influence of democratic socialism in shaping public policy in Canada is due in no small part to his leadership over the forty-five years he held public office.

Bibliography

Douglas, T. C. *The Making of a Socialist*. Edmonton: University of Alberta Press, 1982.

McLeod, Thomas H., and Ian McLeod. *Tommy Douglas: The Road to Jerusalem*. Edmonton: Hurtig, 1987.

Whitehorn, Alan. *Canadian Socialism: Essays on the CCF-NDP*. Toronto: Oxford University Press, 1992.

Patrick Malcolmson

William O. Douglas

Born: October 16, 1898; Maine, Minnesota
Died: January 19, 1980; Washington, D.C.

U.S. jurist and Supreme Court justice (1939-1975)

William Orville Douglas (WIHL-yuhm OHR-vihl DUHG-luhs) was the son of a minister. His father died when he was a small child, and he grew up in poverty in Yakima, Washington. Douglas was struck by polio as a youngster and spent many hours hiking in the mountains to gain strength in his legs. Throughout his life he was an avid outdoorsman. He graduated from Whitman College in Washington State in 1920 and from Columbia University Law School in 1925. He was married four times, with the first three marriages ending in divorce. He had one daughter and one son by his first wife, Mildred Riddle Douglas.

After graduating near the top of his law school class at Columbia, Douglas worked briefly for a New York law firm before becoming a professor at Yale Law School. President Franklin D. Roosevelt named Douglas to serve on the Securities and Exchange Commission in 1936. Roosevelt later appointed Douglas to a seat on the U.S. Supreme Court in 1939, when Douglas was only forty years old.

Judicial Performance

Douglas's impoverished childhood gave him a special concern for people who were mistreated by others because they were poor, were members of minority groups, or held beliefs that differed from those of most people in society. During Douglas's years on the Supreme Court, he contributed to many decisions expanding rights concerning speech, religion, discrimination, and criminal defendants.

Douglas was extraordinarily independent. He did not shy away from controversy. Douglas was criticized by members of Congress because he so frequently favored the rights of individuals over granting expanded authority to the government.

He also received personal criticism because he was thrice-divorced and eventually married a woman forty years younger than himself. There were several unsuccessful efforts by Douglas's critics in Congress to initiate impeachment proceedings against him. Impeachment is the mechanism for removing high officials from office for misconduct and it is the only way to remove life-tenured justices from the U.S. Supreme Court.

Douglas's Importance

Douglas was a prolific writer, authoring many books in addition to his opinions in Supreme

William O. Douglas *(Library of Congress)*

Judicial Activism

"Judicial activism" is a term used by critics to describe the actions of judges who allegedly exceed the proper limits of their authority. The label may be applied, for example, when judges' decisions affect policy issues that the critics believe should be under the control of the legislative or executive branches of government. It is also used to describe the rulings of judges who allegedly fail to follow the Constitution's words or to respect existing judicial decisions. The term may be directed at either liberal or conservative judges. The conservative critics of William O. Douglas accused him of engaging in judicial activism by creating rights, such as the right to privacy, that are not clearly described in the Constitution. By contrast, liberal critics have accused other justices of improperly creating special rights for businesses.

Court cases. When Douglas disagreed with decisions made by a majority of justices on the Supreme Court, he was quick to express his own views in dissenting opinions. Many of his most famous judicial opinions defined new rights. For example, in *Douglas v. California* (1963), Douglas's opinion established that poor people convicted of crimes are entitled to have the government provide an attorney for them when they seek to appeal their convictions. In his most famous and controversial decision, *Griswold v. Connecticut* (1965), Douglas's opinion established a constitutional right to privacy, even though the word "privacy" is not in the Constitution. This right has been used to protect individuals against interference by government when they make decisions about their marriages and families as well as controversial matters such as abortions. Douglas retired from the Supreme Court in 1975 after being disabled by a stroke. He was one of its longest-serving justices. Douglas died five years later at the age of eighty-one. He will always be remembered as one of the Supreme Court's strongest defenders of individual rights.

William O. Douglas in his Washington, D.C., office in 1939, shortly before being nominated to the Supreme Court by President Franklin D. Roosevelt. *(AP/Wide World Photos)*

Bibliography

Douglas, William O. *The Court Years, 1939-1975: The Autobiography of William O. Douglas.* New York: Random House, 1980.

———. *Go East, Young Man.* New York: Random House, 1974.

Wasby, Stephen L. *"He Shall Not Pass This Way Again": The Legacy of Justice William O. Douglas.* Pittsburgh, Pa.: University of Pittsburgh Press, 1990.

Christopher E. Smith

Alexander Douglas-Home

Born: July 2, 1903; London, England
Died: October 9, 1995; The Hirsel, Coldstream, Berwickshire, Scotland

Prime minister of Great Britain (1963-1964)

Alexander Frederick Douglas-Home (a-lehk-ZAN-dur FREH-duh-rihk DUHG-luhs-HEWM) was born a Scottish aristocrat. Holding the courtesy title of Viscount Dunglass as a young man, he attended Eton College and Christ Church, Oxford. He excelled at cricket. In 1936, he married Elizabeth Alington; they had four children. From 1951 (at the death of his father) to 1963 he was generally referred to as Lord Home; in 1963 he renounced his titles and was known thereafter as Sir Alec Douglas-Home.

Early Victories and Defeats

In 1929, the young Dunglass ran for Parliament as a Conservative and lost. In 1931, he tried again and won. In 1936, he became personal private secretary to the Conservative prime minister, Neville Chamberlain. In 1938, Dunglass accompanied Chamberlain to Munich, where Czechoslovakia was partitioned, and he supported Chamberlain's policy of appeasement. When World War II began, Dunglass' political fortunes plummeted. After recovering from a serious operation, he served in Winston Churchill's government for several months before the general election of 1945.

The House of Lords

When his father died in 1951, Dunglass became the fourteenth earl of Home and entered the House of Lords. Churchill appointed him minister of state for Scotland, and in 1955 Prime Minister Anthony Eden named him secretary of state for the commonwealth. He served for five years, supporting Eden on British actions during the Suez Crisis. He was deputy leader of the government in the House of Lords from 1956 to1957 and leader from 1957 to 1960.

The nation was surprised when in 1960 Prime Minister Harold Macmillan appointed Home foreign secretary. Because he could not present the government's ideas in the House of Commons, many wondered whether he could do the job. Home soon showed, however, that he possessed the requisite knowledge, political experience, and strength of character. He was known for his staunch opposition to communism and for opposing the United States on several issues, such as admitting China to the United Nations. Home

Alexander Douglas-Home *(Library of Congress)*

425

British prime minister Alexander Douglas-Home (right) in 1964 with Canadian prime minister Lester Pearson. *(Library of Congress)*

faced problems in Africa and with the United Nations. He also helped lead Britain's unsuccessful application to join the European Economic Community (the Common Market).

Prime Minister

In October, 1963, Macmillan resigned, and Home was asked to form a new government. In order to do so, he renounced his titles. In his year as prime minister, Sir Alec Douglas-Home wrestled, not always successfully, with his country's economic woes. He was noticeably ill at ease when he had to appear on television. In foreign affairs, he had to deal with problems in Cyprus, Cuba, Nigeria, Rhodesia, and Indonesia—and with the new Lyndon Johnson administration in the United States.

Defeat and After

After the Conservative Party's defeat in 1964, Douglas-Home yielded the party's leadership to Edward Heath. He continued to speak out on foreign affairs, and from 1970 to 1974 he was Heath's foreign secretary. He visited China and tried to negotiate a settlement in Rhodesia. He was not greatly involved in Britain's successful reapplication to join the Common Market. In 1974, he retired from politics and was made a life peer as Baron Home of the Hirsel.

The Lords and the Leadership

When Prime Minister Harold Wilson considered naming his successor in 1963, he faced a problem: Alexander Douglas-Home was an earl. He was a member of the House of Lords and was thereby ineligible to sit in the House of Commons. In previous centuries, many lords had been prime ministers. Since 1911, however, a more democratic Britain had assumed that a prime minister must be a commoner. Although over the years, several lords had been serious candidates for the job, the problem did not come to a head until Douglas-Home, the fourteenth earl of Home, was asked to form a government. Home solved the problem by becoming a commoner himself. Parliament had recently passed a law allowing peers to renounce their titles. Lord Home therefore resigned all of his titles except knight of the thistle (knights are not peers) and became Sir Alec Douglas-Home. He then won a by-election and entered the House of Commons to be prime minister.

He wrote three books. Until felled by a stroke in 1992, he often spoke in the House of Lords.

A Career of Service

Douglas-Home did not possess noteworthy intellectual gifts or originality. He was dedicated to public service, however, and his good judgment and cool temperament allowed him to serve well. Although his brief tenure as prime minister was not distinguished, he will be remembered as an effective foreign secretary. His charm and toughness inspired loyalty and made him a good leader during difficult times.

Bibliography

Barber, James. *The Prime Minister Since 1945*. Oxford, England: Blackwell, 1991.

Shell, Donald, and Richard Hodder-Williams, eds. *Churchill to Major: The British Prime Ministership since 1945*. Armonk, N.Y.: M. E. Sharpe, 1995.

Young, Kenneth. *Sir Alec Douglas-Home*. Teaneck, N.J.: Fairleigh Dickinson University Press, 1971.

George Soule

Alexander Downer

Born: September 9, 1951; Adelaide, Australia

Australian political leader, foreign minister (named 1996)

Alexander John Gosse Downer (a-lehk-ZAN-dur JON GOS DOW-nur) is the son of Sir Alexander Downer, who served as minister for immigration and Australian high commissioner in Great Britain, and Mary Gosse. He studied at the elite Geelong Grammar School near Melbourne and then went to Britain and attended Radley College, Oxford. He spent the major phase of his undergraduate education at Newcastle University in England. There he excelled in athletics while impressing professors with his intellectual prowess. He met Nicola (Nicky) Robinson, whom he married in 1978. By this time, after a brief stint in banking, he had joined the Australian diplomatic service as a political appointee of the Liberal Fraser government. Once the Liberal Party became the opposition party in 1983, Downer served as party spokesman in a variety of fields, including arts, housing, and trade. Eventually he was seen as a rising star in a party that seemed to be coming closer to power after being in opposition for so long.

In the Family Tradition

The Liberal Party, led by free-market radical John Hewson, unexpectedly failed to gain power in the general election of 1993, in which they had been widely favored. The Liberals had spent years in the political wilderness under a variety of leaders, and the need for new leadership was paramount. Downer emerged as a natural choice to lead the party in a time of confusion, as he was a young face yet had a powerful sense of the party's tradition through his family (not only through his father but also through his grandfather, who had been premier of South Australia).

Downer became Liberal leader on May 23, 1994. The course of his leadership did not go as smoothly as he may have hoped. His accent seemed far too upper-class for the populist climate of Australian politics. Far from being a spokesman for the ordinary Australian that had traditionally been the backbone of the Liberal constituency, Downer's public manner seemed stilted and uninspiring. As the Australian government led by Paul Keating became more popular, former Liberal leader John Howard saw a chance to regain control of the party at an opportune time. In December, 1994, Downer stood

Alexander Downer *(AP/Wide World Photos)*

down from his post, knowing that he faced a challenge from Howard that he would certainly lose.

Asian Instability

Upon Howard's victory in March, 1996, Downer was given the post of foreign minister, a traditional one for defeated party rivals. The Liberal platform had deemphasized the Keating government's orientation toward Asia and instead stressed the rebuilding of ties with the United States. However, Downer soon found himself almost totally preoccupied with Asian and Pacific events, including the Sandline crisis in New Guinea: The government of that country, with some Austra-

Australian foreign minister Alexander Downer meeting with U.N. secretary-general Kofi Annan in Geneva, Switzerland, in 1997. *(AP/Wide World Photos)*

The South Pacific Summit of 1997

In July, 1997, tremendous embarrassment was caused to the Australian government when a memo intended to be secret was released to the public. This memo, marked "AUSTEO" for Australian Eyes Only but accidentally left on a hotel table in Cairns, Queensland, was directed to Australian foreign service officers in preparation for the upcoming South Pacific Summit. The memo made demeaning remarks about the corruption and inefficiency of several Pacific Island nations and stated that the Cook Islands and Nauru were "on the brink of insolvency." The storm over this disclosure dominated the media coverage of the summit, far overshadowing the substantive social and environmental issues the nations had originally met to discuss. Alexander Downer sought to reassure Pacific leaders that the document did not reflect official policy. Fijian leader Sitiveni Rabuka decided to make similarly insulting remarks about Australians, whereas Nauru's president, Kinza Clodumar, sharply condemned the tacit racism he saw in the memo's language. On July 20, Downer officially apologized for the memo. Nevertheless, many judged that Australia's relationship with its South Pacific neighbors had been seriously damaged.

lian collusion, had employed foreign mercenaries to put down a rebellion on the island of Bougainville. Another regional embarrassment occurred with a secret memo that was made public before the South Pacific Summit in 1997. The problems of human rights in China and the heightening nuclear tension between India and Pakistan were also important elements on Downer's agenda.

All these, however, were overshadowed by the Asian economic crisis that led to the resignation of President Suharto of Indonesia in May, 1998. Massively populated Indonesia is Australia's closest Asian neighbor, and Downer faced renewed challenges in formulating a responsible yet forward-looking Australian policy. After two years of the Howard government, Downer was generally regarded by the Australian public as a good foreign minister.

Bibliography
Dever, Marianne, ed. *Australia and Asia: Cultural Transactions*. Honolulu: University of Hawaii Press, 1997.

Henderson, Gerard. *A Howard Government? Inside the Coalition*. New York: HarperCollins, 1995.

_____. *Menzies' Child: The Liberal Party of Australia*. Rev. ed. Sydney: HarperCollins, 1998.

Robinson, Ronald. *Pathways to Asia: The Politics of Engagement*. St. Leonards, New South Wales, Australia: Allen & Unwin, 1996.

Nicholas Birns

José Napoleon Duarte

Born: November 23, 1926; San Salvador, El Salvador
Died: February 23, 1990; San Salvador, El Salvador

President of El Salvador (1984-1989)

José Napoleon Duarte (hoh-ZAY nah-poh-lay-OHN DWAHR-tay) was the second of three sons born to José Jesús and Amelia Fuentes Duarte. The father, a self-employed tailor and a political activist, had won a modest fortune in the country's national lottery, so young Duarte and his brother Rolando were sent to the United States for a college education. He received an engineering degree from the University of Notre Dame, South Bend, Indiana. This connection with the United States was to serve Duarte well in his later political career.

Early Political Career

Duarte entered politics as a member of the Christian Democratic Party (PDC) and served as mayor of El Salvador's capital city, San Salvador, for three successive two-year terms (beginning in 1964, 1966, and 1968). An honest and capable administrator, he won the support of the city's poor as well as its middle class.

In 1972 Duarte ran for president on a centrist, multiparty coalition called the National Opposition Union (UNO). He ran against the government-sponsored candidate, Colonel Arturo Molina, of the Party of National Conciliation (PNR). When the votes were counted, Molina took an early lead as votes from the government-controlled countryside were counted. When the returns of the city balloting began to be tabulated, however, it was clear that Duarte had overtaken the government-backed candidate. Suddenly public announcements of election results were terminated. After a lengthy pause, the government announced that Molina had won the presidency. In the widespread protest and disorder that followed, Duarte was arrested, imprisoned, and ultimately exiled from the country.

Duarte's Presidency

In 1979 the president of El Salvador, General Carlos Humberto Romero, was ousted in a coup. A junta composed of both civilians and military officers took over the government. Leftist guerrillas refused to accept what they considered to be only cosmetic political change. Open conflict between Left and Right erupted. Duarte returned

El Salvadoran president José Napoleon Duarte at a 1986 press conference in Peru. *(Reuters/Anibal Solimano/Archive Photos)*

José Napoleon Duarte and his minister of defense reviewing troops in 1985. *(Reuters/Archive Photos)*

from exile in Venezuela. In 1980 he accepted an appointment to a reorganized junta. Three years later, in an open election monitored by foreign observers, Duarte won the first democratically held presidential election in El Salvador's history. Despite the democratization process, El Salvador suffered a devastating civil war throughout Duarte's term of office.

El Salvador's Civil War

Continuing throughout the decade of the 1980's and into the 1990's, the battle between Salvadorean government forces and the Farabundo Martí Front for National Liberation (FMLN) proved to be both costly and bloody. Right-wing death squads sought out political opponents and assassinated them. The leftists, in turn, killed government officials in the countryside as well as a half dozen American military advisers. Most of the eighty thousand casualties that occurred during the war came at the hands of government troops, and many thousands of refugees fled the country. Duarte and his administration had little control over the army.

Despite American military aid averaging more than $300 million annually to the Salvadorean army, the war ended in a stalemate. Peace finally came to El Salvador on January 16, 1992, with the signing of a treaty between the government and the rebel FMLN.

The new chief executive received substantial aid from the U.S. government, which saw in Duarte an acceptable leader in the fight against the leftist revolutionaries, the Faribundo Marti for National Liberation (FMLN). No previous Salvadorean president had been able to establish such a close relationship with the United States as had the country's newly elected leader. Duarte opened a dialogue with the rebels, but he was unable to bring an end to the civil war.

Furthermore, Duarte failed to keep many of the promises that he made during his presidential campaign. Land reform, a major issue, was never implemented satisfactorily. The army responded more to U.S. threats to terminate military aid than they did to the orders from their commander in chief. Nevertheless, the country's political structure changed enough to become a legitimate multiparty system during Duarte's administration.

In the 1989 national elections, Duarte's Christian Democratic Party was unable to retain the presidency for the ensuing five-year term. Roberto Cristiani, the U.S.-educated candidate of the rightist Nationalist Republican Alliance (ARENA) party, won the office. Duarte himself did not run for reelection; he was suffering from terminal stomach cancer and died in 1990, shortly after surrendering his sash of office to the ARENA winner. Although Duarte died before peace returned to El Salvador, he and his administration acted as a political bridge between the authoritarian, military-dominated government that preceded his own and the freely elected, if conservative, administration that followed.

Bibliography

Baloyra, Enrique. *El Salvador in Transition*. Chapel Hill: University of North Carolina, 1982.

Duarte, José N. *My Story*. New York: Putnam, 1986.

Montgomery, Tommie Sue. *Revolution in El Salvador*. 2d ed. Boulder, Colo.: Westside Press, 1995.

Carl Henry Marcoux

Alexander Dubček

Born: November 27, 1921; Uhrovec, Slovakia, Czechoslovakia
Died: November 7, 1992; Prague, Czechoslovakia

Head of Czech Communist Party (1968-1969), chairman of Czech Federal Assembly (1989-1992)

Alexander Dubček (ah-lehk-ZAHN-dur DEWB-chehk), the son of Štefan and Pavlina Dubček (a cabinetmaker and a domestic servant), was born shortly after his parents returned to his father's hometown in western Slovakia. The couple, both determined socialists, had met and married in the United States, to which they had immigrated before World War I. In 1925 Dubček's father, a member of the Czechoslovak Communist Party, moved the family to Frunze (Pishpek), in Kir-

ghizia, a Soviet republic, in response to Soviet appeals to help build socialism through modernization and industrialization. The family later moved to Nizhni Novgorod (Gorky) to work in the automobile industry. In Gorky, after completing his education, Dubček worked in an industrial cooperative. The family left the Soviet Union in November, 1938, due to the Stalinist purges. As a locksmith in 1939, Dubček joined the illegal, newly formed Slovak Communist Party, and during World War II he worked in an armaments factory. In 1944 he was wounded twice while fighting with partisans in the Slovak National Uprising against the Nazis and the Slovak puppet state.

The Communist Party

After the war, Dubček married Anna Ondrušová in 1945. The couple had three sons, Milan, Pavol, and Peter. He worked in a yeast factory and quickly rose through the ranks of the Slovak Communist Party, becoming party secretary of Trenčín district in western Slovakia in 1949, the year after the Communists seized control of Czechoslovakia. Between 1951 and 1955, he was elected as a deputy to the National Assembly (the national parliament), while serving as a member of the Central Committee of the Slovak Communist Party in Bratislava and later as regional secretary of the Banská Bystrica region in Central Slovakia. At the same time he pursued legal studies at Comenius University in Bratislava.

Realizing his potential, the party sent him in 1955 to study for three years in Moscow at the College of Political Science of the Central Committee of the Communist Party of the Soviet Union. In 1958, Dubček received a doctorate with

Alexander Dubček *(Archive Photos)*

The Prague Spring, 1968

In response to a faltering economy, a growing sense of Slovak nationalism, severe cultural repression, and the failure of de-Stalinization in Czechoslovakia, the Central Committee of the Czechoslovak Communist Party, led by the moderate Alexander Dubček, attacked the leadership of Antonín Novotný in December, 1967. On January 5, 1968, Novotný was ousted and was replaced as first secretary of the party by Dubček. To try to meet the problems of the country, Dubček relaxed political, social, and economic controls. On April 9 the government issued its twenty-four-thousand-word "Czechoslovakia's Road to Socialism" program, including political plurality; freedom of the media, speech, and religion; the right to assemble, to organize, and to own private property; an independent judiciary; the introduction of small businesses; and greater trade with the West.

As the reforms continued, the Soviet Union and its allies urged Dubček not to let the liberalizing programs go too far. After several unsuccessful attempts to rein in the movement, Czechoslovak and Soviet leaders met in eastern Slovakia, where they reached a compromise to allow Czechoslovakia control of its internal affairs. Despite the agreement, however, Soviet leader Leonid I. Brezhnev believed that the situation was getting out of control and that socialism had to be saved at any cost in Czechoslovakia. During the night of August 20-21, Warsaw Pact nations, minus Romania, invaded the country and put an abrupt halt to the reforms.

honors. Upon his return to Czechoslovakia, he was appointed chief secretary of the Slovak Communist Party in Bratislava and became a member of the Central Committees of both the Slovak and the national Czechoslovak Communist parties. In 1960 he was reelected both to the National Assembly and as a secretary of the national party. Two years later he became the highest-ranking Slovak member of the Central Committee Presidium (the ten-member ruling organization of the party) and a secretary of the Central Committee of the Slovak Communist Party, becoming its first secretary in 1963.

Because of a stagnant economy, a rising tide of Slovak nationalism, and cultural repression, in late 1967, Dubček led the move against Antonín Novotný, the hard-line leader of Czechoslovakia, replacing him in January, 1968. In control of the party and the country, Dubček launched his liberalizing campaign to create "socialism with a human face," becoming the symbol of the Prague Spring. As a result of the reforms, Dubček became immensely popular in Czechoslovakia and the West but unpopular in the Soviet bloc. Dubček resisted Soviet demands to halt his policies; his refusal resulted in the invasion of Czechoslovakia by Warsaw Pact troops during the night of August 20-21, 1968. The Soviets seized Dubček and other members of the presidium and took them to Moscow, where they were forced to cancel many of the reforms. Returning to Prague, Dubček urged his country to cooperate with the invasion forces while he tried unsuccessfully to salvage parts of his programs.

After 1968

Starting in 1969, during what the Soviets called the normalization process in Czechoslovakia, Dubček was slowly removed from his positions of authority. Under pressure, in April, Dubček resigned his position as first secretary of the Czechoslovak Communist Party, but shortly thereafter he was elected chairman of the Federal Assembly, the successor to the National Assem-

Czechoslovakian leader Alexander Dubček (center) greeting Walter Ulbricht, head of the East German Communist Party, in 1968. *(Archive Photos)*

bly. In a form of political exile, the government appointed him ambassador to Turkey in January, 1970. In May the party expelled him, and he was recalled home the next month. Returning to Czechoslovakia, Dubček received a job with the Slovak forestry administration in Bratislava, retiring in 1981 and remaining in relative obscurity under constant police surveillance.

Dubček's Slovak Exile

After being stripped of his membership in the Communist Party in 1970, Alexander Dubček became a political nonentity in Czechoslovakia. His political career over, he received a meaningless job working for the Slovak forestry administration in Bratislava. Under intense official criticism and police scrutiny, he protested the regime and his and his family's treatment in letters to various government agencies. Upon one such letter's release in the West in 1975, officials stated that he could leave the country at any time, an offer Dubček refused. In January, 1988, in an interview with the Italian communist newspaper *L'Unita*, Dubček noted great similarities between his earlier reforms and those of then-current Soviet leader Mikhail S. Gorbachev. Later that year, in November, the Czechoslovak government granted him permission to travel to the University of Bologna to receive an honorary degree.

Political Comeback

During the November, 1989, "velvet revolution," Dubček returned to public life, addressing demonstrators against the regime in both Bratislava and Prague. With the fall of communism in Czechoslovakia, Dubček was briefly considered for the presidency of the republic. Instead he was again elected chairman of the Federal Assembly in December, 1989, serving until June, 1992. Dubček became the chairman of the Social Democratic Party in 1992. He traveled abroad extensively, meeting world leaders and receiving several honorary doctorates. In 1990 the European Parliament awarded him the Andrei Sakharov Prize for Human Rights. Although opposed to the breakup of Czechoslovakia, Dubček was the favorite for the position of president of the soon-to-be independent Slovak Republic. However, he died as the result of injuries received in an automobile accident outside Prague in early September.

Bibliography

Dubček, Alexander. *Dubček Speaks*. New York: Tauris, 1990.

_____. *Hope Dies Last: The Autobiography of Alexander Dubček*. Edited and translated by Jiri Hochman. New York: Kodansha International, 1993.

Shawcross, William. *Dubček*. New York: Simon and Schuster, 1970.

Gregory C. Ference

W. E. B. Du Bois

Born: February 23, 1868; Great Barrington, Massachusetts
Died: August 27, 1963; Accra, Ghana

U.S. scholar, civil rights activist, and cofounder of NAACP (1910)

William Edward Burghardt Du Bois (WIHL-yuhm EHD-wurd BURG-hahrd dew-BOYZ) was born and raised in Massachusetts. Following graduation from high school he attended Fisk University, Harvard University, and the University of Berlin. In 1895 he received his Ph.D. from Harvard University and began his career as an intellectual and social leader of African Americans.

The Scholar

W. E. B. Du Bois was the first African American to receive a Ph.D. in the United States. While

W. E. B. Du Bois *(Library of Congress)*

many Americans identify Du Bois as an activist, he was also one of the outstanding scholars of his era. From 1894 to 1896 Du Bois taught at Wilberforce University in Ohio. He then taught sociology for a year at the University of Pennsylvania before serving as professor of economics and history at Atlanta University from 1897 to 1910. He returned to Atlanta University as chair of the Sociology Department from 1934 to 1944.

Du Bois's doctoral dissertation *The Suppression of the African Slave Trade, 1638-1870,* was a scientific study of the problem of race in the world. It was later published as the first volume in the Harvard Historical Series. His book *The Philadelphia Negro,* published at the beginning of the twentieth century, was one of the first major sociological works published in the United States. His most enduring work was *The Souls of Black Folk,* published in 1903. In it Du Bois philosophically addressed the problem of race in the United States and argued the need for African Americans to receive a higher education in order to provide leadership for the black community and to achieve status in the larger society.

Du Bois published numerous other books throughout his life. In addition, he was editor of *The Crisis,* the publication of the National Association for the Advancement of Colored People (NAACP) from the inception of the group until 1934. In 1940 he started *Phylon, a Journal of Race and Culture* at Atlanta University. All together, Du Bois published an estimated four thousand works throughout his life.

The Activist

W. E. B. Du Bois described color as the greatest problem of the twentieth century, and he dedicated his life to studying the issue and fighting

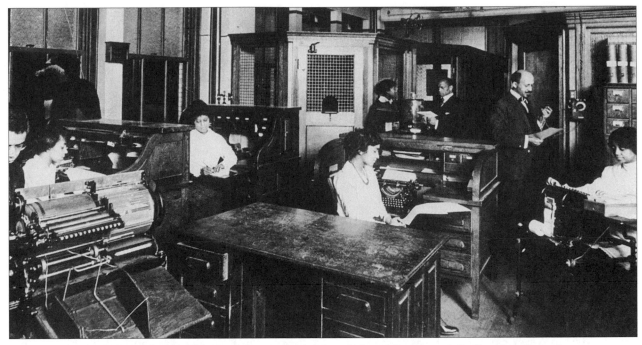

W. E. B. Du Bois (talking on intercom at right) and his publications staff. *(Archive Photos)*

for equality for African Americans. He emerged as one of the great leaders of the African American community when he challenged Tuskegee University president Booker T. Washington's view of race relations in the United States. Washington argued that African Americans should stay on farms and learn vocational skills that would be useful to the larger society. These skills,

The NAACP

In 1905 a group of men under the leadership of W. E. B. Du Bois met in Niagara Falls, Canada, and wrote a list of demands in order to secure full citizenship for African Americans. In 1909 the leaders of the Niagara Movement were invited to a meeting on Abraham Lincoln's birthday by Mary White Ovington, William English Walling, and Henry Moskowitz. From this meeting came an agreement to form an organization dedicated to the abolition of segregation and to obtaining equal education for black and white children, the franchise (the vote) for African Americans, and the enforcement of the Four-teenth and Fifteen Amendments to the U.S. Constitution. In May, 1910, the National Association for the Advancement of Colored People (NAACP) was created. Du Bois became the editor of the NAACP's monthly magazine *The Crisis,* a position he held until 1934. He was also director of publicity and research. In 1934 he resigned from the NAACP and became chair of the Sociology Department at Atlanta University. He returned to the NAACP in 1944 as director of publicity and research. In 1948 he left the NAACP again following disagreements with the organization's leadership.

Du Bois Moves to Ghana

Throughout the twentieth century, W. E. B. Du Bois had been interested in the common problems of Africans and African Americans as seen through his work with the Pan African Congress. Following numerous frustrations and conflicts with the U.S. government, he joined the Communist Party. In 1961 he renounced his U.S. citizenship. Kwame Nkrumah, the president of Ghana, invited Du Bois to edit the *Encyclopedia Africana*. Du Bois then moved to Ghana with his wife, Shirley Graham Du Bois, and became a citizen of that African nation. When Du Bois died in 1963, Nkrumah gave him a funeral befitting a head of state. Dignitaries from around the world attended; however, the U.S. government did not send a representative to pay tribute to Du Bois.

he maintained, would create an economic foundation that would lead to acceptance of African Americans by the larger white society. In 1895 Washington appeared to accept segregation by saying that in the aspects of life that were purely social, African Americans could be as separate as the five fingers on the hand.

Du Bois denounced Washington for condoning segregation and shifting the responsibility for achieving equality to African Americans. He argued that African Americans had to speak out against oppression and discrimination, and he stated that the responsibility for the race problem in the United States rested with the larger white society. Du Bois also argued that the black community had to produce its teachers and leaders through the education of the Talented Tenth—those African Americans who had the opportunity to receive a liberal arts education.

W. E. B. Du Bois became the leader of the African American community in its effort to secure full citizenship and equality. In 1905 he led a meeting at Niagara Falls, Canada, which drew up a list of resolutions. It called for freedom of speech, suffrage, recognition of the basic principles of human brotherhood, an end to distinctions based on race, and respect for the working man. In 1909 these African American leaders met with white activists and created the National Association for the Advancement of Colored People. Thus began Du Bois's long association

An elderly W. E. B. Du Bois being presented with a Soviet peace prize, the International Lenin Prize, at the Soviet embassy in Washington in 1960. *(AP/ Wide World Photos)*

with the dominant civil rights organization in the United States.

Du Bois was also interested in the link between African Americans and Africans. He envisioned African Americans as the leaders of the cause and interests of black people throughout the world, especially in Africa, which was largely colonized by European countries. He rejected the beliefs of Marcus Garvey, who argued that African Americas should leave the United States and return to Africa. Instead, Du Bois became a leader in the pan-African movement. In 1911 he helped organize and attended the First Universal Races Congress in London, England. Then, in February, 1919, Du Bois led the first Pan African Congress in Paris, France. In attendance were sixteen African Americans, twenty West Indians, and twelve Africans. Four more Pan African meetings were held, the last in 1945 in Manchester, England. Du Bois's international involvement extended beyond the pan-African movement. In 1945 NAACP members W. E. B. Du Bois and Walter White attended the founding convention of the United Nations in San Francisco, California, as observers accredited by the U.S. State Department.

In the post-World War II era, Du Bois became frustrated over the United States' failure to resolve its racial problem. Politically, he moved further to the left. In 1951 he was indicted by the U.S. government under the McCarran Act after he and other leaders of the Peace Information Center refused to register as foreign agents. After being cleared of the charges, Du Bois traveled to Africa, China, and the Soviet Union. In 1961 he joined the American Communist Party and moved to Ghana, where he died two years later.

An Assessment

W. E. B. Du Bois was one of the most notable scholars and social activists of the twentieth century. He dedicated his intellectual and personal energies to the resolution of the race problem. His disillusionment with the American failure to resolve this issue resulted in his joining the Communist Party during the Cold War. This association for many years prevented him from receiving the recognition he deserved for his contributions to society.

Bibliography

Lewis, David L. *W. E. B. DuBois: Biography of a Race, 1896-1919*. New York: H. Holt, 1993.

Logan, Rayford Whittingham, ed. *W. E. B. Du Bois: A Profile*. New York: Hill and Wang, 1971.

Marable, Manning. *W. E. B. DuBois: Black Radical Democrat*. Boston: Wayne, 1986.

Rudwick, Elliot. *W. E. B. Du Bois: Voice of the Black Protest Movement*. Urbana: University of Illinois Press, 1982.

William V. Moore

John Foster Dulles

Born: February 25, 1888; Washington, D.C.
Died: May 24, 1959; Washington, D.C.

U.S. secretary of state (1953-1959)

John Foster Dulles (JON FO-stur DUH-lehs) was born in Washington, D.C. The families of his father and his mother included prominent missionaries and diplomats. Diplomatic experience began early for Dulles. At the age of nineteen, he served as secretary of the Chinese delegation at the Second Hague Conference. After passing the bar in 1911, he went to work for Sullivan and Cromwell, a law firm with extensive Wall Street connections and international clients. With his career under way, Dulles married in 1912, and for the next five years he traveled extensively in

John Foster Dulles *(Library of Congress)*

South and Central America representing American corporate interests.

World Wars I and II

World War I (1914-1918) offered new diplomatic opportunities. The United States entered the war in 1917, but Dulles was disqualified from the draft. Dulles spent time in Central America encouraging those nations to declare war on Germany. He returned home and served on the War Trade Board. After the war he accompanied President Woodrow Wilson to France for peace treaty negotiations and remained behind to continue negotiations with Austria, Hungary, and Turkey.

Dulles was part of the group that worked out the Dawes Plan with Germany in 1924, and he worked on a plan to stimulate a Polish economic recovery in 1927. The election of Franklin D. Roosevelt to the U.S. presidency in 1932 caused Dulles to assume the role of foreign policy critic. He aligned himself with the isolationist wing of the Republican Party for the next decade. During foreign policy debates of the period 1941 to 1953—during and after World War II—Dulles took a moderate approach and never aligned with either the isolationists or the internationalist wing of the Republicans. As foreign policy adviser to Thomas Dewey in the 1948 election, be believed that avoiding controversial foreign policy topics would be the key to Republican victory.

The Early 1950's

Comments by Dulles concerning the Soviet Union and international communism were moderate before 1953, given the context of the time. Despite occasional jabs at the atheistic stance of communism and references to the Soviet "octopus," Dulles never agreed with the policy of mili-

South-East Asia Treaty Organization delegates at a 1967 meeting; John Foster Dulles was instrumental in the establishment of SEATO in 1954. *(Library of Congress)*

The Korean War Settlement

On June 12, 1950, communist troops from North Korea invaded South Korea. The United States joined a U.N. force sent to repel the invasion. In October, Chinese forces joined the North Koreans, and the bloody fighting continued for thirty months. After Dwight D. Eisenhower was elected president, John Foster Dulles joined the negotiators working to arrange a cease-fire agreement.

The most emotional issue that emerged was the arrangement of prisoner exchanges. Indignation mounted in the United States as the communists used the return of American prisoners as a bargaining chip with no regard for humanitarian concerns. The United States was reluctant to return prisoners to North Korea and China, because many claimed that they would face prison, torture, or death if they returned. The South Koreans complicated negotiations in June, 1953, by releasing twenty-eight thousand North Korean prisoners without consulting the United States.

Opposition to the cease-fire arose at home, led by politicians supported by the powerful China Lobby, a group of journalists and academics resolved to keep communist China isolated from the world. It took all of Dulles's diplomatic talent to prevail, and he learned along with the rest of the United States that resolving Cold War conflicts would never be easy.

The Southeast Asia Treaty Organization (SEATO)

After the French defeat in Indochina in 1954, John Foster Dulles believed that Southeast Asia needed a collective security agreement to prevent further communist aggression. He arranged for eight nations to meet in Manila beginning on September 6, 1954. The result was a very open-ended commitment that was directed toward resisting communist aggression only. At home, the treaty drew criticism from conservative Republicans who believed that it was inadequate to provide regional security. During the 1950's, such pacts proliferated. In the 1960's and 1970's, SEATO became a symbol for the overcommitment of U.S. power.

tary confrontation with the Soviet Union that was advocated by conservative foreign policy critics. Dulles believed that the Soviet Union was a threat, but he also believed that diplomatic solutions could solve the problems of the Cold War.

The Republican foreign policy platform in the 1952 presidential election bore little of Dulles's influence. He was pragmatic and believed that it was the best platform possible, given the feuding between Republican Party factions. For both his party loyalty and his years of experience, Dulles was named secretary of state when Dwight D. Eisenhower won the election of 1952.

Zenith of Power

Dulles faced three major issues as secretary of state in 1953. First, the position he held had steadily declined in power and influence in the national security bureaucracy. Second, the Department of State had been crippled by charges that its career diplomats had been soft on communism. Third, Dulles's ability to conduct Cold War negotiations was hampered by the Eisenhower New Look military policy, which focused on nuclear weapons development and the threat of massive nuclear retaliation as the chief means of responding to Soviet challenges. Dulles dealt with the first two issues decisively but continued to struggle with the third throughout his diplomatic career. Dulles never received much credit for his role in reorganizing the national security bureaucracy. By 1959 most major policy recommendations reached Dulles's office before they

U.S. secretary of state John Foster Dulles (left) in London with a British official at the height of the Suez Crisis of 1956. *(Express News/Archive Photos)*

reached President Eisenhower. Dulles showed a mastery of bureaucratic organization.

The charges that there were communists and communist sympathizers in the Department of State had left many career diplomats in limbo since 1950. Dulles oversaw the completion of the loyalty hearings begun by President Harry S Truman. He also pressured diplomats associated with Truman's policies, such as George F. Kennan, to resign. Dulles was a target for critics who saw such actions as blatant Republican partisanship, and they remain some of the most controversial and frequently debated topics of his career.

The first task that Dulles faced was negotiating an end to the Korean War. Even as the fine points of those negotiations remained unsolved, the world was shocked in 1954 by the collapse of French military power in the face of a communist offensive in Indochina. The most vivid memory from the Geneva Conference that followed occurred when Dulles refused to shake hands with the Chinese delegate, Zhou Enlai. Nonetheless, Dulles worked doggedly for a peace settlement that was much better than anyone had expected when the conference began.

From 1954 to 1956, Dulles worked to forge security agreements in Southeast Asia and the Middle East to strengthen collective security in Europe. In the confident spirit of the United States in the 1950's, these commitments seemed prudent and appropriate. Later events would reveal that American power was overextended, and Dulles received much of the blame.

Last Years

The Suez Crisis of November, 1956, taxed the diplomatic talents of Dulles to the limit. Just before the U.S. presidential election (in which Eisenhower was reelected), a coordinated attack was launched by English, French, and Israeli forces to seize the Suez Canal in Egypt. At the same time, Russian troops invaded Hungary to preempt a Hungarian defection from the Warsaw Pact. Any U.S. response to the Suez Crisis would be likely to anger both the invaders and the Arab nations that Dulles had courted so arduously. The U.S. response to Hungary was a feeble offer of medical supplies, despite earlier promises to assist any nation that sought to break away from Soviet domination. Almost overnight, the Cold War colossus that Dulles had labored to create began to unravel. At home, much to Dulles's dismay, President Eisenhower responded enthusiastically to Soviet premier Nikita Khruschev's plea for peaceful coexistence and summit diplomacy.

Dulles discovered that he had colon cancer and resigned on April 15, 1959. He died in Washington, D.C., five weeks later. His talent and long career could have ranked him as one of the great secretaries of state, but he served at a time when diplomats and their achievements were eclipsed by a growing reliance on overwhelming military power in international relations.

Bibliography

Gaddis, John. *Strategies of Containment*. New York: Oxford University Press, 1986.

Guhin, Michael. *John Foster Dulles: A Statesman and His Times*. New York: Columbia University Press, 1972.

Hoopes, Townsend. *The Devil and John Foster Dulles*. New York: Little, Brown, 1973.

Immerman, Richard H. *John Foster Dulles: Piety, Pragmatism, and Power in U.S. Foreign Policy*. Wilmington, Del.: Scholarly Resources, 1999.

Marks, Frederick W. *Power and Peace: The Diplomacy of John Foster Dulles*. Westport, Conn.: Praeger, 1993.

Michael Polley

Maurice Duplessis

Born: April 20, 1890; Trois-Rivières, Quebec, Canada
Died: September 7, 1959; Schefferville, Quebec, Canada

Canadian political leader, premier of Quebec (1936-1939, 1944-1959)

Maurice Le Noblet Duplessis (moh-REES leh noh-BLAY dew-pleh-SEE) was the son of a prominent judge who had held office as a Conservative member of the Quebec National Assembly. His mother was of Irish and Scottish descent, and his Catholic education and family life proved to be a powerful influence. Educated at the seminary in Trois-Rivières, and then at Laval University in Montreal, he graduated with a degree in law in 1913. Duplessis practiced law in his father's firm and soon established himself as a remarkable orator, winning the Conservative

Maurice Duplessis *(Library of Congress)*

nomination in Trois-Rivières in 1923. Defeated in the provincial election, Duplessis returned in 1927 to win a seat in the National Assembly. He held the seat for the next thirty-two years, until his death in 1959.

Founding the Union Nationale

Duplessis became the leader of the Quebec Conservative Party in 1933. The Liberal Party was divided; one wing, formed by a group of young reformers, called itself L'Action libérale nationale (ALN). The Conservatives and the ALN agreed to an alliance in order to oppose Quebec's Liberal Party government under Premier Louis Alexandre Taschereau. The coalition came close to defeating Taschereau in the 1935 election. The most important issue during the election was corruption. Throughout the following year, Duplessis made brilliant use of his political skills, bringing to light in the legislature evidence of this corruption. Taschereau was forced to resign, and the Union Nationale swept the election in 1936.

Duplessis was a Conservative, and his first government was a disappointment to many of the reform-minded Liberals who had helped found the Union Nationale. His government inaugurated a scheme for farm credit and overhauled labor legislation allowing the government to set wages. However, little of the reform program of the ALN was instituted, and its former members soon left the Union Nationale. Duplessis's hold on the party was thus consolidated.

Premier of Quebec

In the election of 1939, the Duplessis government was defeated. Duplessis was dangerously ill during the following two years, suffering from both pneumonia and diabetes. His recovery, both physically and politically, was an enormous feat. Known for living the high life, he drastically altered this lifestyle to maintain his health. He also campaigned tirelessly for the two years leading up to the election in 1944; he defeated the Liberals by a narrow margin. No longer the brash and overconfident politician, Duplessis was now a more prudent and serious political leader. He would remain premier of Quebec for the next fifteen years.

During these years, the Duplessis government protected and advanced the powers of the Quebec provincial government over—and sometimes against— the federal government in Ottawa. Duplessis was a firm supporter of the Catholic Church, but he made it clear that the provincial government and not the church would control Quebec.

Maurice Duplessis in 1955, two-thirds of the way through his fifteen-year second term as premier of Quebec. *(AP/Wide World Photos)*

The Union Nationale Party

The Union Nationale Party was founded two weeks prior to the 1935 Quebec provincial election as a coalition of reform-minded Liberals, Conservatives, and Quebec nationalists. Paul Gouin and Maurice Duplessis were its leaders. Maurice Duplessis consolidated his hold on the leadership the following year, and the party developed into an electoral machine designed to keep the Duplessis government in office. Its principles and ideas were mainly a reflection of those of its leader. Duplessis was both a Quebec nationalist and a conservative. He was a firm protector of Catholicism, was conservative on issues regarding the rights of workers, and believed that Quebec must provide a hospitable environment for English Canadian business and industrialization. Because the party was largely an expression of Duplessis, it did not long survive his death. Its place in Quebec politics was taken by the Parti Québécois, a left-wing nationalist party that led the Quebec government four times between 1976 and 1998.

Duplessis also held the cabinet post of attorney general, and he used that position to close businesses that were in any way affiliated with communism or unorthodox religious beliefs. His government enacted progressive legislation to ensure a minimum wage, provided assistance to people to purchase homes, promoted industrialization, and built hospitals, schools, and universities, It prepared the way for the modernization of Quebec that has come to be known as the "quiet revolution." At the same time, Duplessis gained the reputation for being a one-man show, and some of his government's actions in the area of civil and political liberties were successfully challenged in the courts. His conservative nationalism nonetheless served to make Quebec a more powerful province and set the stage for the contemporary independence movement.

Bibliography

Black, Conrad. *Duplessis*. Toronto: McClelland and Stewart, 1977.

Laporte, Pierre. *The True Face of Duplessis*. Montreal: Harvest House, 1960.

McRoberts, Kenneth. *Quebec: Social Change and Political Crisis*. 3d ed. Toronto: McClelland and Stewart, 1988.

Nish, Cameron, ed. *Quebec in the Duplessis Era, 1935-1959: Dictatorship or Democracy?* Toronto: Copp-Clark, 1970.

Patrick Malcolmson

François Duvalier

Born: April 14, 1907; Port-au-Prince, Haiti
Died: April 21, 1971; Port-au-Prince, Haiti

Dictatorial president of Haiti (1957-1971)

François Duvalier (frahn-SWAH dew-VAH-lee-ay) was born in a slum near the Haitian National Palace in Port-au-Prince to an unemployed black schoolteacher father, Duval Duvalier, and a Haitian mother, Uritia Abraham, who worked in a bakery. The U.S. occupation of Haiti from 1915 to 1934 by American white marines was repeatedly met by violent resistance movements that stimulated cognizance of Haiti's African roots in young black intellectuals such as Duvalier.

An avid reader of Voodoo practices, including using the pain-killing capability of narcotic plants, Duvalier graduated from the University of Haiti School of Medicine in 1934 and served as a hospital staff physician until 1943. Duvalier (widely known by his nickname, Papa Doc) had four children with his wife, Simone (Mama Doc). His only son, Jean-Claude (Baby Doc), succeeded him as dictator.

Rise to Power

Duvalier's popularity with Haiti's rural ethnic populace escalated as he directed American-funded efforts toward eradicating malaria and yaws, both of which had reached epidemic proportions. Duvalier served as director of public health from 1946 to 1948 and as minister of public health and labor from 1949 to 1950 under President Dumarsais Estime, his former instructor. He resisted the policies of Paul E. Magloire, who deposed Estime in a bloodless coup in 1950.

Duvalier directed underground forces against Magloire from 1954 to 1956, thus creating domestic unrest that gave him the support of the rural ethnic population to whom he promised to bring economic and political reform. The Haitian economy at the time reflected the nation's political and racial divisions, with the Catholic French-speaking mulatto (racially mixed) elite controlling the wealth while the Creole-speaking Voodoo black majority remained poor. Following Magloire's resignation, Duvalier became president on September 22, 1957, via an undoubtedly fraudulent election. In April of 1961 he was unconstitutionally reelected president, and on June 14, 1964, Duvalier revised the Haitian constitution to proclaim himself president for life. Duvalier declared, "I am a giant capable of eclips-

François Duvalier *(Library of Congress)*

449

Haitian president François Duvalier in his office in 1963. *(Archive Photos)*

The Tonton Macoutes

Duvalier formed the Volunteers for National Security, known as the Tonton Macoutes, a palace army responsible only to the president, in July, 1958, following several unsuccessful coup attempts. The Tonton Macoutes answered only to Duvalier, and their sole purpose was to protect him and keep him in power.

Paid minimal salaries, the Macoutes financed themselves by stealing from the Haitian populace. They instilled fear throughout society by practicing Voodoo. Duvalier proceeded to dissolve the Haitian legislature, outlaw all political parties and labor unions, attack the power structure of the Roman Catholic Church, and arrest, torture, and murder thousands of alleged dissidents. By mixing belief in

ing the sun" at his inaugural speech, garnering unquestioned authority from uneducated Haitian peasants by claiming to be an incarnation of the Voodoo lord of the cemetery.

Voodoo and Politics

Voodoo is a Haitian religion of African origin. It comprises the central element of society in Voodoo villages called combites, wherein 85 percent of Haitians live. Open Voodooism was suppressed by several governmental authorities prior to François Duvalier. Peasants were often forced to swear allegiance to the Roman Catholic Church. Such practices gave rise to the often-quoted Haitian proverb, "Haiti may be 80 percent Catholic, but it is 100 percent Voodoo."

Duvalier's legitimization of Voodoo gained him support from local Voodoo priests, easily the most influential Haitian community leaders. He utilized them to control his superstitious and uneducated compatriots; the priests spread reports regarding his great powers and seances, secret Voodoo ceremonies such as zombification, and sacrifices to the spirits. Establishing his campaign headquarters in local Voodoo temples, Duvalier was elected president on September 22, 1957, by the largest majority in Haitian democratic history. Harvard University researcher Wade Davis penetrated the secret societies of rural Haiti and discovered that altars of Bizango temples were decorated with images of Duvalier. The Voodoo colors, red and black, were utilized by Duvalier to create the new national flag of Haiti.

Haiti and the Cold War

Haitian involvement in the Cold War between the United States and the Soviet Union began when Fidel Castro surprised the world by leading a revolution in December, 1959, that overthrew the government of Cuba. The island of Cuba is 60 miles (97 kilometers) west of Haiti and 580 miles (805 kilometers) southeast of Florida. Castro's communist regime established strong military ties to the Soviet Union.

When Duvalier announced his opposition to communism, American policy makers allocated more than $50 million in direct economic and military aid—more than half of which went to train and supply Duvalier's private guard, the Tonton Macoutes, at a U.S. Marine base in Haiti. After American money had already firmly established Duvalier's dictatorship, President John F. Kennedy halted all military aid to Haiti in response to Duvalier's brutality and corruption.

the supernatural with military force, Duvalier created a police state capable of controlling the thought and behavior of Haitians at every level of society. Duvalier nearly died from a massive heart attack complicated by diabetes on May 24, 1959, giving Clement Barbot, ruthless head of the

Macoutes, temporary control over the country. Barbot directed the defeat of a thirty-man Cuban invasion but made the mistake of reveling in his success. Upon his recovery, Duvalier suspected that Barbot was attempting to undermine his power and jailed him on trumped-up charges of

When François Duvlier's son Jean-Claude appeared in his place, saluting troops on his father's sixty-fourth birthday (April 14, 1971), rumors flew about "Papa Doc's" health. Indeed, François Duvalier died ten days later. *(AP/Wide World Photos)*

treason. Pretending to be a born-again Christian, Barbot was released after sixteen months. He was later killed attempting to stir up a revolt within the Macoutes, who afterward remained loyal to Papa Doc.

Persecution of All Opposition

The May, 1961, assassination of Rafael Trujillo, dictator of the Dominican Republic, apparently instilled in Papa Doc such paranoia that he declared martial law so that he could freely act against all suspected rivals. Described by one historian as being "as shrewd and evil as Adolf Hitler," Duvalier even purged the facilities of youth agencies such as the Boy Scouts and outlawed their existence. Duvalier persecuted his nemeses in the Roman Catholic Church: He expelled Monsignor François Poirier and other church officials from the country for refusing to pray to him as Haiti's spiritual leader using a new version of the biblical Lord's Prayer that Duvalier wrote to glorify himself. The Vatican finally excommunicated Duvalier when he sacrificed pigs as a blood offering to Voodoo spirits on the steps of the Gonaives Cathedral. U.S. president John F. Kennedy, a Roman Catholic, terminated all Haitian military aid in May, 1963, in response to the Tonton Macoutes laying siege to the Dominican embassy in Port-au-Prince.

Papa Doc rarely went out in public during his later life and reportedly retreated deeper and deeper into Voodoo mysticism, with which he is said to have attempted spirit communication using the severed heads of his adversaries. He wrote several books on Voodoo, and rumors surfaced that he suffered at least one heart attack per year before dying at age sixty-four, twice the average Haitian life expectancy. Papa Doc amended the Haitian constitution to allow himself to choose his successor, his nineteen-year-old son Jean-Claude—who continued his father's legacy of corruption as "Baby Doc."

Bibliography

Abbott, Elizabeth. *Haiti: The Duvaliers and Their Legacy*. Rev. ed. New York: Simon and Schuster, 1991.

Condit, Erin. *Francois and Jean-Claude Duvalier*. New York: Chelsea House, 1989.

Davis, Wade. *The Serpent and the Rainbow*. New York: Warner, 1985.

Diederich, Bernard, and Al Burt. *Papa Doc*. New York: McGraw-Hill, 1969.

Gringas, Jean-Pierre O. *Duvalier: Caribbean Cyclone*. New York: Exposition Press, 1967.

Laguerre, Michel. *Politics and Voodoo Still a Potent Combination in Haiti*. New York: Macmillan, 1988.

Weinstein, Brian, and Aaron Segal. *Haiti: The Failure of Politics*. New York: Praeger, 1992.

Daniel G. Graetzer

Jean-Claude Duvalier

Born: July 3, 1951; Port-au-Prince, Haiti

Dictatorial president of Haiti (1971-1986)

Jean-Claude Duvalier (ZHO KLOHD dew-VAH-lee-ay) is the only son of Haitian dictator François Duvalier (also called Papa Doc). A pampered child, Jean-Claude was also an eyewitness to his father's brutal abuse of power. He quickly mastered the ability to manipulate and oppress others and to defend himself at all costs. After graduating from secondary school in Port-au-Prince, Duvalier briefly attended law school at the University of Haiti. He married Michele Bennett on May 27, 1980, in a wedding so lavish it was recorded in the Guinness Book of World Records. It cost his poverty-stricken country more than $3 million and included a $100,000 fireworks display. His mother Simone (also called Mama Doc), whom Duvalier has often referred to as his inspiration, and his eldest sister, Marie-Denise, who continued in her role as presidential secretary, were his unofficial but primary advisers.

World's Youngest Chief of State

François Duvalier amended the Haitian constitution in January, 1971, to allow himself personally to select his successor, who would also be given the title president for life. He also gave himself the power to select his successor's twelve-member advisory cabinet. Duvalier died three months later, on April 21, 1971. Jean-Claude then became the youngest chief of state in the world at age nineteen—after the Haitian assembly declared him to be twenty-one years old, the legal age for holding Haitian office.

The Voodoo belief that Papa Doc would rule the Haitian people through his son resulted in Jean-Claude immediately be-ing nicknamed Baby Doc. American and European political analysts with no understanding of the power of Voodoo in Haitian culture predicted immediate anarchy and revolution. However, the widespread fear of Voodoo actually created the smoothest governmental transition in Haiti's turbulent history. Baby Doc's first major presidential act involved disbanding his father's brutal Ton-

Jean-Claude Duvalier with his wife, Michelle. *(Archive France)*

453

Jean-Claude Duvalier surrounded by his security forces. *(AP/Wide World Photos)*

The 1986 Revolt

Several violent demonstrations occurred throughout Haiti in late 1985 and early 1986 against government corruption and extravagance, high unemployment, terrible living conditions, and the absence of political freedom. Unrest grew until it could no longer be repressed by Jean-Claude Duvalier's regime. As history often records in the downfall of dictators, Duvalier's collapse began when he offered a few token reforms. They resulted in the oppressed citizens

becoming enraged as they imagined life under a more liberal government. Violent governmental crackdowns on Port-au-Prince rallies commemorating the victims of the Duvalier regime resulted in the worldwide publicizing of human rights abuses. The United States again reduced financial assistance. As the situation deteriorated, "Baby Doc" looted government coffers for the final time of his fifteen-year reign and escaped to a life of luxury in France.

tons Macoutes, a palace army responsible only to the president, and restructuring his security forces under his own Leopard Battalion. The Leopard Battalion's stated purpose was to fight communism, a purpose that impressed U.S. policy makers enough to dedicate millions of dollars in assistance to Haiti. However, Baby Doc had a thirst for money that was as intense as his father's thirst for power and blood.

Continued Legacy of Corruption

Jean-Claude Duvalier initially promised economic reforms and a liberalization of his father's harsh policies, but it soon became evident that his many promises would remain unfulfilled and were made solely to attract foreign investors. Businesses began relocating to Haiti because of cheap peasant labor; Duvalier kept wages low to maximize his own profits. Already the Western hemisphere's poorest nation, Haiti became even poorer under Baby Doc, who pledged to "continue the Duvalier revolution with the same fierce energy and intransigence as my father." As Duvalier diverted millions of public dollars into overseas bank accounts, the vast majority of Haitians lived in poverty. By 1985, 80 percent of Haitians were illiterate, life expectancy was forty-three years, and the average income was under $350 dollars per year. Duvalier paid no attention to the poverty that lay beyond the gates of his national palace—which received $17 million in renovations ordered by his wife. Duvalier eased up on repression only when the American government was considering renewal of financial assistance.

Eventually, following widespread revolts against his corrupt regime, Duvalier departed Haiti on February 7, 1986, on a U.S. Air Force cargo plane bound for France. The Haitian government has since sought to recover more than $200 million in compensation through the French courts.

Bibliography

Abbott, Elizabeth. *Haiti: The Duvaliers and Their Legacy.* Rev. ed. New York: Simon and Schuster, 1991.

Condit, Erin. *François and Jean-Claude Duvalier.* New York: Chelsea House, 1989.

Davis, Wade. *The Serpent and the Rainbow.* New York: Warner, 1985.

Gringas, Jean-Pierre O. *Duvalier: Caribbean Cyclone.* New York: Exposition Press, 1967.

Laguerre, Michel. *Politics and Voodoo Still a Potent Combination in Haiti.* New York: Macmillan, 1988.

Tate, Robert J. *Haiti: Land of Poverty.* Lanham, Md.: University of America Press, 1982.

Weinstein, Brian, and Aaron Segal. *Haiti: The Failure of Politics.* New York: Praeger, 1992.

Daniel G. Graetzer

Abba Eban

Born: February 2, 1915; Cape Town, South Africa

Long-time Israeli diplomat, minister of foreign affairs (1966-1974)

Abba Solomon Eban (AH-bah SO-loh-mon EE-bahn) was born Aubrey Solomon. Along with his parents, he immigrated to England while still an infant. His father died shortly thereafter, and he took the name Eban from his stepfather. In 1937, he received his bachelor's degree from Queen's College, Cambridge, where he excelled in debate and the Arabic and Persian languages; he had already learned Hebrew as a child. In 1938, he earned a master's degree with high honors. He soon became active in the Zionist movement, which he had joined at age seventeen. He served

Abba Eban *(Library of Congress)*

in the British army in the Middle East during World War II, rising to the rank of major. He remained there following the war, marrying Susan Ambache in 1945; they had two children, Eli and Gila.

The Creation of Israel

From 1939 through 1946, Eban translated and edited works in Hebrew and Arabic under the name Aubrey Eban. As he became fully aware of the calamity suffered by Europe's Jews in World War II, he determined to remain in Jerusalem and work for the creation of a Jewish state in Palestine. His opportunity came at the age of thirty-two, when he was made a member of the United Nations Special Commission on Palestine.

Palestine was then a British protectorate, and Eban, through the exercise of his diplomatic skills, helped to bring about the partition of that territory into Arab and Jewish sections. The partition led to the creation of the state of Israel. By 1948, Eban was representing the fledgling nation in the United Nations. He sought support for Israel around the world, especially in the United States. Eban proved to be a fine orator as well as a distinguished scholar. He spoke with a cultivated British accent, and his delivery could be mellifluous or acerbic as his subject matter demanded. Because of his urbanity and cosmopolitan air, the Jews of the Diaspora responded to him with a special warmth. He was very popular in the United States.

Diplomatic and Political Career

After having served in a number of important posts at Allied headquarters in Jerusalem between 1942 and 1947, Eban was named liaison officer to the United Nations. At the birth of Israel in 1948, he was appointed by the provisional

Abba Eban visiting the museum at the site of the Dachau concentration camp in Germany in 1970. With him are former camp inmates. *(AP/Wide World Photos)*

The Kinneret Operation

In 1955, the Soviet-Egyptian alliance and the rearmament of Arab states caused Israel to feel that the balance of power in the region was shifting against it. Should the situation continue, Israel feared, its enemies would be encouraged to attack. Abba Eban was pressing the United States for twenty-four jet planes and auxiliary weapons, which he believed would redress the imbalance. Following an initial coolness, John Foster Dulles, the American secretary of state, seemed by the end of the year close to a favorable response.

Then, on December 10, Syrian guns fired on Israeli fishermen on Lake Tiberias (the Sea of Galilee), also known as Lake Kinneret. The next night, Israeli raiders crossed into Syria. Six Israelis were killed, but the raiders killed seventy-three Syrians. Many more were wounded or missing in the action at Kinneret. The international community condemned the Kinneret Operation as a terrible overreaction to Syrian provocation. Although Eban eloquently defended the raid in the U.N. Security Council, he privately believed that long-term goals had been sacrificed to the short-term gains associated with instant response. A majority in the Security Council voted to condemn Israel's retaliatory action, and military aid from Israel's allies was delayed.

U.N. Resolution 242

On June 19, 1967, shortly after the Israeli victory in the Six-Day War (June 4-10, 1967), the Israeli cabinet adopted a resolution that called for a pullback to international borders in exchange for peace and normal diplomatic relations with Egypt and Syria. Within days, foreign minister Abba Eban communicated this proposal to the U.S. government. After two months of consideration, the Israeli government modified its position, but neither the United States nor the new Israeli ambassador, Yitzhak Rabin, was informed of the changes. In November, 1967, the U.N. Security Council passed Resolution 242. It called for Israel's withdrawal from the territories, the end of belligerence among all parties, and the recognition of secure boundaries. However, the wording was sufficiently ambiguous that Israel could say that it was not being asked to withdraw from "all" captured territory, and the Arab states could say they were not asked to make "full" peace with Israel.

government as its representative to the United Nations. He subsequently headed the Israeli mission to that body until 1953. He served as vice president of the U.N. General Assembly in 1953 and was the Israeli ambassador to the United States from 1950 to 1959. In 1959, he was elected to the Knesset, Israel's legislative body, initially serving the government as minister without portfolio.

In 1960, Eban was named minister of education and culture, a post in which he served until 1963. He was deputy prime minister from 1963 to 1966 and minister of foreign affairs from 1966 to 1974. In the latter office, Eban's diplomatic skills proved invaluable to his country during the Six-Day War with Arab neighbors in 1967 and during the Yom Kippur War in 1973. He was intimately associated with every important Israeli leader during the first thirty years of the nation's existence. Yet, despite his unstinting efforts on Israel's behalf, he never achieved his country's highest honor: He never served as prime minister.

From 1974 onward, Eban served as a member of the Knesset's commission on foreign affairs and security, counseling Labor Party leaders on foreign-policy decisions. He was appointed to several offices, conferences, and committees on science and technology in emerging nations, within the United Nations and elsewhere. He was elected to membership in both the World and the American Academies of Arts and Sciences. He

Abba Eban (left) talking with former Israeli defense minister Moshe Dayan. *(Bernard Gotfryd/Archive Photos)*

taught at Columbia University and at the Institute of Advanced Study at Princeton University. He holds honorary degrees from thirteen universities and colleges in the United States and Israel.

Literary Accomplishments

During his days as an active diplomat and politician, Eban was very popular in the United States—and not only within the Jewish community. He was much sought after for interviews and guest appearances on public-affairs television shows. His articulateness and gift for oratory constituted an advantage that his Arab counterparts could seldom overcome. He was so skilled on television that in 1984 he hosted a series, *Heritage: Civilization and the Jews*, on the Public Broadcasting Service.

English was Eban's first language, and he used it so masterfully that from 1939 through 1987 he translated, edited, and authored seventeen books. In addition, he contributed articles in English, French, Hebrew, and Arabic to a variety of learned journals. The quantity and quality of this literary output is especially striking when seen within the context of the whirlwind of diplomatic and political activity in which Eban was involved during virtually the whole of his adult life. His writings on Israel cannot be read as objective analysis, yet his prose is very moving. He makes no pretense of being a coolly detached observer, since he considers the history of his young nation a brave and noble adventure.

Bibliography

Ben-Gurion, David. *Israel: A Personal History*. Translated by Nechemia Myers and Uzy Nystar. New York: Funk & Wagnalls, 1971.

Eban, Abba. *Abba Eban: An Autobiography*. New York: Random House, 1977.

Horovitz, David, ed. *The Jerusalem Report. Shalom, Friend: The Life and Legacy of Yitzhak Rabin*. New York: Newmarket Press, 1996.

Patrick Adcock

Félix Éboué

Born: December 26, 1884; Cayenne, French Guiana
Died: May 17, 1944; Cairo, Egypt

Colonial administrator of French Equatorial Africa during World War II

Born to French West Indian parents of African descent, Adolphe-Félix-Sylvestre Éboué (ah-DOHLF fay-LEEKZ seel-VEHST-ruh ay-BWAY) was educated in France. His career as a colonial administrator included twenty-seven years of service in Oubangui-Chari (now the Central African Republic), notably at Mobaye, Bambari, Bangassou, and Bozoum. In Oubangui-Chari, he wrote books on local customs and languages. He met writer André Gide, who was impressed by Éboué's intelligence and wit. Sent to Guadeloupe in 1936, he was the first French colonial governor of African descent. This posting was quickly followed in 1938 by an appointment as colonial governor of Chad.

Administrator with a Conscience

A portly, serene man with a darker complexion than most of the Africans he ruled, Éboué was respected even by those whites in the colony who at first resented a black superior. His frequent tours of the huge territory, even during the rainy season, kept him in touch with every tribe and interest. Deafness gave him a certain awkwardness, but those who met him were quickly impressed by his good humor and integrity.

As a liberal, a French patriot, and a black man, Éboué hated Germany's Nazi regime, which occupied France while he was governor of Chad. Although he informed General Charles de Gaulle in private of his sympathy for the Free French, Éboué was determined not to do anything rash that might provoke an invasion of Chad by Italian-ruled Libya. The commander of Éboué's own troops wanted to collaborate with the Nazis. Others pressed for quick action. Yet Éboué never wavered in his determination to continue the war and to do so wisely.

On July 3, 1940, Éboué was the first important colonial governor to rally his colony to the side of de Gaulle's Free French. He did so at a time when most French colonial officials were declaring support for pro-Nazi Vichy France or remaining neutral. Provid-

French Equatorial Africa governor-general Félix Éboué (left) welcoming Charles de Gaulle, the leader of free France, to Chad in 1942. (Library of Congress)

ing a major psychological boost to the French resistance at its bleakest moment, Éboué boldly evaded Vichy's efforts to neutralize his authority and was promptly rewarded by de Gaulle with the governorate-general of all of French Equatorial Africa on November 12, 1941. French Equatorial Africa's capital, Brazzaville, soon became the headquarters of the Free French prior to their move to London.

Complications immediately arose in the colony of Gabon. The colonial governor, Pierre Masson, aligned Gabon with the Free French. The following day, however, he reversed his decision. He was apparently influenced by the criticism of the Roman Catholic bishop of Libreville—and by the arrival of two Vichy warships and two high Vichy colonial appointees. Gabon thereafter became the scene of a civil war between the Free French, based in Cameroon, Chad, and the Middle Congo, on one hand, and Vichy forces on the other. In early September the Free French took Mayumba, occupied N'Gounie Province, and

laid siege to Lambarene. Vichy forces abandoned Lambarene on November 5. Four days later these forces combined with others from Cameroon, which had previously swept through Wole N'Tem Province, to take Libreville. After Port-Gentil surrendered to the Free French on November 11, further Vichy opposition ceased.

Liberating Influence

Although his children were still in France and, because of their color, were doubly vulnerable to Nazi retaliation, Éboué lived up to the respect of de Gaulle. De Gaulle's position on decolonization was profoundly changed by his relationship with the governor-general. By the end of 1942, Free French forces had swept the Italians from the southern Libyan province of Fezzan, while British troops invaded northeastern Libya from Egypt.

As an administrator, Éboué saw that Chad needed economic help when its exports were stopped by the war. On November 8, 1941, he

French Equatorial Africa

The federation of French colonies known as French Equatorial Africa was created in 1910 from a model developed earlier in French West Africa. Encompassing some of the most difficult and remote regions ever colonized by Europeans, it included four territories: Gabon, Middle Congo, Oubangui-Chari, and Chad. These colonies yielded great wealth in the form of wood, rubber, diamonds, cotton, and later oil and mineral ores.

Each territory was headed by a governor responsible to a governor-general in the capital, Brazzaville. The federation's revenues were raised through customs duties and other taxes, which were sent to Brazzaville. This process was difficult and often unequal. For example, Gabonese revenues aided construction of railways

elsewhere from which Gabon derived no benefits, even though it needed railroads for its own development. Meanwhile, no taxes at all were collected from large areas of Chad.

The federation was changed into a "group of territories" in April, 1957, as a result of the Loi-Cadre (Enabling Act) of June, 1956. The federation was abolished in September, 1958. By 1960 French Equatorial Africa had become the independent, but ill-prepared, nations of Gabon, Chad, the Central African Republic (formerly Oubangui-Chari) and the Congo (formerly Middle Congo). Attempts by the four to replace the federation with a cooperative political structure failed. Close economic relations and ties with France have continued.

French Africans in World War II

On June 18, 1940, the government of the Third French Republic surrendered to Nazi Germany. The Germans occupied the northern three-fifths of France, while the pro-Nazi Vichy government controlled the remainder. Meanwhile, in London, General Charles de Gaulle called for the formation of a Free French movement to keep Frenchmen in the war on the Allied side. He hoped to use the resources of France's vast empire to liberate the mother country. French authorities in North and West Africa rejected his appeals, while those in Cameroon and French Equatorial Africa rallied to his side in July and August, 1940. This support was largely the work of the governor of Chad, Félix Éboué.

Brazzaville became the headquarters of the Free French, who participated in British efforts to remove the Italians from Libya. The British purchased Gabonese okoume, a wood excellently suited for airplane construction. French Morocco, Algeria, and Tunisia later became battlegrounds as Allied forces swept toward Italy. Thousands of Africans served in the Free French forces in Africa and Europe and subsequently received pensions. These veterans would be important in upholding close ties with France after the war. In early 1944 the Free French government sponsored the Brazzaville Conference, which planned for the postwar liberalization of the colonial regime. The liberalization was in part a recognition of the wartime contributions of French Africans.

---

sent his famous circular on the indigenous politics of French Equatorial Africa to all subdivision heads. This circular was one of the principal working documents for the Brazzaville Conference in February of 1944, which marked the beginning of the decolonizing process in France's African possessions.

As the first and greatest of the Free French leaders in Africa, Éboué served as governor-general from December 30, 1941, until his death in Cairo before the end of the war. After the liberation of Paris his body was interred in the Pantheon. His memory is honored throughout Africa and in France with schools, hospitals, and streets named after him. His role in shaping French colonial policy made him a symbol of African liberation after his death. During decolonization, Éboué's was one of only three "foreign" names not expunged from former French colonies, the others being de Gaulle's and Pierre-Paul-François de Brazza's.

Bibliography

Manning, Patrick. *Francophone Sub-Saharan Africa, 1880-1985*. Cambridge, England: Cambridge University Press, 1988.

Thompson, Virginia, and Richard Adloff. *The Emerging States of French Equatorial Africa*. Oxford, England: Oxford University Press, 1960.

Weinstein, Brian. *Éboué*. New York: Oxford University Press, 1972.

West, Richard. *Congo*. New York: Holt, Rinehart & Winston, 1972.

White, Dorothy S. *Black Africa and de Gaulle: From the French Empire to Independence*. University Park: Pennsylvania State University Press, 1979.

Randall Fegley

Anthony Eden

Born: June 12, 1897; Windlestone Hall, near Bishop Auckland, Durham, England
Died: January 14, 1977; Alvediston, Wiltshire, England

Prime minister of Great Britain (1955-1957)

Robert Anthony Eden (RO-burt AN-tho-nee EE-dehn) was born the third son and fourth child of Sir William Eden, Baronet, and Lady Sybil Frances Grey. He attended school at prestigious Eton and then answered the call to arms during World War I. He enlisted in the King's Royal Rifle Corps in September of 1915 and was dispatched to France. Eden was decorated for heroism under fire and rose to the rank of brigade major by war's end in 1918. After the war, Eden attended Christ Church College of Oxford University, graduating in 1922 with first-class honors in oriental languages (Persian and Arabic).

Early Political Career

Upon graduation, Eden was induced to run for the parliamentary seat of Spennymoor in 1922 on the Conservative Party ticket. Though his bid was unsuccessful, he found his vocation in politics. His lengthy tenure as a Conservative member of Parliament began in 1923 with his election to the Warwick and Leamington seat. Eden exhibited an early interest in foreign affairs, and in 1926 Foreign Secretary Sir Austen Chamberlain appointed him as his parliamentary personal secretary. Eden carried out various assignments as lord privy seal (to which he had been appointed in 1933) during the coalition ministry of Prime Minister Ramsay MacDonald. These included missions to Rome, Berlin, Moscow, and the Saarland. Eden was well positioned to become Britain's League of Nations envoy (June, 1935) and then, on December 22, 1935, foreign affairs secretary in the cabinet of Prime Minister Stanley Baldwin.

As foreign secretary, Eden was confronted by a steady escalation in global tensions over the expansionist policies of Japan in the Far East (with its potential threat to Australia and to the British Raj in India), Italian aggression in the horn of Africa, and Nazi Germany's rearmament in violation of the provisions of the Treaty of Versailles. He showed considerable personal initiative and enjoyed a large measure of autonomy during Baldwin's ministry. The prime minister seldom interjected himself into the sphere of foreign affairs and was content to leave Eden to his own devices in his area of expertise. Eden's first serious crisis was Italy's attack upon Ethiopia. At this stage, he adhered to an appeasement policy

Anthony Eden *(Library of Congress)*

463

British prime minister Anthony Eden (left) shakes hands with French premier Guy Mollett in 1956, signaling their agreement in handling the Suez Crisis. *(Library of Congress)*

that opposed Winston Churchill's views on the necessity of taking a tougher stand against Fascist Italy and Nazi Germany. Eden permitted German leader Adolf Hitler to remilitarize the German Rhineland. (This militarization was against conditions of the Versailles Treaty, signed after World War I.) Eden issued only a mild protest. When the Spanish Civil War broke out, Eden studiously maintained a stance of strict neutrality.

Resignation and Wartime Career

Neville Chamberlain, who became prime minister on May 28, 1937, proved to be much more assertive a leader than Baldwin and was less inclined to delegate to cabinet members. On several occasions he made foreign policy decisions without consulting Eden. Friction arising from the foreign secretary's having been passed over in the decision making festered into a minor crisis, culminating in Eden's resignation from his post on February 20, 1938.

Upon the outbreak of World War II in September of 1939, Eden was named to head the Dominions Office. He served in this capacity until Churchill became prime minister in May, 1940. From

Appeasement

From the time that the Treaty of Versailles was signed after World War I, there was a small but vocal segment of British public opinion that considered treaty provisions to have been unduly harsh to the vanquished Germany. German governments used these guilt feelings effectively. By the mid-1930's, the most influential public figures in Britain were committed to the idea of dismantling the Versailles system. To forestall conflict, they were willing to go to great length to "appease" Germany by catering to alleged German grievances. Adolf Hitler was able to use appeasement sentiment to achieve rearmament,

to remilitarize the Rhineland, and to annex Austria. Furthermore, with the assent of British prime minister Neville Chamberlain at the Munich Conference, Hitler occupied the Sudeten region of Czechoslovakia (the Sudetenland). While a jubilant Chamberlain asserted that the accord had brought "peace in our time," the rest of Czechoslovakia was rendered vulnerable. The March, 1939, seizure of all of Czechoslovakia by Germany in breech of the Munich Agreement permanently discredited the appeasement policy—World War II followed within six months.

The Suez Crisis

Egyptian president Gamal Abdel Nasser had, since taking power in 1955, exhibited a fiercely independent nationalism in his dealings with former colonial powers such as England and France. On July 26, 1956, Nasser announced that Egypt was taking over the Suez Canal Company. This move was viewed by British prime minister Sir Anthony Eden and French premier Guy Mollet as a threat to their shipping through this strategic waterway.

On October 26, a secret meeting at Sevres, France, between French, British, and Israeli representatives mapped out a plan for joint military action. On October 29, Israeli forces invaded Egypt's Sinai Peninsula, and on October 31, Brit-ain and France launched joint military operations against Port Said at the canal's headway.

International condemnation was immediate, and France and Britain had to use their U.N. Security Council vetoes to squelch U.N. sanctions. Threats by the Soviet Union and, more tellingly, pressure from the United States— where president Dwight D. Eisenhower was reportedly quite annoyed at being kept in the dark about these operations—led to an Israeli ceasefire and to the withdrawal of Franco-British forces on November 6. A United Nations Emergency Force administered the clearing of the canal, which reverted to Egyptian control.

U.N. observers driving their white Jeeps into contested territory during the 1956 Suez Crisis. *(National Archives)*

465

May to December, 1940, Eden was war secretary, then from December, 1940, to July, 1945, he took his second tenure as foreign secretary.

The last year of the war took its toll on Eden's health and on his personal life—his first marriage, to Beatrice Helen Gervase, was fast deteriorating. The couple had married in 1923. Eden was incapacitated with a duodenal ulcer and was devastated by the news of his oldest son Simon's death in action during the July, 1945, election campaign. Though Eden was reelected to his parliamentary seat, the government fell to the Labour Party, led by Clement Attlee. During the course of 1946, the Edens separated, and their divorce was finalized in 1950.

Return to Government

In October, 1951, upon the Conservatives' electoral victory and Churchill's return to power, Eden became foreign secretary for the third occasion and was acknowledged deputy leader. In 1954 Eden was named a knight of the order of the garter by Queen Elizabeth II, and he succeeded Churchill as prime minister upon the latter's retirement on April 6, 1955. Eden's tax-reduction measures and a well-conducted media campaign assured the Conservative Party of a comfortable majority in the ensuing parliamentary elections. Though his government's domestic policy proved extremely popular, it was, ironically, Eden's forte, foreign policy, that initiated his ministry's downfall. The Suez Crisis left his government humiliated and Eden himself in a physically debilitated state. He suffered from bile duct disorders that necessitated drug treatments throughout the remainder of his life. On January 9, 1957, he retired for reasons of health and was succeeded by Harold Macmillan.

In 1961 Eden was made first earl of Avon and entered the House of Lords. He had married for the second time, in 1952, to Anne Clarissa Spencer-Churchill. He was the author of four autobiographical works: *Full Circle* (1960), *Facing the Dictators* (1962), *The Reckoning* (1965), and *Another World: 1897-1917* (1976). He died at his estate on January 14, 1977, and was survived by his second wife.

Bibliography

Carlton, David. *Anthony Eden: A Biography*. London: Allen Lane, 1981.

Charmley, John. *Descent to Suez: Diaries, 1951-1956*. London: Weidenfeld & Nicolson, 1986.

Dutton, David. *Anthony Eden: A Life and Reputation*. New York: Arnold, 1997.

James, Robert Rhodes. *Anthony Eden*. London: Weidenfeld & Nicolson, 1986.

Peters, Anthony R. *Anthony Eden at the Foreign Office, 1931-1938*. New York: St. Martin's Press, 1986.

Raymond Pierre Hylton

Edward VII

Born: November 9, 1841; Buckingham Palace, London, England
Died: May 6, 1910; Buckingham Palace, London, England

King of Great Britain and Ireland (1901-1910)

Albert Edward (AL-burt EHD-wurd), the eldest son of Queen Victoria and Prince Albert, was born in Buckingham Palace. As an infant, he was made prince of Wales. Edward was a difficult child. He was educated in a strict fashion, first at home and later at both Oxford and Cambridge. In 1860 he toured Canada and the United States. In 1863 he married Alexandra, the daughter of the King of Denmark. They had five children. Their second son became King George V in 1910. Their youngest daughter, Princess Maude Charlotte Mary Victoria, married Prince Charles of Denmark, who later became the first king of Norway.

The Life of a Prince

Queen Victoria lived until Prince Edward was fifty-nine years old, so he spent most of his life as an heir-apparent. Because the queen lived in virtual retirement after her husband's death in 1862, the prince and princess of Wales filled the royal place on many public occasions. Edward often traveled abroad, notably to Ireland (many times) and to Egypt. In 1875 he toured India, visiting the courts of many rajahs. Because he traveled often to France, Germany, and Russia, he became familiar with continental society.

His London home, Malborough House, was the center of fashionable society, a place where aristocrats rubbed shoulders with newly wealthy men and women. His life was not blameless. In 1871 he shocked the nation when he was named in a divorce suit. Such sexual indiscretions—and his indefatigable taste for gambling, shooting, food, parties, and other luxuries—vexed his mother greatly. She did not trust him with state secrets or allow him any occupation or authority. Yet he was popular with the British people, probably because he shared so many of their amusements, such as the theater and sports, especially racing.

Edward the King

Queen Victoria died on January 22, 1901, and Edward's coronation took place in August. King Edward VII (EHD-wurd thuh SEH-vehnth) was not interested in domestic or colonial matters, but he observed foreign affairs keenly. With the ap-

Edward VII *(Library of Congress)*

467

The British royal family, posing with the visiting Russian royal family, in the first decade of the twentieth century. King Edward VII is seated to the right of Czar Nicholas II at the center of the group. *(Library of Congress)*

The Shadow of Victoria

Prince Albert Edward, who became King Edward VII, lived most of his life in the shadow of his mother, Queen Victoria. She and her husband, Prince Albert, closely supervised his rigorous education. When he attended Oxford and Cambridge, the queen insisted that he live under strict supervision. When Prince Albert died after visiting Edward, the queen was convinced that Edward had somehow caused his father's death. "I never can or shall look at him without a shudder," she wrote, and she never completely forgave him.

Queen Victoria guided Edward's choice of a wife: She had to be a Protestant princess. When he visited India in 1868-1869, the queen planned every major detail. Although his relations with his mother gradually became more cordial, she resented his growing popularity, and she deplored the fast set of adulterers, cigar-smoking gamblers, and Americans that congregated about his London residence.

Mother and son disagreed strongly on many matters of foreign affairs, and she judged him too indiscreet to share state secrets. He was allowed to represent the monarchy on ceremonial occasions, and he organized the ceremonies of the queen's Golden Jubilee in 1887. Until 1892, however, Victoria denied him access to many official government documents. She would not approve any plan to give Edward even a token occupation or to give him any real preparation for his eventual rule.

Edward's 1908 Visit to Russia

As prince of Wales, Edward had visited Russia to attend state funerals. Relations between England and Russia had been strained since the Crimean War of 1854-1856. By the time he became Edward VII, Anglo-Russian relations were even more important, for the Triple Alliance of Germany, Austria, and Italy was threatening the peace. In 1907 Britain and Russia signed an agreement that, although unimportant in itself, seemed to signal closer ties. In 1908, even though protesters at home complained that he was hon-oring a tyrant, King Edward met with Czar Nicholas II at Reval (in what later became Estonia). Edward greatly impressed his hosts with his knowledge of Russia, and the visit was a resounding social success. Although little was agreed upon, Edward's understanding with the czar strengthened the ties between the two nations. Yet the talks also made the German government worried that something sinister was afoot, and thus they added to the circumstances that led to World War I.

proval of the Foreign Office, he conducted discussions with other sovereigns and their representatives. Unlike his mother, he shared much of this information with his son, the prince who would succeed him as King George V. Even so, he was not consulted as much as he desired. He did not get on well with many important politicians. To a degree that later eras find hard to imagine, many disagreements had to do with diplomatic protocol, with offering or declining to offer honors and decorations.

Edward VII continued to travel, especially to France. He gained a reputation at home and abroad as a uniquely effective diplomat. The Germans deplored his influence. His visit to Paris in 1903, undertaken over the objections of the British Foreign Office, helped strengthen the friendship between Britain and France in what Edward dubbed the Entente Cordiale. This agreement drew the two nations together in opposition to the Triple Alliance of Germany, Austria, and Italy. He visited Russia in 1908, also to build an alliance. In contrast, his relations with his nephew, the German kaiser, had never been smooth. Edward made many unsuccessful visits attempting to bring about closer ties between Britain and Germany.

By 1909 the king's health was beginning to fail. Years of cigars, champagne, and rich food had left him notably overweight and short of breath. By the next spring, he coughed incessantly and could not sleep. After a series of heart attacks, he died on May 6, 1910.

A King's Role

Edward VII had modest intellectual gifts and accomplishments, and he led a life of self-indulgence. His attention span was short, and he was easily bored. Even late in life he was subject to childish rages. Yet all who knew him said that he could be generous and kind-hearted. He was often sexually unfaithful to his wife, but otherwise he treated her with respect and consideration.

The power of the sovereign had been whittled away during his mother's reign. Even so, Edward felt his duty to a changing England and to its mission in the world. When he was prince of Wales, landed aristocrats mingled at his London home with men of new wealth. His natural charm and his many contacts with royalty and statesmen all over Europe enabled him, perhaps without planning it, to influence his nation's foreign policy. That influence was probably not as great

Edward VII (seated, center, with cane) with the royal party at Sandringham, in Commodore Wood. *(Archive Photos/ Popperfoto)*

as it seemed at the time; even the Entente Cordiale had been well prepared by others. Yet one biographer points out that the king's policies of vigilance were exactly those that soon saved Britain in World War I.

Bibliography

Cowles, Virginia. *Edward VII and His Circle*. London: Hamish Hamilton, 1956.

Heffer, Simon. *Power and Place: The Political Consequences of King Edward VII*. London: Weidenfield & Nicolson, 1998.

Hibbert, Christopher. *The Royal Victorians: King Edward VII, His Family and Friends*. Philadelphia: J. B. Lippincott, 1976.

Magnus, Philip. *King Edward the Seventh*. New York: E. P. Dutton, 1964.

Massie, Robert K. *Dreadnought: Britain, Germany, and the Coming of the Great War*. New York: Random House, 1991.

St. Aubyn, Giles. *Edward VII: Prince and King*. New York: Atheneum, 1979.

George Soule

Edward VIII

Born: June 23, 1894; Richmond, Surrey, England
Died: May 28, 1972; Paris, France

King of Great Britain and Ireland (1936) who abdicated the throne

Prince Edward Albert Christian George Andrew Patrick David (EHD-wurd AL-burt KRIHS-tyuhn JOHRJ AN-drew PA-trihk DAY-vihd) was the son of King George V and Queen Mary and the great-grandson of Queen Victoria. Throughout his lifetime he carried numerous titles, including prince of Wales, earl of Chester, duke of Windsor, and king of England. He and his five younger siblings spent their early years at various royal estates throughout England. At the age of twelve, Edward entered the Royal Naval College at Osborne on the Isle of Wight. He continued his education at the Dartmouth Naval College and Oxford University. When World War I began in 1914, Edward was made a second lieutenant in the First Battalion of the Grenadier Guards. He never engaged in active combat because of his status as prince of Wales and the heir to the throne. He served behind the front lines in France, Italy, and Egypt in 1916. Over the next two decades, the prince of Wales became a popular figure among the British because of his personal charm, his sympathetic stance toward the poor and unemployed, and his private efforts toward social reform.

A Brief Reign

At the death of his father in January, 1936, Edward acceded to the throne as Edward VIII (EHD-wurd thuh AYTH) for a brief reign that ended in his abdication by the end of the year. From the start, he embraced the modern era—he was the first British king to fly to his coronation ceremony. His immediate reduction of the number of grants usually received by the ruling monarch met huge popular approval. Edward further garnered support by taking measures to minimize unemployment and to relieve poverty, as he had done when he was president of a national fund during the war. His sympathy for Germany and his support of British prime minister Neville Chamberlain's policy of appeasement of Adolf Hitler worried some European heads of state, but they were accepted by most of Great Britain.

Abdication

Popular opinion of Edward had soured immensely by the end of the year, however, as rumors about his involvement with a divorced American woman named Wallis Simpson multiplied. In December, Edward declared his intention to marry Mrs. Simpson. To avert a potential constitutional disaster, he formally abdicated the

Edward VIII *(National Archives)*

throne and left England to live a life of exile in France. Over the next four decades Edward was sporadically involved in political affairs, and he was the governor of the Bahama Islands from 1940 to 1945.

By his own account, Edward believed that he made only two innovations during his short tenure as king: his unprecedented flight to his coronation and his giving permission for the yeoman of the guard to shave their beards if they chose. Despite the brevity of his reign, his choice to abdicate the throne for the woman he loved rather than to compromise the integrity of the monarchy set an important precedent that later generations would look to when scandals involving adultery and divorce touched the monarchy during the reign of Queen Elizabeth II.

Wallis Simpson, the woman for whom Edward VIII abdicated the British throne. *(Library of Congress)*

Bibliography

Beaverbrook, Lord. *The Abdication of King Edward VII*. Edited by A. J. P. Taylor. Atheneum, N.Y.: Beaverbrook Newspapers Limited, 1966.

Bloch, Michael. *The Secret File of the Duke of Windsor*. New York: Harper and Row, 1988.

Ziegler, Philip. *King Edward VIII: A Biography*. New York: Alfred A. Knopf, 1991.

Susanna Calkins

The Abdication Crisis

Edward, Prince of Wales, was introduced to Wallis Warfield Simpson, an American divorcée from Baltimore, Maryland, in 1931. While she was still married to her second husband, an intimate romance between them flourished over the next several years. When Edward acceded to the throne, his long-standing relationship with Mrs. Simpson become an increasingly contentious issue. In October of 1936, she petitioned for a divorce from her husband. Although the British press initially practiced self-censorship, rumors about Mrs. Simpson's divorce and the likelihood of her marriage to the king abounded throughout European and American newspapers. Most British people, and many government officials, did not wish to see the king involved in a marriage in which Mrs. Simpson would be Edward's wife but not the official queen. Prime Minister Stanley Baldwin, backed by most of Parliament, stated his refusal to legalize such a marriage.

On December 10, Edward signed the Instrument of Abdication to avoid escalating the affair to a full-fledged constitutional crisis. By this document, Edward formally renounced his rights to the British throne so that he would be free to marry Mrs. Simpson. The duke of York, Edward's younger brother, became King George VI, and Edward and his wife formally become the duke and duchess of Windsor.

Dwight D. Eisenhower

Born: October 14, 1890; Denison, Texas
Died: March 28, 1969; Washington, D.C.

U.S. military leader during World War II, president of the United States (1953-1961)

Dwight David Eisenhower (DWIT DAY-vihd I-zehn-howr) was the son of deeply religious parents descended from German and Swiss immigrants. His family moved from Texas to Abilene, Kansas, where he grew up and became known as "little Ike" among his schoolmates. Eisenhower's early years held few clues to his future greatness. He finally received an appointment to the U.S. Military Academy at West Point, New York, choosing a soldier's career even though his parents were staunch pacifists. He graduated from the academy in 1915, sixty-first in a class of 164, and was assigned to Fort Sam Houston, Texas. There he met Mamie Geneva Doud, and on the day of his promotion to first lieutenant (July 1, 1916) they were married.

Rise to Prominence

During World War I (1914-1918), Eisenhower was in charge of a tank training center near Gettysburg, Pennsylvania. After the war ended, a pivotal opportunity came to him: admission to the Army's Command and General Staff School at Fort Leavenworth, Kansas. In 1926 Eisenhower graduated first in his class of 275 top army officers. He came to the notice of important army leaders and in 1933 was appointed aide to General Douglas MacArthur, the army chief of staff in Washington, D.C.

Early in 1941, following the outbreak of World War II, the army staged the biggest peacetime exercises of its history, and Eisenhower was appointed chief of staff of the U.S. Third Army in Louisiana. Owing to his brilliant war-games plan, Eisenhower's force routed the U.S. Second Army (including a tank division commanded by friend and fellow future hero, George S. Patton, Jr.). Eisenhower's superior performance earned him a promotion to brigadier general and the admiration of General George C. Marshall, MacArthur's replacement as army chief of staff. Marshall brought Eisenhower to Washington, D.C., to serve in the army's war plans division after Pearl Harbor was bombed by Japanese airplanes on December 7, 1941. He was promoted to major general in March, 1942.

Supreme Commander

In June, 1942, Eisenhower was named commanding general of U.S. forces in Europe, and he

Dwight D. Eisenhower *(Library of Congress)*

was promoted yet again, to lieutenant general. His advancement over several qualified senior officers was spectacular, especially considering he had never before held a combat command. Subsequently, he was given command of all Allied forces that invaded North Africa (November, 1942). In February, 1943, he was promoted to the rank of four-star general, the highest rank achievable in the army at the time. In July, 1943, he organized the Allied invasion of Sicily and, later that year, of all Italy.

In December, 1943, Eisenhower was named supreme commander of all U.S., British, and free French forces, with the charge to plan and carry out a massive cross-channel invasion of the European continent. Known as Operation Overlord, it began on June 6, 1944 (D day), when Allied forces landed on the beaches of Normandy, France. The Normandy invasion was successful, and in December Eisenhower received the newly created rank of five-star general.

After the war, Eisenhower replaced Marshall as army chief of staff (November, 1945). In 1948 he retired from active duty to become president of Columbia University and write a book about his wartime experiences, *Crusade in Europe* (1948). By 1950 he was back in uniform, at the request of President Harry S Truman, to serve as supreme commander of a new military alliance in Europe called the North Atlantic Treaty Organization (NATO).

Thirty-Fourth President

In 1952 there were deep divisions in the country caused by the Korean War (1950-1953). At the urging of some Republicans, Eisenhower ran for the presidency. He defeated Democratic opponent Adlai E. Stevenson and was inaugurated at age sixty-two. He ran for a second term in 1956 and again defeated Stevenson. Eisenhower delegated broad powers to presidential aides and cabinet members. He created the Department of Health, Education, and Welfare in 1953 and worked for a reduction in government spending,

The Normandy Invasion

At the Trident Conference, held at Washington, D.C., in May, 1942, President Franklin D. Roosevelt of the United States and Prime Minister Winston Churchill of Great Britain agreed on a combined military venture to invade Nazi-controlled Europe. General George C. Marshall, U.S. army chief of staff, and General Dwight D. Eisenhower, U.S. commander of Allied forces in Europe, were both considered for the position of supreme commander of the Allied Expeditionary Force to oversee Operation Overlord, as it was called. In December, 1943, however, President Roosevelt chose Dwight D. Eisenhower because he felt he could not spare Marshall from his post.

The Normandy invasion was to be the largest seaborne invasion in history, landing huge amounts of equipment and great numbers of troops on the beaches of Normandy in northern France. Eisenhower's preparations included assembling and training soldiers in England, stockpiling needed materiel, building two artificial harbors to be floated over and sunk off the landing site, and planning a fake invasion to deceive the Germans.

By June 3, assault troops and naval support forces were ready. The weather had turned bad, however, and the success of the operation depended on low tides for the landing vessels and clear skies for air support. On June 5, with only a chance of good enough weather, Eisenhower made his final decision to proceed. D day began early on June 6, 1944, took the Germans by surprise, and was considered a success by nightfall.

The International Atomic Energy Agency

Early in his presidency, Dwight D. Eisenhower began urging that atomic energy be harnessed for peaceful purposes rather than employed for nuclear weapons to be used in warfare. In December, 1953, in a major speech to the United Nations, he suggested that all nations with nuclear capability help establish a U.N. agency to assist in developing and promoting peaceful uses of atomic energy. His program was called Atoms for Peace. Delegates responded enthusiastically. In 1957, according to Eisenhower's proposal, the United Nations created the International Atomic Energy Agency (IAEA) to try to ensure that nuclear materials intended for beneficial activities were not used for military purposes. The IAEA was given responsibility for inspecting nations suspected of violations.

a policy that resulted in a surplus in the U.S. Treasury by 1956. His focus on the economy led to a decrease in conventional U.S. military forces but a buildup of nuclear weapons. He also encouraged the world to use atomic energy for peaceful purposes by helping to establish the International Atomic Energy Agency. Civil rights was beginning to become a significant issue in the

General Dwight D. Eisenhower with paratroopers in England on the eve of the D-Day invasion of Europe. *(Library of Congress)*

U.S. president Dwight D. Eisenhower addresses the nation on television to announce the disintegration of U.S.-Soviet summit talks in 1960. Talks broke down in the wake of the U2 incident, in which the United States denied the existence of a U.S. spy plane shot down over the Soviet Union. *(National Archives)*

Israel to withdraw their invasion forces from Egypt after its president, Gamal Abdel Nasser, had seized the Suez Canal. Just before leaving office, Eisenhower broke off diplomatic relations with Cuba when new Cuban dictator Fidel Castro made his country a communist state.

When Eisenhower returned to the United States from Europe in June, 1945, he was greeted with a hero's welcome. His gifts for grand strategy, tact, and diplomacy in working with other military commanders and world leaders, his optimism, and his luck all helped him forge an unparalleled consensus among the Allies and an effective fighting force to defeat the Axis powers (principally Germany and Italy) during World War II. His recognized leadership won him the presidency, and he in turn gave Americans eight years of general peace and prosperity.

mid-1950's. Eisenhower was by no means in the forefront of the push for ending segregation, but he did order military units to Little Rock, Arkansas, when its governor defied federal school desegregation orders in 1957.

Eisenhower confronted communism by declaring the Eisenhower Doctrine—promising military or economic aid to any Middle Eastern country attempting to resist communist aggression. However, he refused to be drawn into the emerging Vietnam conflict. Despite serious health problems in 1956, he handled the Suez Crisis with skill: He forced Britain, France, and

Bibliography

Ambrose, Stephen E. *Eisenhower: Soldier and President*. New York: Simon and Schuster, 1990.

Divine, Robert A. *Eisenhower and the Cold War*. New York: Oxford University Press, 1981.

Eisenhower, David. *Eisenhower: At War, 1943-1945*. New York: Random House, 1986.

Andrew C. Skinner

Elizabeth II

Born: April 21, 1926; London, England

Queen of Great Britain and Northern Ireland (from 1953)

Elizabeth Alexandra Mary (ee-LIH-zah-behth a-lehk-ZAN-drah MEH-ree) was born into the British royal family during an era when the British monarchy still presided over the world's largest empire. Elizabeth's grandparents, King George V and Queen Mary, were popular monarchs who had projected an image of tradition and nineteenth-century formality. The values of maintaining tradition would become an important element of Elizabeth's life and career. When she was ten years old, Elizabeth saw her father, the duke of York, crowned King George VI. Her father, a rather shy and quiet man, was not prepared to assume the responsibilities of king. However, in 1936, following the death of her grandfather the king, her uncle, King Edward VIII, renounced the throne in order to marry Wallis Warfield Simpson, an American divorcée. This sudden turn of events not only made her father the king but also assigned Princess Elizabeth the role of heiress-presumptive to the British throne.

Heiress Presumptive

Princess Elizabeth's parents were determined to repair the damage to the monarchy caused by the abdication of Edward VIII. Accordingly, they embraced traditional royal responsibilities. King George VI and Queen Elizabeth (who, after 1952, would be known as the queen mother) became quite popular throughout the British Empire. Much of this popularity, especially in the United Kingdom, was based on their positions of leadership during World War II. Following the war, Britain's world position was greatly diminished, but the monarchy performed a stabilizing role as Britain's empire gradually disappeared. By 1946 Princess Elizabeth was starting to perform official public duties. Her first appearance in a par-

liamentary proceeding occurred in 1946, when King George VI, Queen Elizabeth, and Princess Elizabeth visited the Parliament of Northern Ireland.

In 1947 Princess Elizabeth married Prince Phillip, a member of the Greek royal family. In 1948 the couple's first child was born and was given the name Charles Phillip Arthur George. In 1950 a second child was born, Princess Anne. Although Elizabeth and Phillip were a young couple starting a family, they were also members of the royal household, with important responsibilities to perform. These responsibilities were not enough to prepare Princess Elizabeth for the

Elizabeth II *(Library of Congress)*

Queen Elizabeth II arriving in Ceylon on a royal tour in the 1950's. *(Library of Congress)*

death of her father, however. The king's illness had gone through various phases of recovery and decline. By 1952 his health had improved, and he was scheduled to visit British possessions in Africa. However, when his health declined again Princess Elizabeth and Prince Phillip were assigned the duty of making the trip in the king's name. While in Kenya, Elizabeth received word that her father had died and that she was queen. She returned to London as the sovereign at the young age of twenty-six.

The Sovereign

In later years, Queen Elizabeth II (ee-LIH-zah-behth thuh SEH-

---

The British Monarchy

Queen Elizabeth II performs important constitutional responsibilities. Under the British system of government, the king or queen is the head of state and performs primarily ceremonial functions. The prime minister is the head of government, responsible for domestic and foreign policy. One of the queen's most important constitutional duties concerns her relationship with the prime minister. In British politics, political parties are much stronger than in the United States. British voters do not directly elect the prime minister. Instead, voters cast ballots for political parties. The party that wins a majority of the seats in the House of Commons is entitled to form a new government, with the leader of the party becoming the prime minister. In such a situation, the queen invites the leader of the victorious party to form a new administration. This reserved power of the monarchy is crucial when no political party has gained a majority in Parliament. If political leaders find it difficult to reach an agreement, the queen or king performs the role of mediator in trying to establish a new government.

Queen Elizabeth II meets with the prime minister on a regular basis. Under the British constitutional monarchy, the sovereign has the right to be informed about government policy, to ask questions, and to warn. Although Queen Elizabeth has no direct control over the policies of her government, she does possess a tremendous amount of knowledge. Having occupied the throne since 1952, she has nearly fifty years of political and international experience; her first prime minister was Winston Churchill. Given this background, prime ministers not only inform her of decisions but listen carefully to any advice she may care to offer.

The Commonwealth Tour

Queen Elizabeth's father, King George VI, was the constitutional head of an empire. Under the empire, Britain occupied a central position in the governance of colonies and other territories. The independence of India in 1948 marked the end of the empire phase and the beginning of a new era in British imperial policy. The British Commonwealth of Nations replaced the British Empire, and Queen Elizabeth became the head of this informal, loosely organized political entity. Designed to foster connections between Britain and the newly independent nations of Africa and Asia, the commonwealth became very important to Elizabeth.

Following her coronation in 1953, Queen Elizabeth II and her husband, Prince Phillip, embarked on a six-month tour of the commonwealth countries. Elizabeth was determined to use the visit to strengthen the monarchy in Britain and around the world. Elizabeth and Phillip, a young, attractive, and energetic couple, were well-received in the commonwealth countries. As a symbol of the links between Britain and its commonwealth, Elizabeth watched as a new royal yacht, the Britannia, entered the service of the Royal Navy. In accepting the Britannia into the service of the Royal Navy, she said that the yacht symbolized the links between the members of the commonwealth.

kuhnd) remarked that she lacked advanced training for her role as sovereign. Indeed, the early days of her reign were traumatic for her as she made the transition from princess to head of state. Her family life was altered, as she became the focal point of attention. Her mother, who had enjoyed a prominent place in British life, had to adjust to her new role as queen mother. Apparently, it was a difficult transition, as she mourned both the loss of her husband and her change in position.

Elizabeth performed her duties as queen with tremendous energy. She met with government and political leaders and made trips to other nation-states and to British possessions. As the British sovereign, Elizabeth became the head of the British Commonwealth, which was conceived as an organization linking Britain with its former colonies. She remained a strong advocate of the commonwealth throughout her reign and resisted efforts to diminish its significance. In 1973, when Britain became a member of the European Economic Community, Queen Elizabeth used one of her royal prerogatives to distance

Queen Elizabeth (left) and the Queen Mother in 1996, photographed on the Queen Mother's ninety-sixth birthday. *(AP/Wide World Photos)*

herself from the policies of the British government. The queen broadcasts an annual Christmas message to the United Kingdom and to the commonwealth; she writes this speech without consulting with members of the British cabinet. In her 1973 address she stated that the British relationship with Europe would not weaken its ties to the commonwealth.

Elizabeth's Reign

Monumental changes happened to the monarchy, Britain, and the British Commonwealth during the reign of Queen Elizabeth II. Although Elizabeth maintained tradition throughout her reign, she also supported changes in the monarchy at pivotal moments. Elizabeth's reign began a transitional period between the formal, traditional styles of other twentieth-century British monarchs and the advent of a less formal, more modern monarchy.

Bibliography

Bradford, Sarah. *Elizabeth: A Biography of Britain's Queen*. New York: Riverhead Books, 1996.

Keay, Douglas. *Elizabeth II: Portrait of a Monarch*. London: Century, 1991.

Reisfeld, Randi. *Prince William*. New York: Pocket Books, 1997.

Michael E. Meagher

Enver Pasha

Born: November 22, 1881; Constantinople, Ottoman Empire (now Istanbul, Turkey)
Died: August 4, 1922; near Baldzhuan, Turkistan (now in Tajikstan)

Leader of Young Turks movement, Turkish minister of war (1914-1918)

Enver (ehn-VEHR), later known by the titles bey (meaning, roughly, governor) and then pasha (a title for a high-ranking official, pronounced pah-SHAH), was the son of a minor civil servant in Constantinople. Enver completed his education in 1902 and became an officer with the Third Army. In 1906, Enver, like many other young officers, became involved in an effort to reform and modernize the Turkish government. When a number of organizations came together to form the Committee of Union and Progress, also known as the Young Turks, Enver quickly rose to a leading position and helped to organize the rebellion of army troops that provoked the revolution of 1908. Sultan Abdul Hamid II, who had ruled Turkey since 1876, stepped down from the throne, and his brother, Mehmet V, became sultan in 1909. From 1909 to 1911, Enver served as a military attaché in Germany.

Rise to Power

A number of nations took advantage of the political instability in Turkey to attempt to seize Turkish territory. In 1911, Italy declared war and seized Libya. Enver took charge of organizing the fighting against Italy in Libya. Following the loss of Libya to Italy, Enver returned to Constantinople. The First Balkan War broke out in 1912, when the Balkan nations of Greece, Serbia, Montenegro, and Bulgaria invaded Turkish lands in Europe. Once again, Turkey was defeated. The loss of Libya and then the lands in southern Europe caused a political crisis in Turkey. In January of 1913, Enver Pasha led a number of Young Turks in seizing control of the government and forcing the sultan to give all government offices to members of the Committee of Union and Progress.

When the Second Balkan War broke out in 1913, Enver Pasha became chief of the general staff of the army. By the end of the Second Balkan War, the Turkish government had become a military dictatorship. Three men held power: Mehmet Talat Pasha, Ahmet Cemal Pasha, and Enver Pasha.

World War I

Europe plunged into war in 1914 as a result of systems of alliances among the European nations; the alliances guaranteed that war between two nations would pull other countries into the fighting. Mehmet Talat and Ahmet Cemal both felt that Turkey should remain neutral. Enver, how-

Enver Pasha posing in full uniform in 1914. *(Archive Photos)*

The Balkan Wars

The political instability in Turkey that followed the revolution of 1908 made it possible for European sections to be broken away from the Ottoman Empire. After the revolution, Austria took over Bosnia and Herzegovina, and Bulgaria declared itself independent of Turkey. The First Balkan War followed in 1912, when the Balkan nations of Greece, Serbia, Montenegro, and Bulgaria, on the basis of secret agreements, invaded the Turkish provinces of Macedonia and Thrace.

Turkey was defeated and lost most of its European lands. The following year, the Balkan allies began quarreling among themselves over the division of the newly conquered territory. The Second Balkan War began when Bulgaria attacked Serbia and Greece. Montenegro, Romania, and Turkey then entered the war against Bulgaria. The Treaty of Bucharest, signed on August 10, 1913, brought the second war to an end, with Turkey holding only a small corner of Europe.

ever, strongly favored Germany. On August 2, 1914, Enver signed a secret treaty with Germany. Germany and Austria went to war against Russia, England, France, and other allied powers immediately afterward. Turkish cooperation with Germany led Russia to declare war on Turkey on November 5. England and France declared war the following day.

Although the Turkish army was not prepared for another major war, Enver sent his troops into

the Russian Caucasus in the winter of 1914-1915. He hoped to provoke an insurrection among the Turkish-speaking people of Russia. Instead, Enver's forces suffered an overwhelming defeat. The war began to look brighter for Turkey when British forces attempting to invade Turkey in the Dardanelles were driven back. Although this restored some of Enver's prestige, it also helped bring a future rival to prominence. The Turkish forces at the Dardanelles were led by Mustafa Kemal, later known as Atatürk.

Among the Russian troops were Armenians from the Caucasus. Some of these Armenians apparently attempted to recruit Armenians living in Turkey to fight against the Turks. In response, Enver's government ordered the deportation of about 1,750,000 Armenians from Turkey to Syria and Mesopotamia. An estimated 600,000 Armenians died of starvation or were killed by the Turkish military during the deportation.

Despite the victory at the Dardanelles, by 1918 Turkish abilities to fight had been exhausted. The war government resigned, and Enver, Talat, and Cemal fled to Germany. Mustafa Kemal (Atatürk) became the nation's

An estimated 600,000 Armenians died, from starvation or at the hands of Turkish soldiers, after Enver Pasha's government ordered nearly two million Armenians to leave Turkey. *(Library of Congress)*

foremost leader and passed a death sentence against Enver. Under Kemal's guidance, the sultanate was abolished and the modern nation of Turkey came into existence.

Exile and Death

Hoping to win support of the newly established Soviet Union for his plans to return to Turkey and overthrow Mustafa Kemal, Enver went to Russia from Germany. He was unable to convince the Soviet leaders to support him, but they did allow him to go to Turkistan to help organize the Soviet Central Asian republics. Once in Central Asia, he turned against the Soviets and joined a local revolt. Enver Pasha died in a battle against the Soviet Red Army.

Enver's Historical Role

Enver played an important part in transforming Turkey into a modern nation. He was also a dynamic and charismatic leader who helped Turkey through the difficult time of the Balkan Wars.

However, he sometimes showed poor judgment. His decision to bring Turkey into World War I proved to be a serious mistake, and his invasion of the Russian Caucasus was disastrous. His government's persecution of the Armenians is still regarded as one of the great evils of the twentieth century.

Bibliography

Kayal, Hasan, and Hasan Kayali. *Arabs and Young Turks: Ottomanism, Arabism, and Islamism in the Ottoman Empire, 1908-1918*. Berkeley: University of California Press, 1997.

Kirakossian, John S. *The Armenian Genocide: The Young Turks Before the Judgment of History*. Madison, Conn.: Sphinx Press, 1992.

Metz, Helen Chapin, ed. *Turkey: A Country Study*. Washington, D.C.: Library of Congress, 1996.

Walker, Barbara K. *To Set Them Free: The Early Years of Mustafa Kemal Atatürk*. Grantham, N.H.: Tompson & Ritter, 1981.

Carl L. Bankston III

The 1908 Revolution in Turkey

Turkey's 1908 revolution is also known as the Young Turk Revolution. The empire established in Turkey by the Ottoman tribe of Turks in the thirteenth century gradually established itself in a territory that stretched around the Mediterranean Sea from Albania to Algeria. By the end of the nineteenth century, however, the empire seemed on the verge of collapse. Western-oriented intellectuals advocated adopting European political institutions as a way of modernizing their country. In 1876, a new ruler, Sultan Abdul Hamid II, came to power and granted a Western-style constitution. The new sultan then proceeded to ignore the constitution and ruled in an authoritarian, repressive manner.

Young military officers and students formed small groups and secret societies to work against the sultan. In 1907, a number of these groups came together to form the Committee of Union and Progress (CUP), also known as the Young Turks. The goals of the CUP were to modernize their country and to restore the 1876 constitution. On July 23, 1908, Young Turk officers in the area of Macedonia that is now part of northern Greece staged a rebellion. At the city of Saloniki, the Committee of Union and Progress, headed by Enver Pasha, proclaimed the restoration of the constitution and threatened to send two army corps to the Turkish capital of Constantinople. In response, Abdul Hamid II allowed elections to parliament, in which Young Turk representatives won most of the seats. In 1909, Abdul Hamid II abdicated in favor of his brother, Mehmet V.

Matthias Erzberger

Born: September 20, 1875; Buttenhausen, Germany
Died: August 26, 1921; near Bad Griesbach, Germany

German political leader and Treaty of Versailles negotiator (1919)

Matthias Erzberger (mah-TEE-ahs AYRTZ-bayr-gur) was the son of a master tailor and postman who became a village official in Buttenhausen. The Erzbergers were one of the few Catholic families in the town. Erzberger attended Catholic elementary and secondary schools, earning top honors in literature and history. In 1894 he entered the Wurttemberg school system as an apprentice teacher, but his interest quickly turned to trade unionism and politics. Erzberger married Paula Eberhard, the daughter of a prosperous merchant, in 1900. As a member of the Catholic Center Party, he was elected to the Reichstag (the German parliament) for the Zentrum seat in southeast Wurttemberg in 1903.

Left-Center Politics

Controversy marked Erzberger's career in politics. The Center Party members espoused a wide range of political philosophies, and Erzberger, with his background in trade unionism and social movements, became identified with those who advocated social justice and financial accountability. In 1906 Erzberger launched a savage attack on the German government's colonial policies. His criticisms led to the resignation of one official and contributed to Chancellor Bernhard von Bülow's decision to dissolve the Reichstag and call for new elections. Reactionaries denounced Erzberger as an enemy of the empire. Erzberger remained in the Reichstag through World War I and continued to insist that politicians maintain a Christian perspective on all issues.

On July 19, 1917, Erzberger undertook his most controversial political action when he sponsored the Peace Resolution in the Reichstag. The resolution asked the government to negotiate an end to World War I—which had been underway since 1914—without seeking territorial gains. Erzberger had decided that further loss of life could no longer be justified. The Peace Resolution brought a cascade of abuse upon him, and military leaders accused him of treason.

Libel Suit and Resignation

The Treaty of Versailles, establishing the terms for peace after World War I, was signed on June 28, 1919. At that time Erzberger was vice chancel-

Matthias Erzberger *(Library of Congress)*

Matthias Erzberger had the thankless task of being Germany's main negotiator at the peace talks in Paris that produced the 1919 Treaty of Versailles. *(Popperfoto/Archive Photos)*

lor and finance minister in a republican government led by Chancellor Gustav Bauer. The harsh terms of the Versailles settlement brought forth a bitter reaction from German nationalists. As Erz-

berger had advocated peace on whatever terms were available, he was their primary target.

Shortly after the treaty was signed, Karl Helfferich, a long-time political opponent, undertook

Bernhard von Bülow's Colonial Policy

Matthias Erzberger caused a sensation by charging that Chancellor Bernhard von Bülow's colonial policy was rife with racism. Erzberger appealed for the application of Christian ethics and declared that Africans had immortal souls just as Germans did. His comments caused an uproar in the Reichstag, bringing derision from conservative members. Von Bülow responded by appointing Prince Ernst zu Hohenlohe as director of colonial administration, and he

charged him with the task of correcting the abuses. Erzberger objected to this appointment, as Hohenlohe's anti-Catholic biases were well known. Under pressure from Erzberger, Hohenlohe resigned in September, 1906. Shortly thereafter, von Bülow dissolved the Reichstag and, in the elections that followed, carried out a campaign accusing Erzberger and the Catholic Center Party with encouraging anticolonial and antinationalist ideas.

a vituperative attack on Erzberger in several newspaper articles. The comments were so vicious that Erzberger sued for libel. The trial lasted several months, with the jury verdict favoring Erzberger. It was a pyrrhic victory, however. In announcing the decision, the judge said that several of Helfferich's accusations appeared to be substantiated. Under this cloud, Erzberger resigned from his post.

During the course of the libel suit, on January 26, 1920, Erzberger was shot and wounded. The assailant maintained that he was motivated by patriotism, and he received a very mild sentence. On August 26, 1921, while walking with a friend in the Black Forest near Bad Griesbach, Erzberger was shot again and killed. The crime was committed by individuals closely associated with violent conservative elements.

Martyr for Peace

Erzberger was, and continues to be, revered by those who rejected the aggressive nationalism prevalent in German politics during the first two decades of the twentieth century. His murder—and the brutal Nazi era, which began in 1933—confirmed Erzberger's worst fears: that a large number of German reactionaries, who hated peace and scoffed at social justice, were prepared to use violent means to wipe out those who disagreed with their extreme nationalistic views.

Bibliography

Epstein, Klaus. *Matthias Erzberger and the Dilemma of German Democracy.* Princeton, N.J.: Princeton University Press, 1959.

Gatzke, Hans. *European Diplomacy Between Two Wars, 1919-1939.* Chicago: Quadrangle Books, 1972.

Willett, John. *Art and Politics in the Weimar Period: The New Sobriety, 1917-1933.* New York: Pantheon, 1978.

Ronald K. Huch

Herbert Vere Evatt

Born: April 30, 1894; East Maitland, New South Wales, Australia
Died: November 2, 1965; Canberra, Australia

Australian politician and diplomat, foreign minister from 1941 to 1951

Herbert Vere Evatt (HUR-burt VEER EH-vuht) came from a working-class family. He and his siblings were raised by their mother after the early death of their father. In 1905, the family moved to Sydney, where Evatt's brother, Clive Raleigh Evatt, became a prominent attorney. Evatt was educated at Fort Street High School and the University of Sydney. He began to practice law in 1918. Stirred by the plight of the common laborer, he became interested in politics, serving in the New South Wales Assembly for twenty years.

Creating a Foreign Policy

Evatt was appointed to the Supreme Court of Australia in 1930. In 1940, he decided to enter federal Australian politics and won a parliamentary seat as a Labor Party candidate. When Labor took power in October, 1941, Prime Minister John Curtin appointed Evatt foreign minister.

Evatt's task was to free Australian foreign policy from its domination by British interests. This necessity was heightened by the outbreak of World War II, notably the entry of Japan into the war in 1941. When it became clear that Britain no longer had the resources to defend Australia from Japan, Australia had to rely on the United States for protection. Evatt made several trips to Washington, D.C. He simultaneously had to refrain from alienating not only Britain but also the many Australians who still strongly identified with Britain. Evatt's performance as foreign minister was widely acclaimed and helped keep support high for the Labor government during wartime. His frequent abrasiveness and intellectual self-confidence, however, meant that he was often more respected by his colleagues abroad than by those in Australia itself. By the end of the

war, Evatt was a respected figure in world diplomatic circles, and the door was open to his memorable participation in the first United Nations (U.N.) General Assembly in 1945.

Leader of the Opposition

After Curtin's death (1945) and the defeat suffered by his successor, Ben Chifley, Labor turned to Evatt to be its leader. He led the party in opposition from 1951 to 1960. Evatt continued to support the small nations for which he had spoken in 1945 at the U.N. General Assembly. He became particularly respected by the leaders of

Herbert Vere Evatt *(Library of Congress)*

487

Australian foreign minister Herbert Vere Evatt (center) serving as president of the U.N. General Assembly in 1949. *(Library of Congress)*

century Australian history. His courage and idealism helped him make a distinctly Australian contribution to modern international relations.

Bibliography

Buckley, K. D. *Doc Evatt: Patriot, Internationalist, Fighter, and Scholar*. Melbourne, Australia: Longman Cheshire, 1994.

Buzo, Alex. *Pacific Union*. Sydney: Currency Press, 1997.

Crockett, Peter. *Evatt: A Life*. Melbourne: Oxford University Press, 1993.

Day, David. *Brave New World: Dr. H. V. Evatt and Australian Foreign Policy, 1941-1949*. St. Lucia, Queensland, Australia: University of Queensland Press, 1996.

Rickard, John. *Australia: A Cultural History*. New York: Longman, 1988.

Nicholas Birns

newly independent Asian states. However, he was in general an ineffective party leader and retired from the position in February, 1960. Although Evatt never became prime minister, he is one of the most beloved figures in twentieth-

The U.N. General Assembly

The first U.N. General Assembly was held in San Francisco in August, 1945. The General Assembly is the U.N. body to which all U.N. member states send delegates and in which all member states have a vote. It began with fifty-one member states. (The U.N. Security Council, by contrast, began with eleven member states—five permanent members and six members that rotated every two years.) When Herbert Vere Evatt arrived at the San Francisco conference, he quickly saw that the large nations that had dominated the war effort—Britain, the United States, and the Soviet Union—were determined to maintain control of the new United Nations through their role on the Security Council. Evatt lobbied not only for Australian representation in the organization but also for the rights of smaller nations in general. His efforts helped Australia to gain respect from independent nations in Asia and the Middle East, and later from the so-called Third World as a whole. Evatt also urged international supervision of atomic weaponry. He later served as president of the General Assembly (1948-1949).

Arthur William Fadden

Born: April 13, 1894; Ingham, Queensland (now Australia)
Died: April 21, 1973; Brisbane, Queensland, Australia

Prime minister of Australia (1941)

Arthur William Fadden (AHR-thur WIHL-yuhm FA-duhn) was the eldest child of a police constable and his wife. He was educated at Walkerston State School. Fadden began work with a gang of cane cutters at the age of fifteen and held various jobs thereafter. He was assistant town clerk (1913-1918) and town clerk (1918) at Mackay. Fadden took a correspondence course in accounting and became a chartered accountant in Townsville. In 1916, he married Ilma Nita Thornber, and they had four children.

Entering Politics

Fadden was an alderman on the Townsville City Council from 1930 to 1933. In 1934 he won a Legislative Assembly seat in Queensland for the Country and Progressive Nationalist Party. He became part of the Queensland Country Party, which was formed in 1936 to provide a conservative organization separate from the United Australia Party. Fadden went into federal politics and was a Country Party member of the House of Representatives from 1936 to 1958, becoming leader of the Country Party in 1941. Early in his federal career, he held various ministerial responsibilities, including air and civil aviation.

Political Power

In the federal election of September, 1940, the coalition government of the United Australia Party and Country Party won the same number of seats as the Australian Labor Party, creating political instability. When the leader of the United Australia Party, Prime Minister Robert Gordon Menzies, went on a four-month visit to London in early 1941, Fadden acted as prime minister in his absence. Menzies resigned as prime minister later that year. Fadden replaced him, leading a United Australia Party-Country Party government. However, he was prime minister only from August 29 to October 7, 1941. Labor members and independents defeated his budget, and John Curtin, the Labor leader, became the next prime minister.

Fadden was leader of the opposition until 1943 and continued to lead the Country Party until March, 1958. In 1949, the Liberal Party, founded by Menzies, entered into a coalition with the Country Party. When Menzies won the 1949 election, Fadden became deputy prime minister and treasurer in the coalition government from 1949 to 1958. He was an influential figure in the government and a successful treasurer, though he

Arthur William Fadden *(AP/Wide World Photos)*

Fadden, Arthur William

Australian troops marching in Sydney before embarking to fight in the Korean War. *(AP/Wide World Photos)*

However, he has sometimes been criticized for indecision and some poor tactical judgments. He was overshadowed by the towering figure of Menzies, whose intellect and presence he lacked. Fadden served effectively as acting prime minister for Menzies during the latter's frequent trips abroad. The two leaders were political allies, but they were not close personally. After leaving politics, Fadden retired in Brisbane and pursued interests on the boards of various businesses.

was sometimes criticized by his rural constituency for compromising on policy issues. He was fortunate to be treasurer during Australia's long period of postwar economic prosperity, but he was also shrewd—he knew when to take advice and when to question it. Fadden stood down as party leader in March, 1958, and did not contest the election in that year. He was succeeded as treasurer by Harold Holt in December, 1958.

Fadden and Menzies

Fadden was an able political campaigner, known for being gregarious and good-natured.

Bibliography

Ellis, Ulrich. *A History of the Australian Country Party*. Melbourne, Australia: Melbourne University Press, 1963.

Fadden, Arthur. *They Called Me Artie: The Memoirs of Sir Arthur Fadden*. Milton, Queensland: Jacaranda, 1969.

Schedvin, C. B. *In Reserve: Central Banking in Australia, 1945-1975*. Sydney: Allen & Unwin, 1992.

Spender, Percy. *Politics and a Man*. London: Collins, 1977.

Russell Blackford

Fadden as Acting Prime Minister

Arthur Fadden was deputy prime minister to Robert Gordon Menzies in 1940-1941. He later became a long-term deputy prime minister in the coalition government led by Menzies after the 1949 election. Fadden held that position from December 19, 1949, until he stood down as leader of the Country Party in March, 1958. As deputy prime minister to Menzies, Fadden was the acting prime minister during Menzies's trips abroad. Notably, it was Fadden who authorized Australian troops to be sent to the Korean War in 1950. Later, after leaving office, Fadden calculated that he had spent a total of 692 days—nearly two years—as acting prime minister in Menzies's absence.

Fahd

Born: 1922 or 1923; Riyadh, Arabia (now Saudi Arabia)

King and prime minister of Saudi Arabia (from 1982)

King Fahd was born Fahd ibn Abd al-Aziz al Saud (FAHD IHB-uhn AB-dal a-ZEEZ al-sah-EWD), meaning Fahd, son of Abd al-Aziz of the House of Saud. Sources vary as to his date of birth. Fahd belongs to the al-Saud family, one of the country's families of royal lineage. His father was Abd al-Aziz bin Abd al-Rahman (known as King Saud or Ibn Saud in the West), the first king of the present-day state of Saudi Arabia. His mother was Hassa bint Ahmad al-Sudayri. Fahd is the eldest of seven sons of Saud and this wife.

Fahd received the traditional schooling for princes at the Princes' School in Riyadh. He then held various political roles such as governor, minister of the interior, and minister of education (the country's first). In 1962 he became second deputy prime minister and second in line for the kingship. In 1975, his half-brother Khalid became king and appointed Fahd first deputy prime minister and crown prince (next in line for kingship). As Khalid's health deteriorated, Fahd assumed more activity and became the major spokesperson for the country; during this time he gained more experience in national and international affairs. He gained a reputation as a competent leader, though he was also known as a playboy who enjoyed gambling and other pursuits. In 1982, Fahd was named king and prime minister.

Role as Saudi Leader

As prime minister, Fahd courted the United States heavily, building close economic and strategic relations. Saudi Arabia is a leading supplier of oil for the United States, and the United States has provided Saudi Arabia with military training and equipment. Under a mutual defense assistance agreement, the United States has a military training mission in the country. The U.S.-Saudi tie as well as Saudi-Arab world ties have sometimes been strained because of the United States' support of Israel. Fahd wields great influence in the Arab world, however, and has been a key player in mediating

Fahd *(Archive France/Archive Photos)*

conflicts. He reestablished various diplomatic relations: with Egypt in 1989, and with Iran in 1991.

Though Fahd is known as king, his official title is "custodian of the two holy mosques." This title bears great religious significance within the Arab world: It deems Fahd the spiritual custodian of Mecca, the largest Muslim pilgrimage site. He plays a crucial role in all governmental decisions, and although Islamic law dictates that decisions must be made by consensus, Fahd ultimately maintains power over all branches of the Saudi government and makes all final decisions. In 1992 he introduced a new Basic Law system of governing based on Shariʿah law of the Wahhabi branch of Islam. The king and the Council of Ministers hold executive power. A Consultative Council of sixty members and a chairman, all appointed by Fahd, can make recommendations, though they have no legislative power. Some observers see Fahd's council as a move toward democracy, whereas others maintain that anyone proposing ideas contrary to Fahd's risks serious repercussions.

Challenges at Home and Abroad

In the early 1980's, a surplus of oil in the petroleum market drove oil prices down. This situation had serious consequences for Fahd's government and Saudi Arabia, which depends on petroleum for the majority of its income. The country has also faced external difficulties from neighbors Iran and Iraq, and in 1990 it became a major player in the Iraq-Kuwait skirmish. The Asian crisis of early 1998 affected world oil prices, as did the recession in Japan, one of Saudi Arabia's biggest oil customers. In addition, it must compete in the oil market against Mexico and Venezuela, two other large oil producers.

Fahd and the Saudi royal family have drawn criticism from a number of quarters. In the 1990's Saudi Arabia faced a mounting external debt in spite of its huge oil revenues. The country's treasury supports the royal family, which numbers in the tens of thousands, by providing its members with salaries and various costly benefits. Saudi Arabian oil has made Fahd the second-richest person in the world, with an estimated personal wealth of $25 billion, and his personal spending habits have been called a drain on the economy. Fahd has been criticized by human rights groups such as Amnesty International for repressive policies limiting freedom of speech and religion; political prisoners and common law criminals have been tortured and forced to confess to crimes. On the other hand, Fahd has been an important and relatively moderate leader in the Arab world. He has also tried to keep standards of living high for Saudis, continuing the tradition begun in the 1970's of providing Saudi citizens with fully or highly subsidized social services.

The Fez Plan

Also known as the Fahd Plan, the Fez Plan was a Middle East peace plan devised by then-crown prince Fahd in 1981. Its goal was the peaceful coexistence of all nations in the region and the resolution of the Arab-Israeli conflict. The eight-point plan called for Arab recognition of Israel's legitimacy as a state and, in turn, Israel's withdrawal from the Arab areas it occupied in 1967. It also endorsed the founding of a Palestinian state. The plan was presented at the Arab Summit in Fez, Morocco, in November, 1981. It was accepted by the Palestine Liberation Organization (PLO) but rejected by other Arab groups and countries, some of whom refused to accept Israel's status as a state. Though not accepted, the Fahd Plan helped further Fahd's position as mediator in Arab affairs.

The Defense of Kuwait

In the summer of 1990, tensions were high between Iraq and the tiny neighboring country of Kuwait. Saddam Hussein's Iraqi government was angry for a number of reasons: Kuwait refused to limit its oil production to Organization of Petroleum Exporting Countries (OPEC) standards, the oil was being taken from an area whose border with Iraq had been disputed for centuries, and Kuwait was pressing Iraq for immediate debt repayments from the Iran-Iraq War. After several unproductive attempts at mediation, Iraq invaded Kuwait on August 2.

King Fahd, along with the leaders of other oil-rich countries, supported Kuwait, seeing Hussein as a serious threat. Because of Fahd's economic and political power in the Arab and Western worlds, the Kuwait invasion rested heavily on Fahd. A few days after, Fahd met with U.S. secretary of defense Dick Cheney. They decided that Fahd would invite U.S. troops to Saudi Arabia to stand behind the demand that Iraq withdraw from Kuwait. At the same time, Fahd tried to dispel the view of Saudi Arabia as an instrument of U.S. strategy by involving other countries in the defensive force against Iraq. Through the efforts of U.S. president George Bush and Fahd, about thirty countries offered aircraft, ships, and troops, to be led by the United States and Saudi Arabia. Attempts at mediation by the United Nations were unsuccessful, and in January, 1991, a military plan called Operation Desert Storm began, with the goal of liberating Kuwait from Iraq.

Fighting in the Persian Gulf War continued for more than a month. During this time Fahd provided a temporary headquarters for the Kuwaiti government. After the liberation, Kuwait's leaders returned home, and foreign troops began withdrawing from Saudi Arabia. Saudi Arabia returned thousands of Iraqi political prisoners of war and gave refuge to Iraqi political dissidents who had recently attempted an unsuccessful coup against Hussein. Fahd and seven other Arab leaders joined forces to create a peacekeeping coalition in the area. Financially, the war resulted in tremendous cost to Saudi Arabia.

Fahd continued the process of modernization in Saudi Arabia while retaining the strict religious laws of the Wahhabi sect of Islam. He is a leading voice in the Arab world and a leader with strong economic and political power. As of the late 1990's, Fahd's health was said to be deteriorating; he suffered from diabetes and a heart condition. Many of his duties were being taken on by his appointed successor, Abdallah.

Bibliography

Abir, Mordechai. *Saudi Arabia in the Oil Era*. Boulder, Colo.: Westview Press, 1988.

Aburish, Said K. *The Rise, Corruption, and Coming Fall of the House of Saud*. New York: St. Martin's Griffin, 1996.

Chapin Metz, Helen, ed. *Saudi Arabia: A Country Study*. Lanham, Md.: Bernan Press, 1993.

Xiomara Arellano

Faisal

Born: c. 1905; Riyadh, Arabia
Died: March 25, 1975; Riyadh, Saudi Arabia

King of Saudi Arabia (1964-1975)

Faisal ibn Abdul Aziz (FI-suhl IHB-uhn AB-duhl a-ZEEZ) was the fourth son of Abdul Aziz bin Abdul Rahman bin Faisal al Saud (Ibn Saud), the founder of the kingdom of Saudi Arabia. Faisal's mother, Tarfa bint Abdullah, who died when he was a small boy, belonged to the al-Sheikh clan, which provided most of Saudi Arabia's religious scholars and leaders. Prince Faisal was raised by his maternal grandparents until he was age ten or eleven. Under their guidance he developed a keen appreciation for learning, scholarship, and religion and completed his study of the Koran. From his father, King Ibn Saud, Faisal learned horsemanship, the art of desert warfare, and political cunning.

Faisal *(Archive Photos)*

Foreign Minister

Prince Faisal was appointed foreign minister by his father, Ibn Saud, in 1919, a position he held until his father's death in 1975. In 1926, Faisal was made the viceroy of the Hejaz, the western portion of the newly created kingdom of Saudi Arabia. As foreign minister, he traveled to Western Europe, the Soviet Union, the United States, and to many places in the Middle East. While abroad, Prince Faisal studied English, Western political systems, culture, agriculture, and industry. During his travels, he witnessed growing Western support for Zionist demands for a Jewish state in Palestine. Faisal opposed both the creation of a Jewish state on Arab land and the Zionist movement. He was not anti-Semitic, but he expected Palestinian and Arab rights to be legally and internationally recognized. U.S. president Harry S Truman's 1947 decision to cast a vote in the United Nations to divide Palestine was a severe diplomatic blow to Prince Faisal and the Arab world.

Crown Prince

In Saudi Arabia, succession to the throne is not automatically given to the king's eldest son. The princes of the royal family vote for an acceptable candidate. King Ibn Saud's deathbed wishes were respected by the royal family when his eldest surviving son, Saud, was declared king and Ibn Saud's second surviving son, Faisal, was made crown prince and premier on November 9, 1953. As crown prince, Faisal traveled abroad, renewing his contacts with Western governments. During his absences, King Saud's lack of aptitude for government and his financial excesses impoverished a country awash in oil revenues. On March 22, 1958, King Saud was forced by agreement among the royal princes to transfer his authority to Faisal to solve Saudi Arabia's economic crisis. Increasing rivalry between the two brothers led Saud to reclaim his authority December 21, 1960. Faisal remained as crown prince and foreign minister. However, within two years, renewed political and financial crises, external threats to the kingdom from Egypt and neighboring Yemen, and Saud's ill health forced Saud to restore Faisal as premier. Meetings of royal, tribal, and religious councils then pressured King Saud to abdicate in favor of Faisal on November 3, 1964.

Saudi Arabia's King Faisal (right) meeting with Egyptian president Gamal Abdel Nasser in Sudan in 1967. *(Archive Photos)*

King of Saudi Arabia

King Faisal married three times. The first two marriages were arranged political unions with daughters of prominent Saudi Arabian families. Both marriages ended in divorce, but each provided Faisal with a son. Faisal's third marriage, to Iffat bint Ahmed al Thunayan, born and educated in Turkey, was a love match. It became a monogamous union (in a country where men were allowed four legal wives) and produced five sons. Iffat, the only wife of a Saudi king to ever be called queen, encouraged Faisal to establish a public education system for Saudi women at elementary, secondary, and higher-education levels. Faisal's nine daughters (from three marriages) were among the first women to be formally educated in Saudi Arabia. All seven of Faisal's sons were educated in the United States.

The Saudi Arabian Economic Crisis of 1958

On March 25, 1958, King Saud transferred his powers to his brother, Crown Prince Faisal, to deal with Saudi Arabia's deepening economic crisis. Saud's expensive and unnecessary public works and palace construction projects, as well as political and economic corruption with the regime, had left Saudi Arabia with an empty treasury, extensive debts, and no money to pay its civil servants. Within two years, Faisal balanced the budget, restored the currency, paid off Saudi debts, and ended needless spending projects. Saudi budget surpluses were invested in the World Bank and the International Monetary Fund. Nonetheless, less than three years later, King Saud removed Faisal as prime minister and resumed his royal powers.

The Yemeni Civil War

On September 27, 1962, Imam Muhammad al-Badr, Yemen's newly ascended king from the Hamiduddin dynasty, was overthrown in a military coup by Colonel Abdullah al-Sallal. Al-Sallal immediately proclaimed a republic, and he requested and received Egyptian military aid. Fearful of an Egyptian plan to overthrow the Saud family in Saudi Arabia, Crown Prince Faisal began five years of financial and military commitment to Imam al-Badr and his royalist supporters. Egypt's defeat in the 1967 Arab-Israeli War (the Six-Day War) led to a Saudi-Egyptian summit that removed al-Sallal and Egyptian troops from Yemen. The 1970 failure of a royalist assault on the Yemeni capital of Sanaa, the possibility of Soviet military support for Yemen's republican forces, and the deposition of Imam al-Badr by the royalists led to an end to Saudi involvement in Yemen.

As crown prince, Faisal had abolished slavery (1962); as king he guaranteed its extinction. He also created a unified government, with religious leaders (*ulema*) as the official interpreters of the *Shariʿa* (the laws of Islam). King Faisal's first five-year plan (1970-1975) established a Central Planning Organization, constructed pipelines for water supply in six major cities, built seven desalination plants, constructed thousands of miles of paved roads, and built twenty domestic airports. He expanded the construction industry, educational system, and health-care system, and he guaranteed employment to all Saudi males.

In foreign policy, King Faisal financed the royalist side in Yemen's civil war, gave financial aid to Arab states hostile to Israel, improved relations with the United States, and condemned communism as a godless ideology. In the early 1970's, U.S. president Richard M. Nixon continued to provide support for Israel without requiring Israel to return conquered Arab lands in Gaza, the West Bank of the Jordan, and Jerusalem. This situation led Faisal in 1973 to pressure the Organization of Petroleum Exporting Countries (OPEC) to stop the flow of Arab oil to the United States. Oil prices and embargoes became Arab tools for diplomacy against the West.

King Faisal was assassinated March 25, 1975, during a public audience at the royal palace in Riyadh, by a nephew, Prince Faisal ibn Musad. The prince was said to be mentally deranged. Faisal's sons established the King Faisal Foundation to continue their father's commitment to humanitarian values by awards recognizing world peace, cancer, scientific and elec-

King Faisal pressured OPEC to stop oil exports to the United States in 1973, resulting in high prices and long lines at U.S. gas stations. *(AP/Wide World Photos)*

tronic advances, and funding for health and education programs and research.

As foreign minister, crown prince, and later king, Faisal ibn Abdul Aziz al Saud brought conservative, puritanical Saudi Arabia into the modern world. His economic and political decisions aided Saudi Arabia's transition from a poor desert nation to a wealthy oil kingdom. He effectively used oil as a weapon to support conservative Arab states, to lure Egypt away from the influence of the Soviet Union, and to foster Arab unity against Israel. Maintaining relations with the United States remained a pillar of Saudi foreign policy in the Cold War era. Faisal's mastery of statecraft and compromise kept Saudi Arabia independent, politically stable, and economically prosperous in an unstable Middle East.

Bibliography

Aburish, Said K. *The Rise, Corruption, and Coming Fall of the House of Saud*. New York: St. Martin's Press, 1995.

Farsy, Fouad, al-. *Saudi Arabia: A Case Study in Development*. London: Stacey International, 1978.

Holden, David, and Richard Johns. *The House of Saud*. New York: Holt, Rinehart and Winston, 1981.

Lacey, David. *The Kingdom*. New York: Harcourt Brace Jovanovich, 1981.

Powell, William. *Saudi Arabia and Its Royal Family*. Secaucus, N.J.: Lyle Stuart, 1982.

William A. Paquette

Faisal I

Born: May 20, 1885; Taif, near Mecca, Arabia (now Saudi Arabia)
Died: September 8, 1933; Bern, Switzerland

First king of modern Iraq (1921-1933)

Faisal I (FI-suhl thuh FURST), also spelled Feisal and Faysal, was the third son of Husain ibn Ali, sherif of Mecca and later king of the Hejaz, and Abidyah Hanem, a cousin, of the Hashemite dynasty. The Hashemite dynasty traced its descent from the Prophet Mohammed through his daughter Fatima. Along with his father and older brothers, Ali and Abdullah, Faisal was taken to Constantinople in honorable captivity in 1891. There he was educated by Arab and Turkish tutors under the watchful eye of the sultan, Abdul Hamid II. In 1905, Faisal married his Hashemite cousin Hazaima; they had three daughters, Azza, Rajha, and Rafia, and a son, Ghazi, the second king of Iraq. The Young Turks Revolt in Constantinople in 1908 brought an end to the sultan's tyrannical rule, enabling Faisal and his family in 1909 to return to Mecca as the guardians of the city's holy sites. In 1913, Faisal was elected to represent the city of Jeddah in the Turkish parliament.

The Arab Revolt

While serving as a parliamentary delegate, Faisal often stopped in Damascus on trips between Mecca and Constantinople. There he became acquainted with secret Arab societies that were planning to overthrow Turkish rule of the Arabs. The brutal executions of suspected Arab dissidents in Damascus in 1915 and 1916 by the Turkish governor, Jemal Pasha, convinced Faisal of the need for an Arab revolt during World War I (1914-1918). Arab leaders were encouraged by the British commitment to Arab independence in an exchange of letters between Sherif Husain and Sir Henry McMahon, the British high commissioner in Egypt, and the Arab Revolt was proclaimed from Mecca on June 2, 1916. Britain assigned T. E. Lawrence as Faisal's political and liaison officer and later placed Faisal's army legions under Sir Edmund Allenby's military command.

From the beginning, Faisal was perceived as the guiding force behind the Arab Revolt's eventual success. The sheer force of his personality and commitment to Arab independence above his own life, family, and possessions rallied the Arabs, who gained control over Arabia, except Medina and Ma'an, by the war's end in 1918.

Faisal I *(Library of Congress)*

King of Syria

Faisal's triumphant entry into Damascus on September 30, 1918, was approved by Allenby. The British designated Faisal to represent the Arab cause at the Paris peace negotiations at the end of World War I. However, the French refused to accept Faisal's installation in Damascus, citing the 1916 Sykes-Picot Agreement with Britain, which placed Damascus and Syria under French control. Ignored by the French in Paris, Faisal continued to believe in Britain's commitment to Arab independence. Upon his return to Damascus, Faisal was elected king of Syria in March, 1920, by the Syrian Congress despite the Allied conference having given the area to France in the Treaty of San Remo. France's opposition to an independent Arab state, and its military presence in Syria, forced Faisal's departure from Damascus on July 20, 1920.

King of Iraq

Faisal left Syria for Italy and later London, where Winston Churchill and Lawrence confirmed a British commitment to place Iraq, a British mandate, under Faisal's rule. Sir Percy Cox, the British high commissioner in Iraq, ar-

ranged for a special election that approved Faisal's acceptance of the Iraqi throne by an overwhelming 96 percent of the vote. On August 23, 1921, Faisal was crowned the first king of modern Iraq. From the beginning of his rule, Faisal I faced opposition among the Muslim Shias in southern Iraq, the Christian Assyrians to the west, and Kurds to the north. Each wanted their own homeland. He was also opposed by the Turks, who claimed oil-rich regions in the north around Mosul. The strong British military presence in Iraq assisted Faisal in consolidating his power base among the diverse Arab populations of the country and defining Iraq's northern border with Turkey.

As Iraq's first king, Faisal maintained a delicate balance among urban nationalists and traditional tribal sheiks and riverain landlords and the conflicting religious demands of his Shia and Sunni subjects. King Faisal's success was attributed to his ability to persuade the British to end the mandate in Iraq early by a series of Anglo-Iraqi treaties in 1922, 1926, and 1930, giving Iraq full independence. Faisal also recognized the need to maintain friendly relations with his Persian, Turkish, and Arab neighbors. In 1930, a reconciliation was affected between King Faisal and King

The Sykes-Picot Agreement of 1916

France had had extensive interests in Syria and Lebanon since 1860, when it had come to the aid of the Christian Maronites against the Druses and Muslims. Syria had French schools and French-run railroads, and the French language was spoken more widely than any other European language there. Sir Mark Sykes and M. Georges Picot negotiated the Sykes-Picot Agreement, signed in London in May, 1916. Although never formally ratified, and later replaced by the San Remo Pact, the Sykes-Picot Agreement advocated the creation of an international administration for Palestine, a British zone

of control over Basra, Baghdad, and Khanikin, and a French zone in Lebanon, coastal Syria, and the Upper Tigris. Damascus, Aleppo, and Mosul were placed under French supervisory control. Russia was to receive Armenian provinces and some Kurdish areas. The agreement did not support Arab independence, as promised in the correspondence between King Husain of the Hejaz and Sir Henry McMahon, and it almost led to a complete rupture in Anglo-Arab relations. Arab nationalists learned of Sykes-Picot in 1917, when the documents were released by the new Soviet government in Russia.

The Anglo-Iraqi Treaty of 1930

Iraq gained independence and admission to the League of Nations when the 1930 Anglo-Iraqi Treaty ended the British mandate over Iraq. Iraq was responsible for all internal matters, but special status was still accorded the British ambassador in Iraq. Regular consultations in foreign policy continued between Iraq and Great Britain in matters of common interest, and a free grant of bases in Iraq was given to the British air force, with Iraqi troops supplying base protection. The treaty was to last twenty-five years from the date of Iraq's admission into the League of Nations.

Ibn Saud of Saudi Arabia, who had overthrown Faisal's brother, Ali, as king of the Hejaz. Faisal convened Iraq's first parliament on July 16, 1925, resolved Turkish-Iraqi boundary disputes in 1926, and built a strong British-trained army and air force. As king, Faisal encouraged increased literacy, greater rights for Muslim women, the preservation of Iraqi's archaeological past, and Arab unity.

The end of the British mandate of Iraq in October, 1932, and Faisal's state visit to London on June 21, 1933, symbolized his exceptional capabilities as king. However, the strain of maintaining such adroit control over Iraq's disparate factions weakened his health. King Faisal I suffered a coronary thrombosis in 1933 while in Switzerland receiving medical treatment.

Faisal's training in Constantinople made him a master of the arts of intrigue and diplomacy. His military prowess in the Arab Revolt displayed his abilities to lead, inspire, and command. His election as a deputy in the Turkish parliament and his extensive British contacts gave Faisal a knowledge of Western ways, manners, and governance. King Faisal was the first true Arab nationalist; his dream was a single, united Arab state in the Middle East. Faisal's personality and intellect created a nation from desert and dissent.

Bibliography

De Gaury, Gerald. *Three Kings in Baghdad*. London: Hutchinson, 1961.

Erskine, Mrs. Stewart. *King Faisal of Iraq*. London: Hutchinson, 1933.

Lawrence, T. E. *Seven Pillars of Wisdom*. Garden City, N.Y.: Doubleday, 1926.

Mack, John E. *A Prince of Our Disorder: The Life of T. E. Lawrence*. Boston: Little, Brown, 1976.

Wallach, Janet. *Desert Queen*. New York: Doubleday, 1996.

William A. Paquette

Geraldine Ferraro

Born: August 26, 1935; Newburgh, New York

U.S. congresswoman (1979-1984) and first woman vice presidential candidate (1984)

Geraldine Anne Ferraro (JEH-rahl-deen AN feh-RAH-roh) is the only daughter of a first-generation Italian-American mother and a successful Italian immigrant businessman. When her father died, her mother was forced to support the family by beading dresses. Despite financial hardships, her mother helped Geraldine graduate from Marymount College in Manhattan in 1956 and attend Fordham University Law School at night while she taught grade school during the day. In 1960 Ferraro received her law degree and married John Zaccaro; in 1961 she was admitted to the New York State Bar, and in 1978 she was admitted to the U.S. Supreme Court Bar. A strong supporter of women's rights, Ferraro used her maiden name professionally in honor of her mother.

Political Beginnings

Like many other women of her era, Ferraro worked to change inequities in the workplace. One of only two women enrolled in her law-school class of 179 at Fordham, she graduated with honors, only to be turned down by Wall Street law firms because she was female. During the 1960's and early 1970's, Ferraro worked part time as a lawyer for her husband's successful real estate business while raising their three children. She also became involved in local politics and helped her cousin, Nicholas Ferraro, district attorney of Queens, New York, get elected to the state senate.

In 1974 her cousin helped her become assistant district attorney in the Investigations Bureau. There she helped create—and in two years headed—the Special Victims Bureau, where she handled rape and family violence cases. Known as a persuasive, tough, but fair prosecutor, she quit her position after four years, dissatisfied

with the fact that she was being paid less than her male peers and with the heavy emotional demands of her work. Seeking to effect real changes in society, in 1978 Ferraro ran for Congress. After a bitter campaign against a conservative Republican opponent, she became the first female representative from the Ninth Congressional District.

Supporter of Women's Rights

In 1979 Representative Ferraro went to Washington and served her constituents on various low-profile committees, developing a reputation

Geraldine Ferraro in 1998 announcing that she would seek the Democratic U.S. Senate nomination from New York; she was defeated for the nomination by Charles Schumer. *(Reuters/Peter Morgan/Archive Photos)*

501

Geraldine Ferraro, the first woman candidate for the U.S. vice presidency, waving with Democratic presidential candidate Walter Mondale in 1984. *(AP/Wide World Photos)*

The 1984 Presidential Election

At the Democratic National Convention in July, 1984, former vice president Walter F. Mondale was named the Democratic Party nominee for president. On July 12, Mondale announced Geraldine A. Ferraro as his running mate. For the first time, a major party had nominated a woman for one of the country's top two offices. Their opponents in the 1984 presidential election were popular incumbent president Ronald Reagan and his vice president, George Bush. By nominating Ferraro, Democratic Party leaders hoped to attract, women, Roman Catholic, Italian-American, and northeastern voters. Critics

quickly attacked Ferraro, claiming that she had limited experience in legislative and military matters. Accusations were also made, and were circulated in the media, concerning her family's taxes and 1978 congressional campaign contributions. Ferraro fought back in a grueling ninety-minute press conference, and then went on to campaign vigorously across the country. On election day, Reagan took forty-nine states and 525 electoral votes, the biggest electoral sweep ever. He also won 56 percent of the female votes. The Democrats received only 13 electoral votes, but they did take 41 percent of the popular vote.

as a hard worker and team player. Voting along party lines brought her to the attention of the Democratic leadership, but she took political risks when necessary to support causes that affected women. Although Catholic, Ferraro supported abortion rights. Frustrated that women often earned less than men for the same work, and that male members of Congress seemed apathetic to the plight of working women, she supported the Equal Rights Amendment (ERA). Ferraro was reelected to the House of Representatives in 1980 and 1982. In 1981 she helped draft the Women's Economic Equity Act. In 1980 and 1982, Ferraro was elected secretary of the Democratic Caucus, where she showcased her abilities on various powerful committees; in 1983 she was appointed to the powerful Budget Committee, where she questioned wasteful defense spending.

First Female Vice Presidential Nominee

In 1984 Ferraro became the first chairwoman of the 1984 Democratic Platform Committee. Her reputation as a skilled politician, combined with her successful work on the party platform, brought her prominence and publicity. At the Democratic National Convention, presidential candidate Walter F. Mondale asked her to be his running mate. Despite their hard work and intense campaigning, however, President Ronald Reagan was overwhelmingly reelected. After the election, Ferraro and her family faced both legal and personal problems. Investigations into her family finances, begun after her nomination, continued, and her son was arrested for cocaine possession. In 1992 she ran for the U.S. Senate and narrowly lost in the Democratic primary.

According to political analysts, while Ferraro had not attracted as many votes as the Democrats thought she would, she was not the reason for the defeat of the Democratic ticket in 1984. On the contrary, Geraldine Ferraro's tenacity and determination, her work for women's rights, and her history-making nomination encouraged more women to be politically active and for the first time made the dream of the first woman vice president or president a real possibility.

Bibliography

Ferraro, Geraldine A., and Linda Bird Francke. *Ferraro: My Story*. New York: Bantam Books, 1985.

Fireside, Bryna J. *Is There a Woman in the House—or Senate?* Morton Grove, Ill.: A. Whitman, 1994.

Lindop, Laurie. *Political Leaders*. New York: Twenty-First Century Books, 1996.

Pollack, Jill S. *Women on the Hill: A History of Women in Congress*. New York: Franklin Watts, 1996.

Lisa-Anne Culp

Andrew Fisher

Born: August 29, 1862; Crosshouse, Ayrshire, Scotland
Died: October 22, 1928; London, England

Prime minister of Australia (1908-1909, 1910-1913, 1914-1915)

Andrew Fisher (AN-drew FIH-shur) was the son of a Scottish coal miner and his wife. He attended a local school. When Fisher was about ten he began to work in the mines after his father became ill. In 1879, he was elected as secretary of the local branch of the Ayrshire Miners' Union. In 1885, Fisher immigrated to the colony of Queensland and worked in various jobs in the mining industry, including engine driving. He married Margaret Jane Irvine on December 31, 1901.

Andrew Fisher *(Library of Congress)*

Early Political Career

In 1891, Fisher became president of both the town of Gympie's branch of the Amalgamated Miners' Association and the town's branch of the Labor Party. He was elected to the Queensland Legislative Assembly in 1893. When he lost his seat in 1896, he returned to engine driving, acted as auditor to the Gympie municipal council, and helped other Labor supporters establish a pro-Labor newspaper, the Gympie *Truth*, to counteract the *Gympie Times*'s strong opposition to the Labor Party.

In 1899 Fisher was reelected to the Legislative Assembly and was secretary for railways and public works in the government of Anderson Dawson. Dawson's was the first Labor government in the Australian colonies, but it lasted for only six days in early December of 1899.

Federal Politics

Fisher joined the 1890's campaign for a federation of the Australian colonies, and he entered federal politics after the creation of the Commonwealth of Australia in 1901. He was a member of the House of Representatives for the electorate of Wide Bay in Queensland from 1901 until his retirement in 1915. He was minister for trade and customs in the Labor government led by John Watson (April-August, 1904) and became leader of the Australian Labor Party in 1907 when Watson resigned. Fisher became prime minister and treasurer in the minority Labor government formed in November, 1908, but the government was narrowly defeated by the Fusion Party in an election six months later.

Fisher became prime minister and treasurer once again following Labor's win in the 1910 election. This government's reforms included the

The Australian Navy

At least from the early 1870's, some leaders of the Australian colonies were concerned about their vulnerability to naval attack. Toward the end of the century, some defense experts, such as William Cresswell, began to call for a substantial Australian navy. In 1903 the new Commonwealth of Australia began amalgamating the small naval forces of the colonies. The British Admiralty was originally opposed to the creation of a significant Australian fleet. Nonetheless, the Fisher government made a decision in February, 1909, to order three destroyers. Brit-ain's attitude changed as Germany began to increase its naval power. The 1909 Imperial Defense Conference recommended Australia's acquisition of a fleet led by an armored battle cruiser. This proposal was implemented quickly, leading to the creation of the Royal Australian Navy. The fleet assembled in Sydney in October, 1913, and was ready for active service when World War I broke out in 1914. It had considerable success against Germany's naval squadron in the Pacific.

provision of maternity allowances, extension of aged and invalid pensions, and the establishment of the Commonwealth Bank. Following Labor's loss in the 1913 election, Fisher became leader of the opposition. The Liberals controlled the House of Representatives but not the Senate, and there was a double dissolution in 1914. Labor won the election, and Fisher became prime minister for a third time. He resigned in 1915 because of ill health and the strain of office.

After Politics

In 1916 Fisher succeeded George Reid as Australian high commissioner in London, and he held that position until 1921. He returned to Australia that year and considered reentering politics, but instead he retired in London in 1922 and lived quietly there until his death.

Fisher was a successful Australian politician, though he was overshadowed by the flamboyant William Morris Hughes, who succeeded him as Labor leader. Although seen in his day as a radical, Fisher left a legacy of sound and lasting reforms. Indeed, these were on a scale that was not equaled by a Labor government until the prime ministership of John Curtin in the 1940's. The reform program of Fisher's government would undoubtedly have been more extensive if not for the stress imposed on Australian society and its economic resources by World War I.

Bibliography

Clark, C. H. M. *The People Make Laws, 1888-1915.* Vol. 5 of *A History of Australia.* Melbourne, Australia: Melbourne University Press, 1981.

Malkin, John. *Andrew Fisher, 1862-1928.* Darvel, Scotland: Walker & Cornell, 1979.

McQueen, Humphrey. *A New Britannia: An Argument Concerning the Social Origins of Australian Radicalism and Nationalism.* 3d ed. Melbourne, Australia: Penguin, 1986.

Russell Blackford

Gerald R. Ford

Born: July 14, 1913; Omaha, Nebraska

President of the United States (1974-1977)

Gerald Rudolph Ford, Jr. (JEH-ruhld REW-dolf FOHRD JEW-nyur), was born in Omaha, Nebraska, to Leslie King and Dorothy Gardner King. His birth name was Leslie Lynch King. After his parents' divorce in 1914, he and his mother moved to Grand Rapids, Michigan. In 1916 his mother married Gerald R. Ford, Sr., the owner of a paint company. His stepfather adopted him and gave him a new name, Gerald R. Ford, Jr. Interested in sports and outdoor activities as a youth, Ford joined the Boy Scouts, where he attained the rank of Eagle Scout. As a senior at South High in Grand Rapids, he was named to the All-State Football Team in 1931 and was awarded an athletic scholarship to the University of Michigan.

When Ford graduated from the University of Michigan in 1935, he was offered contracts to play for the Detroit Lions and the Green Bay Packers. Ford chose instead to accept a position as assistant line coach for the junior varsity team at Yale University and head coach of the boxing team. In 1941 Ford earned a law degree, graduating in the top third of his class. He practiced law in Michigan for a year before enlisting in the U.S. Navy. He served as a lieutenant commander during World War II and earned ten battle stars.

The Congressman's Congressman

At the end of the war Ford returned to Grand Rapids, where he practiced law and became active in politics. In 1948 Ford was elected to the House of Representatives from Michigan's Fifth District. In the same year he married Elizabeth Bloomer Warren, a former Martha Graham dancer. The Fords have four children, Michael, John, Steven, and Susan.

Ford served as a Republican member of the U.S. House of Representatives from 1949 to 1973. In 1961 he was named the "Congressman's Congressman" by the American Political Science Association. He was chosen Republican Conference Chairman in 1963 and became the House minority leader in 1965, serving in that position until 1973. During the 1960's, Ford and the Senate minority leader, Everett Dirksen of Illinois, appeared on a series of televised press conferences nicknamed "The Ev and Jerry Show." Ford and Dirksen presented the Republican views on current issues. In 1967, in a speech from the House floor, Ford criticized President Lyndon B. Johnson's handling of the Vietnam War. Ford advocated increased bombing of communist forces and a blockade of North Vietnam.

Gerald R. Ford *(Library of Congress)*

President of the United States

On the resignation of Spiro T. Agnew in 1973, President Richard Nixon appointed Ford vice president. In 1974 Nixon resigned rather than face impeachment because of his involvement in the Watergate scandal. Gerald Ford then became president. He was the first person in U.S. history to have occupied both the presidency and vice presidency without being elected to either office. In his inaugural speech, Ford referred to the turmoil caused by Watergate, saying, "My Fellow Americans, our long national nightmare is over." He selected former Governor Nelson Rockefeller of New York as his vice president and asked all members

U.S. president Gerald R. Ford on September 8, 1974, making his most famous and controversial public statement—announcing that he was granting former president Richard M. Nixon a full presidential pardon. *(Library of Congress)*

Ford Pardons President Nixon

On June 17, 1972, five burglars broke into the Democratic National Committee Headquarters in the Watergate office building in Washington, D.C. They were carrying telephone wiretapping equipment and spy cameras. When it was discovered that members of the Committee to Re-Elect the President (CREEP) were responsible for the break-in, President Richard M. Nixon denied any knowledge of or involvement in the incident. In May, 1973, the Senate Watergate investigation committee began televised hearings that went on for a number of months. It became clear that Nixon had lied—he had been actively involved in attempts to cover up the burglary. After the House of Representatives instituted impeachment proceedings, Nixon resigned rather than face impeachment charges.

Upon Nixon's resignation, Vice President Gerald R. Ford became president. On September 8, 1974, Ford granted Nixon a "full, free, and absolute pardon" for all offenses committed during his administration. Ford had decided to do this without consulting party leaders, the special Watergate prosecutor, or members of Congress. The public, as well as many members of Congress, were angered by the pardon, but Ford maintained that the pardon was "the right thing to do." He justified his position by saying that a prolonged investigation of Nixon would not be good for the country and that it was time to "heal the wounds." Understanding the severity of the criticism, Ford voluntarily appeared before a congressional committee to answer questions about his decision. President Ford's controversial pardon of Nixon was a factor in his loss of the presidential election in 1976.

The *Mayaguez* Incident

On May 12, 1975, the Cambodian Khmer Rouge government fired on the American merchant ship *Mayaguez*, which was sailing in the Gulf of Siam, some 60 miles (97 kilometers) off the coast of Cambodia. Cambodian sailors boarded the ship and took its crew as prisoners. At the time of the incident, the United States had no diplomatic relations with the Cambodian regime. President Gerald R. Ford believed that failing to act would endanger the prestige of the United States around the world. He said that the United States "must act upon it now, and act firmly." Calling the Cambodian action an "act of piracy," Ford sent military forces to rescue the crewmen. The U.S. position was that the *Mayaguez* was in international waters. Naval and military forces were successful in rescuing the crewmen, although forty-one Americans were killed during the operation, and another fifty were wounded.

---

of the cabinet and heads of government agencies to remain in their positions.

One of Ford's first acts was to grant Nixon a full pardon, prohibiting any criminal charges that Nixon might have faced in connection with Watergate. Because of the negative reaction to the pardon, Ford voluntarily appeared before a subcommittee of the House of Representatives to explain his decision. On the economic front, Ford fought to control inflation and vetoed a number of appropriations bills that would have increased the budget deficit. Among his major goals were reducing taxes and easing controls on businesses.

When South Vietnam fell to North Vietnam in 1975, Ford oversaw the evacuation of American personnel from Saigon. In April of 1975 he ordered the airlift of 237,000 anticommunist Vietnamese refugees, most of whom were taken to the United States. A month later, Cambodians of the Khmer Rouge seized the American merchant ship *Mayaguez* in the Gulf of Siam. Calling this action an act of piracy, Ford sent military forces to rescue the crewmen. Although the mission was successful, forty-one Americans were killed during the operation. In other areas of foreign policy, the Ford administration provided aid to both Israel and Egypt in an attempt to persuade the two countries to accept a truce agreement. Ford also met with Soviet Union leader Leonid I. Brezhnev. In their first summit meeting, they set new limitations on nuclear weapons.

In August, 1976, Ford won the Republican Party's presidential nomination in a close race against Ronald Reagan. When Ford lost the election to Jimmy Carter, he retired from politics. Carter, in his acceptance speech, thanked Ford "for all he has done to heal our land."

Bibliography

Ford, Gerald R. *A Time to Heal: The Autobiography of Gerald R. Ford*. New York: Harper & Row, 1979.

Greene, John Robert. *The Presidency of Gerald R. Ford*. Lawrence: University of Kansas Press, 1995.

Vestal, Bud. *Jerry Ford, Up Close: An Investigative Biography*. New York: Coward, McCann & Geoghegan, 1974.

Judith Barton Williamson

Francis Michael Forde

Born: July 18, 1890; Mitchell, Queensland (now Australia)
Died: January 28, 1983; Brisbane, Queensland, Australia

Australian deputy prime minister (1941-1945; 1945-1946) and prime minister (1945)

Francis Michael Forde (FRAN-sihs MI-kuhl FOHRD), widely known as Frank Forde, was educated at a local state school and the Christian Brothers' College at Toowoomba. Before entering politics, he worked as a teacher, telegrapher, and electrical engineer. In February, 1925, he married Veronica O'Reilly in Wagga Wagga, New South Wales. They had four children.

Political Career to 1946

Forde was Labor member for the seat of Rockhampton in the Queensland Legislative Assembly from 1917 to 1922, when he resigned to move into federal politics. He was member for Capricornia in the federal lower house, the House of Representatives, from 1922 to 1946.

In 1929 he became honorary minister in the Australian Labor Party (ALP) government led by James Scullin, and he was appointed minister for trade and customs in February, 1931. After Labor's electoral defeat at the end of 1931, he became deputy leader of the party. In October, 1935, he ran for the leadership after Scullin stood down. He was defeated unexpectedly—and by only one vote—by John Curtin. Curtin went on to become one of Australia's greatest Labor prime ministers.

From 1941 to 1945, during World War II, Forde was deputy prime minister to Curtin and minister for the army, a position of great importance and sensitivity at the time. At the time of Curtin's death on July 5, 1945, Forde was acting prime minister. He was then prime minister for seven days, from July 6 to July 12, until the party could choose its new leader. Joseph Benedict (Ben) Chifley, whom Curtin had named as his successor, was chosen. Forde retained his position as deputy and was minister for the army and minister for defense in the first Chifley ministry.

Electoral Defeat and After

Forde lost his seat in the September, 1946, federal election, in which Labor was returned with a reduced majority. The deputy position was then assigned to Herbert Vere Evatt, the attorney general and a former High Court judge. Forde was rewarded with the position of Australian high commissioner to Canada in Ottawa, where he served from 1946 to 1953. He then returned to Brisbane to become the ALP's Queensland political organizer.

In 1954, Forde attempted to make a comeback in federal politics, standing unsuccessfully for the seat of Wide Bay. However, he won the state seat of Flinders in a by-election the following

Francis Michael Forde *(Library of Congress)*

509

Australian army minister Francis Michael Forde inspecting U.S. soldiers serving in Australia in 1942. *(Library of Congress)*

tin and then by Ben Chifley. He lost two leadership contests in frustrating circumstances, both times from the position of deputy leader of his party. He was a hard-working, loyal, and affable politician whose time in politics spanned forty years, most of them in the federal parliament. He played a major role in Curtin's wartime government, which introduced important social reforms to benefit returned servicemen and working people more generally. During the last months of Curtin's prime ministership, Curtin's health was fragile, and much of the burden of Australian involvement in the war effort fell heavily on Forde's shoulders at a critical and difficult time.

year. He was reelected in 1956 but lost the seat by one vote in 1957. Forde lived in retirement in Brisbane until his death at the age of ninety-two.

Forde's Place in History

Forde's career has been neglected by historians because he was overshadowed first by John Cur-

Bibliography

Crisp, L. F. *Ben Chifley: A Political Biography*. London: Angus & Robertson, 1977.

Spender, Percy. *Politics and a Man*. London: Collins, 1977.

Russell Blackford

The Re-establishment and Employment Act

During the war years of the early 1940's, the Labor Party government was determined to introduce social reforms. At the end of 1942, a ministry of postwar reconstruction was created. The government planned to create a postwar society with full employment and a comprehensive scheme of social security. It introduced such measures as improved maternity allowances and unemployment benefits.

The Re-establishment and Employment Act, which came into force in mid-1945, contained a comprehensive scheme of rights for returned servicemen, including controversial provisions for preference in employment. Such provisions were greeted with suspicion by trade unions while being condemned by the returned servicemen's lobby for not going far enough. The act also had broader provisions for social reconstruction, including the establishment of an important new body, the Commonwealth Employment Service. This body was meant to find employment for former servicemen and munitions workers but was given a broader role to help the unemployed.

Francis Ferdinand

Born: December 18, 1863; Graz, Austria
Died: June 28, 1914; Sarajevo, Bosnia-Herzegovina

Assassination victim whose death sparked World War I

As one of the many archdukes of Austria from the Habsburg dynasty, Francis Ferdinand (FRAN-sihs FUR-dih-nand) grew up among sump- tuous palaces and luxurious estates. Since 1848 his uncle, Emperor Francis Joseph, had ruled the Austro-Hungarian Dual Monarchy, one of the great powers of Europe. Francis Ferdinand and his cousins were trained to uphold the customs and traditions of this important aristocratic family.

Heir to the Throne

With the mysterious death of Crown Prince Rudolph in 1889, probably in a double suicide pact with a lover, Francis Ferdinand—also known as Franz Ferdinand (German pronunciation FRAHNTZ FEHR-dee-nahnt)—unexpectedly became the heir apparent. The archduke's prickly and proud personality did little to make him popular either at the imperial court or with the common people. His only kindness seemed to be directed toward his immediate family, and his family relationships caused serious trouble between himself and the emperor. In 1900 Francis Ferdinand insisted on marrying Countess Sophie Chotek from Bohemia, who, while of a distinguished noble family, was not considered of sufficient aristocratic rank to marry a future emperor. Francis Joseph reluctantly allowed them a morganatic marriage: Under this type of arrangement she did not gain the imperial status and rights equivalent to those of her husband. Francis Ferdinand was also forced to renounce the future rights of his children (the couple eventually had a daughter and two sons) to inherit the throne.

Because of Emperor Francis Joseph's dislike for his heir, he gave him little to do besides the usual ceremonials (which often reinforced the unequal status of his wife). Yet the heir apparent tried to develop a shadow government from his palace residence, the Belvedere, planning for the day when he would assume the throne. Politically he was an archconservative absolutist, disliking modern ideas such as socialism and liberalism. He saw, however, that the monarchy needed to adapt to modern times. He especially recognized the danger of growing ethnic tensions. While some key advisers of the emperor saw Serbian agitation as the monarchy's main problem, Francis Ferdinand wanted to avoid war

Francis Ferdinand with his wife, Sofie. *(Archive Photos)*

Artist's rendition of the 1914 assassination of Francis Ferdinand and his wife in Sarajevo. *(Archive Photos)*

in the Balkans. Instead he blamed the dualistic structure of the empire, which since 1867 had granted the Hungarians, or Magyars, substantial autonomy. Whatever his plans to deal with nationalism, he never got the chance to put them into practice.

Assassination

In June, 1914, the emperor ordered Francis Ferdinand to supervise military maneuvers in Bosnia-Herzegovina. Meanwhile, members of the Serbian secret police had organized a conspiracy of young Bosnian Serb students to assassinate Francis Ferdinand during his visit to Bosnia's capital, Sarajevo. During the official motorcade through Sarajevo on June 28, one of the quickly trained students managed to throw a bomb at the archduke's automobile, but he missed. Later that day, because of a confusion in the change of route, the archduke's automobile stopped in front of another conspirator, Gavrilo Princip, who shot the archduke and his wife Sophie at point-blank range. Francis Ferdinand's death provided some imperial leaders with an excuse to

Ethnicity in the Austrian Empire

In 1910 more than 51 million people lived together under the Habsburg emperor, but they increasingly saw themselves separated by ethnicity. The growing popularity of nationalism—the idea that ethnic groups should form their own sovereign states—was Austria's intractable problem. Constitutionally, the emperor reigned over three sections of the empire. First, in the Austrian portion, the dominant Germans composed merely 35 percent of the population. The more numerous Czechs, Poles, Ruthenians (Ukrainians) and Italians, bitter about their subordinate status, often obstructed political action.

Second, in Transleithania, the Hungarians, or Magyars, made up almost half the population and held all the political power. The large numbers of Romanians, Germans, Slovaks, Ruthenians, Croats, and Serbs were determined to resist the "magyarization" program, which forced them to use the Hungarian language. Third, in the imperial province of Bosnia-Herzegovina, many Muslims, Croats, and Serbs resented their conquest in 1878 and annexation in 1908. It was a group of radical Serbs who killed Francis Ferdinand in protest.

provoke war against Serbia. By August, 1914, the war had expanded to become World War I, which not only toppled the Habsburg dynasty and destroyed the Dual Monarchy of Austria-Hungary but also changed the course of the twentieth century.

Bibliography

Brooke-Shephard, Gordon. *Archduke of Sarajevo: The Romance and Tragedy of Franz Ferdinand of Austria*. Boston: Little, Brown, 1984.

Cassels, Lavender. *The Archduke and the Assassin: Sarajevo, June 28th, 1914*. New York: Stein and Day, 1985.

Pauli, Hertha. *The Secret of Sarajevo: The Story of Franz Ferdinand and Sophie*. New York: Appleton-Century, 1965.

Remak, Joachim. *Sarajevo: The Story of a Political Murder*. New York: Criterion Books, 1959.

Brian A. Pavlac

Francis Joseph I

Born: August 18, 1830; Schönbrunn Palace, near Vienna, Austria
Died: November 21, 1916; Schönbrunn Palace, near Vienna, Austria

Emperor of Austria (1848-1916)

Francis Joseph I (FRAN-sihs JOH-sehf thuh FURST) was born at a time when his family was trying to maintain not only its position as rulers of Austria, the leading German state, but also its control over a vast multicultural empire. The old order that Klemens von Metternich (1773-1859), the rigid Austrian minister, had helped restore after the defeat of Napoleon was falling apart. In 1848, revolutions swept Europe. Because of the crisis, weak-minded Emperor Ferdinand was persuaded to relinquish the throne in favor of his eighteen-year-old nephew.

Francis Joseph I *(Library of Congress)*

Triple Threats

Francis Joseph was faced with three threats that challenged his rule and his empire. First was nationalism, and second was the concept of democratic rule: These two major forces of the nineteenth century were incompatible with the structure of the Habsburg Empire. Third was the rising power of Prussia, which threatened Austria's position as head of the German states.

Immediately upon becoming emperor, Francis Joseph abolished the Austrian constitution and put down the republican movement in Hungary, his major non-German possession, by force. His efforts to retain the Italian states of Lombardy and Venetia within the empire resulted in war with France and the loss of Lombardy. In 1866, in a short but decisive war, Prussia defeated Austria to become the leading German state. Austria was forced out of the German Confederation and lost Venetia to the newly founded kingdom of Italy.

In 1867, to cope with the growing problem of Hungarian nationalism, Austria gave Hungary almost equal status with Austria in the creation of the Austro-Hungarian Empire. The rights of other minorities within both Hungary and Austria, especially those of the Slavs, were largely ignored. In 1871, after a short war with France, Prussia asserted its control over the German states through the establishment of a unified German nation-state. The growth of its powerful neighbor to the north threatened Austria's long-time position in Europe.

The Balkan Crisis

Increasingly, Francis Joseph's government was drawn into the growing crisis in the Balkans, which was complicated by antagonisms among three religions (Catholic, Muslim, and Eastern

Orthodox), the waning power of the Ottoman Empire, and the political ambitions of Serbia. The Serbs saw themselves as leader of a South Slav or Yugoslav movement. Fearing unrest in its southern provinces, the Austro-Hungarian government sought to curb Serbian expansion by denying Serbs access to the Adriatic Sea. The Austro-Hungarians cut Serbian access to the south by supporting the independence of Montenegro and Albania. They threatened a cutoff to the north by occupying (in 1878) the provinces of Bosnia and Herzegovina, taken from the Ottomans—provinces the Serbs claimed as rightfully theirs.

A Tragic Personal Life

Francis Joseph remarked toward the end of his long life that no tragedy was spared him. His empress refused to fulfill her duties; her increasing eccentricities and her aimless wanderings finally resulted in her assassination in 1898. His brother Maximilian's short career as emperor of Mexico ended in front of a revolutionary firing squad. The apparent double suicide of his son, Crown Prince Rudolf, and Rudolf's mistress in 1889 has never been satisfactorily explained. By 1908, the diamond jubilee of his reign, a lonely old man could recall few satisfactions other than that the festivities were taking place in

Francis Joseph's brother Maximilian, briefly the emperor of Mexico, was executed in 1867 by Mexican troops. *(Archive Photos)*

The Habsburgs

One of Europe's oldest ruling families, dating from the tenth century, the Habsburgs were noted for acquiring territories through diplomacy and marriage rather than by military means. The envied fertility of Habsburg women assured the continuance of the dynasty. The height of Habsburg power and influence occurred during the reign of Charles V (1519-1556), who reigned over Germany, Austria, Hungary, Spain, Holland, Belgium, most of Italy, and the overseas Spanish Empire. The greatest Habsburg ruler is thought to have been Maria Theresa, mother of sixteen, among them the ill-fated Queen Marie Antoinette of France. Although the office was elective, the Habsburgs managed to become Holy Roman emperors or German emperors for nearly four hundred years. Removed by Napoleon Bonaparte, the Habsburgs became emperors of Austria, a title they retained until the end of World War I in 1918.

Nationalism

Generally defined as emotional attachment to an ethnic or political group, nationalism assumes two forms: cultural and political. Cultural nationalism—emotional attachment to an ethnic group, usually defined by language or religion—is old. The Jewish nation is an example. Political nationalism is more recent, a product of the French Revolution exploited by Napoleon Bonaparte to achieve French dominance of Europe. Other countries followed the French example. The nineteenth century was the age of nationalism with the establishment of the German and Italian nation-states. The American Civil War was a manifestation of nationalism, as was the return to power of the emperor in Japan in 1867. Nationalism, or the self-determination of peoples, was one of the more important of President Woodrow Wilson's Fourteen Points at the end of World War I.

a city he had helped create. Between 1857 and 1888 Vienna had been transformed from an unsanitary medieval city into a metropolis with broad avenues and imposing public buildings.

On October 6, 1908, Francis Joseph signed an order that would eventually destroy his government: Bosnia-Herzegovina became a province of the Austro-Hungarian Empire.

The Imperial Opera in Vienna, Austria, was built between 1861 and 1869, during a period in which Francis Joseph oversaw Vienna's transformation into a cosmopolitan city. *(Archive Photos)*

Assassination of the Archduke

The death of Crown Prince Rudolf resulted in Francis Joseph's nephew, Archduke Francis (or Franz) Ferdinand, becoming heir to the thrones of Austria and Hungary. Married to a Czech, Ferdinand was known to be sympathetic to the political aspirations of the Slavs—alarming the Serbs, who favored continued unrest among the Slavs. At the same time, the crown prince was in favor of curbing the privileges of the Hungarians, arousing their hostility. In short, there were many who opposed Francis Ferdinand becoming emperor.

The crown prince and his wife accepted an invitation to attend military maneuvers to be held June 28, 1914, in Sarajevo, the capital of the newly acquired province of Bosnia. During the visit, the driver of the automobile carrying the imperial couple was given wrong directions. He brought the automobile to a stop a few feet from a Bosnian-Serb assassin, who proceeded to shoot both Francis Ferdinand and his wife dead.

The End of the Dynasty

Determined to destroy the Serbian threat, Austria-Hungary, backed by its alliance with Germany, issued an ultimatum to Serbia. Serbia, backed by Russia (in turn backed by France and Britain), rejected the ultimatum. The alliance system plunged Europe into World War I in August, 1914. In Vienna, Francis Joseph, now eighty-four

and deeply discouraged, continued his accustomed routine. On November 21, 1916, in a country shivering and starving, with its armies in retreat, Francis Joseph died. The empire and the dynasty he had spent his life defending and upholding died two years later when another nephew, now crown prince, and his family were forced into exile.

A Cautious Reappraisal

The reign of Francis Joseph has typically been regarded as a failure—a vain attempt to halt political progress. However, given the ethnic warfare that began raging in the 1980's and 1990's in the region that was once the Austro-Hungarian Empire, such criticism has become a bit more muted.

Bibliography

Brooke-Shephard, Gordon. *Archduke of Sarajevo: The Romance and Tragedy of Franz Ferdinand of Austria*. Boston: Little, Brown, 1984.

Haslip, Joan. *The Lonely Empress: A Biography of Elizabeth of Austria*. New York: World, 1965.

Palmer, Alan. *Twilight of the Habsburgs: The Life and Times of Emperor Francis Joseph*. New York: Grove Press, 1994.

Wheatcroft, Andrew. *The Habsburgs*. New York: Viking, 1995.

Nis Petersen

Francisco Franco

Born: December 4, 1892; El Ferrol, Galicia, Spain
Died: November 20, 1975; Madrid, Spain

Dictatorial ruler of Spain (1939-1975)

Francisco Franco (frahn-THEES-koh FRAHN-koh) was born Francisco Paulino Hermenegildo Teódulo Franco y Bahamonde. He was born into a naval family but attended Spain's infantry academy in Toledo. A young Franco led troops against the Berbers in Morocco and then, in 1922, commanded his country's foreign legion. He married Carmen Polo in 1923. By age thirty-three Franco had achieved the rank of brigadier general. He was named director of a military academy in 1928, but Spain's liberal Republican government closed it in 1931. Franco remained neutral during Spain's political turmoil of the

Francisco Franco *(Library of Congress)*

early 1930's, serving both liberal and conservative governments equally well. He helped organize the conservative administration's violent repression of a rebellion in Asturias in 1934 and later rose to the title of chief of the general staff. In 1936 Spain's newly elected liberal government removed him from this position and made him garrison commander in Tenerife, in the Canary Islands, far from the Spanish mainland.

Franco and the Spanish Civil War

When a military uprising initiated the Spanish Civil War on July 17, 1936, Franco was flown from the Canary Islands to Morocco to assume command of the elite Spanish troops stationed there. Franco enlisted the intervention of the fascist regimes of Germany and Italy to help him move his troops to Spain. As he approached Madrid in September, the question of who would lead the new rebel government had to be addressed. The logical answer was Franco, who on October 1, 1936, became *Generalissimo* of the armed forces and chief of the government. The original plan was that Franco would lead the Nationalist forces to final military victory and then provide a smooth transition to a more permanent conservative government, most likely in the form of a restored monarchy. The Spanish Civil War lasted until March, 1939, however, and by then *el Caudillo* (a term meaning "leader," but akin to the German führer and Italian duce) had so consolidated his power that it was obvious that his regime would be anything but temporary.

An Outcast Franco, an Outcast Spain

The first years of Franco's dictatorship were marked by severe political repression, brought about by Franco himself, and economic hardship,

Francisco Franco saluting the crowd from a hotel balcony in Salamanca, Spain, in 1937. *(National Archives)*

brought about in large measure by the world's reaction to the nature and behavior of Franco's regime. Franco used his absolute power to outlaw labor strikes, civil marriages, divorce, and public meetings, while imposing strict censorship and mandating religious education. At the same time, his dictatorship empowered the various factions that made up the coalition of conservative traditionalists that he represented, among them the fascist Falange and the Catholic Church.

Franco refused Adolf Hitler's request for help in World War II. Still, while he officially adopted a neutral position during the war, his sympathies clearly lay with the Axis (the alliance including Nazi Germany and Fascist Italy). This situation changed

The Spanish Civil War

The Spanish Civil War (1936-1939) was a power struggle between Spain's leftist and rightist political factions. The leftists were socialists and other liberals, including communists, who sought a Republican (nonmonarchist) Spain with a virtually nonexistent Catholic Church and a more egalitarian society and economic system. The rightists included Falangists (fascists fiercely devoted to Spanish nationalism), monarchists, the Catholic Church, the aristocracy, big business, and the military; they sought a classic, traditional Spain. The two sides had alternated in power in the five years before the civil war. When elections returned power to the Left in 1936, the Right decided to take action. It made its move a few months later in a military uprising beginning on July 17, 1936.

Led by Francisco Franco and aided by the Germans and Italians, the Right (Nationalists) made relatively easy, if slow and bloody, work of its leftist (Loyalist or Republican) adversaries. The Republicans received limited aid from Russia for a time, but none (except for some volunteer fighters) from the United States or other Western countries, who respected an arms embargo on the war. The Republicans were more divided among themselves than the more disciplined Nationalists were; they were also simply outnumbered and outgunned.

The war was over on March 28, 1939, leaving behind some one million dead. Thousands of people were executed and killed in horrifying acts of violence such as the bombing of the town of Guernica, depicted in the Pablo Picasso painting of the same name.

Spain Joins the United Nations

In 1953 the Vatican supported Francisco Franco and his regime by recognizing Catholicism as the only religion in Spain and by granting Franco a role in choosing Catholic prelates in his country. In the same year Franco signed a treaty with the United States to allow American military bases on Spanish soil. These two events symbolized the legitimacy of Franco's regime in the eyes of the international community, and they opened the door to Spain's entry into the United Nations in 1955. This event ended a nine-year boycott by the international body. Spain, at last, had officially joined the civilized nations of the post–World War II era.

in 1943, when it became obvious that the democratic Allies would win. In an effort to win approval from the rest of the world, Franco retreated from totalitarianism, but his shift was not dramatic, and it came too late to satisfy the rest of the world. The United Nations imposed a diplomatic boycott on Franco's Spain in 1946, and Spain was blocked from the North Atlantic Treaty

Alcalá Zamora (center), president of Spain's Second Republic, and members of his cabinet. The politically tumultuous years of the republic, proclaimed in 1931, led to the Spanish Civil War in 1936. *(National Archives)*

Organization (NATO) and the Marshall Plan for rebuilding war-torn Europe. Franco and his country were isolated, outcasts, and Spain's economy, devastated since the Civil War, lay in ruins.

Legitimacy and Change

The agreement that Franco signed with the Vatican in 1953 and the treaty he negotiated with the United States to bring American bases to Spain in the same year brought legitimacy to Franco's regime. Spain was allowed entry into the United Nations in 1955. The treaty with the United States, in particular, brought much-needed external capital. (It would not be enough to solve Spain's ongoing economic woes, however.) The answer to this problem lay inside Spain, in a group called *Opus Dei* (God's work), whose members the once anticapitalist Franco called on to develop the country's economy. The *Opus Dei* technocrats practiced an economic philosophy that reconciled capitalism with the Catholic Church, and the liberal policies that they instituted led Spain into the modern economic world in the 1960's.

Perhaps in response to the growing discontent of his people or to the new, more liberal attitudes present in the Catholic Church, Franco relaxed social and political restraints in the mid-1960's. He eased censorship, granted more religious freedom, and allowed direct election of legislative representatives. In 1969, twenty-two years after he declared Spain a monarchy (albeit a monarchy without a sitting monarch) and claimed the power to name his successor, Franco selected Don Juan Carlos, the grandson of Spain's last king, to sit on the throne upon his death.

The End of an Era

Franco died on November 20, 1975. Only one foreign head of state, Chile's dictator Augusto Pinochet, attended the funeral. In contrast, leaders (or their representatives) and royalty from all over the world witnessed the coronation of King Juan Carlos, who almost immediately began a process that would produce a new and democratic Spain, the likes of which Franco never would have allowed. A majority of Spaniards celebrated the change, although others longed for the stable, conservative days of *el Caudillo*.

Bibliography

Carr, Raymond, and Juan Pablo Fuzi Aizpurua. *Spain: Dictatorship to Democracy*. London: George Allen & Unwin, 1979.

Payne, Stanley G. *The Franco Regime: 1936-1975*. Madison: University of Wisconsin Press, 1987.

Preston, Paul. *Franco*. New York: Basic Books, 1994.

Keith H. Brower

Felix Frankfurter

Born: November 15, 1882; Vienna, Austria
Died: February 22, 1965; Washington, D.C.

U.S. jurist and Supreme Court justice (1939-1962)

Felix Frankfurter (FEE-lihkz FRANK-fur-tur) was born in Vienna of Jewish parents. He immigrated to New York's Lower East Side as a boy of twelve. He attended the City College of New York from 1899 to 1902 and then entered Harvard Law School, graduating with an LL.B. in 1906. He immediately took a job as assistant U.S. attorney in New York, working with Henry Stimson, later to be U.S. secretary of state and secretary of war. Frankfurter served the government until offered a position teaching law at Harvard, which he

Felix Frankfurter *(Library of Congress)*

accepted in 1914. In 1919 he married Marion A. Denman.

Legal Career

Frankfurter taught at Harvard until 1939, while participating actively in liberal political and legal causes. He was one of the original founders of the American Civil Liberties Union (ACLU), was a legal adviser to the National Association for the Advancement of Colored People (NAACP), and was active in the defense of Nicola Sacco and Bartolomeo Vanzetti in their celebrated trial and appeal. Frankfurter participated in a number of important Supreme Court cases, arguing in *Bunting v. Oregon* (1917) and *Adkins v. Children's Hospital* (1923) that state governments have the power to regulate employment relationships. He became an early supporter of and adviser to President Franklin D. Roosevelt, who appointed him to the U.S. Supreme Court in 1939.

Mr. Justice Frankfurter

Frankfurter's scholarship led him to adopt a skeptical view of the Supreme Court's role. In most areas of constitutional law he believed that the court should exercise self-restraint, deferring to the laws created by legislatures whenever possible. He voted consistently to uphold the extension of federal power under the commerce clause in the U.S. Constitution, just as he usually supported state criminal procedures unless they could be shown to be outrageously unfair. For example, in *Adamson v. California* (1948) and *Wolf v. Colorado* (1949) he voted to uphold questioned state criminal methods despite his view that the same procedures, at the federal level, were unconstitutional.

The Sacco and Vanzetti Case

In April, 1920, Niccola Sacco and Bartolomeo Vanzetti were tried and convicted of robbing and murdering a paymaster and guard in South Braintree, Massachusetts. They were sentenced to death. Sacco and Vanzetti were anarchists who feared deportation, and both were armed at the time of their arrest. The evidence against them was ambiguous, and the state was allowed to enter much prejudicial testimony about their radical politics and Italian immigrant background. Frankfurter strongly believed that an injustice had been done. He assisted with their appeals, wrote a short but powerful book, *The Case of Sacco and Vanzetti* (1927), and attempted to muster public support for commutation of their sentences. In spite of Frankfurter's efforts (and those of many others), Sacco and Vanzetti were electrocuted in 1927. As a result of the case, Frankfurter became widely but falsely conceived of as a supporter of radicals and radical causes.

Frankfurter was not a radical liberal activist. Yet in a case in which a state obtained criminal evidence by forcibly pumping it from a defendant's stomach, Frankfurter voted to overturn the conviction. He thus became known for attempting to apply broad standards of fundamental fairness to constitutional issues. His judging technique was not destined to prevail in the Supreme Court, however, and Frankfurter found himself in the minority in many cases. This became increasingly true after the appointment of Earl Warren as chief justice in 1953. Yet Frankfurter's influence on the Court cannot be measured entirely in terms of cases won and lost. His skeptical technique, his willingness to engage in sometimes fierce argumentation, and his role as a gadfly in pressing advocates during oral argument deepened and matured the Court's consideration of many cases, even when Frankfurter himself did not prevail.

Frankfurter also had a penchant for writing concurring opinions rather than accepting the opinion of the Court, which allowed him to express his sometimes idiosyncratic views. Frankfurter also became known for his dislike of embroiling the Supreme Court in political controversies. Thus he argued in *Colegrove v. Green* (1946) that the Court should not hear legislative reapportionment cases. Although his view prevailed in *Colegrove v. Green*, the Supreme Court later reversed itself in *Baker v. Carr* (1962) to establish the "one person, one vote" rule. Frankfurter's passionate dissent in *Baker v. Carr* was the last important opinion he prepared. Soon thereafter he suffered a stroke, and he resigned when it became clear that his recovery was insufficient to permit him to continue to work. He died in Washington, D.C., three years later.

Bibliography

Baker, Liva. *Felix Frankfurter*. New York: Coward-McCann, 1969.

Hirsch, H. N. *The Enigma of Felix Frankfurter*. New York: Basic Books, 1981.

Hockett, Jeffrey D. *New Deal Justice: The Constitutional Jurisprudence of Hugo L. Black, Felix Frankfurter, and Robert H. Jackson*. Lanham, Md.: Rowan & Littlefield, 1996.

Urofsky, Melvin I. *Felix Frankfurter: Judicial Restraint and Individual Liberties*. Boston: Twayne, 1991.

Robert Jacobs

Malcolm Fraser

Born: May 21, 1930; Melbourne, Victoria, Australia

Prime minister of Australia (1975-1983)

John Malcolm Fraser (JON MAL-kuhm FRAY-zur) was educated at Melbourne Church of England Grammar School and Oxford University before becoming a grazier (sheep rancher). He entered Australian politics in 1955 when he became the Liberal Party member for the electorate of Wannon in the House of Representatives. In 1956 he married Tamara "Tamie" Beggs.

Political Career

Fraser held various posts under a succession of Liberal prime ministers, starting with Robert Gordon Menzies. In 1971 he took a prominent

Malcolm Fraser *(Express Newspapers/Archive Photos)*

role in the dispute within the Liberal Party that led to John Gorton's resignation and his replacement by William McMahon as party leader and prime minister. McMahon subsequently lost the 1972 federal election to Gough Whitlam, the leader of the Australian Labor Party, and was replaced by his deputy, Billy Snedden. Whitlam defeated Snedden in an early election in 1974, and Fraser became leader of the Liberal Party in 1975.

In late 1975, the Whitlam government still controlled the lower house of federal Parliament, the House of Representatives, but the opposition, led by Fraser, had obtained effective control of the Senate. A deadlock was reached when the Senate refused to pass the appropriation bills to provide finance for the federal budget. The crisis was resolved, controversially, when the governor-general, Sir John Kerr, dismissed the Whitlam government on November 11. Fraser was made caretaker prime minister pending an election. Fraser's Liberal Party and National Country Party (later called the National Party) coalition easily won the election on December 13, 1975, and Fraser won further elections in 1977 and 1980.

Defeat and Retirement

The Australian economy experienced growth under Fraser's prime ministership, but it went into recession in 1982 after an explosion in wages. Despite the recession, many observers believed that Bill Hayden, the Labor leader, could not win an election against Fraser. Labor's best chance seemed to be with Bob Hawke, a charismatic front-bench parliamentarian and former president of the Australian Council of Trade Unions. On February 3, 1983, Fraser called an election for March 5, but not before Hayden suddenly resigned in favor of Hawke. Hawke campaigned

Australian prime minister Malcolm Fraser (left) on a visit to the White House in 1976. To the right of Fraser is U.S. president Gerald R. Ford. *(Archive Photos)*

with the key idea of a need to build consensus in the Australian community in order to overcome the nation's social and economic problems. He won the election by a comfortable majority. After this defeat, Fraser resigned as leader and left the Parliament.

After his resignation from Parliament, Fraser continued to be a force in Australian and international politics. He worked to end apartheid in South Africa and has been vocal on a number of political issues, especially as a high-profile opponent of racism.

The Liberal and National Parties

In the Australian political system, the Liberal Party of Australia and the National Party of Australia are allied to form a single front against the more left-wing Australian Labor Party (ALP). The Liberal Party was created in 1945. (A different party of the same name had existed from 1913 to 1917). It is oriented toward business and usually has moderately conservative policies. The National Party mainly represents rural interests. It was created in 1920 as the Australian Country Party but changed its name to National Country Party in 1975 and then to National Party of Australia in 1982. When the coalition is in power, ministers are chosen from both parties. The Liberal Party leader becomes prime minister, while the leader of the National Party becomes deputy prime minister.

A Controversial Figure

Fraser was the most successful Liberal Party politician since Sir Robert Menzies, and he was possibly the only conservative-leaning politician of his time who was a match for Gough Whitlam in parliamentary debate. As prime minister he aroused strong feelings because he originally came to power by engineering a constitutional crisis rather than by winning an election. Even though he went on to success in three elections, some observers argue that Fraser was nonetheless weakened by a question mark concerning the legitimacy of his government. He is often criticized for failing to make structural reforms to the Australian economy of the kind that were introduced by the Hawke government in the mid-1980's.

Bibliography

Ayres, Philip. *Malcolm Fraser: A Biography*. Melbourne, Australia: Heinemann, 1987.

Kelly, Paul. *November 1975: The Inside Story of Australia's Greatest Political Crisis*. Sydney: Allen & Unwin, 1995.

Renouf, Alan. *Malcolm Fraser and Australian Foreign Policy*. Sydney: Australian Professional Publications, 1986.

Summers, Anne. *Gamble for Power: How Bob Hawke Beat Malcolm Fraser: The 1983 Federal Election*. Melbourne, Australia: Nelson, 1983.

Weller, Patrick. *Malcolm Fraser PM: A Study in Prime Ministerial Power*. Melbourne, Australia: Penguin, 1989.

Russell Blackford

Hedy Fry

Born: 1941; Trinidad

Canadian political figure, named secretary of state for multiculturalism and the status of women (1996)

Hedy Fry (HEH-dee FRI), a member of the Liberal Party of Canada and a cabinet minister in the government of Jean Chrétien, was born on Trinidad, a small Caribbean island. Fry would eventually marry and have three sons. Pressure from her political life eventually contributed to the breakup of her marriage. Fry took a feminist approach to politics; this approach, she said, reflected in particular the influences of a grandmother and a group of Irish nuns who had taught her in Trinidad.

A Medical Career

Fry chose medicine as her initial career path, obtaining her medical degree from the Royal College of Surgeons in Dublin, Ireland. She moved to Canada and began a lucrative medical practice in the early 1970's. She practiced for twenty-two years in the Vancouver, British Columbia, area. Her medical career included involvement with significant committee work. In 1977 she became president of the British Columbia Federation of Medical Women. Later in the 1980's she became a member of a committee that prepared a brief to a special commission examining issues related to reproductive technologies.

Entering Politics

The Liberal Party warmly welcomed her in the early 1990's when she indicated an interest in running for the Parliament in the next federal election. She had attained some local prominence and was a woman in an occupation still dominated by males. Fry became one of several rising-star Liberal candidates whom party leader Chrétien appointed to represent the party. (Normally, the nomination would have to have been obtained through an election involving local party members.) The Vancouver riding (district) that Fry chose to seek was not an easy one: It was represented by Kim Campbell, then the prime minister of Canada. During the 1993 election campaign, however, Campbell's popularity plummeted, aiding Fry in becoming the first woman ever to defeat a sitting prime minister in an election.

Parliament

Because of her part in the Liberals' significant victory in the elections, media commentators assumed that Fry would be appointed to Chrétien's first cabinet, perhaps even in the important position of minister of health. Other events, however, interceded to prevent the expected move. Nota-

Hedy Fry *(Courtesy of the office of Hedy Fry)*

The Canadian Medical Association

Founded in 1867, the Canadian Medical Association (CMA) is a voluntary organization that represents medical practitioners in Canada. By the late 1990's, the organization's membership was more than forty-three thousand. Included within the CMA's ranks are a number of subsidiary organizations. Hedy Fry, a future Liberal cabinet minister, headed two of these: the Vancouver Medical Association from 1988 to 1989 and the British Columbia Medical Association from 1990 to 1991. From 1992 to 1993 Fry also headed the Canadian Medical Association's Multiculturalism Committee, a body charged with studying issues relevant to practitioners of health in an increasingly varied nation, both racially and ethnically. Fry's involvement in the health field led some to speculate that she might be appointed minister of health after her party's election win in 1993. Fry, however, received a reprimand from the British Columbia College of Physicians and Surgeons over a prescription. She reached the cabinet three years later as secretary of state for multiculturalism and the status of women.

bly, Fry received a public reprimand from the British Columbia College of Physicians and Surgeons for changing a person's name on a prescription. Instead of serving in the cabinet, Fry spent her initial parliamentary period outside the main corridors of power. She participated in committee work along with other members of Parliament. She served on a special committee to recommend reforms to social security and on a permanent committee on health. In 1995 she spoke at an international women's gathering in Beijing, China, and made a name for herself when she publicly criticized American actress Jane Fonda for promoting an unhealthy level of thinness among women.

Cabinet Minister

In a cabinet shuffle in 1996, Chrétien appointed Fry to a junior cabinet position as secretary of state for multiculturalism and the status of women. Essentially, her position reflected her life experience. She became the first woman of color to occupy the post. During her time in the cabinet, which continued after she was reelected in the 1997 federal election, Fry angered both her supporters and critics. To some, her feminist views were too radical. To others, she was not doing enough to promote her views around the cabinet table. Feminist groups were especially critical of her, because they faced cutbacks in government funding.

Bibliography

Greenspon, Edward, and Anthony Wilson-Smith. *Double Vision: The Inside Story of the Liberals in Power*. Toronto: Doubleday Canada, 1996.

Martin, Lawrence. *Chrétien: Volume 1, the Will to Win*. Toronto: Lester Publishing, 1995.

McLaughlin, David. *Poisoned Chalice: The Last Campaign of the Progressive Conservative Party?* Toronto: Dundurn Press, 1994.

Steve Hewitt

Alberto Fujimori

Born: July 28, 1938; Lima, Peru

President of Peru (took office 1990)

Alberto Fujimori (ahl-BEHR-toh few-jih-MOH-ree), the son of Japanese immigrants to Peru, began his public career as an educator. He pursued agriculture and environmental studies in France and the United States. Following graduation he began teaching at the National Agrarian University in Lima, rising to the position of rector at that institution.

He soon began hosting a program on a local television channel in Lima entitled *Getting Together*, which addressed the contemporary problems facing the country. The exposure led him to enter politics, for in the decade of the 1980's Peru was suffering under disastrous conditions, both politically and economically. The incumbent president, leftist Alan García, had unsuccessfully attempted to create an economy independent of foreign investment and to nationalize the country's banking system. In 1990 the country's inflation rate had reached a staggering annual figure of 8,000 percent.

The 1990 Election

Fujimori decided to make a bid for the country's presidency, although he was a political novice. He founded a movement called Change 90 and promised to revitalize the economy and control the terrorism that had become endemic in the country. Opposing him was a coalition of traditional leftist parties and, on the right, the internationally famous author Mario Vargas Llosa. Although Vargas Llosa was expected to win, he failed to secure the necessary majority vote and was forced into a runoff election. Fujimori had come in a surprising second and proceeded to defeat Vargas Llosa in the ensuing election. The voting public had become increasingly skeptical of the system of politics as usual and turned instead to the political neophyte, Fujimori. He

became president of Peru on July 28, 1990.

The new chief executive immediately implemented a series of political and economic changes designed to curb Peru's runaway inflation, control illegal drug manufacture, and open the country's economy to privatization. Moreover, in a massive reorganization of the country's bureaucratic structure, he dismissed more than seven hundred judges and demoted or discharged hundreds of police and military officers for corruption and fraud.

Alberto Fujimori at a press conference shortly after winning the Peruvian presidency in June, 1990. *(Reuters/ Anibal Solimano/Archive Photos)*

Peruvian soldiers helping hostages escape from the Japanese ambassador's residence in Lima in 1997. *(AP/Wide World Photos)*

Fujimori Assumes Greater Powers

Fujimori encountered stiff resistance from the old-line politicians in Peru's congress. On April 6, 1992, he decided to dissolve that body, to suspend the constitution, and to impose censorship on the press. The Peruvian military establishment supported the president in this unilateral action. Utilizing more direct political and eco-

nomic control, Fujimori was able to put an end to hyperinflation and encourage an upswing in the economy.

The Shining Path

A terrorist group known as the Shining Path, organized in the southern Peruvian Andes and led by a former academic, Abimael Guzmán from Ayacucho, had plunged Peru into a virtual civil war by the early 1990's. The group used kidnappings and assassinations to eliminate their political enemies. Fujimori gave the Peruvian army a free hand in combating the Shining Path. The army finally succeeded in capturing Guzmán and his top subordinates on September 12, 1992, breaking the back of the movement and generally restoring peace to the country. Guzmán and his subordinates were tried by a military court and sentenced to life imprisonment under close confinement.

The 1995 Election

Fujimori's political opposition accused him of disrupting the country's democratic process, and he turned to the people for support in the presi-

Change 90

Alberto Fujimori adopted this name for his grass-roots political campaign to capture the presidency of Peru in 1990. His movement lacked professional staffing and advisers. Fujimori made a series of promises: to reduce runaway inflation, to create new jobs, to control the illegal drug traffic, and to regain the confidence of foreign investors. Although his campaign did not provide the specifics for the implementation of these goals, the voters, tired of the promises

of the traditional office seekers, backed this political novice and elected him to the presidency. Once in office, Fujimori developed a plan of action that first addressed the country's most critical problems, inflation and criminal activity. In the financial field, he had the technical assistance of a foremost Peruvian economist, Hernando de Soto. By the end of his first term in office, Fujimori had started Peru on the road to political and economic recovery.

The 1997 Hostage Crisis

On December 17, 1996, a fourteen-person team, members of the radical Túpac Amaru Revolutionary Movement (MRTA), seized the Japanese embassy in Lima during a holiday reception held by the Japanese government for prominent Peruvian and foreign dignitaries. Their goal was the release of approximately 430 members of the MRTA being held in prison by the Peruvian government. The MRTA had established a reputation for terrorism and wholesale killings. Once gaining control of the embassy, the heavily armed guerrillas released most of the guests attending the function but retained seventy-two high-ranking foreign and Peruvian private and public officials, including President Alberto Fujimori's brother.

For 126 days, Fujimori negotiated with the terrorists, seeking to reach some compromise on the prisoner issue. Meanwhile the Peruvian army began the construction of a tunnel under the embassy in a plan to recapture the building. On April 22, the army crashed through the first floor of the embassy from the tunnel below. At the same time, another highly trained task force broke into the building from the outside.

Surprised by the emergence of the heavily armed military unit from the tunnel beneath the first-floor ballroom, the terrorists fled to the second floor and sought to regroup. There they were met by the task force that killed all the MRTA hostage holders. All but one of the hostages were rescued. The hostage was killed, as was one army officer, during the ensuing firefight. Despite the ruthless extermination of the terrorists, Fujimori received acclaim throughout Peru as well as general approval outside the country for the successful operation.

dential election of 1995. The voters endorsed his program by returning him to office with 65 percent of the popular vote. His defeated opponent was a former secretary-general of the United Nations, the venerable Javier Pérez de Cuéllar.

Peru's economy improved in the 1990's. The national debt was reduced, and foreign investment was attracted to the country once more. Fujimori could count on the continued support of the army, the World Bank, foreign investors, and the

Three South American presidents meeting in September, 1998, to resolve a long-standing border dispute between Peru and Ecuador. From left to right, Jamil Mahuad of Ecuador, Fernando Henrique Cardoso of Brazil, and Alberto Fujimori of Peru. *(AP/Wide World Photos)*

general Peruvian population, which benefited from his programs of spending on a variety of public works designed to increase employment.

Bibliography

Méndez, Juan E. *A Certain Passivity: Failure to Curb Human Rights in Peru.* New York: America's Watch Committee, 1987.

Palmer, David S., ed. *The Shining Path of Peru.* New York: St. Martin's Press, 1992.

Poole, Deborah. *A Time of Fear.* London: Latin American Bureau, 1992.

Stern, Peter A. *Sendero Luminoso.* Albuquerque: University of New Mexico Press, 1995.

Vargas Llosa, Alvaro. *The Madness of Things Peruvian: Democracy Under Siege.* New Brunswick, Conn.: Transaction, 1994.

Carl Henry Marcoux

J. William Fulbright

Born: April 9, 1905; Sumner, Missouri
Died: February 9, 1995; Washington, D.C.

Longtime U.S. senator (1945-1974)

James William Fulbright (JAYMZ WIHL-yuhm FUHL-brit) was raised in the family of a prosperous, self-made Arkansas businessman. In 1925 he graduated from the University of Arkansas, Fayetteville. An outstanding student and athlete, he received a Rhodes Scholarship to Oxford University in England, graduating there in 1928. Fulbright studied law at George Washington University, in the District of Columbia, and received his law degree in 1934. Two years earlier he married Elizabeth Kremer Williams, with whom he had two daughters.

Early Career

Fulbright became an attorney with the Department of Justice in 1934, but the following year he accepted a position teaching law at George Washington University. In 1936 he accepted a position at the Law School of the University of Arkansas and returned to Fayetteville, where he could also take care of the business interests of his family. Because of his political connections, in 1939 he was elected president of the University of Arkansas, becoming the youngest university president of the time. For the same political reasons, however, he was removed from the presidency two years later.

He overcame this humiliating setback in 1942, when he successfully ran for Congress as a Democrat from the third district of Arkansas. He distinguished himself as a young congressman with the Fulbright Resolution, proposing creation of an international organization to support world peace.

Senator

Fulbright was elected to the Senate in 1944, and he served for almost thirty years. The following year he supported legislation to charter the United Nations and introduced a bill to finance the scholarships in international education that would come eventually to bear his name. From 1955 to 1959 he was chairman of the Senate Committee on Banking and Currency. He was chairman of the Senate Committee on Foreign Relations from 1959 to 1974. In the latter position he formulated some of his most famous internationalist positions. He advised President John F. Kennedy not to invade Cuba in 1961. He opposed President Lyndon B. Johnson in 1965 regarding

J. William Fulbright *(Library of Congress)*

533

Senator J. William Fulbright speaking to reporters in front of the Supreme Court building in August, 1958. Fulbright had filed a "friend of the court" brief in *Aaron v. Cooper*, urging the Court to allow Arkansas to delay integration of Little Rock schools for two and a half years. *(AP/Wide World Photos)*

The Fulbright Scholarships

In 1945 Senator Fulbright proposed legislation that was approved by President Harry S Truman the following year as the Fulbright Act. It established scholarships for American scholars, professors, and graduate students to study and do research abroad and for foreign scholars and students to come to the United States. The program was expanded by the Fulbright-Hayes Act of 1961. Nearly a quarter of a million individuals had participated in this program by the end of the twentieth century. The scholarships are budgeted principally through the U.S. Informa-

tion Agency, although there is also a smaller program through the Department of Education. Administration of the program occurs principally through the Council for the International Exchange of Scholars, the Institute for International Exchange, and binational Fulbright commissions or foundations in more than one hundred countries. The presidentially appointed Board of Foreign Scholarships has broad policy and supervisory responsibility for the program. There is also a Fulbright Alumni Association for those who have participated in the program.

the invasion of the Dominican Republic, arguing that the United States was exaggerating the threat of communist influence.

Initially he supported President Johnson in the buildup of American forces in Vietnam after attacks on U.S. destroyers in the Gulf of Tonkin in 1964. These attacks led to the Gulf of Tonkin Resolution, escalating the war. Learning later that several of the assumptions for that resolution were unfounded, Fulbright became one of the most vehement and influential opponents of the war. He argued that the military buildup in Vietnam represented an "arrogance of power" (the title of a book he

President Bill Clinton congratulating his mentor, J. William Fulbright, at Fulbright's eighty-eighth birthday celebration in 1993. *(Reuters/Gary A. Cameron/ Archive Photos)*

published in 1966). He maintained that only a negotiated settlement would end the conflict in Vietnam. During 1966 future President Bill Clinton worked as a mail clerk in the office of Senator Fulbright.

Throughout the Cold War Fulbright supported détente with the Soviet Union. He had a stellar record as a liberal politician and supported the Senate's censure of Senator Joseph McCarthy in 1954. However, as a southern politician bent on his political survival, he opposed or gave only listless support to civil rights legislation. Fulbright's political career ended in 1974 with a surprise upset by his opponent in the Democratic primary for his Senate renomination. Retired from the Senate, he became a lawyer in Washington, D.C., and engaged extensively in writing and giving lectures. Just before his death he was honored by President Clinton with the Medal of Freedom.

Bibliography

Brown, Eugene. *J. William Fulbright: Advice and Dissent*. Iowa City: University of Iowa Press, 1985.

Powell, Lee Riley. *J. William Fulbright and His Time: A Political Biography*. Memphis, Tenn.: Guild Bindery Press, 1996.

Woods, Randall Bennett. *Fulbright: A Biography*. Cambridge, England: Cambridge University Press, 1995.

Edward A. Riedinger

Indira Gandhi

Born: November 19, 1917; Allahabad, India
Died: October 31, 1984; New Delhi, India

Prime minister of India (1966-1977, 1980-1984)

Indira Gandhi (ihn-DEE-rah GAHN-dee), born Indira Priyadarshini Nehru, was the daughter of Jawaharlal Nehru, the first prime minister of independent India. She studied at Oxford University and in 1942 married Feroze Gandhi, a journalist, who died in 1960. They had two children in the 1940's. After serving as India's minister of information between 1964 and 1966, she ran for leadership of the ruling Congress Party and became India's first woman prime minister in 1966. Except for a period between 1977 and 1980, she was India's prime minister from 1966 to 1984.

Indira Gandhi *(Library of Congress)*

Economic Initiatives

Gandhi's first priority in office was to make India independent in food production in order to combat widespread poverty and hunger. She sought to utilize both internal and external sources to develop India's economy. The government of the United States provided India with a $100 million loan following Gandhi's appeal for economic aid. India also received a promise of approximately $133 million from France, Italy, the United Kingdom, and the Netherlands, and a credit of $330 million from the Soviet Union. The dynamic energy of her various domestic and international initiatives caused some alarm among conservative and radical Indian politicians alike. However, she reiterated that her policy goals were essentially those of her father: "socialism, secularism, and democracy."

Party Politics

The Congress Party, which had guided India through its long independence movement, was weakened by political disruptions in many areas and lost public support in the 1967 elections. A combination of external pressures and internal strife led to a factional breakup of the party in November, 1969. Earlier, in July of that year, Gandhi had nationalized the largest banks in India as part of a strategy of economic reform. She was formally expelled from the Congress Party, an action she declared to be illegal. Allying with left-wing groups who supported her socioeconomic policies, Gandhi formed her own party and was successful in the 1971 elections. The New Congress Party, as it was called, won approximately 327 seats. It was also resoundingly successful in provincial elections in the following year, winning fourteen of sixteen states.

War with Pakistan

When the British had left India in 1947, they divided the subcontinent into India and Pakistan. Pakistan itself was split into two sections—one to the east, the other to the west of India. Human rights violations and genocide by West Pakistan against the ethnically different residents of East Pakistan led to a huge flow of refugees from East Pakistan into eastern India. They sought safety and sanctuary, mainly in West Bengal. India's slender economic resources were considerably strained by the huge increase in the population of the region. Diplomatic relations with Pakistan were strained as well, and the two nations went to war in 1971. In about two weeks, Indian forces were deci-

Indian prime minister Indira Gandhi in 1971 at India-Iraq talks. At right is Saddam Hussein, at the time the vice president of Iraq. *(Archive Photos)*

sively victorious and took ninety-three thousand Pakistani troops prisoner. East Pakistan was formally declared independent and renamed Bangladesh with its own sovereign government.

The State of Emergency in India, 1975-1977

In June, 1975, Indira Gandhi was found by the Allahabad High Court to have committed electoral malpractices during the 1971 campaign and was barred from public office for six years. Refusing to resign, Gandhi used the Maintenance of Security Act to arrest hundreds of her political opponents, requested the president to declare a state of emergency (June 26, 1975), and imposed press censorship (a first in independent India). She committed serious human rights violations and implemented an economic program to decrease inflation, increase employment, and encourage manufacturing. Parliament approved the emergency, and the Supreme Court of India overturned the Allahabad Court's rul-

ing. Gandhi called for elections in March, 1977. A volatile campaign resulted in defeat for Indira Gandhi and her party. The Janata came to power with Prime Minister Morarji Desai heading a coalition that immediately dismantled and revoked the emergency. The emergency demonstrated that the world's most populous democracy could suddenly be converted by an elected leader into a dictatorship—and could just as suddenly return to democratic systems. The vulnerability of democracy in 1975 resulted in a stronger, more articulate Indian press and public opinion, both strongly committed to the survival of freedom and civil rights in modern India.

The 1984 Assault on the Golden Temple

The Sikh religious community, centered in Punjab, India, follows the spiritual teachings of Guru Nanak (1469-1538). The Golden Temple in Amritsar is one of the most sacred places of worship for this religion, which emphasizes brotherhood and community. During the 1980's, Sikh militants agitated, at times violently, for a separate homeland, to be called Khalistan. Under leader Bhindranwale, they converted the Golden Temple into an armed camp. This challenge to Indian authority resulted in the storming of the temple by Indian armed forces in June, 1984. Numerous militants were killed, and Sikhs vehemently protested the army action. Possibly in retaliation for having ordered the attack on the temple, Sikh members of Indira Gandhi's personal bodyguard assassinated Gandhi on October 31, 1984.

Technology

Leading a developing nation, Gandhi's government was committed to the expansion of India's electrical supply through the use of nuclear power plants. India also exploded an underground nuclear device on May 18, 1974, making India the world's sixth nuclear nation. In April, 1975, in cooperation with the Soviet Union, India became the eleventh nation to put a satellite in outer space.

State of Emergency

Droughts in 1973-1974 and the global oil crisis of 1973 caused serious economic setbacks for Indira Gandhi's reform program. Some Congress-led provincial governments were publicly accused of corruption. Opposition to the Gandhi government had coalesced by 1975 in the form of the Janata Front. In June of 1975, a judge ruled that, because of abuses during the 1971 elections, Gandhi had to give up her seat in Parliament and remain out of politics for six years. Gandhi refused. She declared a state of emergency, which lasted until early 1977, creating a political and constitutional crisis. Human rights violations during this period resulted in disillusionment with her government, and in the 1977 elections Gandhi lost not only the prime minister-

Indira Gandhi attending a concert at the Royal Festival Hall, London, with Britain's Prince Charles and prime minister Margaret Thatcher in 1982. *(Express Newspapers/Archive Photos)*

ship but also her own seat in Parliament. She was denounced across India for having subverted the country's democratic systems by declaring the state of emergency.

The Janata came to power under the prime ministership of Morarji Desai, who immediately revoked the state of emergency. Gandhi managed to win a by-election in 1978, and she returned to Parliament to lead the official opposition. The government was badly divided, and the Janata was unable to govern effectively. The inability of the Janata to rally parliamentary support forced a call for new elections in January, 1980. Gandhi returned with a strong parliamentary majority, although her party, now named Congress (I), took only 42 percent of the popular vote. In June, 1980, Gandhi's politically influential son and heir apparent Sanjay Gandhi was killed in an air crash. His older brother, Rajiv, assumed the family responsibility and easily won his brother's parliamentary seat.

Gandhi's Second Term

Communal and religious problems in the Punjab and Assam regions dominated Indira Gandhi's second term in office. Violence between religious and ethnic groups was increasing in many parts of India. In the summer of 1984 her government confronted militant Sikhs directly by attacking a Sikh shrine and stronghold, the Golden Temple. This assault is thought to be a major reason why Sikh members of her personal bodyguard assassinated her a few months later, on October 31, 1984. Rajiv Gandhi succeeded her as prime minister.

Bibliography

Bhatia, Krishan. *Indira: A Biography of Prime Minister Gandhi*. New York: Praeger, 1974.

Jaykar, Pupul. *Indira Gandhi: A Biography*. New York: Viking, 1993.

Malhotra, Inder. *Indira Gandhi: A Personal and Political Biography*. Boston: Northeastern University Press, 1991.

Ranee K. L. Panjabi

Mahatma Gandhi

Born: October 2, 1869; Porbandar, Gujarat, India
Died: January 30, 1948; New Delhi, India

Leader of Indian independence movement, pacifist, and president of Indian National Congress (1925-1934)

Mohandas Karamchand Gandhi (MOH-hahn-dahs KUH-rahm-chuhnd GAHN-dee), known throughout the world as Mahatma (mah-HAHT-mah) Gandhi, was the son of the prime minister of the small principality of Porbandar. "Mahatma" is not a name but an Indian term for a person of great wisdom and selflessness—a "great soul." Mohandas Gandhi was married at thirteen to a girl of the same age, Kasturba Makanji, the illiterate daughter of a merchant. The marriage lasted sixty-two years and produced three surviving sons, Devadas, Harilal, and Manilal. In 1888 Gandhi went to England to study law. He returned to India in 1891, and then moved to South Africa in 1893 as a consultant for a Muslim ship-owning and trading company owned by the Dada Abdulla family.

Beginnings of Leadership

Gandhi became a political leader soon after becoming a victim in three violent and humiliating racial incidents following his arrival in South Africa. (Indians in South Africa were required by law to be deferential to Europeans.) In 1894 the legislature of the Natal region of South Africa sought to pass the Franchise Amendment Bill, denying Indians the right to own property or vote despite their payment of an annual additional tax. Gandhi exerted pressure on the secretary of state for the colonies, Joseph Chamberlain, and the British government in London. This pressure resulted in a law that established voting rights for all British subjects.

Imperial colonialism prompted Gandhi to develop a philosophy of self-reliance to help Indians in South Africa raise their self-esteem and resist injustice. Gandhi himself served as doctor in his own home. He insisted that his family and staff had to share household tasks, including menial ones that were, in Indian society, the traditional jobs of Untouchables (*harijans*). He refused to send his sons to local schools where the medium of instruction was English. Nevertheless, during the Boer War in 1899, Gandhi, a pacifist who believed that loyalty to empire would result in political dividends for Indians, established an ambulance corps of stretcher bearers and hospital workers. He won a medal for services at the Battle of Spion Kop.

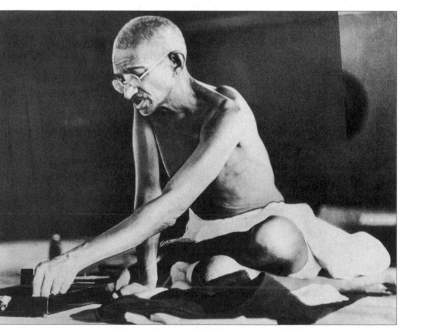

Mahatma (Mohandas) Gandhi. *(Archive Photos)*

540

Reform in South Africa

In South Africa Gandhi founded and edited the weekly magazine *Indian Opinion*, printed in three languages, to educate Indians about politics. He and his staff lived in tents and practiced self-reliance on a ninety-acre farm outside Durban. This community was the forerunner of similar centers, or *ashrams*, in South Africa and India. Inspired by nineteenth-century American writer Henry David Thoreau's essay "Civil Disobedience," Gandhi developed a method of nonviolent *satyagraha* (truth-force or firmness in truth). The success of this method helped him soften the Asiatic Registration Bill, or Black Act, though he was jailed in the struggle. His compromise produced the Indian Relief Bill, which recognized all Hindu and Muslim marriages and removed unfair taxes.

Mahatma Gandhi in 1925, using a spinning wheel; Gandhi urged Indians to produce their own cloth rather than wear machine-made clothing. *(Library of Congress)*

Working Toward Indian Independence

Gandhi returned to India in 1914. His first Indian *satyagraha* was effected in 1916 in the cause of indigo farmers in Champaran. The first time he used fasting for a public cause was in 1918, when he won a pay increase for exploited textile workers. The spinning wheel (*charkha*) for producing *khadi*, or coarse cotton fabric, became his symbol for indigenous identity through cottage industries. In 1919 six thousand unarmed peasants were massacred in Jallianwala Bagh, Amrit-

---

The Zulu Rebellion

The trouble that became known as the Zulu Rebellion started in Natal (a part of South Africa) in 1906 when the Zulu chief urged nonpayment of a tax imposed upon his people by the British. The disturbance worsened when he speared the British officer who had come to collect the tax. Mahatma Gandhi, although he sympathized with the Zulus, thought that he should not oppose the British, whose empire, he believed, existed for the welfare of the world. Accordingly, he formed an Indian Ambulance Corps that assisted the wounded on both sides of the conflict. His role lasted for six weeks, and it entailed the breakup of his household at Johannesburg and difficult marches by him and his ambulance corps. In addition to preparing and dispensing prescriptions to wounded white soldiers, Gandhi attended to Zulus wounded either in battle or as tortured political prisoners.

Satyagraha

Mahatma Gandhi developed the idea of *satyagraha* (which has been variously translated as truth-force, soul-force, or firmness in truth) to resolve conflicts—whether between Indian nationalists and the British Raj, between peasants and landlords, or between husbands and wives. *Satyagraha* challenges the assumption that in any conflict there must be winners and losers. For Gandhi the point was to achieve harmony. He believed that even an adversary must be trusted, because distrust is a sign of weakness and will not foster cooperation.

Satyagraha first appeals to reason but ultimately appeals to the heart. Rather than being a doctrine of mass action, it is a personal creed. The *satyagrahi* wants nothing beyond the illumination of love and truth. Gandhi first used *satyagraha* in Natal (in South Africa) in 1913 to effect a compromise between cane planters and their Indian laborers. He then employed it in a dispute between Indian employees and the Durban municipality. His greatest *satyagraha* movements, however, were in India in the cause of independence.

Mahatma Gandhi (center) toward the end of his life, after Britain had agreed to Indian independence on the condition that India be partitioned into two countries. *(Library of Congress)*

sar, by troops under Brigadier General Reginald Dyer. This unconscionable violence ended Gandhi's faith in Britain. Gandhi returned his medals from the Boer War and Zulu Rebellion, burned piles of European clothing to symbolize an end to tyranny, and called for a nationwide strike in order to bring the colonial government to a standstill and to lead to Indian home rule.

Master of Gestures

Dressed in a simple loincloth (*dhoti*) and sandals, Gandhi managed to turn his passive resistance and civil disobedience into moral and political victories. After he led the Dandi salt march of 1930, in defiance of the British monopoly on salt production, he was imprisoned yet again. With the achievement of the Gandhi-Irwin Pact in 1931, he called off nonviolent protests in exchange for the release of all *satyagrahis*—nonviolent protesters—from jail. The British arranged for a Round Table Conference in London to include Hindus, Muslims, Christians, Indian princes, and landowners, with Gandhi representing the Indian National Congress.

Gandhi met with King George V, famous scholars and leaders at Oxford and Cambridge Universities, and unemployed English mill workers in Lancashire—who cheered him on despite his being the cause of their unemployment. However, the conference itself failed, and in India Gandhi quickly found himself back in prison in protest against the English plan for a separate electorate for Untouchables. Such a policy, he believed, would defeat home rule.

Partition and Martyrdom

After retiring from Congress in 1934, Gandhi remained in touch with Indian leaders Jawaharlal Nehru and Vallabhai Patel. He based himself in an *ashram* in Wardha, accepted new disciples (even from the West), and sent a "Quit India" resolution to Congress, calling for Britain's immediate withdrawal. Imprisoned once again, he was released only after his wife's death and the deterioration of his own health.

By 1944 the British had agreed to independence on the condition that India would be partitioned into two new states: Viceroy Louis Mountbatten would oversee the establishment of an independent Muslim state (Pakistan), headed by Mohammed Ali Jinnah. Partition led to racial violence and atrocities. Gandhi, accepting responsibility for the situation, began a fast that ended only after a Hindu-Muslim peace pact was signed. The agreement was signed less than two weeks before Gandhi was assassinated by Nathuram Godse, a member of a militant Hindu group.

Gandhi's death led to the waning of religious violence in India and Pakistan, though it did not unite Hindus and Muslims. However, Gandhi's influence reached far beyond India's borders. His philosophy of nonviolence influenced human rights leaders in the West, including Martin Luther King, Jr.

Bibliography

Easwaran, Eknath. *Gandhi the Man: The Story of His Transformation*. Tomales, Calif.: Nilgiri Press, 1997.

Gandhi, Mohandas K. *An Autobiography: The Story of My Experiments with Truth*. Translated by Mahadev Desai. London: Jonathan Cape, 1966.

Gold, Gerald. *Gandhi: A Pictorial Biography*. New York: Newmarket Press, 1983.

Parekh, Bhiku. *Gandhi*. New York: Oxford University Press, 1997.

Severance, John B. *Gandhi: Great Soul*. New York: Clarion Books, 1997.

Keith Garebian

Rajiv Gandhi

Born: August 20, 1944; Bombay, India
Died: May 21, 1991; Sriperumbudur, Tamil Nadu, India

Prime minister of India (1984-1989)

Rajiv Ratna Gandhi (rah-ZHEEV RAHT-nah GAHN-dee) was the eldest son of Indira Gandhi, who was prime minister of India from 1966 to 1977 and again between 1980 and 1984. His grandfather was Jawaharlal Nehru, India's first prime minister (1947-1964). Rajiv was educated at India's most exclusive school, Doon School at Dehra Dun. He then went to England to study at Trinity College, Cambridge University (1963-1964), and at the Imperial and Scientific College of the University of London (1964-1968). He did not receive a degree from either university. While he was at Cambridge he met a young Italian woman, Sonia Maino, who had gone to Cambridge to study English. They were married on February 25, 1968. They had a son, Rahul (b. 1970), and a daughter, Priyanka (b. 1972). Gandhi showed little interest in politics but loved flying and joined Indian Airlines in 1968. He was a commercial pilot in India from 1972 to 1981.

Entry into Politics

Gandhi's younger brother, Sanjay Gandhi, was a rising political star, but he was killed while flying his own plane in 1980. Consequently, Rajiv resigned from Indian Airlines and joined his mother in politics. He inherited his brother's constituency, Amethi, in Uttar Pradesh, in north India. He was elected to India's lower house, the Lok Sabha, in 1981; in 1983 he became a general secretary of the Congress (I) Party.

Prime Minister of India

On October 31, 1984, shortly after the assassination of his mother by her Sikh bodyguards, Rajiv Gandhi became prime minister of India. Indians admired his modesty and the fact that he seemed to represent a break with the old corrupt politics. This situation did not last long, however, and his prime ministership is often described as "ill-starred." He emphasized technology as the means to modernize India, and he favored economic liberalization. He encouraged foreign investment and began to abolish the system for granting industrial licenses. In December, 1984, he was reelected with the largest margin in Indian history (83.67 percent), but his luck soon began to change. On December 3, 1984, an accident occurred at a pesticide factory owned by an

Indian prime minister Rajiv Gandhi discussing problems in Sri Lanka at a 1989 press conference in New Delhi. *(Reuters/Archive Photos)*

544

Indian subsidiary of Union Carbide in Bhopal, Madhya Pradesh. A large quantity of poison gas was released into the air, killing four thousand people and poisoning another twenty thousand.

Political Troubles

From 1985, Gandhi came under increased criticism from older politicians who resented the younger people he had brought into the govenment. He seemed to do everything in a hurry, without consulting the older politicians, including the president of India, Zail Singh. Singh eventually accused Gandhi of acting in an unconstitutional manner. He was also being challenged by his sister-in-law, Maneka, the widow of his younger brother, who claimed leadership of the Nehru dynasty.

Political Downfall

In 1987 scandals erupted that were to dog Gandhi for the next two years and to earn his

Rajiv Gandhi at the 1987 Commonwealth Conference in Vancouver, Canada, speaking with President Desmond Hoyte of Guyana. *(Reuters/ Andy Clark/Archive Photos)*

government a reputation for corruption. V. P. Singh, the minister of defense, opened an inquiry into reported kickbacks from the Swedish company Bofors to Gandhi's friends. This and other scandals caused the press increasingly to accuse

Jammu and Kashmir

When the British left India in August, 1947, they partitioned it into the sovereign nations of India and Pakistan. Pakistan was a state created for the Muslim population. The various states of India had to choose which country to join. The ruler of Jammu and Kashmir chose India even though more than 90 percent of the people living there were Muslim. India and Pakistan have fought two wars directly over Kashmir since 1947. By the 1980's, Muslims in Kashmir were in open rebellion, and a secessionist movement had developed. Pakistan assisted this movement, but the policies of Indira Gandhi and Rajiv Gandhi, who increasingly centralized power in India, were the major cause of Muslim hatred for the Indian government. Farooq Abdulla was elected chief minister of the state in 1983, but the following year he was ousted from power, and Indian troops were sent in to keep the peace. Guerrilla warfare there became more widespread. Only the existence of some 300,000 Indian military personnel kept an uneasy peace in Kashmir, where between twelve thousand and twenty thousand people have been killed.

The 1987 Sikh Rebellion

In 1984 the prime minister of India, Indira Gandhi, ordered troops to invade the Golden Temple in Amritsar, the Sikhs' holiest shrine, to clear it of terrorists. Apparently as a result of the anger this engendered, she was assassinated by her Sikh bodyguards in 1984. This act led to anti-Sikh riots in India in which thousands of people were killed. In July, 1985, the new prime minister, Rajiv Gandhi, signed an agreement with the Sikh leader Sant Longowal in order to reduce tensions in the Sikh-dominated Punjab region. However, Longowal was assassinated in his own village, and the government did not live up to its promises. (Among them were to make Chandigarh the capital of the Punjab and to grant Sikhs some of their demands, such as increasing their representation in the Indian army.) Violence returned as the Sikhs, some of whom wanted to separate from India, created a state of virtual civil war in the Punjab in 1987. The split among the Sikhs, with those Sikhs who had been trying to cooperate with the central government coming under increased criticism, and the inability of the Punjab government to maintain law and order, caused the Indian government to dismiss the Punjab government and impose president's rule in May of 1987.

the government of being corrupt, and Gandhi's popularity plummeted. Singh was forced to resign in April of 1987, and he quickly became Gandhi's leading opponent.

In the summer of 1987 the monsoon failed, and India suffered one of the worst droughts in one hundred years, causing severe economic and personal hardship. In the by-elections of 1987, Gandhi's party, Congress (I), suffered defeat in a number of provinces. Gandhi did have some success in international affairs, including participation in 1985 in the birth of the South Asian Association for Regional Cooperation, but his intervention in Sri Lanka was to be his downfall.

Sri Lanka was divided between the Sinhalese and Tamils. Some of the Tamils had organized themselves into a militant, separatist group, the Liberation Tigers. They armed themselves and, by the mid-1980s a civil war was raging on the northeast part of the island. As a result, Gandhi insisted on sending Indian troops into Sri Lanka to defeat the Tamils in 1987. Although Indian troops remained there until 1990, the mission failed, and violence continued. As a result of his failed economic policies, the scandals, and continued violence in the Punjab and other Indian provinces, especially Kashmir, Gandhi had become so unpopular that he lost the prime ministership in the general elections of November 29, 1989.

Assassination

In March, 1991, Gandhi refused to support the prime minister Chandra Shekhar, forcing general elections to be held in May. Public opinion polls indicated that Gandhi's party would return to power. During the campaign he flew to Madras and then drove to Sriperumbudur, in the countryside. There he and twenty other people were assassinated by a Tamil woman with a bomb; she was a member of a Tamil Tiger team of terrorists.

Bibliography

Merchant, Minhaz. *Rajiv Gandhi: The End of a Dream*. New Delhi: Viking, 1991.
Nugent, Nicholas. *Rajiv Gandhi: Son of a Dynasty*. London: BBC Books, 1990.

Roger D. Long

Alfonso García Robles

Born: March 20, 1911; Zamora, Michoacán, Mexico
Died: September 2, 1991; Mexico City, Mexico

Mexican diplomat, winner of 1982 Nobel Peace Prize

Alfonso García Robles (ahl-FOHN-soh gahr-THEE-ah ROH-blays) became one of Mexico's greatest diplomats. He was possibly the best educated member of the Mexican political elite. His particular concern became disarmament and world peace. García Robles completed many tasks for the United Nations and developed a long association with the United States.

Early Years

Born in the state of Michoacán during the bloody years of Mexico's revolution and civil war from 1911 to 1920, García Robles finished his secondary and preparatory studies in Guadalajara before initiating law studies at the Universidad Autónoma de México from 1931 to 1933. He also received a diploma from the International Law Academy at The Hague in 1938. A particularly impressive accomplishment was obtaining his law degree from the University of Paris and serving on its faculty. Finally, García Robles completed graduate studies at the National Law School in Mexico's national university.

A career foreign officer, García Robles became a member of the Mexican delegation to Sweden from 1939 to 1941. During World War II, he served as the director-general of political affairs and the diplomatic service with the Ministry of Foreign Affairs from 1941 to 1946. Here he argued strongly for Mexico to forge an alliance with the United States against the Axis powers. After World War II, García Robles represented Mexico to the United Nations from 1946 to 1957. As if to symbolize Mexico's growing world presence, he also served as director of the Political Affairs Division of the United Nations at the same time he represented Mexico.

García Robles returned to Mexico in 1957 to serve as head of the Department of International Organizations and as director in chief of the European, Asian, and African Department in the Ministry of Foreign Relations. He handled both of these assignments from 1957 to 1961. Then he was named Mexico's ambassador to Brazil from 1962 to 1964. During that period, García Robles sympathized strongly with the populist regime of João Goulart and protested the military takeover of Brazil that began in 1964.

Alfonso García Robles *(The Nobel Foundation)*

547

Alfonso García Robles addressing the U.N. General Assembly in 1976. *(AP/Wide World Photos)*

Success and Strategy

García Robles's diplomatic career blossomed from 1964 to 1970. Officially, he was the subsecretary of foreign relations during these years, but

his major accomplishment was the 1967 Treaty for the Denuclearization of Latin America, known as the Treaty of Tlatelolco. It was a diplomatic masterstroke because it involved the much-publicized defense of disarmament without assuming any political risk. The treaty, which included many protocols to be signed by the nuclear powers and by countries with colonies in the Americas, attempted to keep nuclear weapons out of Latin America. It was never ratified by Argentina and Brazil, the only nations in the area suspected of having nuclear ambitions. However, it permitted Mexico to embrace the cause of nuclear disarmament. Later it earned García Robles a share—along with Swedish disarmament advocate Alva Myrdal—of the 1982 Nobel Peace Prize.

García Robles's strategy at this time was to make occasional appearances on the international and regional diplomatic stages and then withdraw to the reality of Mexico's internal development and its relations with the United States. This approach suited Mexican president Gustavo Díaz Ordaz, who exhibited no interest in traveling to Europe and instead met many times with U.S. presidents Lyndon B.

García Robles and Disarmament

The possibility of nuclear warfare horrified Alfonso García Robles, as it did statesmen everywhere. In 1967 he concluded a successful treaty prohibiting the deployment of nuclear weapons in Latin America. During the Cuban Missile Crisis of 1962, U.S. president John F. Kennedy had impressed García Robles by agreeing to take down U.S. missile sites in Turkey if the Soviet Union would remove its atomic missiles from Cuba. Because of the serious danger caused by the Soviets having put their nuclear

forces on full alert during the Cuban Missile Crisis, however, García Robles determined to have all Latin American nations agree to forbid the development of nuclear weapons throughout the region. Only Brazil and Argentina refused to sign the resulting Treaty of Tlatelolco. Partially for that reason, García Robles insisted successfully that Mexico devote its diplomatic emphasis away from South America. He predicted correctly that Brazil and Argentina would follow their nuclear ambitions secretly.

Johnson and Richard M. Nixon. In Latin America, Mexico's profile was low, and many South American governments felt little identification with Mexico. Despite the importance of maintaining an independent foreign policy as a counterweight to its economic dependency upon the United States, Mexico paid less attention to the rest of the world than to the United States.

Final Years

García Robles returned to the United Nations to serve as ambassador from Mexico from 1971 to 1974. The author of twenty books and more than three hundred articles, García Robles became recognized as a learned authority upon foreign relations and international law. As a testimony to his influence within political circles, García Robles was appointed a member of the Institute of Economic, Political, and Social Studies of the government's political party, the Insti-

tutional Revolutionary Party, in 1972. In Mexico, he culminated his professional career in 1975 as secretary of foreign relations until 1976. Abroad once more, García Robles served as head of the Mexican delegation to the U.N. Committee on Disarmament from 1976 to 1982 before a final term from 1982 to 1988.

Bibliography

Grayson, George W. *Oil and Mexican Foreign Policy*. Pittsburgh, Pa.: University of Pittsburgh Press, 1988.

Purcell, Susan Kaufman. *Mexico in Transition: Implications for U.S. Policy*. New York: Council on Foreign Relations, 1988.

Riding, Alan. *Distant Neighbors*. New York: Knopf, 1985.

Smith, Peter. *Mexico: The Quest for a U.S. Policy*. New York: Foreign Policy Association, 1980.

Douglas W. Richmond

Marcus Garvey

Born: August 17, 1887; St. Ann's Bay, Jamaica
Died: June 10, 1940; London, England

U.S. black nationalist leader, founder of Universal Negro Improvement Association (UNIA)

The son of a bricklayer, Marcus Mosiah Garvey (MAHR-kuhs moh-ZI-ah GAHR-vee) was raised among the black peasantry of St. Ann's Bay, Jamaica, and educated at the local Church of England school. Though later in his life he became a Roman Catholic, he was baptized into the Wesleyan Methodist church. He left school in his early teens to work as a printer's apprentice, first in his hometown and later in Jamaica's capital city, Kingston. There he became involved in the organizing work of the International Typographical Union. He also began to print his own political pamphlets and to enter local elocution contests, modeling the style of his speeches on the sermons he had heard preached. The early skills he developed as a writer, printer, organizer, and speaker were all later well utilized in his career of political activism.

Marcus Garvey *(Library of Congress)*

Universal Negro Improvement Association

In his early twenties, Garvey spent a few years living and working in Central America and Great Britain. In London he took college courses and met West Indian and African intellectuals who were supporters of Pan-Africanism and opponents of colonialism. When Garvey returned home to Jamaica, he set about founding a benevolent association based on the uplift or self-help principles and separatist policies exemplified by Booker T. Washington's Tuskegee Institute in Tuskegee, Alabama. He and his girlfriend, Amy Ashwood, founded the Universal Negro Improvement Association (UNIA) in Kingston in 1914.

Hoping to found a technical school for blacks in Jamaica under UNIA auspices, Garvey traveled to the United States in 1916 in order to raise money for the plan. Introduced to African American and West Indian radical intellectuals in New York City, he decided to remain there. He reformulated the UNIA as a nationalist Harlem-based organization in 1917-1918. He began publication of the UNIA's newspaper, *Negro World*, in August of 1918. Garvey served as editor of the paper and printed his race-conscious editorials on its front page. The paper eventually featured special pages reporting on the news of local UNIA divisions, a women's page, and sections in French and Spanish.

Garvey's first marriage to Amy Ashwood Garvey ended in divorce in June, 1922. His second marriage, in July, 1922, was to another fellow Jamaican and UNIA activist, Amy Jacques Garvey. A skilled manager, speaker, editor, and writer, Amy Jacques Garvey emerged as an important leader in the Garvey movement in her own right. Her book *Garvey and Garveyism* (1963) is the primary memoir of the movement. She and Marcus Garvey had two sons.

Political Repression

The UNIA quickly gained in popularity, reaching its heyday by 1924. West Indian migrants and African Americans alike responded to its "race first" black nationalist platform, its radical anti-colonial stance, and its program of economic uplift. The fervor with which Garvey gained support soon drew him to the attention of federal and colonial officials, and from 1919 onward the Garvey movement was subjected to steady political repression. *Negro World* was banned as seditious in many regions of the world under colonial rule, and Garvey and his activities were placed under close surveillance in the United States. In 1922 Garvey was arrested on mail-fraud charges stemming from the sale of stock in the Black Star Line, a steamship company. Brought to trial in 1923, he was convicted. After the failure of an appeal, he was imprisoned at the Atlanta Federal Penitentiary in February, 1923. President Calvin Coolidge pardoned him in November of 1927, but Garvey was subjected to immediate deportation. He never returned to the United States.

After Deportation

Following his release from prison, Garvey reestablished a political career in Jamaica. He operated a new headquarters and mass meeting place for the UNIA in Kingston and hosted international conventions there. He ran for local political office under the umbrella of the People's Political Party, which he founded, and he published the *Blackman* newspaper. In 1934 he moved the UNIA headquarters to London, where he lived for the rest of his life. He spoke regularly in Hyde Park on issues of African independence and published a journal, the *Black Man*. He traveled to Toronto, Canada, for UNIA conventions in the summers of 1937 and 1938, where he inaugurated the African School of Philosophy, a workshop and mail-order course designed to train UNIA organizers.

Garvey died of a cerebral hemorrhage just as World War II was in its beginning phases. He was in many ways a man before his time, whose ideas reached fruition long after his passing. Although he never personally set foot on African soil, he

The Universal Negro Improvement Association (UNIA)

Marcus Garvey founded the Universal Negro Improvement Association (UNIA) in Kingston, Jamaica, in 1914 as a self-help organization. The organization was reformulated as a black nationalist organization in New York in 1917-1918. Fueled by post-World War I "New Negro" radicalism, the UNIA held weekly mass meetings at Liberty Hall. Its business wing, the African Communities League, developed black enterprises, including the Negro Factories Corporation, which founded small businesses in New York, and the Black Star Line. The UNIA sponsored juvenile divisions, and its auxiliaries included the Black Cross Nurses, the Universal African Legions, and a motor corps.

The UNIA boasted several hundred local chapters by the early 1920's. Although it was strongest in the industrialized cities of the Northeast and Midwest, it had grassroots support throughout the United States, as well as in Africa and the Caribbean. Annual international conventions held in New York drew hundreds of delegates, and high-profile UNIA parades were mounted through the city streets. The UNIA was hampered from without by surveillance and repression, and from within by discord and factionalization. Support for the UNIA waned with the deportation of Marcus Garvey in 1927, but local chapters continued to exist into the 1940's and beyond. Centralized leadership shifted from New York and London to Cleveland and Philadelphia after Garvey's death in 1940.

The Black Star Line

The UNIA's Black Star Line shipping company was incorporated in 1919. Operated out of UNIA headquarters in New York, it went bankrupt and was dissolved among the legal difficulties surrounding Marcus Garvey's arrest in 1922. The line was plagued by economic, labor, and repair problems throughout its short-lived existence. It nevertheless served as a powerful propaganda tool for the UNIA. Important as a black-owned and black-operated enterprise, its main ship was used for trade between the Caribbean and New York. Although plans to expand into a transatlantic passenger line linking New York and Liberia never transpired, the Black Star Line was used to bring members into the UNIA. It became an enduring symbol of the UNIA's Back to Africa program. It was succeeded by a second UNIA shipping enterprise, the Black Cross Navigation and Trading Company, which existed between 1924 and 1927. Both shipping lines were used successfully by the UNIA to spread the word about the organization and to carry organizers to the Caribbean and Central American ports, where they founded new UNIA chapters or helped to strengthen those already in existence.

Marcus Garvey in the ceremonial uniform he wore at many United Negro Improvement Association functions. (*Archive Photos*)

was a strong inspiration to leaders of African independence movements. His ideas of black pride and self-sufficiency gained renewed popular appreciation in the cultural and political environments of the 1960's. He was declared Jamaica's first national hero in 1964. His remains are interred at the Marcus Garvey Memorial in Kingston.

Bibliography

Clarke, John Henrik, ed. *Marcus Garvey and the Vision of Africa*. New York: Vintage, 1974.

Garvey, Marcus. *Philosophy and Opinions of Marcus Garvey*. Compiled by Amy Jacques Garvey. 2 vols. 1923. Reprint. New York: Atheneum, 1986.

Lewis, Rupert. *Marcus Garvey: Anti-Colonial Champion*. London: Karia, 1987.

Lewis, Rupert, and Patrick Bryan, eds. *Garvey: His Work and Impact*. Rev. ed. Trenton, N.J.: Africa World Press, 1991.

Martin, Tony. *Race First*. Westport, Conn.: Greenwood Press, 1976.

Stein, Judith. *The World of Marcus Garvey*. Baton Rouge: University of Louisiana Press, 1986.

Barbara Bair

Charles de Gaulle

Born: November 22, 1890; Lille, France
Died: November 9, 1970; Colombey-les-Deux-Eglises, France

French military and political leader, president of France (1958-1969)

Charles André Joseph Marie de Gaulle (CHAHRL ahn-DRAY zhoh-SEHF mah-REE deh GOHL) was born into a professional noble family with a long and distinguished tradition of service to the French state. He inherited from his father, Henri, his love for history. His passionate nature was inherited from his mother, Jeanne. De Gaulle graduated from the French military academy of Saint-Cyr and served with distinction in World War I before being wounded and captured by the Germans at the Battle of Verdun (1916). He was hailed by his commander, Marshal Philippe Pétain, as "in all respects an officer without equal." Following the war he lectured and wrote on military affairs, achieving distinction as an expert on mechanized armored warfare. In 1922 he married Yvonne Vendroux; they had three children, Geneviève, Anne, and Philippe.

Scholar and Soldier

After World War I, de Gaulle was sent to Poland as a trainer of Polish army officers. On his return to France in 1921, he taught military history at Saint-Cyr. In 1924, he published his first book, *Discord Among the Enemy*, analyzing the reasons for Germany's defeat in 1918. Also in 1924 he graduated with distinction from the War College. Following a brief stint at Mainz, in 1925, Captain de Gaulle joined the staff of Marshal Pétain, vice president of the Supreme Defense Council. He began writing a book under Pétain's supervision in 1927 (published as *France and Its Army* in 1938). He was promoted in the fall of 1927 and assumed command of the Nineteenth Light Infantry Battalion at Trier in Germany. In 1929 he was posted to Beirut to serve in the Army of the Levant. Upon his return to Paris in 1931, de Gaulle served at the Secretariat of the Supreme

Defense Council and shortly afterward published *The Edge of the Sword*, which was an expanded version of his 1927 lectures on leadership delivered at the War College. This book delineated his personal image of a successful military leader, who was primarily a "man of character" commanding people's loyalty.

During 1933 and 1934 de Gaulle's critique of French military strategies and his own military ideas took shape. In *Toward the Professional Army* he presented a powerful case for mechanized warfare. His ideas found support from a handful

Charles de Gaulle *(Library of Congress)*

Free French troops in North Africa in 1942. *(Library of Congress)*

promoted to the rank of brigadier general. He was given command of the Fourth Armored Division, which acquitted itself creditably in the Battle of Montcornet (1940).

Political Career

As early as 1939, de Gaulle had conceived of a "second war," a war to be waged from what he called the "vital space" of the French Empire. After Germany occupied France in June of 1940, he positioned himself to play an active role in this second war. With remarkable audacity and speed, he procured aid from the Allies, chiefly the British. He launched his Free French movement, which sought to incorporate the French imperial territories and to weld the French resistance movement into a massive force to protect the sovereign

of readers, most notably Paul Reynaud, a Radical member of the Chamber of Deputies. Reynaud argued for an armored striking force in 1935. World War II broke out in 1939. On March 21, 1940, Renaud became prime minister of France, and on May 24 of that year Colonel de Gaulle was

The Free French Movement

The Free French movement, composed of French exiles in England, was launched in London by Charles de Gaulle on June 18, 1940. The purpose was to wage a military struggle against the German army in France—the German army had been in France since June 10, 1940—and a political struggle against the French collaborationist regime at Vichy, formed on July 3. The Free French operated under the command of de Gaulle, who had identified himself with France. His aims was to liberate his country and have its rights recognized by the Allied powers. The British prime minister, Winston Churchill, recognized and supported this movement. In London

De Gaulle succeeded in forming the Council for the Defense of the Empire on October 27 and, on September 22, 1941, the French National Committee.

The Free French integrated the underground resistance movement in France by organizing the National Resistance Council and the French Forces of the Interior in 1943. It also rallied the French colonies in Africa and Asia under its banner and successfully aided the Allied forces in Africa against the Italians and the Germans. After the Allied landing on D day (June 6, 1944) in Normandy, De Gaulle became the president of the provisional government of liberated France.

The Fall of the Fourth Republic

The Fourth Republic of France, created on October 13, 1946, fell for a variety of reasons. The Republic lacked strong leadership. Charles de Gaulle, the most imposing figure in French government, had resigned as president of the provisional government in January, 1946. (De Gaulle was opposed to the Fourth Republic's parliamentary system.) There was a critical lack of decision making, as the three ruling parties (the Christian Democrats, the Socialists, and the Communists) caused *immobilisme*, or postpon-

ment of political decisions. There was also a nationalist revolution in the French African colony of Algeria, where native Algerians and the French colonials were struggling for power. The colonials revolted against their own government on May 13, 1958, and de Gaulle was invited to assume leadership of France on June 1. Two days later the National Assembly authorized his government to revise the constitution. The Fourth Republic was replaced by the Fifth Republic on October 4, 1958.

integrity of France. De Gaulle succeeded in his efforts.

After the liberation of France at the end of the war, the reconstruction of the French polity

proved to be an uphill battle for the general. His vision of a united and orderly republican France ran counter to French political tradition since the French Revolution in the eighteenth century—

French president Charles de Gaulle meeting with U.S. president Richard M. Nixon during a state visit in 1969, the last year of de Gaulle's presidency. *(Library of Congress)*

and more recently since the establishment of the Third Republic. De Gaulle resigned his position as the head of the provisional government on January 20, 1946, and remained politically quiescent throughout the period of the Fourth Republic (1946-1958). He returned to power in June, 1958, in the midst of the crisis stemming from a nationalist revolt in French Algeria, a French colony in Africa.

De Gaulle became president of the Fifth Republic on December 21, 1958. Though the Fifth Republic has been criticized by politicians, polemicists, and historians—a famous French historian called it a "hidden monarchy"—it was based on de Gaulle's overriding concern for unity, which he equated with national strength. He successfully extricated France from the Algerian quagmire by the Évian Accord in the spring of 1961, confirmed by the referendum of April, 1962.

The 1960's

De Gaulle preferred presidentialism to parliamentarianism. Therefore, through a referendum in 1962, he had the constitution amended to call for election of the president by direct universal suffrage. Presidentialism produced benefits for France: stability, prosperity, and a leadership role in Europe. Though the middle years of the 1960's were the Gaullist golden years, the president's halcyon days were coming to an end.

The events of May-June, 1968, starting with the student revolt of May 3 and rapidly escalating into a massive student-worker revolution coupled with the resurgence of the communists, presented a serious challenge. De Gaulle managed to survive it, largely because of his remarkable charisma. He was, however, nearing eighty and was tired and uneasy about his political future. De Gaulle resigned his presidency on April 28, 1969. In November, 1970, he died in isolation at Colombey in the midst of writing his memoirs. Until the end of his life he remained what he had declared himself to be many years ago: "a free Frenchman" who believed "in God" and "in the future of [his] fatherland."

Bibliography
Cogan, Charles G. *Charles de Gaulle: A Brief Biography with Documents*. Boston: Bedford Books, 1996.

Gough, Hugh, and John Home, eds. *De Gaulle and Twentieth Century France*. London: Edward Arnold, 1994.

Johnson, Douglas. "The Political Principles of General de Gaulle." *International Affairs* 41, 1965: 650-662.

Lacouture, Jean. *De Gaulle*. 2 vols. Translated by Patrick O'Brian (vol. 1) and Alan Sheridan (vol. 2). New York: Simon and Schuster, 1991-1992.

Shennan, Andrew. *De Gaulle*. London: Longman, 1993.

Narasingha P. Sil

George V

Born: June 3, 1865; Marlborough House, London, England
Died: January 20, 1936; Sandringham, Norfolk, England

King of Great Britain and Ireland (1910-1936)

Prince George Frederick Ernest Albert (JOHRJ FREH-duh-rihk UR-nehst AL-burt) was the younger son of Albert Edward, Prince of Wales, and Princess Alexandra of Denmark. Because he was not in direct line for the throne, George was allowed to choose a naval career. On January 14, 1892, his elder brother, Albert Victor, duke of Clarence, died of pneumonia. Prince George therefore became heir presumptive, second in the succession after his father. He was created duke of York on May 24, 1892. On July 6, 1893, he married his distant cousin, Princess Mary of Teck, who had originally been betrothed to his late brother. His grandmother, Queen Victoria, died on January 22, 1901, and his father became King Edward VII. Shortly thereafter Prince George was made prince of Wales. Nine years later, on May 6, 1910, following King Edward's unexpected death from heart failure, he ascended the throne as George V (JOHRJ thuh FIHFTH).

The Constitutional Crisis

Shortly after his succession, George V was required to mediate a crisis between the House of Commons and the House of Lords. To finance their program of social reform during the last years of the reign of Edward VII, the Liberal ministry sought to reform the tax system. Their efforts were eventually successful, but only after a bitter struggle with the House of Lords. Determined to avoid future confrontations, the Liberal majority in Parliament intended to reduce the power of the peers. This revision of the British constitution was opposed by the Conservatives until they learned that George V supported the changes and that he was willing to create enough Liberal peers to pass the measure. The king had schooled himself in the duties of a constitutional monarch from the time that he became heir apparent. Because parliamentary reform had the support of the people, it had the patronage of George V.

World War I

No sooner had George V weathered the crisis in Parliament then he was forced to deal with a series of problems ranging from the loss of the RMS *Titanic* in 1912 to the renewed militancy of the British women suffragists to the stormy passage of an Irish home rule bill, which was to take

George V *(Library of Congress)*

557

Because Prince George was not directly in line for the British throne, he was able to embark on a naval career as a young man. *(Library of Congress)*

effect in September, 1914. World War I, which erupted suddenly in August, 1914, changed forever the course of the history of Great Britain as well as the personal life of George V. His first cousin, William II of Germany, became his enemy, and another cousin, Nicholas II of Russia, would perish with his entire family before the war ended in November of 1918. George V and Queen

George V and World War I

When Great Britain entered World War I on August 4, 1914, the wave of patriotic fervor that swept across the nation was accompanied by an anti-German hysteria which often resulted in violence. George V refused to condone such behavior, and throughout the conflict he advocated a sensible approach to the treatment of enemy aliens and conscientious objectors.

Throughout the war, George V visited allied troops in the field with little regard for his personal safety. On October 28, 1915, while reviewing a unit of the Royal Flying Corps, he was thrown from a horse and seriously injured. Once he was fully recovered he resumed his duties with enthusiasm. Often with Queen Mary, he visited the wounded, bringing comfort to them and their families. King George did not shield his family from the risks of the conflict; his two eldest sons, Edward, Prince of Wales, and Prince Albert, later George VI, both saw action during the war. George V kept himself informed of every aspect of the war. Throughout the conflict he was able to provide sensible counsel to his ministers as the struggle against the Central Powers moved to a successful conclusion on November 11, 1918.

The British Navy

In the late nineteenth century, British naval superiority was challenged by technological innovations in the design of warships. Launched in 1906, H.M.S. *Dreadnought* was the prototype of the new ironclad vessel, and during the next decade Britain attempted to build four dreadnoughts a year to keep pace with Germany, which had initiated a similar naval building program. This rivalry was a contributing factor to their going to war with each other in 1914.

The British navy did not play a strategic role in World War I, which was primarily a land-based struggle. The failure of the Admiralty to coordinate operations with the General Staff led to total defeat in the Dardanelles campaign of 1915. In 1916, the results of the Battle of Jutland, the only major engagement between the British and German high-seas fleets during the war, were inconclusive. For the remainder of the war the British navy spent its energies protecting Allied shipping from attack by German submarines.

Mary never failed in their support of Britain's war effort, and the king visited the troops regularly. He actually suffered a severe injury while on such a tour in 1915, but he did not allow it to stop him from performing his duties. He felt deeply the sacrifices his people made for the war effort, and he worked with unfailing energy to ensure that postwar Britain would be a place worthy of heroes. In 1917 George V discarded his German surname, Saxe-Coburg Gotha, in favor of the name Windsor.

Postwar Britain

A generation of young men was slaughtered in the trenches of World War I, and the economy of Great Britain was crippled by the tremendous cost of the conflict. The bright future envisioned by George V faded before renewed violence in Ireland and seemingly endless labor unrest. In 1920 Ireland was divided into two states, but the civil war continued. Successive British governments formed by the Liberal, Labour, and Conservative

George V (left) with Russian czar Nicholas II. *(Library of Congress)*

Parties failed to solve the nation's problems, and in 1926 a general strike almost immobilized Britain. Throughout these troubled times, King George worked with each successive government, giving each prime minister his full support and always advising a cautious course of action. This unpretentious, sensible monarch who sought to do his duty as he saw it became for his people the symbol of everything that was good about Britain.

The Silver Jubilee

In the 1930's, Great Britain slowly began to recover from the most severe economic effects of the war in spite of the Great Depression that began with the collapse of the New York stock market in October, 1929. This global financial disaster accelerated a movement toward totalitarianism in a number of European nations, but British democracy seemed to grow stronger despite adversity. This was due in part to the faith of George V in the ability of his people to determine their own destiny. He maintained his unswerving devotion to the principles of constitutional monarchy, which set an example his subjects followed. In 1935, to celebrate the twenty-fifth anniversary of his reign, the British people honored King George with a Silver Jubilee. The aging monarch was almost overwhelmed with the outpouring of devotion shown him during the year. It was a fitting tribute to a remarkable man, and an appropriate climax to a successful reign. On January 20, 1936, after a brief illness, King George V died of heart failure.

Bibliography

Gore, John. *King George V: A Personal Memoir.* London: J. Murray, 1949.

Halperin, John. *Eminent Georgians: The Lives of King George V, Elizabeth Bowen, St. John Philby, and Nancy Astor.* New York: St. Martin's Press, 1995.

Nicolson, Harold. *King George the Fifth.* London: Constable, 1952.

Rose, Kenneth. *King George V.* London: Weidenfeld and Nicolson, 1984.

Sinclair, David. *Two Georges: The Making of the Modern Monarchy.* London: Hodder and Stoughton, 1988.

Clifton W. Potter, Jr.

George VI

Born: December 14, 1895; Sandringham, Norfolk, England
Died: February 6, 1952; Sandringham, Norfolk, England

King of Great Britain and Ireland (1936-1952)

On December 14, 1895, Prince Albert Frederick Arthur George (AL-burt FREH-duh-rihk AHR-thur JOHRJ), the second son of the duke and duchess of York, was born at Sandringham, the favorite residence of his grandfather, the prince of Wales. On the death of his great-grandmother, Queen Victoria, in January, 1901, his grandfather ascended the throne of Great Britain as Edward VII. Nine years later, on the death of King Edward on May 6, 1910, his father succeeded to the crown as George V. Because he was the second son, and thus not in the direct line of succession, Prince Albert was allowed to choose a naval career. In 1920 he was named duke of York, and three years later he married Lady Elizabeth Bowles-Lyon. In 1926 their daughter, Elizabeth, was born; four years later, she was joined by her sister, Margaret-Rose. The duke and duchess lived with their daughters far from the glare of publicity, but that peaceful existence ended with the death of George V in 1936.

The Abdication Crisis

On January 20, 1936, Edward VIII became king; less than a year later he went into exile. For months the king had been involved with a twice-divorced American woman, Wallis Warfield Simpson. His intention to marry her was strongly opposed by a number of clergymen and politicians. The majority of his subjects were unaware of the impending constitutional crisis because of a voluntary news blackout; thus the abdication of Edward VIII on December 11, 1936, came as a shock to many. Suddenly the duke of York, who treasured his privacy above all else, became George VI (JOHRJ thuh SIHKSTH), and his elder brother, now the duke of Windsor, left for France.

World War II

Immediately after he became king, George VI was briefed by his ministers on a crisis potentially far more serious than his brother's abdication. In March, 1936, Germany had violated the Treaty of Versailles (the treaty signed after Germany's defeat in World War I) by sending troops into the demilitarized Rhineland. Adolf Hitler was now threatening to take over his neighbors. Great Britain and France were unprepared for another major war. In March, 1938, they issued only mild protests when Nazi Germany seized Austria. In November, 1938, they bought a temporary peace by surrendering to the Germans that part of

George VI *(Library of Congress)*

George VI visiting British troops and observing exercises on the Thames during World War II. *(Library of Congress)*

Czechoslovakia known as the Sudetenland. George VI did not personally approve of the appeasement of Hitler, as this policy came to be called, but he was bound to support his ministers and their policies because they represented the will of the electorate.

After 1918 many Britons had longed for a return to an isolationist policy, and during the 1930's pacifism was very popular among the younger generation. The British government had actively supported the cause of disarmament, and now, on the eve of Hitler's seizure of the rest of Czechoslovakia in March of 1939, Britain was almost defenseless. On March 21, 1939, Hitler began to make territorial demands of Poland. At last convinced that the policy of appeasement was a failure, Britain and France announced their intention to defend the territorial integrity of Poland. Having signed a nonaggression pact with the Soviet Union in August, 1939, Hitler decided to test French and English resolve on September 1, 1939, when he invaded Poland. World War II had begun.

The early months of the war were relatively quiet, but in the early spring of 1940, Hitler unleased a full-scale invasion of most of Europe. As nations fell one by one to the German army, Prime Minister Neville Chamberlain resigned, and George VI was at last free to ask Winston Churchill to form a coalition government and be prime minister. The king believed that Churchill was the one man capable of leading Great Britain to ultimate victory. Churchill was a wise choice. From June, 1940, until the United States officially entered the war in Decem-

The Battle of Jutland

At the age of twenty, Prince Albert (George VI) saw action in the Battle of Jutland as a junior officer aboard HMS *Collingwood*. Early on the morning of May 31, 1916, the British Grand Fleet under Admiral Sir J. R. Jellicoe engaged the German High Seas Fleet under Admiral Reinhard Scheer in the largest sea battle in history. Having temporarily suspended unrestricted submarine warfare on Allied and neutral shipping, the German high command sought to cripple the British navy by trapping and destroying the British cruiser fleet that was patrolling the North Sea. Faulty recon-naissance by the Germans failed to discover that the main British fleet was also in the area, and the Germans almost were caught in the trap they had planned for the lightly armed cruisers.

More than 250 vessels of various sizes were involved in the battle, which left 6,097 British sailors dead. The Germans suffered 2,545 casualties. The British lost fifteen ships, and the Germans eleven. During the night the German fleet regained the safety of German waters. It never gave battle again, remaining at Wilhelmshaven until the end of the war.

Independence for India

Two years after World War II ended, another major event occurred during the reign of George VI: England granted independence to India, its last great colonial holding. During their years of controlling India, the British had provided their subjects with certain benefits that helped make independence feasible, even inevitable. The use of English as a second language allowed Indian leaders to transcend the maze of languages and dialects that divided their people. Technological advances such as the steam locomotive, the telegraph, and the radio helped to bind the various provinces and principalities together. By offering a first-class education to Indians of talent and ability, the British trained the men and women who would eventually win independence for the Indian people.

The British authorities in India had been able to quell violent disturbances and outbreaks of terrorism by using force, but they could not resist the campaign of nonviolence conducted by Mohandas K. (Mahatma) Gandhi. Early in 1947, Louis Mountbatten (Admiral Lord Mountbatten) was appointed viceroy of India and charged with the task of preparing India for independence. With speed and efficiency he accomplished his commission, and on August 15 the British Parliament approved the necessary legislation. To prevent further clashes between Hindus and Muslims, the British province of India was divided into two countries: India and Pakistan.

---

ber, 1941, Britain stood alone against the might of Germany.

Beginning in July, 1940, the German air force launched a relentless bombing campaign against Britain. Although German bombing of Britain—the "Blitz"—reduced much of London and other major cities to rubble, Germany ultimately lost the Battle of Britain. Hitler could not break the spirit of the British people. George VI and Queen Elizabeth were always there, climbing over the ruins to inspire and comfort the victims of the air raids. They were a constant inspiration to a nation under siege. Germany finally surrendered in May, 1945, and its ally, Japan, followed in September.

Postwar Britain

Although exhausted and already in failing health, George VI never stopped encouraging and inspiring his people in peacetime as he had done during the war. When the Labour Party won a stunning victory in 1945, George VI supported their policy of austerity as the best way to restore Britain's prosperity. The only bright moment in that dreary period in Britain's recovery was the marriage of Princess Elizabeth to Philip Mountbatten in November, 1947. Because George VI's health continued to deteriorate, the young couple assumed many of the duties that normally would have devolved upon the king. They were on a state visit to several Commonwealth countries when King George died in his sleep on February 6, 1952. As a man who saw his duty and did it, King George VI had helped to save his nation.

Bibliography

Bradford, Sarah. *The Reluctant King: The Life and Reign of George VI, 1895-1952*. New York: St. Martin's Press, 1990.

Howarth, Patrick. *George VI: A New Biography*. London: Hutchinson, 1987.

Judd, Denis. *King George VI, 1895-1952*. New York: Franklin Watts, 1983.

Sinclair, David. *Two Georges: The Making of the Modern Monarchy*. London: Hodder and Stoughton, 1988.

Wheeler-Bennett, John W. *King George VI: His Life and Reign*. New York: St. Martin's Press, 1965.

Clifton W. Potter, Jr.

John H. Glenn, Jr.

Born: July 18, 1921; Cambridge, Ohio

U.S. astronaut and senator (1974-1998)

John Herschel Glenn, Jr. (JON HUR-shuhl GLEHN JEW-nyur), was born to John H. and Clara Glenn. In 1943 he attended Muskingum College in New Concord, Ohio. That same year he married Anna Castor. They had a son Dave and daughter Lyn. By 1944 he had joined the U.S. Marine Corps and served in combat in the South Pacific.

Military Career

Glenn's twenty-three-year career in the Marine Corps started in the South Pacific during World War II. In 1943 he received two distinguished flying crosses (DFCs) and ten air medals. During the Korean War, he received five more DFCs and

John H. Glenn, Jr. *(Library of Congress)*

an air medal with eighteen clusters. After the Korean War, Glenn became a test pilot, and in 1957 he flew from Los Angeles to New York in the nation's first nonstop supersonic flight. He earned yet another DFC.

Astronaut

In his last six years as a Marine, Glenn was a Project Mercury astronaut. In 1959 he became one of seven volunteer astronauts in the "Man-in-Space" program. On February 20, 1962, Glenn made a three-orbit flight aboard the Mercury capsule *Friendship 7*. The flight lasted 4 hours and 56 minutes and covered a distance of 81,000 miles (130,000 kilometers) at an altitude of 160 miles (257 kilometers). As the first American to orbit the earth, he became a peacetime hero.

Politics

Glenn's first try at politics came at the age of forty-three, in a 1964 race for the Ohio Democratic U.S. Senate nomination. Glenn had to withdraw for health reasons. In 1966 Glenn became a vice president of Royal Crown Cola and president of Royal Crown Cola International. In 1970 Glenn ran again for the Democratic Senate nomination and was defeated in the Democratic primary. In 1974, at the age of fifty-three, Glenn won the Democratic U.S. senatorial primary in Ohio and was elected. It was his first elected office. Glenn viewed his public service in the office of the Senate as an extension of his earlier public service as a Marine and astronaut.

Entering national politics late in life, Glenn possessed experience that not many could match, yet at the same time, he lacked political expertise. He had to train himself in a new profession while still under the influence of his former profession. His name was synonymous with his former oc-

U.S. senator John Glenn at the 1998 news conference at which it was announced that he would become, at age seventy-seven, the oldest American to experience space flight. *(AP/Wide World Photos)*

cupation as astronaut, and, as a result, he faced a challenge in establishing his new identity—and his credibility—as a senator. He had emerged from his former career with certain personal traits, attitudes, values, and abilities firmly established. Some of these characteristics proved to be political strengths, some proved to be weaknesses. In 1984 Glenn sought the Democratic nomination for president. Glenn was regarded as the most serious challenge to former Vice President Walter F. Mondale, and he was thought by many to be the Democrat with the best chance of defeating President Reagan. Running a weak second in the first primaries of 1984, however, he withdrew from the race.

Glenn continued to serve in the Senate, maintaining a twenty-four-year political career. By 1998 he had decided to retire at the end of his term. Another interest had caught his attention, however. In 1995 he was a member of the Senate Special Committee on Aging, and he became interested in the similarity in the effects of aging and of space flight on the body. Over the next few years, he worked diligently and succeeded in turning this interest into an offer from NASA to become a crew member on a 1998 space shuttle flight. The flight occurred between October 29 and November 7, 1998. At seventy-seven, Glenn became the oldest person to have gone into space.

Bibliography

Cole, Michael D. *John Glenn, Astronaut and Senator*. Hillside, N.J.: Enslow, 1995.

Fenno, Richard F., Jr. *The Presidential Odyssey of John Glenn*. Washington, D.C.: CQ Press, 1990.

Van Riper, Frank. *Glenn: The Astronaut Who Would Be President*. New York: Empire, 1983.

David J. Dranchak

The Nuclear Nonproliferation Act

In 1977 Senator John Glenn was named to the Senate Foreign Relations Committee. Shortly thereafter, President Jimmy Carter signed into law a piece of legislation of which Glenn was the major author, sponsor, and strategist: the Nuclear Nonproliferation Act of 1978. It was designed to restrict the spread of nuclear material from peaceful to military uses. This act gained Glenn a reputation as a capable legislator on a nationally important subject. He was able to contribute in the area of arms control, thus affecting the outcome of the Strategic Arms Limitation Talks (SALT II) proposal. The time Glenn spent on the Foreign Relations Committee was well invested and boosted his standing as a senator.

Charles Albert Gobat

Born: May 21, 1843; Tramelan, Switzerland
Died: March, 16, 1914; Bern, Switzerland

Swiss public servant and peace activist, winner of 1902 Nobel Peace Prize

Charles Albert Gobat (CHAHRL al-BAYR goh-BAH) was born into an affluent clerical family. He studied widely, at the Universities of Basel, Heidelberg, Bern, and Paris, taking his doctorate summa cum laude at Heidelberg in 1867.

Lawyer, Lecturer, and Public Servant

Gobat entered private legal practice in Bern and lectured on law at the university. In 1882 he was appointed superintendent of public instruction for the Bern canton (state), a position he held for thirty years. He initiated revision of the Primary Education Act, improved teacher-student ratios, promoted the sciences and modern languages, and supported federal subsidies for vocational and technical schools.

Gobat was elected to the Grand Council of Bern, and in 1884 he became a member of the Swiss Council of States. From 1890 until his death, he was a member of the Swiss National Council. He also wrote a two-volume history of Switzerland, which was published in 1899 and earned him great acclaim.

An Avid Interparliamentarian

From the inception of the Interparliamentary Union in 1888, Gobat was an enthusiastic participant in this peace organization. In 1892 he presided over the union's annual conference in Bern. He secured the use of Switzerland's National Assembly chambers, establishing a tradition for conferences to come. Gobat became general secretary and director of the union's Interparliamentary Bureau, positions he held for two decades. His functions included facilitating communication among pacifist parliamentarians, arranging annual conferences, editing (and often writing) the union's monthly review, and promoting initiatives in member parliaments.

Gobat was a strong advocate of international arbitration. In 1899 the first Peace Conference at The Hague and the resulting conventions gave him hope for future peace initiatives. In 1902 Gobat spearheaded a new Swiss policy to submit any and all commercial treaty disputes to the Permanent Court of Arbitration. That same year, Gobat was named a corecipient of the Nobel Peace Prize. In 1904, at the Interparliamentary Union Conference in St. Louis, Gobat led a group that successfully petitioned U.S. president Theodore Roosevelt to convene the Second Hague Peace Conference.

Charles Albert Gobat *(Library of Congress)*

The Interparliamentary Union

In 1888 the English pacifist William Randall Cremer and the Frenchman Frederic Passy joined to establish the Interparliamentary Union. This organization was devoted to bringing together parliamentarians from the various nations of the world for the discussion and promotion of peace. For their work, Passy was awarded the Nobel Peace Prize in 1901, and Cremer was awarded the prize in 1903. At the union's 1892 session in Bern, Switzerland, where only twelve nations were represented, the union stressed expanding its membership. The Interparliamentary Bureau was established as an administrative office to support the activities of the annual meetings. The Interparliamentary Union was not without internal strife. Nationalist sympathies sometimes colored the debate, and the British parliamentarians opposed strong executive leadership in the organization. In 1909 the Interparliamentary Union moved its headquarters to Brussels, Belgium. The following year, it was awarded the Nobel Peace Prize for its work in bringing together statesmen in the cause of peace.

International Peace Bureau

In 1906 Gobat assumed leadership of the International Peace Bureau, an organization of independent peace societies and workers. Under Gobat, the bureau became more outspoken. When the Inter-Parliamentary Union moved its headquarters to Brussels in 1909, the Peace Bureau became Gobat's primary focus. Gobat tried to influence international dispute resolution. In 1911 he privately attempted to prevent Italy from going to war with Turkey. That same year, he published a book entitled *The Nightmare of Europe*, criticizing the 1871 Franco-German peace treaty over the regions of Alsace and Lorraine. Seeing the situation continue to deteriorate, Gobat arranged a meeting of French and German parliamentarians in Strasbourg in May of 1913. His concerns were justified: The following year World War I erupted across Europe. On March 16, 1914, Gobat collapsed while addressing a meeting of the Peace Bureau. He died within an hour.

Gobat was a fiery advocate for peace. He worked tirelessly, devoting all his spare time to pacifist exploits. He wrote extensively and lectured widely, inspiring many to join the peace movement. The organizations he helped to build became part of the foundation for international diplomacy in the twentieth century.

Bibliography

Abrams, Irwin. *The Nobel Peace Prize and the Laureates: An Illustrated Biographical History, 1901-1987.* Boston: G. K. Hall, 1978.

Cot, Jean Pierre. *International Conciliation.* Translated by R. Myers. London: Europa Publications, 1968.

Lipsky, Mortimer. *The Quest for Peace: The Story of the Nobel Award.* South Brunswick, N.J.: A. S. Barnes, 1966.

Simon, Werner. "The International Peace Bureau: Clerk, Mediator, or Guide?" In *Peace Movements and Political Cultures.* Edited by Charles Chatfield and Peter Van Dungen. Knoxville: University of Tennessee Press, 1988.

Barry Stewart Mann

Robert H. Goddard

Born: October 5, 1882; Worcester, Massachusetts
Died: August 10, 1945; Baltimore, Maryland

U.S. rocket-science pioneer

Robert Hutchings Goddard (RO-burt HUH-chihngz GO-durd) displayed an early interest in science as he grew up in Massachusetts. He received a B.S. from Worcester Polytechnique Institute in 1908 and M.S. and PhD degrees in physics from Clark University in 1910 and 1911, respectively. Teaching at Clark University and conducting rocket experiments consumed his early adult years. He conducted aeronautical research for the U.S. military during World War I and wed Esther Catherine Kisk, nineteen years his junior, in June, 1924.

Robert H. Goddard *(NASA)*

Rocket Research and Tests

Influenced by H. G. Wells's novel *The War of the Worlds*, Goddard dreamed of space travel throughout his life—which was filled with ongoing experiments to develop efficient high-altitude rockets. By 1914 he had received patents that covered broad principles such as using a combustion chamber with a nozzle to exhaust burning gases and the use of a multistage rocket. By 1917 his pioneering work brought him modest support from the Smithsonian Institution, especially for meteorological research. During World War I, Goddard demonstrated his primitive rockets to the U.S. Army. The Army's initial interest waned with the war's end.

The publication of *A Method of Reaching Extreme Altitudes* in 1919 under the auspices of the Smithsonian Institution brought Goddard fleeting fame as a "mad scientist" figure who dreamed of rockets to the moon. Goddard shunned such publicity and continued, rather secretly, to conduct tests on rockets. By 1921 he realized that liquid-fuel rockets were more feasible than solid-fuel systems for high-altitude travel and he focused on a gasoline-liquid oxygen fuel. In 1926, with a fuel-injection system of his design, Goddard produced a nose-driven device that provided more thrust than its own weight. On March 16 of that year, Goddard achieved a first: He launched a liquid-propelled rocket that traveled 41 feet (12.5 meters) in the air, settling 184 feet (56 meters) from its launch site. Continuing developmental work, he switched to tail-driven rockets and conducted a series of tests on these models.

Significant Support and Funding

This work intrigued Charles Lindbergh, whose visit to Goddard in 1929 resulted in Guggen-

A Method of Reaching Extreme Altitudes

Seeking funds to expand his early solid-fuel rocket experiments, Robert Goddard sent a report of his work to the Smithsonian Institution. In 1919, after working for two years with the Smithsonian's support, Goddard revised the report to include his tests with high-efficiency solid-fuel rockets. It was published that year by the Smithsonian as *A Method of Reaching Extreme Altitudes*. This small book contained Goddard's theory of rockets and many calculations based on his theoretical analyses and experimental trials. In a concluding section, Goddard theorized that a multistage rocket could achieve high-altitude flight and reach the moon. The press, focusing on the possibility of space travel, mocked Goddard as a mad scientist. This sensationalist reaction to Goddard's carefully crafted scientific work reinforced his desire for privacy and secrecy. However, the report was a seminal work on aeronautics and rockets; it made Goddard the spiritual leader of modern rocket science and technology.

heim Foundation funds for expanded rocket research. This support allowed Goddard to move from New England to Roswell, New Mexico, where he established a rocket-testing laboratory in 1930. For most of the next decade, he conducted a range of experiments, incrementally and painstakingly revising his rocket designs. He pioneered using a nozzle for thrust, demonstrating that a rocket would function in a vacuum, using liquid fuel, controlling a rocket with gyroscopes, using a multistage rocket, using deflector vanes for stabilization and guidance, and devising various rocket engines and pumps. Essentially, Goddard had invented nearly every piece of a workable space rocket.

The Lone Pioneer

Unfortunately, Goddard's interest in secrecy kept much of this technology from other American rocket scientists during his lifetime. During World War II Goddard again worked with the U.S. Army and Navy, focusing his efforts at the Naval Engineering Experiment Station from 1942 until his death in 1945. In 1961 the U S. government honored Goddard's pioneering rocket research by establishing the Goddard Space Flight Center in Maryland.

Robert H. Goddard posing with a rocket prototype. *(Library of Congress)*

Goddard, Robert H.

Bibliography

Emme, Eugene M., ed. *The History of Rocket Technology*. Detroit, Mich.: Wayne State University Press, 1964.

Lehman, Milton. *Robert H. Goddard: Pioneer of Space Research*. Reprint. New York: Da Capo Press, 1988.

Von Braun, Wernher, Frederick I. Ordway III, and Dave Dooling. *Space Travel: A History*. New York: Harper & Row, 1985.

Winter, Frank H. *Prelude to the Space Age*. Washington, D.C.: Smithsonian Institution Press, 1983.

H. J. Eisenman

Joseph Goebbels

Born: October 29, 1897; Rheydt, Germany
Died: May 1, 1945; Berlin, Germany

Nazi Germany's minister of propaganda (1933-1945)

Paul Joseph Goebbels (POWL YOH-sehf GOO-behlz) was the third of five children in a working-class Catholic family. A childhood illness, probably osteomyelitis, left Joseph with a shortened right leg, a club foot, and arrested physical development. The boy became a reader, idolizing historical and fictional heroes, but lonely in his own social life. These tendencies were reinforced by his rejection for military service in World War I.

The Young Nazi

Goebbels completed his doctorate at Heidelberg. Cultural liberalism, love affairs, and anti-bourgeois political views dominated his student days. Failing to gain employment as a writer for the mainstream press, Goebbels in 1924 approached local Nazi groups. He was a member of Gregor Strasser's northern branch of "socialist" Nazis until 1926, when Adolf Hitler picked him to be party leader (*Gauleiter*) for Berlin. As Berlin *Gauleiter*, Goebbels developed a corps of Nazi street fighters to combat the communists and a newspaper, *Der Angriff* (the attack), which was pro-Hitler and anti-Semitic.

Goebbels was elected to the Reichstag (the German parliament) in May, 1928, reflecting the Nazi Party's growth in Berlin despite the party's poor showing nationally. In September of that year, Hitler gave Goebbels full authority over Nazi propaganda. The party's showing at the next Reichstag election in September, 1930, was enormously helped by the Great Depression and serious unemployment. Goebbels improved his own party status when, in 1931, he married Magda Quandt, an attractive divorcée who was already on friendly terms with Hitler. The Goebbels' marriage produced six children. In 1932 the Nazi Party fought two presidential elections and two

Reichstag elections. Goebbels became one of Hitler's closest advisers. Although disappointed at not being on Hitler's first cabinet list on January 30, 1933, he was added to the cabinet on March 14, 1933, as minister for enlightenment and propaganda.

Minister of Propaganda

The ministry's most powerful instrument for influencing public opinion was radio. Radio broadcasting was a government monopoly. Thousands

Joseph Goebbels *(Library of Congress)*

The Goebbels Diaries

Portions of Joseph Goebbels's diaries were recovered starting in 1945, and they were soon widely used and accepted almost at face value by many historians. This acceptance gave remarkable credence to a man who was a professional propagandist. To be sure, some of Goebbels's tendencies are predictable—Hitler is presented in heroic terms, although Goebbels shares the stage.

However, many historians have accepted Goebbels's version of his youthful acquaintances, girlfriends, and early contacts with Hitler and the Nazi Party, even when these are at variance with the recollections of others. The Goebbels version, with its colorful language, is fascinating, but it must be compared with, and weighed against, other sources.

Nazi propaganda minister Joseph Goebbels (left) with Hermann Göring, commander of the German air force, the Luftwaffe, in 1936. *(Library of Congress)*

of cheap radio receivers were sold to increase the listenership. There was a relatively small number of newscasters and script writers, and they were easy to organize. The private press—newspapers, periodicals, and books—was "guided" through negotiations. Art and music were supposedly also under the ministry, but in practice Hitler himself insisted on being the supreme judge of these fields. Goebbels was especially interested in film production. German film attendance quadrupled from 245 million in 1933 to more than 1 billion in 1943. *Wünschkonzert* (1940) and *Die Grosse Liebe* (1942), both musicals, topped the box office. *Jud Süss* (1940) was the most popular of the anti-Semitic films.

The late 1930's were a low point in Goebbels's influence. His 1938 love affair with the Czech film star Lida Baarova endangered both his marriage and his political position. Evidence suggests that in order to regain his influence with Hitler, Goebbels took an active role in the November 9, 1938, Kristallnacht attack on the Jews. Also, during Hitler's bloodless diplomatic triumphs of 1936-1938 and his military victories of 1939-1940, there was little need for propaganda to exaggerate the importance of Nazi successes.

Wartime Leader

The German failure to take Stalingrad (1942-1943) created a need for clever propaganda to disguise the reality. Goebbels treated Stalingrad as a tragic defeat, but one that would not affect the eventual outcome of the war. Lesser defeats he often denied until they could be labeled unimportant. As Allied air raids reached the Berlin area, Goebbels was conscientious in visiting bombed neighborhoods, and as Hitler and other Nazi leaders began avoiding public appearances, Goebbels was by 1945 the regime's only prominent public speaker. Hitler, on the day of his suicide—April 30, 1945—appointed Goebbels chancellor to succeed him. On the following day, however, Goebbels chose death for his children, his wife, and himself.

Bibliography

Fraenkel, Heinrich, and Roger Manvell. *Doctor Goebbels: His Life and Death*. New York: Simon & Schuster, 1960.

Reimann, Viktor. *The Man Who Created Hitler*. London: William Kimber, 1977.

Reuth, Ralf Georg. *Goebbels*. New York: Harcourt Brace, 1993.

K. Fred Gillum

Joseph Goebbels stirring a crowd with his oratory. *(Library of Congress)*

Mikhail Gorbachev

Born: March 2, 1931; Privolnoye, Russia, U.S.S.R.

Reformist Soviet leader, last general secretary of the Soviet Union's Communist Party (1985-1991)

Mikhail Sergeyevich Gorbachev (myih-kuh-EEL syihr-GYAY-yeh-vyihch gawr-buh-CHOF) was born into a peasant family in Privolnoye, in the Stavropol region. Mikhail's academic ability was recognized at an early age, and he was able to attend Moscow University, an unusual honor for a rural student. After completing a law degree at the university, he returned to Stavropol with his wife, Raisa M. Titorenko Gorbacheva, in 1955. The Gorbachevs had one daughter, Irina, born in 1957. They lived in Stavropol until 1978, when Gorbachev went to Moscow as the Central Committee secretary in charge of agriculture.

Mikhail Gorbachev speaking at a 1990 press conference. *(Reuters/Frederiqu Lengaigen/Archive Photos)*

Building a Career

Gorbachev's political career began when he became a Komsomol activist. At eighteen he received the Order of the Red Banner of Labor (1949) for his work in agriculture. Gorbachev's political involvement continued at Moscow University, where he joined the Communist Party (CPSU) in 1952 while pursuing a law degree. After graduation in 1955, Gorbachev worked for the Komsomol and later the Communist Party in Stavropol. Eventually he rose to first secretary of the Communist Party of the Stavropol region (1970). His successes in agriculture there attracted the attention of the Politburo in Moscow. Gorbachev was elected to the Central Committee of the Communist Party in 1971. He owed his agricultural success both to his own studies and to his wife's sociological research among the collective farmers. Gorbachev's agricultural reforms attracted the notice of the Moscow leadership because agriculture had long been a major weakness in the Soviet economy.

Gorbachev also benefited from the fact that the Stavropol region had several health spas favored by the top Communist Party elite. As regional first secretary, Gorbachev met members of the ruling Politburo, most notably Yuri Andropov, head of the KGB, widely regarded as the most capable member of the Brezhnev administration.

In 1978 Gorbachev was brought to Moscow to serve as the Central Committee secretary in charge of agriculture. From there the path to the top was relatively short. Gorbachev was recognized as the most able of the younger men in the aging Politburo. After Brezhnev died in 1982, he served as unofficial second secretary under the ailing

Soviet leader Mikhail Gorbachev (right) in 1991 with Russian prime minister Ivan Silayev at the Moscow airport. *(Reuters/Tass/Archive Photos)*

general secretary of the Communist Party, Andropov (from 1982 to 1984), and his equally ill successor, Konstantin Chernenko (in 1984 and 1985). Gorbachev gradually gained recognition within the Soviet Union and abroad. His 1984 meetings with Prime Minister Margaret Thatcher in England established him on the world stage. In March, 1985, Chernenko died, and the Polit-

---

Glasnost and *Perestroika*

Shortly after coming to power, Mikhail Gorbachev launched a campaign of *glasnost* (openness), which gradually and selectively revealed truths about the Soviet past and permitted a freer atmosphere in literature and the arts. *Glasnost* went far beyond the thaw of the 1950's and permitted greater freedom of expression than ever before for Soviet citizens. In 1987 Gorbachev introduced *perestroika* (restructuring), a program of economic reform that would allow greater self-management in the state sector and limited private enterprise. The reforms were designed to decentralize the Soviet economy, although the majority of the economy would remain state-owned. As soon as privatization of the land was raised as a possibility, great controversy arose within the Communist Party, since many believed that collectivized agriculture was a cornerstone of the Soviet system. *Glasnost* proved difficult to control, and the economic reforms more difficult to implement than Gorbachev had anticipated. By the early 1990's, he could no longer fully control the reforms he had launched.

The Union Treaty

The fifteen Soviet republics were bound to the Soviet Union by a constitution that promised considerable autonomy but in fact established a unitary state allowing each republic little freedom. In the atmosphere of reform in the late 1980's, nationalist sentiments grew within the republics. Some, such as the three Baltic republics of Latvia, Lithuania, and Estonia, called for independence, whereas others sought greater autonomy. The voices of independence grew during the Mikhail Gorbachev years, leading to the use of force in Georgia in 1989 and in the Baltic in 1991. In an effort to appease the republics, Gorbachev first used rhetoric and persuasion and later promised a new union treaty with greater rights for the republics. On August 19, 1991, on the eve of the signing of the new treaty, conservatives among the party leadership staged a coup in which they held Gorbachev hostage. Gorbachev was released because of the efforts of Boris Yeltsin (the president of the Russian Republic), assisted by mass demonstrations and international interests. The republics refused to sign the treaty, and the movement toward the dissolution of the Soviet Union progressed quickly in late 1991.

U.S. president Ronald Reagan and Mikhail Gorbachev take a break from meetings at the White House to pose for photographers in 1987. *(Reuters/Denis Paquin/Archive Photos)*

buro selected Gorbachev as general secretary of the Communist Party.

Gorbachev's Reforms

As first secretary, Gorbachev launched a reform program in 1985. He began with *glasnost* (openness) and expanded his program to *perestroika* (or restructuring). The path of reform was not an easy one. Within the Communist Party, opposition grew from both those who believed reform was proceeding too slowly and those who thought reform was progressing too rapidly. A controversial aspect of the Gorbachev reforms was his campaign to curb alcohol consumption. Alcoholism was a pervasive problem in Soviet society. Gorbachev's initiative limited where and when vodka and other alcoholic beverages could be sold. The plan backfired, as Russians turned to bootlegging to ensure that their supply of vodka remained available.

As the Soviet Union became more open, political reforms were launched, and competitive elections began. The old Supreme Soviet was transformed into a largely popularly elected Congress of People's Deputies with a smaller standing Supreme Soviet that functioned as a real legislature. In 1988 Gorbachev became president of the Soviet Union as well as general secretary of the Communist Party, gradually relying more on his presidential role and reducing the dominance of the party in Soviet society. In an effort to pacify all the opposition groups, Gorbachev retreated from some of the reforms. He began to pursue a zig-zag path of reform and retreat, alienating his opponents on the Right and the Left. Furthermore, growing anti-Soviet sentiments in the republics were undermining the future of the union.

International Successes

While Gorbachev was having difficulties at home, his international successes were growing. Rapprochement with the United States began with a summit meeting with U.S. president Ronald Reagan in 1985. Relations improved dramatically with all the Western states, and the Cold War between East and West began to evaporate. Gorbachev's reforms encouraged some client states in Eastern Europe to pursue reform, whereas others—hard-liners—tried to prevent reform. The Soviet Union failed to support hard-liners in East Germany and Czechoslovakia, and their hold on power crumbled. In 1989 the hated Berlin Wall fell, and by late 1990 reformers controlled most of Eastern Europe.

Legacy of Reform

Gorbachev's reforms were a two-edged sword that profoundly changed the Soviet system and perhaps hastened its collapse. Gorbachev's place in history is assured as the man who brought down the Berlin Wall and contributed to the end of the Cold War. His domestic legacy is a mixed one. Although he initiated reforms, the Soviet system collapsed before reforms could take permanent root. After the demise of the Soviet Union, Gorbachev formed a research foundation and devoted his time to lecturing and writing.

Bibliography

Brown, Archie. *The Gorbachev Factor*. Oxford, England: Oxford University Press, 1997.

Doder, Dusko, and Louise Branson. *Gorbachev: Heretic in the Kremlin*. New York: Penguin, 1991.

Gorbachev, Mikhail. *Perestroika: New Thinking for Our Country and the World*. New York: Harper and Row, 1987.

Wieczynski, Joseph L., ed. *The Gorbachev Encyclopedia*. Salt Lake City, Utah: Schlacks, 1993.

Norma C. Noonan

Al Gore

Born: March 31, 1948; Washington, D.C.

Vice president of the United States (took office 1993)

Since his father served in the U.S. Congress for nearly three decades, young Albert Arnold Gore, Jr. (AL-burt "AL" AHR-nuhld GOHR JEW-nyur), grew up mixing with the Washington elite. Gore attended Harvard University, earning a bachelor of arts degree in government in 1969. After graduation, he enlisted in the army and served as an army reporter in Vietnam. Upon leaving the military in 1971, Gore was hired as an investigative reporter and, later, as an editorial writer, for the Nashville *Tennessean*. In addition to his journalism career, Gore also gained experience as a home builder, a land developer, and a livestock and tobacco farmer in Tennessee.

Al Gore *(Library of Congress)*

U.S. Congress

In 1974, Gore entered Vanderbilt University's law school but left in 1976 to run for a seat in the U.S. House of Representatives. Gore won the primary election against eight other Democratic candidates and went on to win the general election. He also ran successfully in the next three elections. In 1980, he gained recognition when he was assigned to study nuclear arms on the House Intelligence Committee.

After a seat for a U.S. senator from Tennessee became vacant in 1984, Gore won election to the Senate by a large margin. Gore focused his attention on health-related matters, nuclear arms control and disarmament, and cleaning up the environment. He also stressed the potential of new technologies, especially computer development.

A Campaign and a Book

At the age of thirty-nine, Gore entered the 1988 presidential race. His campaign was based on traditional domestic Democratic policies as well as on foreign policy issues. Gore gained a strong following in the South but failed to develop a national following. Consequently, Gore withdrew from the presidential nomination race in mid-April.

In 1990, Gore was reelected as U.S. senator from Tennessee. His son, Albert, was seriously injured when he was hit by an automobile, so Gore decided not to seek the presidency in 1992. During that time, he made his mark by writing his best-selling book, *Earth in the Balance: Ecology and the Human Spirit*, expressing his concern, ideas, and recommendations for conservation and the global environment.

Vice President

In 1992, Bill Clinton chose Gore as his running

mate in the presidential campaign. With Gore's experience in foreign and defense policy, expertise in environmental and new technology issues, and image as a strong family man, he provided an excellent complement to Clinton's strengths. After a fierce campaign in which they urged voters to opt for change and a way out of economic recession, Clinton and Gore claimed victory over the George Bush-Dan Quayle Republican ticket. Gore was inaugurated as the forty-fifth vice president of the United States on January 20, 1993. At least partly because of greatly improved economic conditions, Clinton and Gore were reelected in 1996. Gore's image, however, became somewhat tarnished after charges of illegal campaign fund-raising.

U.S. vice president Al Gore (right) with Alabama governor Fob James in 1998 after viewing extensive tornado damage in Alabama and Georgia. *(Reuters/ Tami L. Chappell/Archive Photos)*

As vice president, Gore enjoyed an unusual degree of access to the president, who relied heavily on Gore's judgment. Gore was a staunch advocate of strong families and technological advancement. Continuing to stress environmental issues, Gore was successful in initiating the

The Summit for America's Future

Between April 27 and 29, 1997, nearly two thousand national leaders participated in the President's Summit for America's Future, held in Philadelphia, Pennsylvania. The overall goal of the event was to initiate a nationwide volunteer program involving millions of individuals and thousands of organizations to help the youth of the United States have a brighter future. Five critical resources were identified as being necessary to help young people succeed in life. The summit sought to ensure that by the year 2000 an additional two million youth would have access to these resources and that five million more youth would have access to at least one of these resources.

The five critical resources identified were a mentoring program with a caring adult, provision for safe after-school activities, child health care, education in a marketable skill, and involvement in youth service activities. Statements about volunteer programs to help American youth were made by President Bill Clinton, former presidents George Bush, Jimmy Carter, and Gerald Ford, former First Lady Nancy Reagan, Vice President Al Gore, and General Colin Powell.

Al Gore arriving in Kuala Lumpur in January, 1998, for the Asia-Pacific Economic Cooperation (APEC) summit meeting. *(AP/Wide World Photos)*

Global Climate Change Action Plan, a public-private partnership to reduce greenhouse gas emissions in the atmosphere dramatically. Gore was also instrumental in breaking the gridlock on the national wetlands policy, in forging a historic partnership between government and industry to develop a new generation of fuel-efficient vehicles, and in unveiling a program to monitor and report on the health of the nation's ecosystems.

Bibliography

Burford, Betty M. *Al Gore, United States Vice President*. Hillside, N.J.: Enslow, 1994.

Walch, Timothy, ed. *At the President's Side*. Columbia: University of Missouri Press, 1997.

Waldrup, Carole C. *The Vice Presidents*. Jefferson, N.C.: McFarland, 1996.

Alvin K. Benson

Hermann Göring

Born: January 12, 1893; Rosenheim, Germany
Died: October 15, 1946; Nuremberg, Germany

German Nazi political and military leader

Hermann Göring (HAYR-mahn GOO-rihng) was the son of an official in the German colonial service, born at Rosenheim, Bavaria. He attended the German military academy and became an officer in the German army in 1914. He served with distinction throughout World War I, becoming the last commander of the famous Richthofen flying circus in 1918, when he won Germany's highest decoration for valor. After the war he worked for the Svenska Lufttraffik in Sweden, where he married a countess, Karin Fock. He then returned with his wife to Bavaria. In 1920 he attended a meeting at which Adolf Hitler was the featured speaker. He fell under Hitler's spell and joined the Nazi Party. In 1931 Göring's first wife died. In 1936 he married actress Emmy Sonnemann; they had one daughter.

Struggles with Hitler

Hitler appointed Göring to command the *Sturmabteilung* (the SA, or storm troopers). In 1923 Göring and the SA played a pivotal role in Hitler's attempt to seize power in Bavaria by force, called the beer-hall putsch. Göring, badly wounded in the attempt, fled the country and developed gangrene. He became addicted to morphine. He returned to Bavaria in 1927 and served as head of the twelve-member delegation the Nazis elected to the Reichstag (parliament) in 1928.

After the Nazi electoral success of 1933, Göring became president of the German parliament. Hitler appointed him to several other important posts in the German government and promoted him to general. Göring played an important role in the purge of the Nazi Party in 1934, when Hitler ordered the execution of Ernst Röhm.

The Rebuilding of Germany

In 1935 Hitler appointed Göring commander in chief of the German air force and minister for air power. In 1936 Hitler placed Göring in charge of the four-year plan, which made him the virtual economic dictator of Germany. Göring became fabulously wealthy and lived like a medieval baron on his palatial estate, Karinhall. He played an important role in the economic recovery of Germany. Göring also participated in German diplomacy during the period before the outbreak of World War II. He was instrumental in the takeover of Austria by Germany in 1938. In 1939

Hermann Göring *(Library of Congress)*

581

London battered by the "Blitz"—the attacks of the German Luftwaffe—in December, 1940. *(Library of Congress)*

he realized that a German attack on Poland might result in another world war, and he tried unsuccessfully to prevent it.

Göring and World War II

Hitler designated Göring as his successor should anything happen to him. In 1940 Hitler promoted him to *Reichsmarschall*. However, the German air force failed to defeat the British Royal Air Force, and German cities began to be bombed by the Allies. Göring fell out of favor with Hitler and lost the confidence of the German people. He sank deeper into drug addiction, lost most of his authority, and spent his time at Karinhall hunting and collecting art, which he looted from Nazi-occupied countries.

In April, 1945, Göring telegraphed Hitler, suggesting that he (Göring) should assume full power in Germany in accordance with his designation as Hitler's successor. Hitler immediately expelled him from the Nazi Party, revoked all his positions in the government, and ordered his arrest, which was never effected. The Americans captured Göring in May and put him on trial for war crimes at Nuremberg in 1946. The Nuremberg Tribunal convicted him and sentenced him to hang, although Göring protested his innocence and conducted an eloquent de-

The Luftwaffe

In 1935 Hermann Göring became the minister for air and the commander of the German Luftwaffe, or air force. Hitler gave him full responsibility for the recruitment and training of pilots and the development of military aircraft. Göring became the architect of the new German air force, guiding its development through the outbreak of World War II. The Luftwaffe was an indispensable component of the German concept of Blitzkrieg (lightning war), which led to spectacular German victories during the period 1939-1941. During the Battle of Britain (an air war fought in the skies over the British isles), however, the Royal Air Force so badly crippled the Luftwaffe that it never fully recovered. Between 1943 and 1945, when British and American bombers attacked civilian targets in Germany, the pilots of the Luftwaffe tried desperately to prevent the bombing. They were unsuccessful, despite the introduction of the world's first operational jet fighter, the ME263.

fense. On October 15, 1946, the night before he was scheduled to hang, Göring committed suicide.

Hermann Göring was a brave soldier and a brilliant administrator and politician. His drug addiction and his love of luxury and artwork all contributed to his undoing. It is possible that he told the truth at Nuremberg when he insisted that he had no knowledge of the atrocities of which the Germans were accused during World War II. Nonetheless, he knowingly permitted many Europeans to become slave laborers and to work in abominable conditions during the war, and he oversaw the bombing of civilian targets during the Battle of Britain. His name will be forever associated with the horrors of World War II.

Bibliography

Irving, David. *Göring: A Biography*. London: Grafton, 1991.

Manville, Roger, and Heinrich Fraenkel. *Göring*. New York: Simon & Schuster, 1962.

Mosley, Leonard. *The Reich Marshal: A Biography of Hermann Göring*. Garden City, N.J.: Doubleday, 1974.

A uniformed Hermann Göring with Archbishop Angelo Roncalli, the future Pope John XXIII, in Rome in 1933. *(Library of Congress)*

Overy, Richard J. *Göring, the "Iron Man."* London: Routledge & Kegan Paul, 1987.

Paul Madden

John Grey Gorton

Born: September 9, 1911; Melbourne, Victoria, Australia

Prime minister of Australia (1968-1971)

John Grey Gorton (JON GRAY GOHR-tuhn) was the son of a prosperous fruit grower at Mystic Park in northern Victoria. He was educated at Sydney Church of England Grammar School, Geelong Grammar School, and Oxford University, where he obtained a second-class honors degree in history. In 1935, while still at Oxford, he married an American student, Bettina Brown. (She died in 1983, and Gorton married Nancy Home in 1993.) On returning to Australia in 1936, he took over the family orchards, then served in the Royal Australian Air Force during World War II, from 1940 to 1944. In 1942 his fighter plane was shot down, and he was badly wounded.

John Grey Gorton *(Archive Photos)*

Early Political Career

After his time in the air force, Gorton returned to Mystic Park. In 1946 he was voted to the Kerang Shire Council as a Country Party candidate. In 1948 he joined the Liberal Party and stood unsuccessfully in a state election the following year. In 1949-1950 he was president of the shire council, but he entered federal politics in 1949, becoming a Victorian senator at the election that brought Liberal Party leader Sir Robert Menzies to power as prime minister.

From 1958 to 1968, Gorton held various cabinet positions in the coalition governments led by Menzies and Sir Harold Holt. In December, 1966, he became minister for education and science; in October, 1967, he also became leader of the government in the senate. When Holt died in a drowning accident at the end of 1967, Gorton became a strong candidate for prime minister.

Gorton as Prime Minister

After a party vote, Gorton became the new leader of the Liberal Party and was sworn into office as prime minister on January 10, 1968. Traditionally, the prime minister of Australia comes from the lower house of Parliament, the House of Representatives, rather than from the Senate, so Gorton resigned his Senate seat and stood successfully for the lower-house seat of Higgins, which had been held by Holt before his death.

Gorton's period of leadership was marked by controversy over military conscription and the involvement of Australian troops in the Vietnam War. Gorton stated that he was "Australian right through to my boots." He sought to take a more independent approach to foreign policy than his predecessor had, showing less enthusiasm than Holt about the war. He acted to limit the number of Australian troops in Vietnam, but Australia

Coalition Government in Australia

In the Australian political system, the Liberal Party of Australia and the National Party of Australia are allied to form a single force in the Parliament. In practice, this coalition is the alternative government to the more left-wing Australian Labor Party. Since 1949 the federal coalition has been suspended for only two brief periods, in 1973-1974 and in 1987. The Liberal Party is oriented toward business and usually has moderately conservative policies, while the National Party mainly represents rural interests. It was created in 1920 as the Australian Country Party but changed its name to National Country Party in 1975 and to National Party of Australia in 1982. When the coalition is in power, ministers are chosen from both coalition parties. The Liberal Party leader becomes prime minister, while the leader of the National Party becomes deputy prime minister.

remained involved. Gorton discouraged overseas investment, extended the federal government's role in education, and strongly emphasized national policy rather than states' rights. He was branded a "centralist" and made powerful enemies among state leaders, such as the premier of New South Wales, Robert Askin, and the premier of Victoria, Henry Bolte.

Gorton narrowly won the 1969 federal election but was embroiled in further controversies, including innuendo about his attractive young private secretary, Ainslie Gotto. In March, 1971, a dispute with the defense minister, Malcolm Fraser, led to Fraser's resignation from the cabinet. In a party room debate that followed, Gorton's supporters sought a vote of confidence in his leadership. When the vote was tied, Gorton stood down and was replaced by William McMahon as party leader and prime minister. Gorton later resigned from the Liberal Party and stood unsuccessfully as an Independent candidate for the Senate in 1975. He was knighted in 1977. In retirement he has remained a commentator on political and social issues.

On a visit to the United States, Australian prime minister John Grey Gorton rides on a golf cart with U.S. president Lyndon B. Johnson at Johnson's Texas ranch. *(National Archives)*

Bibliography

Henderson, Gerard. *Menzies' Child: The Liberal Party of Australia*. Rev. ed. Sydney: HarperCollins, 1998.

Reid, Alan. *The Gorton Experiment*. Sydney: Shakespeare Head Press, 1971.

Trengrove, Alan. *John Grey Gorton: An Informal Biography*. Melbourne, Australia: Cassell, 1969.

Russell Blackford

Antonio Gramsci

Born: January 23, 1891; Ales, Sardinia, Italy
Died: April 27, 1937; Rome, Italy

Italian Communist leader and Marxist theorist

Antonio Gramsci (ahn-TOH-nee-oh GRAHM-shee) had a poor and sickly childhood made worse by an accident at the age of four which left him with physical deformation and life-long disability. His father was imprisoned in 1897, making the family's poverty deeper. Although from a poor and isolated region of Italy, Gramsci educated himself and won a scholarship to the University of Turin in 1911. Gramsci became a leading voice in Italian socialism and Marxist philosophy.

Revolutionary Turin

During the 1890's the Italian city of Turin was a center for working-class activism. In this indus-

Antonio Gramsci

trial town, "workers' socialism" and powerful labor unions had taken root. When Gramsci arrived at the university, it was at the heart of a politically charged arena. Gramsci joined the Turin section of the Italian Socialist Party (PSI) in 1914 and contributed articles to its main publication, *Il Grido del Popolo* (the cry of the people). Gramsci was a student of philosophy and history, but his political interests soon focused on the revolutionary potential of the farmers of Southern Italy. Gramsci began to write about adapting socialist tactics to the needs of Italy and finding ways to ally the industrial workers with the poor people of the countryside.

Gramsci's thinking brought him to espouse revolutionary change in Italy. He strongly supported the Socialist International and its policy of abstention from World War I. Italian socialists were able to help keep Italy out of the war for several years by proclaiming that the workers of the world should seek international solidarity rather than fight for the imperial powers of Europe. Eventually Italy joined the war, but Gramsci remained firm, becoming the leading voice for radical socialism. He found himself disillusioned with labor unions and the reform-minded policies of the center of the PSI. In his writings he opposed Italy's entrance into the war and supported international socialism. He was inspired in 1917 by the success of the Bolshevik Revolution in Russia.

The Italian Communist Party

The end of World War I brought mixed results for Italy. The economy in 1919 was struggling, and returning soldiers had difficulty finding jobs. Labor unrest and anxiety were everywhere. The PSI was fragmented among those who urged

L'Ordine Nuovo

In May of 1919, the newspaper *L'Ordine Nuovo* (new order) was founded in Italy by Antonio Gramsci. Gramsci was a leading thinker in Italian socialism, and *L'Ordine Nuovo* became a major voice in the movement. One of the significant events in Italian socialism occurred between 1919 and 1920. It was known as the Turin Factory Council Movement. The Factory Council Movement emerged in 1919 during a series of strikes by Italian labor unions. These "workshop committees" were seen by Gramsci and *L'Ordine Nuovo* as equivalent to the "soviets" of the Russian Revolution of 1917. *L'Ordine Nuovo* attempted to inspire the workers to revolutionary struggle and to encourage the Factory Councils to overthrow the labor unions in the hope that a spontaneous uprising might develop. Such a revolt did not happen, and more moderate elements maintained control of the Italian Socialist Party and most of the unions. *L'Ordine Nuovo* and its followers broke away to form the Italian Communist Party in 1921. *L'Ordine Nuovo* became the daily paper of the Communist Party.

revolutionary struggle and the majority of socialists who sought modest reform and greater workers' rights. Gramsci led among the more radical voices. He founded the newspaper *L'Ordine Nuovo* (new order) and provided inspiration for the Turin Factory Council Movement. The *L'Ordine Nuovo* group believed in spontaneous revolutionary activity as a way to empower the workers. As he developed his own ideas of Marxist philosophy, Gramsci began to see revolution as a way of creating a new and more democratic culture for common people. Gramsci opposed a terrorist or underground movement with authoritarian tendencies. He favored spontaneous action which could lead to the liberation of working people. Eventually the tension between the majority elements of the PSI with the radical groups split the party. Gramsci and *L'Ordine Nuovo* broke away with other radicals in 1921 and established the Italian Communist Party (PCI). The PCI hoped to gain recognition from the Communist International in Moscow and thus to be part of an international movement. The new PCI, with only twenty-five thousand members, began as an isolated splinter party.

Although he had opponents in the party, Gramsci was recognized as a major theorist, and he was even its leader in 1924. Among Gramsci's contributions were his original thinking and democratic style. He saw Marxism as a philosophy of liberation that must be adapted to the specific culture and circumstances of people. Gramsci felt that revolutions begin with the everyday lives of working people, and he emphasized mass movement as the only authentic revolutionary process. He wrote of a creative Marxism that could liberate without dictatorship. With the rise of Fascism, dark days came, but the PCI struggled for the liberation of Italy and arose as the most prominent party on the Left in postwar Italy.

Prison and Philosophy

Gramsci was arrested in 1926 with other communist leaders. The fascist regime sought to destroy all its opposition, and Gramsci was seen as a serious threat because of his leadership of the PCI and his intellectual prowess. His health gradually declined over the ten years of his incarceration, and he died shortly after his release. The legacy of those years is his writings, known as the *Prison Notebooks* (1929-1936). Gramsci refined his thinking and made his greatest philosophical contributions during this time.

Gramsci cautioned against the idea that one model of revolution could work everywhere. His interest in culture and adaptation to national cir-

The Italian Communist Party

The Italian Communist Party (PCI) was formed in January, 1921, in Livorno, Italy. The party began as a radical splinter of the Italian Socialist Party. These "radical socialists" had been inspired by the Russian Revolution of 1917 and believed that Italy was ripe for revolution. The majority of Italian Socialists and their trade-union followers were more moderate and espoused gradual reform for workers' rights. Thus, the PCI broke away as a tiny faction, but in the years after World War II the Communists became the leading left-wing party. From the beginning the PCI, led by Antonio Gramsci and Palmiro Togliatti, argued that com-

munism must reflect the national culture of a people and that there are many models for socialism. The "Via Italiana" or "Italian Way" to socialism led to the PCI becoming a legal participant in postwar Italian democracy. The Communists became increasingly moderate and were often elected to government. In the 1990's the PCI dropped the name "Communist" and became the Democratic Party of the Left (PSDI). Italian communism was the model for "Eurocommunism" and the idea that a communist party can play a legitimate role in democracy.

cumstances offered flexibility in the communist movement. This approach created the opportunity for the PCI to be independent of Moscow in

the postwar era and to be a legitimate participant in Italian democracy. Later PCI leaders would draw from Gramsci the inspiration for the "Via Italiana al Socialismo," and these leaders played a large part in helping Italian democracy to survive in the aftermath of Fascism and defeat in World War II.

Gramsci's Mark

Antonio Gramsci rose from poverty to become a leading Marxist philosopher of the twentieth century. Although he always dreamed of a world revolution, Gramsci is primarily an example of hope in the struggle against oppression and poverty. Gramsci exemplified the importance of ideas in making history.

Bibliography

Cammett, John M. *Antonio Gramsci and the Origins of Italian Communism*. Stanford, Calif.: Stanford University Press, 1967.

Gramsci, Antonio. *Selections from the Prison Notebooks*. New York: International Publishers, 1980.

McLellan, David. *Marxism After Marx*. New York: Harper and Row, 1979.

Anthony R. Brunello

Inspired by the writings of Karl Marx (above), Antonio Gramsci became a leading Marxist theorist and Italian Communist Party Leader. *(Archive Photos)*

Herbert Gray

Born: May 25, 1931; Windsor, Ontario, Canada

Long-time Canadian political figure, minister of industry, trade, and commerce (1980 to 1982), solicitor general (1993-1997), deputy prime minister (beginning 1997)

Herbert Eser Gray (HUR-burt EE-zur GRAY), a veteran Canadian politician at the center of power for more than thirty years, was born in Windsor, Ontario, in 1931. He received his post-secondary education at the School of Commerce at McGill University and later at Osgoode Hall Law School in Toronto. In 1967 he married; he and his wife Sharon had two children.

A Career in Politics

In 1962, at the age of thirty-one, Gray was elected for the first time to the Canadian House of Commons. He captured a riding (district) from his home city of Windsor for the Liberal Party. Including his first victory, he would win his seat eleven straight times between 1962 and 1997.

Four years after being elected, Gray made his first step up from the anonymous political ranks when he became the chair of the House of Commons Standing Committee on Finance, Trade, and Economic Affairs. He served in this capacity until 1968. After the 1968 election, in which the Liberal Party under Pierre Elliott Trudeau won a majority government, Gray's ascendancy continued. He was now one position below the cabinet. From 1968 to 1969 he was parliamentary secretary for the minister of finance; minister of finance is the most important cabinet position other than prime minister. In 1969 Gray reached the cabinet in a junior position as a minister without portfolio—meaning that he was a cabinet minister without a specific area of responsibility. The following year, he achieved greater responsibility when Prime Minister Trudeau appointed him as the minister of national revenue, the position responsible for taxation. In 1972 he became the minister of consumer and corporate affairs.

In and Out of the Cabinet

After the 1974 election, in which the Liberals won a majority, Gray found himself demoted from the cabinet. This period would last until 1980. It included a short period in opposition, 1979-1980, after the Progressive Conservative Party under Joe Clark defeated the Liberals in 1979. A year later, however, Trudeau and the

Herbert Gray *(AP/Wide World Photos)*

The Gray Report

The issue of Canada's relationship to the United States became especially controversial in the 1960's and early 1970's. Many nationalists in English-speaking Canada feared that the United States had too much economic control over the Canadian economy. Some who felt this way belonged to the Liberal Party of Canada, in power from 1963 to 1979. Among them were Walter Gordon, finance minister during the 1960's, and Herb Gray.

The government of Pierre Trudeau appointed Gray to head a committee to look into American control of the Canadian economy. The result was the 1971 Gray Report, which cataloged the extent of American control and called for an effort by the federal government to reverse the situation. In 1973 the Trudeau government created the Foreign Investment Review Agency as a measure to monitor and control foreign investment in Canada.

Liberals returned to power in a federal election. Gray, now seen as a steadying influence because of his repeated success at getting elected and his standing as a senior member of the government, could not be denied a place in the cabinet. He served as minister of industry, trade, and commerce from 1980 to 1982. For a brief period in 1982 he was the minister of regional economic expansion before becoming president of the Treasury Board, another cabinet position, from 1982 to 1984.

The year 1984 was a pivotal one for the Liberals and Herbert Gray: Pierre Trudeau retired, and his replacement, John Turner, was unable to win widespread support. The federal election proved a disaster for the party, as its membership in Parliament was drastically reduced by the Progressive Conservative Party under Brian Mulroney. Gray managed to avoid the fate that had befallen many of his colleagues. Because of his lengthy experience and stature, he would play an important role over the next nine years with the

Liberals, who now served as the official opposition to the governing party. In 1993 Gray was in the cabinet once again after the Liberal Party under Jean Chrétien replaced the Progressive Conservatives. By now the elder statesman of the party, Gray served first as solicitor general and then, in 1997, as deputy prime minister. Although he was never a flashy personality or a spectacular politician, Gray's political legacy is an important one that should not be underestimated.

Bibliography

Clarkson, Stephen, and Christina McCall. *Trudeau and Our Times*. Toronto: McClelland and Stewart, 1990.

Graham, Ron. *One-Eyed Kings: Promise and Illusion in Canadian Politics*. Toronto: Collins, 1986.

Greenspon, Edward, and Anthony Wilson-Smith. *Double Vision: The Inside Story of the Liberals in Power*. Toronto: Doubleday Canada, 1996.

Steve Hewitt

Alan Greenspan

Born: March 6, 1926; New York, New York

Chairman of U.S. Federal Reserve Board (named 1987)

Alan Greenspan (A-luhn GREEN-span) was raised by his mother and grandparents, Russian Jewish immigrants, after his parents' divorce when he was six. He attended New York City public schools and spent two years at the prestigious Juilliard School of Music before a brief tour with a swing band. Recognizing his limitations, however, and with a bent for economics, he distinguished himself at New York University's School of Commerce, where he earned a B.A. (1948), an M.A. (1950), and, later, a doctorate (1977). He was briefly married to Joan Mitchell (1952) and, much later (1997), married Andrea Mitchell of NBC News.

Government Service

In between stints at his business consulting firm, Townsend and Greenspan, which he headed after his partner's death in 1958, Greenspan became connected with official Washington in 1968. A conservative Republican, he became presidential candidate Richard M. Nixon's director of domestic policy research; he also served in other capacities. However, it was not until July, 1974, that Greenspan held a full-fledged federal position. At that time President Nixon, shortly before his resignation, appointed Greenspan to be the chairman of the Council of Economic Advisers. He was sworn in by Nixon's successor, President Gerald R. Ford. When Democrat Jimmy Carter was elected president in 1976, Greenspan returned to his economic consulting firm in New York City.

After advising both presidential candidates Ronald Reagan and George Bush in the Republican Party primaries of 1980, Greenspan was given various assignments by President Reagan. His most notable was as chairman of the bipartisan National Commission on Social Security Re-

form in 1982-1983. The committee made recommendations about the program's future viability. In 1987 an unexpected opening occurred for chairman of the Federal Reserve Board (often simply called "the Fed"), America's central bank. Greenspan was highly recommended by two previous holders of the job, several senior government officials, and especially the business community. (Greenspan was a director on several prestigious corporate boards.) He was appointed

Alan Greenspan enjoying a light moment at a 1998 Senate Budget Committee hearing. *(Ron Sachs/CNP/ Archive Photos)*

U.S. Federal Reserve Board chairman Alan Greenspan (right) talking with Senate Banking Committee chairman Donald Riegle. *(Reuters/Mike Theiler/Archive Photos)*

Rand. Like her, he believed strongly in the "rational selfishness"—but also in the efficiency and even morality—of laissez-faire capitalism, unfettered markets, and minimum government regulations. In his position as chairman of the Federal Reserve Board, he would have a major role in deciding monetary and credit policies that would greatly affect the United States' economic growth, income, and employment levels, the international value of the U.S. dollar, and trends in business cycles.

Greenspan as Chairman

According to most observers, Greenspan has performed well in juggling the economic and political contradictions and tradeoffs inherent in his chairman's job. He was reappointed by both Republican President George Bush in 1991 and Democratic President Bill Clinton in 1996. Along the way, Greenspan and "the Fed" faced numerous crises.

Early in Greenspan's first term, on October 19,

by President Reagan and confirmed by the U.S. Senate on August 11, 1987.

Greenspan the economist was greatly influenced by social philosopher and novelist Ayn

The Council of Economic Advisers

Created by the Employment Act of 1946 as amended in 1953, the Council of Economic Advisers (CEA) consists of three economists appointed by the U.S. president with the consent of the Senate. The CEA's primary purpose is to provide policy recommendations to the president. The CEA is part of the executive branch of the federal government. The Council of Economic Advisers analyzes the national economy and advises the president on economic developments. It also appraises the federal government's economic programs and policies and makes recommendations, assists in the preparation of the president's economic reports to

Congress, and prepares its own annual report.

Whereas at the outset the council's members were inclined to give their own individual viewpoints, over time a more unified approach has developed. Despite fluctuations in the degree of its influence, the council's proposals affecting taxing, spending, and even monetary matters—primarily the responsibility of the Federal Reserve Board—are often considered important. As CEA chairman from 1974 to 1976, Alan Greenspan focused on fighting the many pressures on Washington to expand government spending during those recessionary years.

The Federal Reserve System

The U.S. Federal Reserve System, managed by the Federal Reserve Board, is exclusively a bankers' bank. Its purpose is to help the United States achieve stable economic growth through its monetary and credit policies. "The Fed," as it is often called, accomplishes this goal through its regulations. The primary general tools of monetary policy are the discount (or interest) rate, open market operations, and reserve requirements. The discount rate is the interest rate charged by each of the regional Federal Reserve banks on loans to financial institutions. Open market operations involve the purchases and sales of U.S. securities in the money and bond markets. Reserve requirements set the minimum cash or cash-equivalent requirements that member banks must hold in reserve. Specific regulations relate to consumer credit requirements. The Federal Reserve System also helps collect and clear checks, supervises banks and other financial institutions, acts as agent for the U.S. Treasury Department, and distributes coins and currency to the public through banks.

The Board of Governors of the Federal Reserve System, its ultimate authority, consists of seven members, mostly professional economists, appointed by the U.S. president and confirmed by the Senate. The board's chairman and vice chairman serve four-year terms that are renewable up to a fourteen-year limit. The board, through its chairman, reports to the U.S. Congress and is often an economic adviser to the president. As board chairman, Alan Greenspan proved to be a steadying economic helmsman.

1987, the New York stock market dropped by 22 percent of its paper value. Greenspan quickly reversed his traditional anti-inflationary policy, providing the necessary liquidity to prevent further asset deflation. In the 1990's, the Federal Reserve Board confronted a series of problems: record federal outlays and budget deficits, and a resulting chronically weak dollar; the savings-and-loan and banking "bail-out" scandals; large-scale corporate downsizing; oil price hikes following the Persian Gulf War; and the reduction of the military establishment after the collapse of the Soviet bloc and the termination of the Cold War.

Then came the Mexican economic and currency crisis, followed by the Southeast Asian economic downturn, both with potentially damaging impacts on the United States. Still, by June, 1998, Greenspan was able to report to the U.S. Congress that the American business environment was the best he had seen in his professional life. Politically, Greenspan has found himself walking a tightrope, because candidates like to run for elections in an employment-creating economic environment, whereas his own priority of low inflation is not in the forefront of most voters' minds. In this respect he has incurred the displeasure of at least two American presidents for his tight-money policy.

Bibliography

Beckner, Steven K. *Back from the Brink: The Greenspan Years.* New York: John Wiley & Sons, 1996.

Greider, William. *Secrets of the Temple: How the Federal Reserve Runs the Country.* New York: Simon and Schuster, 1987.

Jones, David M. *The Politics of Money: The Fed Under Alan Greenspan.* New York: New York Institute of Finance, 1991.

Rand, Ayn. *Capitalism: The Unknown Ideal.* New York: Signet/Penguin Books, 1966.

Peter B. Heller

Andrei Andreyevich Gromyko

Born: July 18, 1909; Starye Gromyki, Belorussia, Russian Empire (now Belarus)
Died: July 2, 1989; Moscow, U.S.S.R.

Soviet leader and diplomat, foreign minister (1957-1985)

Andrei Andreyevich Gromyko (uhn-DRYAY-ih uhn-DRYAY-yeh-vyihch gro-MEE-koh) was the son of peasant parents, Andrei Matveyevich and Olga Evgenyena Gromyko. His mother encouraged his interest in books and education, which enabled him to earn a degree in economics and do postgraduate studies in Minsk and Moscow during the mid-1930's. He was awarded a doctorate of economics by Moscow State University after he published *The Export of American Capital* in 1957, for which he used the pseudonym G. Andreyev. He married Lydia Dmitrievna and had two children, Anatoly and Emilia. Gromyko joined the Communist Party in 1931.

Andrei Andreyevich Gromyko *(Library of Congress)*

Early Diplomatic Service

Gromyko finished his postgraduate studies in 1936 and then for three years was a research associate in the Institute of Economics of the Academy of Sciences. During this period Joseph Stalin purged many members of the government, creating a need for individuals to serve in the diplomatic corps. In 1939 Gromyko was appointed director of the division of the Commissariat of Foreign Affairs that dealt with the United States, partially because of his previous study of the English language. Late in the year he was appointed consul of the Soviet embassy in the United States.

In 1943 Gromyko was appointed ambassador to the United States. During World War II he was very active in diplomatic efforts to coordinate Russia's military operations and those of the countries fighting on the Western Front. He headed the Soviet delegation to the Dumbarton Oaks Conference and participated in the Allied summit meetings at Yalta and Potsdam in 1945. In 1946 he became the permanent representative of the Soviet Union to the Security Council of the United Nations and a deputy foreign minister. In 1949 he was appointed first deputy minister of foreign affairs. In 1952 Gromyko was made a candidate member of the Central Committee of the Communist Party; he became a full member in 1956. During 1952-1953, he was ambassador to the United Kingdom. After serving as first deputy minister from 1953-1957 he was appointed minister of foreign affairs for the Soviet Union in February, 1957.

Foreign Minister

Because of the fact that during most of his career Gromyko was not identified with any par-

Soviet foreign minister Andrei Andreyevich Gromyko (lower right) speaking at the United Nations in 1961. Behind him are (left to right) U.N. secretary-general Dag Hammarskjöld, Frederick Bland of Ireland, and Andrew Cordier. *(Agence France Presse/Archive Photos)*

Nuclear Test Restrictions, 1963

Prior to 1963, there were no regulations concerning the testing of atomic or nuclear weapons. In the 1940's and 1950's most tests had been conducted in the atmosphere, causing destruction where the test was conducted and allowing radioactive material to be carried great distances by the wind. The Nuclear Test-Ban Treaty, signed in 1963, was a significant step forward, benefiting people and the environment. It was a landmark in the history of the Cold War. The treaty banned tests that were above ground, under water, or in outer space. Therefore, only underground tests could be conducted by those who signed this treaty. Although only three of the five nuclear powers of the time signed the treaty, it was a major breakthrough in the Cold War: Until this treaty, the relationship between the United States and the Soviet Union was one in which each side sought to gain something at the expense of the other. This treaty signified that Cold War diplomacy did not have to be a win-or-lose proposition—rather, both countries could benefit through cooperation. When the treaty was first signed, questions were raised as to whether it would be possible to verify compliance. Within a few years satellite technology was developed that made cheating virtually impossible.

The 1944 Dumbarton Oaks Conference

This conference, named for the Washington, D.C., mansion in which it was held, dealt with proposals for what was to become the United Nations. Meeting from August 21 to October 7, 1944, representatives from China, the Soviet Union, the United States, and the United Kingdom tried to create a more effective international organization to replace the League of Nations. The goal of the new organization was to achieve world peace through international law. Binding international laws would be adopted by the countries through this organization. However, it was recognized that the more powerful countries should have a stronger voice concerning threats to international peace. Thus it was agreed at this conference that the United States, the United Kingdom, and the Soviet Union (later expanded to include China and France) should have veto power in the U.N. Security Council. Only two major issues were unresolved at this conference: the range of issues that should be subject to Security Council veto power and the number of constituent republics within the Soviet Union that should have a vote in the U.N. General Assembly. These issues were resolved at the Yalta Conference in 1945. Having reached agreement on most central points at the Dumbarton Oaks Conference, the San Francisco Conference in 1945 drew up the Charter of the United Nations.

Gromyko was instrumental in the adoption of the 1963 Nuclear Test-Ban Treaty that banned atmospheric nuclear tests—shown is a U.S. bomb test in 1962. *(U.S. Naval Photographic Center)*

ticular faction within the Russian Communist Party, he was able to serve as foreign minister for twenty-eight years and in four Soviet administrations. In a period when much of what occurred in the Soviet Union was not known by the outside world, he gave continuity of contact and style in foreign relations. He was the leading negotiator for the Soviet Union in times of crisis; he met personally with President John F. Kennedy during the Cuban Missile Crisis. He also sought changes in the international arena.

One of his first achievements was the 1963 Nuclear Test-Ban Treaty. Since

Europe had experienced two world wars in the twentieth century, Gromyko pushed for high-level contacts between the Soviet Union and other countries and sought to lessen tensions in Europe. He negotiated the Renunciation of Force Treaty with the Federal Republic of Germany (West Germany). He also assisted in the development of the 1975 agreement that recognized the post-1945 borders in Europe as legitimate. During his service as foreign minister, he encouraged the strengthening of détente with the United States. This resulted in treaties dealing with research in space (1967), nuclear nonproliferation (1968), nonnuclear weapons on the seabed (1971), biological and toxic weapons (1972), and the landmark Strategic Arms Limitation Talks (SALT I) agreement in 1972, with its codicil in 1974. Gromyko continued to seek the lessening of tensions in the Strategic Arms Limitation Talks agreement of 1979 (SALT II), but it was never fully ratified.

Final Areas of Service

Having been a member of the Central Committee for seventeen years, Gromyko was elevated to the Politburo (the inner circle of advisers) in 1973 and served in this capacity until 1988. It was Gromyko who nominated Mikhail Gorbachev to become the general secretary of the Communist Party and leader of the Soviet Union in 1985. Later that year, he was replaced as foreign minister and was elected president of the Supreme Soviet of the Soviet Union, technically the head of state, but actually a largely ceremonial position. During a period of radical changes by Gorbachev in 1988, Gromyko resigned as president and from the Politburo. In early 1989, he was removed from the Central Committee of the Communist Party. He had served the Soviet Union for fifty years and had been a part of all but its first government.

Bibliography

Arbatov, Georgi. *The System: An Insider's Life in Soviet Politics.* New York: Random House, 1992.

Gromyko, Andrei. *Memoirs.* Translated by Harold Shukman. New York: Doubleday, 1989.

Kennan, George F. *At Century's Ending: Reflections 1982-1995.* New York: W. W. Norton, 1996.

Taubman, William. *Stalin's American Policy: From Entente to Detente to Cold War.* New York: W. W. Norton, 1982.

Donald A. Watt

Heinz Guderian

Born: June 17, 1888; Kulm, Germany (now Chelmno, Poland)
Died: May 14, 1954; Schwangau bei Füssen, Bavaria, West Germany

German general, World War II military leader

The son of a German officer, Heinz Wilhelm Guderian (HINTZ VIHL-hehlm gew-DAY-ree-ahn) was educated in Cadet School and in 1908 was commissioned into the 10th Hanoverian Jaeger (light infantry) Battalion commanded by his father. In 1913 he was selected for the *Kriegsacademie* (war college) for further instruction in military science. That same year, on October 1, he married Margarete Goerne; the Guderians had two sons. In World War I, Guderian rose steadily as a staff officer on the divisional, corps, and army levels on the western front.

Heinz Guderian *(Deutche Presse/Archive Photos)*

A New Type of Army

Following the war, Guderian was one of the four thousand officers (out of a surviving thirty-two thousand) chosen to remain in the greatly reduced German army. His main activity between the wars was to oversee the creation of a powerful German armored force based on the tank (in German, *Panzerkampfwagen*, or *Panzer* for short). From 1931 to 1935, as chief of staff to the inspector general of transport, Guderian argued for the establishment of a strong tank force. Guderian received backing from German dictator Adolf Hitler, and by 1935 three panzer divisions had been created, with Guderian in command of the Second Panzer Division. His 1937 book, *Achtung Panzer!* (warning, tank!) outlined how the new weapon should be used in breaking open the enemy's front line and charging forward to sow confusion and disruption. These were crucial tactics of the Blitzkrieg (lightning war) that would prove so effective in Poland, France, and Russia.

Blitzkrieg in Operation

When Germany overran Poland in September, 1939, beginning World War II, Guderian commanded the XIX Panzer Corps. He led the same forces in May, 1940, during the German invasion of France and the Low Countries. He was halted by Hitler's orders only miles from Dunkirk, where the British Expeditionary Force was trapped against the sea. Given the unexpected reprise, the British evacuated their army to fight another day.

Guderian's greatest challenges came with Operation Barbarossa, the German invasion of the Soviet Union in the summer of 1941. As commander of the Second Panzer Army, in the first six weeks of the campaign he won a brilliant series of victories against the Red Army, encircling and capturing hundreds of thousands of Russian troops. By July, within 100 miles (160 kilometers) of Moscow, he was halted by Hitler and ordered to support a German drive toward Ukraine and the Crimea. Guderian and other German generals argued against the shift, but by the time Hitler had relented and the attack on Moscow resumed, it was almost winter. Guderian's panzers ground to a halt within 30 miles (48 kilometers) of the Soviet capital.

German military commander Heinz Guderian talking with troops at the Russian front in 1941. *(Library of Congress)*

The Road to Defeat

Hitler relieved Guderian of his command for failure during the Russian counteroffensive in December, 1941. Guderian remained inactive until February, 1943, when he was appointed inspector general of the armored forces. He worked closely with Armaments Minister Albert Speer to restore and even increase German armor production. He was approached by officers plotting against Hitler; Guderian neither joined nor betrayed them.

The day after the failure of the July 20, 1944,

The Development of the Tank

Armored fighting vehicles were designed as long ago as the fifteenth century by Leonardo da Vinci, but it was not until 1916 that they were introduced into combat, to break the stalemate of the western front of World War I. Called "tanks" by the British to conceal their purpose, they were known by the Germans as *Panzerkampfwagen* (armored war vehicles) or *Panzers*.

The first tanks were slow, lightly armed, and inefficient. In the 1920's and 1930's, military engineers developed the weapon into a more potent, powerful, and flexible fighting machine. Light, medium, and heavy tanks were built for their respective tasks of scouting, infantry support, and tank-to-tank combat. The installation of radios allowed larger tank formations to be coordinated by a single commander. The German army developed entire Panzer units (and later, Panzer armies) based around the tank. These units combined tanks with motorized infantry and artillery, supported by air power, in an effective striking force that won many of Germany's early victories in World War II.

German tanks under the command of General Heinz Guderian advancing into the Soviet Union in 1941. *(National Archives)*

bomb plot to kill Hitler, Hitler appointed Guderian chief of the general staff of the army high command. As chief of staff, Guderian had no real power and little influence, since Hitler had become thoroughly disillusioned with all professional military men. On March 21, 1945, Guderian was dismissed, and on May 10, as the war was ending, he was taken prisoner by the U.S. Army. In 1951, Guderian published *Erinnerungen eines Soldaten* (memoirs of a soldier), which was a best-seller in Germany and was translated into English in 1952 as *Panzer Leader*. He died in May, 1954.

Bibliography

Dupuy, Trevor N., Curt Johnson, and David Bongard, eds. *Harper Encyclopedia of Military Biography*. New York: HarperCollins, 1992.

Guderian, Heinz. *Panzer Leader*. Reprint. New York: Da Capo Press, 1996.

Keegan, John. *The Second World War*. New York: Viking, 1989.

Keegan, John, and Andrew Wheatcroft. *Who's Who in Military History*. New York: William Morrow, 1976.

Polmar, Norman, and Thomas B. Allen. *World War II: The Encyclopedia of the War Years, 1941-1945*. New York: Random House, 1996.

Michael Witkoski

Che Guevara

Born: June 14, 1928; Rosario, Argentina
Died: October 9, 1967; La Higuera, Bolivia

Communist revolutionary leader in Cuba and South America

Ernesto Guevara de la Serna (ehr-NAY-stoh gay-VAH-rah day lah SEHR-nah) was the eldest of five children born of aristocratic parents in the eastern Argentinean town of Rosario. His architect father and politician mother helped to nurture his interest in leftist politics and sociology. The young "Che" (pronouced CHAY and translated as "buddy" or "chum") Guevara joined the Partido Union Democratica and read widely, especially the works of Karl Marx, Friedrich Engels, Sigmund Freud, and, most significantly, Chilean communist poet Pablo Neruda. Throughout his teens, he protested the policies of Argentine dictator Juan Perón.

Guevara's close relationship with his ailing paternal grandmother apparently influenced him to enter medical school at the University of Buenos Aires, from which he graduated as a doctor of medicine and surgery in 1953. During his medical school years, Guevara went on bicycle, motorcycle, and hitchhiking trips throughout much of South America. He worked for a time as a nurse in a leper colony. He attempted to visit the United States but was denied entrance by immigration officials in Florida. During one trip in 1951, he met Salvador Allende in Chile, and his travels generally made him aware of the plight of the very poor, including the descendants of indigenous tribes in northern Argentina.

Development of a Revolutionary

The combination of reading Marxist political ideology and experiencing the covert operations of the U.S. Central Intelligence Agency (CIA) in Guatemala led Guevara to the conclusion that armed and violent revolution was not only defensible but also necessary in order to create more equitable societies. In Mexico City in 1954,

Guevara met Nico Lopez, who introduced him to Raúl and Fidel Castro, at that time émigrés from Cuba during the regime of Fulgencio Batista. Guevara served them both as a doctor and as a guerrilla officer, eventually achieving the rank of major. Guevara helped in Castro's unsuccessful 1956 invasion attempt on the south coast of Cuba's Oriente Province.

The Castro brothers, with Guevara as chief political and military adviser, then set up camp in the Sierra Maestre Mountains of Cuba, from where they engaged in a successful guerrilla war over the next two years. They eventually defeated Batista and assumed control of the Cuban

Che Guevara *(Library of Congress)*

Revolutionary Che Guevara (right) with Cuban leader Fidel Castro in 1960. *(Library of Congress)*

government in January, 1959. Guevara acquired the stature of philosophical mastermind behind the Cuban communist revolution: He was noted both for his strict military training and for his status as one of the leading apologists in the Western Hemisphere for Leninist communism. Guevara developed the philosophy that military revolution was necessary in order to effect not only political, but especially a social, revolution. In the early years of Fidel Castro's communist dictatorship in Cuba, Guevara's philosophies turned from a more orthodox, Moscow-style communism toward an indigenously Cuban communism that looked to communist China and Mao Zedong as much as it had previously viewed the Soviet Union and Vladimir Lenin as models.

A Countryside Revolution

Guevara, as Cuba's minister for industry, signed a landmark five-year trade agreement with the Soviet Union in 1960 which sent Cuban sugar in return for oil, machinery, and other finished industrial products. Even so, Guevara increasingly viewed Mao as his philosophical

Che Guevara in Guatemala

After receiving his medical degree in 1953, Guevara traveled to La Paz, Bolivia, during the time of the National Revolution. Disillusioned there, he went to Guatemala in December, 1953, and supported himself by selling encyclopedias and writing articles about Incan and Mayan ruins. Guevara even held a minor governmental post as an inspector of agrarian reform under the regime of leftist president Jacobo Arbenz Guzman in 1954. Although by this time Guevara considered himself a Marxist, he refused to join the Communist Party, which disqualified him from any sort of governmental medical appointment. When the Arbenz regime was overthrown later in 1954 by

forces under the direction of Colonel Carlos Castillo Armas, Guevara briefly attempted to organize a resistance movement before going to Mexico City in September, 1954. There he met Nico Lopez as well as Raúl and Fidel Castro. Guevara's sojourn in Guatemala is significant because he saw there at first hand the covert influence that the U.S. Central Intelligence Agency (CIA) could exert in foreign countries. By the time Guevara went to Mexico in the fall of 1954, he had become convinced that the goal of a just society for all people would probably require armed revolution.

A Symbol of Revolution

Che Guevara became a living legend in the early 1960's because of his status as a spokesperson for violent revolution in order to reformulate societies into a more equitable and humane *polis*. Utilizing the theories of Franz Fanon and Regis Debray, Guevara proselytized his *foco* strategy: developing a mobile guerrilla base of peasants who would serve both military and political-philosophical functions. Unlike capitalistic or monarchical societies, the revolutionary communist *foco* philosophy demanded that its members be complete and complex individuals whose labor and life's work would be meaningful and dignified.

Guevara's international appeal as a revolutionary symbol exists not only because of his philosophical theories and courageous actions but especially because of the mystery and personal charisma that his character exuded. Che's temporary disappearance in Cuba in the early 1960's and his violent death in Bolivia in 1967 combined to form a media figure that was strident yet mysterious, righteous yet willing to support violent means to reach a more equitable end. Several generations of North American college students recognize Guevara's face from a widely distributed poster of him with beret, beard, and mustache, flowing locks of hair, and an intent expression emanating from dark brown eyes.

model because of the Chinese leader's belief that the peasants in the countryside should begin the revolution, which will then spread to the urban centers. From 1960 to 1965, Guevara became increasingly disenchanted with Soviet communism because of what he perceived as its dehumanizing elements. Guevara theorized that large-scale Soviet communism merely traded

Che Guevara (right) with Raúl Castro, Fidel's brother, in Mexico City for the Cuban Anniversary Meeting in 1964. *(AP/Wide World Photos)*

one sort of worker exploitation for another. In February, 1965, while speaking at the Organization for Afro-Asian Solidarity at Algiers, Guevara denounced the Soviet Union as a "tacit accomplice of imperialism" because it did not trade exclusively with communist-bloc countries.

Castro, well knowing Cuba's dependence upon Soviet trade, financial support, and military power, believed that he had no recourse but to place Guevara in a less visible position within the government. Although Guevara's formal status within the Castro regime did not change, his influence and his visibility dropped dramatically after the Algiers speech. Guevara's disappearance from sight resulted in rumors of his deportation or even death. There were reported sightings of Guevara in various African countries—especially the Congo, where he was supposedly organizing revolutionary forces. Late in 1965, Guevara surfaced in Cuba and took a contingent of 120 Cubans to the Congo in an unsuccessful attempt to turn the "Kinshasa rebellion" there into a communist revolution.

Death of a Revolutionary

Che Guevara's final campaign occurred in the Bolivian jungle. In the middle of 1966, Guevara began what would be nearly eighteen months of revolutionary activities among the Bolivian peasantry. There was dissension among various factions of Bolivian communists as Guevara attempted to import to Bolivia his *foco* strategies: creating a mobile guerrilla base in which the participants are not only military operatives but also politically astute apologists for social revolution. Guevara's Bolivian activities were perhaps doomed from the beginning, since revisionist historians have unequivocally proved that CIA agents had infiltrated various factions in the Bolivian revolution and likely had direct involvement in Guevara's capture by the Bolivian army on October 8, 1967. He was executed the following day.

Bibliography

Gonzalez, Luis J., and Gustavo Sanchez Salazar. *The Great Rebel: Che Guevara in Bolivia*. New York: Grove Press, 1969.

Guevara, Ernesto. *La Guerra de Guerillas*. Havana: Cuban Government, 1960.

Guevara, Ernesto, and Fidel Castro. *Socialism and Man in Cuba*. New York: Pathfinder, 1989.

James, Daniel. *Che Guevara: A Biography*. New York: Stein & Day, 1969.

Rodriguez, Carlos, et al. *Che Guevara, Cuba, and the Road to Socialism*. New York: Pathfinder, 1991.

Richard Sax

Guo Moruo

Born: November 10 or 16, 1892; Sha-wan, Sichuan Province, China
Died: June 12, 1978; Beijing, China

Chinese writer and longtime political figure

Guo Moruo (GWO MO-RWO), also written Kuo Mo-jo, was born into a prosperous merchant-landlord family. He was something of a playboy and a rebel, and he was twice expelled from school for participating in antigovernment demonstrations. He studied medicine in Japan but never practiced.

Literary Intellectual

In 1917, Guo began his prolific writing career, translating poems by Rabindranath Tagore. In 1921 he was influential in starting the Creation Society; his first book of poetry (*The Goddesses*) was published that same year. This was a period of great linguistic experimentation and innovation in China. In a comment on Johann Wolfgang van Goethe published in 1922, Guo wrote, "Literature should be a kind of revolutionary manifesto against established morality and established society." In 1923 he began to develop an interest in Marxism. He earned his living by freelance writing and teaching. His essays, poems, and plays were emotional and personal. In 1925 Guo joined the Kuomintang (KMT). During the Northern Expedition, he became a leader in the KMT Political Department. In 1927, when KMT leader Chiang Kai-shek attacked the Communists, Guo joined the Chinese Communist Party. Seeking safety in Japan in 1928, he settled into a highly productive literary life, producing novels, plays, and essays and translating radical Western literature.

Through War and Revolution

When war erupted in 1937 between China and Japan, Guo returned to China. The Nationalist government appointed him to head the Propaganda Section of the National Military Council. However, antileftist feeling caused his transfer to a less sensitive post in 1940—one, however, that gave him freedom and opportunity to write. He published several historical dramas and scholarly works on intellectual history and archaeology.

When World War II ended in 1945, Guo was active in efforts to form a working partnership between the KMT and the Chinese Communist Party (CCP). As civil war between the two parties intensified, he moved to Manchuria in

Guo Moruo in 1951. *(Sovfoto)*

Guo Moruo (front, second from right), president of China's Academy of Sciences, at a 1951 peace conference in Vienna, Austria. *(National Archives)*

1948, behind the Communist lines. He followed the Communist leaders to Beijing in early 1949 and became a part of the new government under Mao Zedong. He organized a Congress of Literary and Art Workers, which met in July, 1949, and urged them to create a "new people's literature and art." From this developed a network of associations for the different creative arts, all di-

The Northern Expedition

After the death of Yuan Shikai in 1916, China's national government, centered in Beijing, became weak and corrupt. Real power gravitated to regional warlords. In South China, Sun Yat-sen's Kuomintang (KMT, the Nationalist Party) developed its own military force. Sun welcomed members of the newly formed Chinese Communist Party into the KMT.

After Sun's death in 1925, his protégé Chiang Kai-shek emerged as leader of the KMT military forces. In July, 1926, Chiang embarked on the Northern Expedition, moving north from the Canton (Guanzhou) area, intending to overthrow the Beijing government and unify the country. With Communist and labor-union support, Chiang was able to take control of Shanghai in March, 1927. The following month he unleashed a violent attack on the Communists, beginning a long campaign to exterminate them, and established a new Nationalist government in Nanjing. In June, 1928, the new government gained control of Beijing.

rected toward mobilizing the talents of artists for political purposes and repressing dissident impulses.

In addition to holding high posts in some of these organizations, Guo was appointed president of the Academy of Sciences in 1949. In this role he negotiated international agreements to share scientific knowledge and helped organize a new University of Science and Technology in 1958, becoming its president. He also politicized the scientific community. He became chairman of the China Peace Committee and traveled widely over the next fifteen years to international conferences designed to publicize the communist point of view. Guo also participated in the program to reform and simplify the Chinese language. Through all this, he continued to be a prolific writer.

Guo's Importance

Guo was one of the few prominent Chinese who were able to maintain important government posts from 1949 until the late 1970's. He was willing to be a front man for the Communist Party, to follow all its changes in viewpoint, and to participate in the persecution of independent and free-thinking literary figures. His own writings have come to be seen more as artifacts than as literature of permanent value and interest.

Bibliography

Guo Moruo. *Five Historical Plays*. Beijing: Foreign Language Press, 1984.

Hsia, C. T. *A History of Modern Chinese Fiction*. 2d ed. New Haven, Conn.: Yale University Press, 1971.

Roy, David Tod. *Kuo Mo-jo: The Early Years*. Cambridge, Mass.: Harvard University Press, 1971.

Paul B. Trescott

Juvénal Habyarimana

Born: March 8, 1937; Gasiz, Gisenyi, Ruanda-Urundi (now Rwanda)
Died: April 6, 1994; near Kigali, Rwanda

President of Rwanda (1973-1994)

Juvénal Habyarimana (zhew-vay-NAHL hah-BEE-ah-ree-MAH-nah) was born of Hutu parents in Gisenyi in northwestern Rwanda. Educated in the Belgian Congo, he spent a year studying medicine before dropping out to join the army. He achieved rapid success as a soldier. In 1961, two years after being commissioned one of the first officers in Rwanda's National Guard, he became chief of staff. In 1965 he was made minister of defense under President Gregoire Kayibanda. Rapid promotions, such as those of Habyarimana, the Congo's Mobutu, and Uganda's Idi Amin, were forced by decolonization. They contributed much to the instability of many of Africa's newly independent nations.

Juvénal Habyarimana *(Reuters/Corbis-Bettmann)*

General and President

The adjustment to independence in 1962 was painful for landlocked, mountainous Rwanda, one of the world's most densely populated countries. Beginning in 1959, clashes between the Tutsi and Hutu ethnic groups resulted in vengeful massacres in which at least twelve thousand Tutsi died and more than 150,000 were driven into exile, mostly north to Uganda. Militant advocates of the more numerous Hutu took power. In 1963 a group of Tutsi rebels invaded, and the army, led by now General Habyarimana, successfully repulsed them. This conflict was followed by more bloodbaths of revenge. Renewed massacres of Tutsis erupted in 1967 and 1973, when Tutsis were purged from all institutions of higher education.

Deteriorating economic conditions and discontent among junior officers led Habyarimana to stage a bloodless coup in July of 1973. Overthrowing the civilian government, he declared himself president. He set to work easing tensions, but his commitment to true ethnic harmony was questionable. He instituted ethnic quotas for all public-sector employment, eliminated identity cards showing ethnic origins, and attempted to mend relations with Burundi and Uganda, both hosts of large numbers of Tutsi refugees. Tutsis were restricted to 9 percent of available jobs. Greatly influenced by and indebted to his wife's clan, he made most official appointments to the northern Hutu, adding regional resentments to ethnic ones.

In 1975 he imposed a single-party system based on his newly formed political party, the National Revolutionary Movement for Development (MRND, or Mouvement Révolutionnaire National pour le Développment). In 1977 Habyarimana joined the leaders of Burundi, Tanzania, and Uganda in founding the Kagera Basin

Tutsis massacred by Hutu militia in 1994; by 1994, bloody civil war in Rwanda had claimed hundreds of thousands of lives. *(Reuters/Corinne Dufka/Archive Photos)*

The Hutu-Tutsi Conflict

Mystery clouds the origins of the ethnic groups of Rwanda and Burundi, countries with similar cultural compositions but differing histories. Twa Pygmies, the region's first inhabitants, constitute only 1 percent of the population. The Hutu, more than 86 percent of the population, are hill farmers descended from Bantu groups farther west. Tutsi pastoralists probably entered the area from the northeast during the 1400's. They became the dominant force, though never representing more than 18 percent of the population. The Tutsi created a feudal system whereby the Hutu gained protection and cattle in return for crops and labor. For at least two hundred years, until independence in 1960, both Rwanda and Burundi were ruled by Tutsi kings. Differing markedly in physical features, the Hutu and Tutsi nonetheless share languages, kinship systems, and religions.

German and, later, Belgian colonialists ruled through Tutsi kings and exacerbated ethnic divisions by unequally distributing resources and education. In 1959, the Rwandan Hutu seized power, and centuries of resentment led to massacres. Seeing events in Rwanda, Burundi's Tutsis instituted repressive measures. Rebellion ensued, and massacres followed. More than a million deaths have resulted from ethnic strife in Hutu-dominated Rwanda and Tutsi-dominated Burundi since 1959.

The Kagera River Basin

The Kagera River of east-central Africa is 300 miles (480 kilometers) long and follows the Rwanda-Tanzania and Uganda-Tanzania borders into Lake Victoria. Burundi's Ruvyironza River, which flows into it, is regarded as the source of the Nile. The area is highly populated, mountainous, with variable rainfall and a reasonably pleasant climate. The region's great potential for hydroelectric power, iron and nickel mining, cash crops, and tourism depends on considerable improvement in energy, roads, railways, and telecommunications.

The Kagera Basin Organization (KBO), founded in 1977, promotes cooperation among the region's governments through the integrated exploitation and management of water and land resources in the basin. The KBOs members are Burundi, Rwanda, Tanzania, and Uganda. Officially known as the Organization for the Management and Development of the Kagera Basin, the KBO has its headquarters and documentation center in Kigali, Rwanda. Sponsored by the World Bank and aided by the United Nations and various donor countries, the KBO in the 1990's concentrated on rail and road transport, intraregional telecommunications, energy, forestation, insect and water hyacinth control, irrigation, pastoral use of marginal lands, and training.

Organization to promote regional development. Throughout the 1980's, his regime was criticized for corruption.

Problems, Agreement, and Unease

Rwanda's political crisis deepened in the early 1990's. A drop in world coffee prices in 1989 led Habyarimana to introduce an extremely unpopular austerity program. Responding to pressures from international aid donors, opponents, and human rights groups, he authorized opposition parties and began a cautious program of political liberalization in July, 1990. In October of that same year the Rwandan Patriotic Front (RPF), a Tutsi-led rebel force of exiles armed by Uganda, invaded from the north. At great cost and in spite of French military support, Rwandan forces were unsuccessful in expelling RPF forces from their camps in the Ruwenzori Mountains. The fighting abated in 1993, but political and ethnic tensions remained dangerously high.

The early 1990's saw growing paranoia in the regime, and Habyarimana retreated from his conciliatory position to one of blaming the Tutsi for all of Rwanda's problems. Mandatory ethnic identity cards were reinstated. Installed for a twenty-two-month term as transitional president, Habyarimana opened peace talks with the rebels and declared that he would accelerate his democratization program. In reality, an uneasy Habyarimana stalled while other East African leaders pressed him to continue his reforms. Meanwhile, Hutu civilian militias, known as the Interahamwe, were trained and armed by the regime to repel the RPF, who immediately resumed their offensive. Several thousand Tutsi were killed in various incidents throughout the country. By 1993 RPF forces had advanced close to the capital, Kigali. Following negotiations in Arusha, Tanzania, in August of 1993, Habyarimana agreed to a power-sharing arrangement with the RPF. U.N. peacekeeping troops were deployed. A solution seemed imminent, even though human-rights groups warned of impending upheavals as Hutu militants began broadcasting exhortations to attack Tutsis.

Assassination and Genocide

On April 6, 1994, following talks in Dar-es-Salaam, Tanzania, the presidential jet carrying

Habyarimana and Burundian president Cyprien Ntaryamira home was shot down by rockets, launched either by the RPF or by hard-line elements of the Hutu Presidential Guard opposing the Arusha Accords. The assassination came at a crucial juncture in negotiations. A vindictive slaughter of Tutsi and moderate Hutus was unleashed by the Interahamwe. Among the first victims was Rwanda's first woman prime minister, Agatha Uwilingiyimana, and her ten Belgian bodyguards. More than a half million Rwandans, including the elderly and children, were killed. Another 1.2 million fled the country. Although unable to stop the genocidal killings, the RPF was able to overthrow the Hutu regime by July, 1994.

Juvénal Habyarimana's rule was a model of how to survive in power under extremely adverse conditions. For two decades Habyarimana's dictatorial rule was unquestioned. However, his lack of political courage and failing commitment to ethnic harmony ultimately led to the worst human-rights violations in Rwanda's already blood-stained history.

Bibliography

Destexhe, Alain. *Rwanda and Genocide in the Twentieth Century*. New York: NYU Press, 1995.

Keane, Fergal. *Season of Blood: A Rwandan Journey*. London: Viking, 1995.

Prunier, Gérard. *The Rwanda Crisis: History of a Genocide*. New York: Columbia University Press, 1995.

Randall Fegley

Alexander M. Haig

Born: December 2, 1924; Philadelphia, Pennsylvania

U.S. security adviser and secretary of state (1981-1982)

Alexander Meigs Haig, Jr. (a-lehk-ZAN-dur MEHGZ HAYG JEW-nyur), was the son of an assistant city prosecutor and World War I veteran. He attended Notre Dame but then fulfilled a childhood dream by entering the United States Military Academy at West Point. Following graduation in 1947, he spent the next thirty-two years in the army, rising to the rank of a four-star general. In 1950 he married Patricia Antoinette Fox and had three children, Alexander, Brian, and Barbara.

Alexander M. Haig *(Library of Congress)*

Military Service

After World War II, Haig became an assistant to General Douglas MacArthur in occupied Japan; he was then an aide during the Korean War. He took part in the Inchon landing. Further studies at the Naval War College, Army War College, and Georgetown University also advanced his rank. During the Vietnam War he commanded the 1st Battalion, 26th Infantry, and received the Distinguished Service Cross for bravery. His expertise in military affairs brought him to the attention of Washington leaders, and he began serving as an aide to the National Security Council (NSC). Thereafter, Haig became a trusted confidant of several presidents. President Gerald R. Ford appointed him North Atlantic Treaty Organization (NATO) supreme commander, and he served in Europe as major general for five years until retirement in 1979.

White House Days

In 1969 Colonel Haig became a military aide and then deputy for national security adviser Henry Kissinger. Because of Kissinger's frequent trips around the world, Haig became instrumental to the functioning of the National Security Council. He developed a close working relationship with President Richard M. Nixon. After Nixon fired White House chief of staff H. R. Haldeman as the Watergate scandal unfolded, he made Haig chief of staff. Haig assisted the president in his defense and communicated Nixon's order to fire the special prosecutor investigating the president. Haig is credited with orchestrating Nixon's resignation and taking the unprecedented step of running the White House as the turmoil grew.

In 1981 President Ronald Reagan appointed Haig secretary of state. Almost immediately he

Alexander M. Haig, who replaced H. R. Haldeman as President Richard M. Nixon's White House chief of staff, listens attentively to Nixon at a 1974 press conference. *(Archive Photos)*

maintained a stable relationship with the Soviet Union during a low point in relations between the superpowers. He continued efforts for peace in the Middle East and began funding military advisers in El Salvador. When Reagan was shot during an assassination attempt in March of 1981, Haig announced to the national press, "As of now, I am in control here in the White House, pending return of the vice president." This statement ignored constitutional succession and appeared as though Haig had assumed more power than appropriate. Haig denied that his intent had been to assume greater authority and later explained that he was attempting to reassure the public in a time of crisis. The statement further

clashed with White House staff over authority for making foreign policy. Haig believed that Reagan had appointed him chief policy maker, and his strong personality led to further disputes. Haig

damaged his relations with White House staff, however. Haig blamed the staff for press leaks damaging to him and took a defensive stance when consulted by presidential advisers.

The National Security Council

Created by act of Congress in 1947, the National Security Council (NSC) serves the president as an advisory, crisis management, and policy-making body. The council grew out of World War II experiences and the new global challenges of the Cold War. The United States needed a coherent and coordinated effort approach among the executive branch and other departments of government for successfully meeting threats to the nation. Depending upon how a president chooses to use the council, its advice can have an enormous impact on the formulation of domestic, military, and for-

eign policy. The council has broad authority to ensure that departments and agencies of the government are communicating and cooperating on vital security matters. The council provides direction and strives for consistency in strategic matters. Membership in the National Security Council has varied. The president is always at the head, and other members usually include the vice president, secretary of state, secretary of defense, other experts in and out of government, and a special assistant or adviser who takes chief responsibility for presenting ideas and options to the president.

U.S. secretary of state Alexander M. Haig meets with President Ronald Reagan in Los Angeles in 1981. Haig had just completed a diplomatic visit to China and other Asian countries. *(AP/Wide World Photos)*

The impasse broke when Haig resigned in 1982 after only eighteen months on the job. After leaving government service, Haig became a consultant for United Technologies, where he had been chief executive officer (CEO) after his retirement from the army. He also founded Worldwide Associates, a private Washington, D.C., consulting firm for international and strategic matters.

Bibliography

Frost, David. *The Next President.* New York: U.S. News and World Report, 1988.

Haig, Alexander. *Caveat: Realism, Reagan, and Foreign Policy.* New York: Macmillan, 1984.

Haig, Alexander Meigs. *Inner Circles: How America Changed the World, a Memoir.* New York: Warner Books, 1992.

Kissinger, Henry. *Years of Upheaval.* Boston: Little, Brown, 1982.

Henry O. Robertson

Haile Selassie I

Born: July 23, 1892; near Harer, Ethiopia
Died: August 27, 1975; Addis Ababa, Ethiopia

Emperor of Ethiopia (1930-1974)

Tafari Makonnen (teh-FAH-rih ma-KOH-nehn), later known as the last Ethiopian emperor, Haile Selassie I (HI-leh seh-lah-SEE thuh FURST), was the youngest of ten children born to a daughter of a minor noble and a prominent politician related to the Emperor Menelik II. He was educated in Christian schools, where he learned European as well as Ethiopian languages and culture. At age thirteen Tafari formally joined the ruling class when he was made, in name at least, the governor of a small territory. At the death of his father, his education continued at the palace school, where he served as one of the emperor's personal servants. In 1908 the emperor gave him full administrative power, first as governor of Darossa, a subprovince of Ethiopia, and then as governor of a larger province two years later. In 1911 Tafari married Woizero Menen, with whom he had four sons and two daughters.

Crown Prince and Regent

After Emperor Menelik died in 1913, his grandson Lij Yasu took the throne. The new emperor, strongly aligned with Islam, soon alienated the large Christian population in Ethiopia. In 1916 Tafari helped engineer a coup that replaced Yasu with Menelik's daughter Zauditu. In reward, Tafari was proclaimed the crown prince and the regent of Ethiopia. He was given the rank of Ras, or duke. As regent, Tafari was expected to act only as a weak executive officer while the Empress Zauditu actually wielded the power. Although the empress and the regent were cordial in public, in private they sought to strengthen their own political positions. From the outset, Tafari worked to solidify his relations with the Ethiopian Orthodox Church, his strongest political alliance. He also worked to improve the qual-

ity of his army and the education of Ethiopian children. In 1923 Tafari used his diplomatic and political ties to obtain Ethiopia's membership in the League of Nations. In fulfilling the conditions imposed by the league, he abolished slavery in Ethiopia a year later.

The Last Emperor

Tafari became a king in 1928. In 1930 Tafari surprised his enemies by attacking the empress

Haile Selassie I *(Library of Congress)*

615

Ethiopian emperor Haile Selassie I addressing his subjects from the balcony of his palace in 1935, speaking of Italy's demands and the likelihood of an Italian invasion. *(Library of Congress)*

The Italian Invasion of 1935

In the early 1930's, Ethiopia was the only independent African state—other than Liberia—still free from European control. Since the nineteenth century, Italy had been watching Ethiopia and waiting for a chance to expand farther into Africa and compete with the other colonial powers. In 1935 Italy marched an Italian army across Somalia and Eritrea into Ethiopia despite the Treaty of Friendship, which had been signed in 1928.

The Italians, led by fascist dictator Benito Mussolini, had post-World War I technology on their side, including artillery, tanks, airplanes, and poison gas. Within eight months, Italy had forced most of Ethiopia into submission. Although Haile Selassie requested help from the League of Nations in Geneva, the league's member states virtually ignored Italy's international aggression for several months. Finally, in January, 1941, nearly six years after the initial invasion, Britain invaded Ethiopia. Britain was responding to Italian threats to British interests in North Africa. Fiercely supported by forces garnered from British, Belgian, and French territories throughout Africa and various volunteer forces, Haile Selassie and his patriots fought off the hostile Italian armies. By the middle of the year the Ethiopians had regained their capital at Addis Ababa, and the emperor was restored to the throne.

The 1974 Revolution

The emperor's last decade in power was very difficult because of severe economic problems, unemployment, and famine. The revolution began with the mutiny of the army's Second Division in which certain high officials, including the governor of Eritrea, were arrested. They captured a town, then an air force headquarters, and then descended on Addis Ababa. To the dismay and amazement of many Ethiopians, Haile Selassie decided to negotiate rather than quash the rebellion's forces. By February, 1974, the army had seized power even as the emperor still attempted to negotiate and provide a legal basis in Parliament for the political shift. In September the emperor was arrested and formally deposed. Ethiopia, ruled by the Provisional Military Revolutionary Council (PMRC), was declared officially a republic.

at her stronghold. He stripped her of her power and forced her to transfer her control of the armed forces to him. At the same time, Tafari methodically deflated threats from his political rivals, clearing his path to imperial power. When the empress died soon after, Tafari was crowned emperor on March 3, 1930. He took the name Haile Selassie I. The name means "might of the Trinity."

As emperor, Tafari immediately developed a program of modernization designed to counteract the years of corruption, disease, and general decline that Ethiopia had undergone. He worked to improve the civil administration and the judicial system and to institute a fiscal program designed to strengthen the economy. He introduced a written constitution which provided for a bicameral government. The government consisted of a Senate appointed by the emperor and a Chamber of Deputies designed to advise the emperor. The constitution further ensured that political and economic decisions would be determined by majority vote in both houses.

Haile Selassie's reforms extended to religious and cultural matters. In the Ethiopian Orthodox Church he appointed bishops, and he made the patriarch of the church the local archbishop. He utilized a new European style of rank and uniform, built new military schools with foreign

Haile Selassie and members of the Ethiopian royal family in exile in London in 1936; they did not return to Ethiopia for four years. *(National Archives)*

617

instructors, and imported more weapons and war planes with foreign pilots. Furthermore, to make the modern Amharic literature more accessible throughout Ethiopia, Haile Selassie introduced large-scale printing into the country so that more books as well as government tracts could be published.

Exile

In 1935 Italy invaded Ethiopia despite the Treaty of Friendship that had existed between the two countries since 1928. After losing a critical battle at Maichen, Haile Selassie went into exile in 1936. His decision to flee disappointed and angered many of his subjects, who expected the emperor to lead the patriotic resistance. Almost penniless and relying on the assistance of European governments, he escaped with his family and a few faithful staff members to England.

The emperor, viewed increasingly as an important symbol of resistance and independence, worked steadily to bring international attention to Ethiopia's plight during his four years in exile. He addressed the General Assembly of the League of Nations in Geneva. He argued that membership in the league guaranteed the equality of all states and that the league was obligated to intervene when one state acted aggressively toward a member state. He returned to Addis Ababa in May, 1941.

Final Years

Throughout the next three decades, Haile Selassie worked to stabilize the political and economic situation of Ethiopia. He initiated major land reforms in 1942 and 1944. In 1955 he revised the constitution so that all adults could vote. In 1960 an abortive coup occurred. In 1974, one year before he died, he was arrested and deposed from the throne in a revolution.

In many ways, the reign and leadership of Haile Selassie I marked Ethiopia's transition into the modern world. His attempts to strengthen Ethiopia politically, economically, and culturally ultimately brought about his downfall in the form of the 1974 *coup d'état* that removed him from power and made Ethiopia an independent republic.

Bibliography

Lockot, Hans Wilhelm. *The Mission: The Life, Reign, and Character of Haile Selassie I*. New York: St. Martin's Press, 1989.

Marcus, Harold G. *Haile Selassie I: The Formative Years, 1892-1936*. Berkeley: University of California Press, 1987.

Mosley, Leonard. *Haile Selassie: The Conquering Lion*. Englewood Cliffs, N.J.: Prentice-Hall, 1965.

Susanna Calkins

William F. Halsey

Born: October 30, 1882; Elizabeth, New Jersey
Died: August 16, 1959; Fishers Island, New York

U.S. naval commander of South Pacific forces in World War II

William Frederick Halsey, Jr. (WIHL-yuhm FREH-duh-rihk HAHL-zee JEW-nyur), was the son of a naval officer. He attended a large number of schools before receiving his appointment to the U.S. Naval Academy from President William McKinley in 1900.

Early Career

As a midshipman, Halsey distinguished himself in athletics, not scholarship. After graduating in 1904, he was assigned to the USS *Missouri*. In 1907 he joined the USS *Kansas*. During the next twenty-five years, Halsey served primarily aboard destroyers. In 1915 he went ashore to spend two years in the Executive Department of the Naval Academy. When the United States entered World War I in 1917, Halsey returned to sea with the Queenstown Destroyer Force. He continued to serve on various destroyers, with brief periods of shore duty.

In 1934 he embarked on his aviation career, reporting to the Naval Air Station in Pensacola, Florida, for flight training. He received his wings as a naval aviator on May 15, 1935, and subsequently took command of the carrier USS *Saratoga*. In 1938 he attained flag rank, and by 1940 he had become commander of the Aircraft Battle Force with the rank of vice admiral. He was on the USS *Enterprise* at the time of the Japanese surprise attack on the U.S. naval base at Pearl Harbor, Hawaii.

The Fighting Admiral

Halsey was not in Pearl Harbor on the morning of December 7, 1941. His carrier division had been assigned to take reinforcements to Wake Island, and their return was delayed. After the attack, the United States immediately declared war on Japan, bringing the United States into World War II. When Halsey received word of the attack, he immediately began searching for the Japanese force, although without success. In the early months of 1942, Halsey began a series of hit-and-run raids on Japanese-held islands. Although these made little strategic contribution, they provided a much-needed boost to morale shattered by Pearl Harbor.

Halsey missed the first two major battles of the war in the Pacific. He arrived too late to participate in the Battle of the Coral Sea. Stress had made inroads in his health, and he was suffering from a skin disorder that rendered him nearly unable to rest. Thus he missed the Battle of Midway, an absence he was to regret for the rest of his life.

William F. Halsey *(Library of Congress)*

Halsey, William F.

A battle cruiser attempting to extinguish the fire on the USS *Princeton*, hit during the battle of Leyte Gulf in 1941. *(Library of Congress)*

The Great Offensives

Recovered from his illness, Halsey was made commander of the South Pacific forces and South Pacific area in October of 1942. While in this command he was promoted to the rank of admiral. In June, 1944, he assumed command of the Third Fleet. His role became increasingly controversial, especially after the Battle of Leyte Gulf. His encounters with two typhoons further damaged his standing. Halsey's flag flew aboard the USS *Missouri* on September 2, 1945, in Tokyo Bay for the signing of the formal Japanese surrender. Subsequently, Halsey shifted his flag to the USS *South Dakota* and returned to the United States, where he hauled his flag down for the last time.

Postwar Career

On December 11, 1945, Halsey took the oath as a fleet admiral. As such, he was immune to mandatory retirement, but he requested to be transferred to the retired list on March 1, 1947. Subsequently he became involved in various civilian business activities and an attempt to preserve the USS *Enterprise* as a national shrine.

Bibliography

Halsey, William F. *Admiral Halsey's Story*. New York: McGraw-Hill, 1947.

Merrill, James M. *A Sailor's Admiral: A Biography of William F. Halsey*. New York: Crowell, 1976.

Potter, E. B. *Bull Halsey*. Annapolis, Md.: Naval Institute Press, 1985.

Leigh Husband Kimmel

The Battle of Leyte Gulf

On October 23, 1944, the U.S. Navy engaged Japanese forces near the Philippine Islands in the largest naval battle of World War II, involving more than 244 ships. American forces were divided into two major groups, commanded by William F. Halsey and Thomas Kinkaid. Lack of communication between the two commanders led to major difficulties. Kinkaid's forces came under heavy fire while Halsey was pursuing a Japanese force far to the north. Kinkaid repeatedly pleaded for relief until area commander Chester W. Nimitz intervened. Halsey reluctantly broke off his attack and turned back to support the main striking force. He remained bitter for the rest of his life about the loss of the chance to destroy the Japanese force he was attacking to the north; he blamed Kinkaid. The Leyte Gulf battle marked the beginning of Halsey's fall from grace. There was talk of retiring him, and only his reputation among the troops as a fighting admiral saved his career.

Dag Hammarskjöld

Born: July 29, 1905; Jönköping, Sweden
Died: September 18, 1961; near Ndola, Northern Rhodesia (now Zambia)

Swedish diplomat, secretary-general of the United Nations (1952-1961), winner of 1961 Nobel Peace Prize

Dag Hjalmar Agne Carl Hammarskjöld (DAHG YAHL-mahr AHNG-neh KAHRL HAH-mahr-shuhld) was the son of Agnes Hammarskjöld (née Almquist) and Hjalmar Hammarskjöld, a professor of law and prime minister of Sweden during World War I. The Hammarskjöld family had served as statesmen and soldiers since the seventeenth century, and Dag Hammarskjöld held various posts in the Swedish government and the United Nations throughout his life. He graduated from Uppsala University in 1935, receiving a bachelor of arts degree, a degree in economics, a bachelor of laws degree, and a doctoral degree in political economy, a subject which formed the basis of his life's work in government and humanitarian service.

Service in the Swedish Government

From 1936 to 1945, Hammarskjöld was appointed undersecretary in Sweden's Department of Finance, and from 1941 to 1948 he served as chairman of the board of the National Bank of Sweden and a member of the Board of Exchange. Together with his brother Bo Hammarskjöld, who was an undersecretary in the Ministry of Social Welfare, Hammarskjöld brought forward legislation that helped to create Sweden's present-day social welfare system.

During World War II, Hammarskjöld developed his skills as an international negotiator by arranging support from the Allied countries for Norway's government-in-exile, although Sweden itself remained a neutral country. In the postwar era, Hammarskjöld held a series of influential posts in the Swedish government, being appointed in 1946 as a finance specialist in the Foreign Office, in 1948 as assistant foreign minister and vice chairman of the executive committee

of the Organization for European Economic Cooperation (OEEC), and in 1951 as minister of state in charge of foreign economic relations. During this time, Hammarskjöld helped to promote economic cooperation between countries by representing Sweden in implementation of the Marshall Plan. (The Marshall Plan provided loans to help European countries devastated by World War II to rebuild their economies.) As vice chairman of the executive committee of the OEEC,

Dag Hammarskjöld *(Library of Congress)*

621

During his nine years in the office, Dag Hammarskjöld (second from left) strengthened the role of the U.N. secretary-general as peace negotiator. *(National Archives)*

Hammarskjöld helped develop and promote joint economic projects which strengthened ties between all Western European countries.

Leadership of the United Nations

In 1951 Hammarskjöld joined the General As-sembly of the United Nations as vice chairman of the Swedish delegation. In April of 1952 he was elected secretary-general of the United Nations, being reelected in 1957. During these nine years Hammarskjöld did much to establish the United Nations' right to act independently from the con-

---

Korean Prisoners of War

During the Korean War (1950-1953), fifteen American airmen (part of the United Nations-led forces fighting on the side of South Korea) were captured by the Chinese. When the war ended, the Chinese refused to release the prisoners and sentenced eleven of them to lifelong sentences on charges of espionage. Since the United States had had no formal relations with China since China's communist revolution, the United States re-quested that the United Nations resolve the problem. The U.N. General Assembly sent Secretary-General Dag Hammarskjöld to negotiate personally with the Chinese for the release of the prisoners of war. The talks, which took place in January, 1955, were difficult but ultimately successful. All the prisoners were released the following summer.

The Congo Crisis

In June, 1960, the Republic of the Congo achieved independence from Belgium. The nation was governed by two opposing factions, with Prime Minister Patrice Lumumba being supported by the Soviet Union and President Joseph Kasavubu by the United States. The civil service and military of the new country were still dominated by Belgian nationals, and the Congolese soon rebelled. Without approval from the Congolese government, Belgium sent in troops to try to restore order. Supported by Belgian troops, the leader of the province of Katanga, Moïse Tshombé, declared his province independent. The Congolese government requested U.N. intervention.

On July 14, the U.N. Security Council approved the sending of an international peacekeeping force to the Congo, and the Opération des Nations Unies au Congo (ONUC) began immediately. As well as ending the Congo crisis before it escalated, the council wanted to prevent other newly independent African nations from becoming battlegrounds between communist and noncommunist superpowers. The Security Council ordered the withdrawal of Belgian forces from the province of Katanga. In time ONUC forces were able to restore civil order, although Katanga remained a breakaway state. In November, 1960, Prime Minister Lumumba was taken prisoner by the Congolese army, and he was later executed by rebel leader Tshombé in Katanga. The U.N. operation in the Congo continued until 1963 and was ultimately successful in persuading Katanga to rejoin the Republic of the Congo.

---

flicting national interests of its member states. He also greatly strengthened the role of the secretary-general as a negotiator for peace in regions of world conflict. The U.N. Secretariat was reorganized and given operating guidelines that defined its status as an independent and impartial body with the right to act in the best interests of world peace.

In 1954-1955, Hammarskjöld personally negotiated the release of American soldiers who had been captured by the Chinese in the Korean War. Throughout his first term as secretary-general, Hammarskjöld developed a policy of using "preventive diplomacy" to ward off conflicts between nations. In the Middle East, he encouraged diplomatic efforts to maintain the armistice agreements between Israel and the Arab states. In 1956 Egypt claimed national jurisdiction over the Suez Canal, causing the Suez Crisis—a confrontation with Israel, Britain, and France. As well as engaging in diplomatic discussions with the nations involved, Hammarskjöld averted military action between these nations by quickly creating the United Nations Emergency Force (UNEF), the first of its kind, to guarantee a peaceful resolution to the crisis. Another Middle East crisis occurred in 1958 when Lebanon and Jordan felt threatened by neighboring Arab states and requested military aid from Britain and the United States. Hammarskjöld again set a precedent by persuading the Middle Eastern states to settle the dispute among themselves and by replacing British and American troops with a U.N. observation group.

Hammarskjöld and the Congo

In 1960-1961, the United Nations attempted to resolve a series of political crises in the Republic of the Congo (later called Zaire, later still the Congo again), newly independent from Belgium. The new country was being torn by internal political factions and by attempts by major Cold War nations (the Soviet Union and various Western countries) to take sides in the conflict. As secretary-general, Hammarskjöld coordinated all the diplomatic negotiations and initiatives that together prevented an outbreak of full-scale war. He fought hard to establish the U.N. role as peace-keeper and arbiter in Africa, where many nations were experiencing political instability as they gained independence. On September 18, 1961, Hammarskjöld was killed in a plane crash while on his way to the rebel province of Katanga to try to negotiate a truce with the Congo's central government. After his death, he was awarded the 1961 Nobel Peace Prize in recognition of his life-long devotion to the cause of global peace and cooperation.

Lifetime Achievement

Under Dag Hammarskjöld's leadership, the United Nations became an active participant and negotiator on behalf of world peace. Although he met significant opposition and criticism for his views, Hammarskjöld successfully transformed the United Nations into an effective international organization which was able to fulfill the aims of its original charter in promoting negotiation and cooperation among nations.

Bibliography

Beskow, Bo. *Dag Hammarskjöld: Strictly Personal.* New York: Doubleday, 1969.

Fredriksson, Gunnar, et al. *Sweden at the UN: Eight Profiles.* Stockholm: Swedish Institute, 1996.

Kellen, Emery. *Dag Hammarskjöld: A Biography.* New York: Meredith Press, 1969.

Wallensteen, Peter. *Dag Hammarsköld.* Stockholm: Swedish Institute, 1995.

Helen Bragg

Warren G. Harding

Born: November 2, 1865; Caledonia (now Blooming Grove), Ohio
Died: August 2, 1923; San Francisco, California

President of the United States (1921-1923)

Warren Gamaliel Harding (WAH-rehn ga-MAY-lee-ehl HAHR-dihng) was born in comparatively modest circumstances in rural Ohio. His father, largely self-trained as a physician, could barely support his family. Harding was raised primarily by his strong-willed mother. Because of his dark complexion, he was suspected of having African American ancestry and often faced prejudice because of it. After graduation from college, Harding, after trying various occupations, settled on becoming a newspaperman. His life changed after he moved to Marion, the county seat. He acquired the *Marion Star*, a small bankrupt paper, and then married Florence Kling DeWolfe, a divorcée and the daughter of the town's richest man. Even more strong-willed than Harding's mother, and a shrewd businesswoman, Florence Harding helped make the *Marion Star* a commercial success and steered her husband into the field of politics, for which he quickly showed he had aptitude.

Ohio's Favorite Son

Harding's talents for politics stemmed from his never taking a firm stand on a controversial subject (such as whether the United States should join the League of Nations), his ability to harmonize and compromise, his gregarious, attractive personality, and his silver-tongued oratorical style. His greatest asset was perhaps his appearance. His dark complexion contrasted with his silver hair and dark eyebrows. A handsome man, Warren G. Harding looked like a president.

A staunch Republican, backed by the growing influence of his newspaper, Harding was elected to the Ohio Senate in 1898. He became lieutenant governor in 1904 but lost the race for governor in 1910. In 1914 he became Ohio's first popularly elected U.S. senator. Harding's career as senator was lackluster. He introduced no important bills, but he also made no enemies. Membership in the Senate suited Harding—but not his ambitious wife. As the Democratic presidential term of the increasingly unpopular Woodrow Wilson drew to a close, the Republican bid for the presidency seemed assured.

The Nomination Battle

Prodded by Florence Harding and by Harry M. Daugherty, an unscrupulous political promoter

Warren G. Harding *(Library of Congress)*

625

U.S. president Warren G. Harding throws out the first ball of the 1922 baseball season in Washington, D.C. *(Archive Photos)*

and fund-raiser, Harding entered the race for the nomination at the Republican Convention in June of 1920 in Chicago. At first his chances seemed slim, but in-house fighting between rival candidates—and the fact that Theodore Roosevelt, who had previously seemed the most logical candidate, had died the year before—opened the way for a compromise candidate. On a Friday afternoon in the wilting summer heat, the weary delegates nominated Warren G. Harding as their candidate for president on the eighth ballot.

A Return to "Normalcy"

By now a seasoned politician, Harding knew

Normalcy

Although it was not coined by Warren G. Harding, as sometimes reported, "normalcy" became one of his favorite words. It helped him gain the presidency but soon assumed broader implications as a form of political conservatism. Normalcy was a longing for less-troubled times, a return to an imagined pre-1914 America and the wisdom of the Founding Fathers. Normalcy meant being against the United States joining the League of Nations. Normalcy supported Prohibition as part of a morally pure America. Normalcy justified a rollback of wages, a continuance of the twelve-hour working day, child labor, high tariffs, and a general deflationary fiscal policy.

The Teapot Dome Scandal

The Teapot Dome scandal was a major scandal of Warren G. Harding's administration. Secretary of the Interior Albert B. Fall secretly leased the Teapot Dome naval oil reserve in Wyoming to private interests for exploitation. Secretary Fall tried to defend his act as a patriotic move, saying it would salvage oil from drainage and provide the Navy with above-ground oil storage to meet a possible threat from the growing naval power of Japan. A supporter of the exploitation of natural resources, Fall antagonized conservationists, who plotted his downfall. He committed perjury before the investigating Senate committee when he failed to reveal the interest-free loans he had received from the private interests involved. For this he received a criminal conviction.

the country's mood. After the emotional trauma of World War I (1914-1918) and the trying peace process, the country longed for simpler, less complicated times. Harding gave the electorate what it wanted. He conducted his campaign largely from his front porch, posing as a genial small-town newspaper editor and family man whose greatest pleasure was to "boviate"—or do nothing requiring effort. The results were spectacular. Harding was swept into office by 60 percent of the popular vote.

Heavy Political Obligations

Despite his mandate, Harding came into office with many political debts that could be met only through patronage. His party had been out of power for eight years, and many party figures wanted jobs in the government. To satisfy the demand, Harding released thousands of positions from civil service protection and turned them into political appointments. Prohibition (which had gone into effect in January, 1920) provided additional positions that lent themselves to corruption. Harry Daugherty was rewarded by being named U.S. attorney general. Charles R. Forbes, another political crony, headed the Veterans Bureau, with its generous appropriations. Albert B. Fall became secretary of the interior. These were appointments that Harding would soon regret. Charles Evans Hughes as secretary of state, Herbert Hoover as secretary of commerce, and Andrew Mellon as secretary of the treasury, however, were good choices.

Harding's presidency saw a number of accomplishments. A Bureau of the Budget was created to bring order to federal finances. In 1922, Hughes, with Harding's support, sponsored the

Warren G. Harding during his 1920 run for the presidency, flanked by (left) Will Hays and vice presidential candidate Calvin Coolidge. *(Library of Congress)*

Washington Naval Conference to limit naval armaments. Harding pressed for U.S. involvement with the World Court. He supported limits on child labor, a shorter work day, and better working conditions for labor.

Scandals Begin to Surface

After a relatively harmonious beginning, by 1923, Harding's presidency was in trouble. Romantic liaisons with the wife of his best friend and with a young woman thirty years his junior posed the threat of blackmail or exposure. Rumors surfaced of the secret leasing of Navy oil reserve lands by Secretary of the Interior Fall. There were also rumors of the corrupt buying and selling of military supplies by Charles Forbes. After a violent confrontation, Harding forced the resignation of his long-time friend Forbes. Daugherty's involvement with graft was common knowledge, although the wily attorney general managed to steer clear of indictment. Harding personally was never tainted by corruption. Nonetheless, as he sadly remarked, he could take care of his enemies; it was his friends who were giving him trouble.

Harding's Last Trip

In June of 1923, a visibly discouraged and physically run-down president decided to take a fence-mending tour across the United States, terminating in Alaska, with speaking stops in the small towns that had been his main support. The trip was not a success. Harding's health and spirits continued to deteriorate. On the boat trip back from Alaska, a Navy plane delivered a secret message that Harding read and then destroyed; its effects were devastating. Canceling all engagements, the presidential party hurried to San Francisco, where President Harding died of heart failure on August 2.

A Second Look

Generally regarded as among the worst—if not the worst—of American presidents, Harding has undergone some historic revisionism. Although limited in ability, Harding was conscientious and hard-working. He wanted to be, and was, a popular president. His tragedy was being caught between the moralistic demands of the time and a Congress that sought to hide its own deficiencies by emphasizing those of the president.

Bibliography

Anthony, Carl S. *Florence Harding*. New York: William Morrow, 1998.

Mee, Charles L. *The Ohio Gang*. New York: M. Evans, 1981.

Murray, Robert K. *The Harding Era*. Minneapolis: University of Minnesota Press, 1969.

Russell, Francis. *The Shadow of Blooming Grove: Warren G. Harding in His Times*. New York: McGraw-Hill, 1968.

Nis Petersen

William Averell Harriman

Born: November 15, 1891; New York, New York
Died: July 26, 1986; Yorktown Heights, New York

U.S. public official and diplomat

William Averell Harriman (WIHL-yuhm AY-veh-rehl HA-rih-muhn) was a child of privilege. His father, Edward H. Harriman, built an American railroad empire during the late nineteenth century. The younger Harriman attended the elite preparatory school Groton, and in 1913 he graduated from Yale University. He married three times. His third wife, Pamela Digby Churchill, served as the U.S. ambassador to France (1993-1997).

Businessman and Diplomat

Harriman began his business career working for the Union Pacific Railroad, which his father had reorganized at the beginning of the twentieth century. He avoided military service during World War I and instead invested his inheritance in new enterprises. In 1918 he organized the Merchant Shipbuilding Company, which soon boasted the largest shipping fleet in the United States. Two years later he established an international investment house on Wall Street named W. A. Harriman and Company. By 1932 he was also acting as chairman of the board for the Union Pacific and the Illinois Central Railroads.

Harriman became involved in politics and diplomacy during the Depression. Although he opposed many New Deal programs, he was drawn into the Democratic Party and Franklin D. Roosevelt's administration by their mutual friend Harry L. Hopkins. Harriman chaired the Commerce Department's Business Advisory Council and actively supported the National Recovery Administration (NRA). As World War II approached, the president relied on Harriman's financial ability as well as his familiarity with Europe. In 1941 he was dispatched to London to help facilitate the lend-lease program, transfer-

ring war materials to the Allies. Two years later he was appointed ambassador to the Soviet Union, where he gained the trust of communist leaders and developed his reputation as a Russian expert.

Ambassador-at-Large

Ambassador Harriman also served President Harry S Truman as an adviser early in the Cold War. After transferring from Moscow to London, the envoy returned to Washington in 1946 to become Truman's secretary of commerce. His next fours years were dedicated to the Marshall Plan, an American program to reconstruct

William Averell Harriman *(Library of Congress)*

The Lend-Lease Program

World War II began in 1939. By early 1941 it appeared likely that the totalitarian regimes in Germany and Japan would win the war and dominate Europe and Asia. The Lend-Lease Act of March 11, 1941, authorized the supposedly neutral United States government to provide war materials and provisions to foreign nations—especially Great Britain, and later China and the Soviet Union. Their independence was considered vital to American security. This abrupt shift in official policy changed the course of the war and measurably increased the American stake in its outcome. The lend-lease program continued after the Japanese attack on Pearl Harbor, totaling roughly $50 billion in foreign aid.

Europe's economy following World War II. During the Korean War he served in several new capacities including special adviser on national security, representative to the North Atlantic Treaty Organization (NATO), and director of the Mutual Security Agency.

During the early 1950's Harriman aspired to become president or secretary of state. When voters abandoned the Democrats in the 1952 presidential election for Republican Dwight D. Eisenhower, however, he settled for New York's governorship in 1954. The businessman-diplomat proved a weak politician and lost his bid for reelection.

New demands for his ambassadorial skills surfaced in the 1960's with the presidencies of Democrats John F. Kennedy and Lyndon B. Johnson. Harriman held several posts in the State Department and often worked as a roaming diplomat. He led U.S. negotiations amid crises in the Congo, Laos, and Vietnam. Perhaps his most critical achievement was the 1963 Nuclear Test Ban Treaty, a limited agreement banning nuclear tests above ground or in space that was signed by the United States, the Soviet Union, and many other countries. During the 1970's and 1980's, Harriman made numerous personal trips to Moscow and always offered his insights to the sitting American president.

William Averell Harriman campaigning for governor of New York in 1934; with him are Hulan Jack and Margaret Truman. *(Archive Photos)*

U.S. ambassador to the Soviet Union Averell Harriman (left) being greeted in London in 1943 by U.S. ambassador to Great Britain John Winant. *(Library of Congress)*

A Statesman's Legacy

Historians have credited Harriman as one of the founding fathers of American Cold War policy. This distinction carries both positive and negative attributes. For example, his support of constructive programs such as lend-lease, the Marshall Plan, and the Nuclear Test Ban Treaty must be balanced against his war-prone strategy for thwarting nationalism and communism in Asia. His lifelong affiliation with international relations, particularly his dealings with the Soviet Union, was crowned in 1982 when he donated $10 million to Columbia University's Russian Institute and it was renamed in his honor.

Bibliography

Abramson, Rudy. *Spanning the Century: The Life of W. Averell Harriman, 1891-1986.* New York: William Morrow, 1992.

Harriman, W. Averell, and Elie Abel. *Special Envoy to Churchill and Stalin, 1941-1946.* New York: Random House, 1975.

Isaacson, Walter, and Evan Thomas. *The Wise Men: Six Friends and the World They Made.* Simon and Schuster, 1986.

Kimball, Warren F. *The Most Unsordid Act: Lend Lease, 1939-1941.* Baltimore, Md.: The Johns Hopkins University Press, 1969.

Jeffrey J. Matthews

Hassan II

Born: July 9, 1929; Rabat, Morocco

King of Morocco (from 1961)

Mawlay Hassan Mohammad ibn Yusuf (mew-LAY HA-suhn moo-HAH-muhd IHB-uhn YOO-soof), a thirty-fifth-generation descendant of the Prophet Muhammad by his daughter Fatima, became the seventeenth sovereign of the Alouite Dynasty, which has ruled Morocco since the early seventeenth century. The eldest son and one of six children born to King Mohammad V, Hassan was educated at the imperial college at Rabat in Arabic literature, Muslim theology, English, French, and Arabic. He studied the law at the University

Hassan II *(Library of Congress)*

of Bordeaux's extension branch in Rabat and passed the qualifying examinations to practice. As a student Hassan enrolled in a training course in the French navy and served aboard the battleship *Jeanne d'Arc*.

Crown Prince Hassan

In 1953, Hassan accompanied his father into exile on Corsica and Madagascar when the French removed them from Morocco for agitating for independence from France. Increased Moroccan opposition to French rule forced France to release Hassan and his father from exile in 1955. In 1956, Hassan led Morocco's delegation to the Franco-Moroccan talks that ultimately brought about the withdrawal of French troops from Morocco and granted Morocco its independence. As crown prince, Hassan was his father's chief deputy, commander in chief of the army, vice premier of the government, and minister of defense. Hassan became king upon the sudden death of his father, Mohammad V, during minor surgery on February 26, 1961.

King of Morocco

Upon his ascension as king, Hassan II (HA-suhn thuh SEH-kuhnd) eschewed his former bachelor lifestyle and refused to establish a harem. In 1961 he married a commoner, Lalla Lotifa Amhourok, who remained in strict seclusion in the Muslim tradition. The king has five children: sons Sidi Mohammad (the crown prince) and Mulay al-Rashid, and daughters Myriam, Asma, and Hasna.

Hassan has devoted considerable energy to eradicating illiteracy in Morocco by constructing primary schools and importing teachers from France. Public works projects have helped reduce the nation's high unemployment rate, but the

The Western Sahara

In 1975, Spain agreed to transfer its former Western Saharan colony, Rio de Oro, to Morocco and Mauritania. The International Court of Justice in The Hague noted that Morocco had had certain legal ties to the Saharan tribes prior to Spanish colonization in 1884 but that Morocco had failed to establish territorial sovereignty to the region. The Western Sahara is rich in phosphates, and neighboring Algeria wanted the region to be independent. To ensure the Western Sahara's incorporation into Morocco, King Hassan ordered a "Green March" of volunteers to claim the land for Morocco. In November of 1975, Morocco's prime minister, Ahmed Osman, led forty thousand peaceful marchers into the Western Sahara shouting the praises of Allah and King Hassan. Eventually 350,000 Moroccans entered the former Spanish colony, claiming it for Morocco.

Algeria refused to accept the Moroccan takeover and has since provided financial and military assistance to Western Saharan rebels known as the Polisario. In 1978, Mauritania surrendered its share of the Western Sahara to Morocco after severe military reversals at the hands of the Polisario. King Hassan remained committed to a "controlled referendum" to determine the Western Sahara's future.

Eventually, instability in Algeria cost the Polisario their key ally. Moreover, Morocco's erection of a 750-mile (1,200-kilometer) sand wall with electronic sensors enclosing half of the Western Sahara and a strong military presence defending the wall have significantly weakened the Polisario position. U.N.-sponsored discussions to resolve the Western Saharan problem continued to break down over voting lists for a referendum on the region's political future. An accord between Morocco and the Polisario to hold a U.N.-supervised election in the Western Sahara was reached in 1997.

increased number of births and college graduates strains Morocco's limited resources. The king's peaceful invasion of the Western Sahara in 1975 was predicated on Hassan's desire to regain a region formerly part of Morocco and to provide increased revenue and employment by taking over the region's phosphate production.

Political Role

While no one contests the fact that Hassan is the absolute ruler of Morocco, the nation has had a series of constitutions. The first was promulgated in 1962, a second in 1972, and a third in 1992. The 1992 constitution was modified in 1996 to permit a second chamber in the country's legislature. King Hassan reputedly governs his nation using the strategy of political dualism, which blends progress toward modern forms of democratic governance with centuries-old practices.

Whereas repression has been used to contain dissent, Hassan has responded to popular demands to increase government accountability, improve the status of women, and maintain the cultural integrity of the Berbers. Parliament's role in running Morocco has increased, political parties are more active and numerous, and the press is allowed to be more vocal. Yet King Hassan is the final national arbiter and decision maker as he prepares Morocco for the time his eldest son becomes king.

King Hassan's governance of Morocco has not been without serious risks. He has escaped numerous leftist plots to overthrow him and two serious military assassination attempts. The first was at his forty-second birthday party in 1971, when ninety-eight guests were killed; the second was in 1972, when his official jet was repeatedly strafed upon reentering Moroccan airspace on

Morocco and the 1991 Gulf War

King Hassan had received financial support from Saudi Arabia in Morocco's war against the Polisario in the annexed Western Sahara region. In return, Iraq's invasion of Kuwait in 1990 brought a request from Saudi King Fahd to Hassan to contribute to the allied coalition challenging Iraqi president Saddam Hussein. Morocco committed about thirteen hundred troops. However, Moroccan opposition parties and unions declared a strike in the kingdom. They denounced

the war and Moroccan participation. Correctly gauging the changing mood of public opinion, King Hassan allowed a pro-Iraqi march, which attracted more than 300,000 demonstrators—a crowd estimated to be larger than the ones that had celebrated Morocco's 1956 independence from France. Protesters criticized the Moroccan troop deployment despite the royal edict banning public discussions of government policies.

orders from high-ranking Moroccan military officials.

Since gaining independence, Morocco has been perceived as pro-Western even though Hassan ordered that U.S. bases be removed from his country in 1964. He has been a tireless voice of moderation in the continuing Arab-Israeli conflict. However, internal opposition does appear against some of the king's pro-Western actions, as when he supplied troops to the allied coalition fighting Iraq in the Persian Gulf War in 1990, and again when Morocco recognized the state of Israel in 1996. Occasionally there is debate about the expense of the Great Hassan II Mosque under construction in Casablanca or the king's numerous palaces, in which he stays as he governs Morocco by moving about the country to see the nation and the people's needs.

King Hassan will be remembered as Morocco's most important twentieth-century leader because of his strategies for guiding his nation into

the modern era of governance. His spiritual guidance, enhanced by his descent from the Prophet Muhammad, his highly regarded international image, and his understanding of the needs of the Moroccan people have enabled him to adapt policy more quickly than conventional Western means in a part of the world known for its volatility.

Bibliography

Bendourou, Omar. "Power and Opposition in Morocco." *Journal of Democracy* 7, July, 1996: 108-122.

Denoeux, Guilain, and Abdeslam Maghraoui. "King Hassan's Strategy of Political Dualism." *Middle East Policy* 5, Jan., 1998: 104.

Hassan, King of Morocco. *The Challenge: The Memoirs of King Hassan II*. London: MacMillan, 1978.

William A. Paquette

Charles James Haughey

Born: September 16, 1925; Castlebar, County Mayo, Ireland

Prime minister of Ireland (1979-1981, 1982, 1987-1992)

Charles James Haughey (CHAHRLZ JAYMZ HAW-kee), three-time prime minister, or taoiseach (pronounced tee-shock), of the Republic of Ireland, was the son of John Haughey and his wife, Sarah Anne McWilliams. John Haughey, who held the title of commandant, was a veteran of the Irish Republican Army (IRA) during the Anglo-Irish War of 1919-1921 and the Free State Army during the Irish Civil War of 1922-1923. The family moved to Dublin, and Charles received his education at Schuil Muire and St. Joseph's Christian Brothers School. He received his bachelor's degree in communications and accounting from University College, Dublin, and his law degree from King's Inn, Dublin. He was admitted to the Irish bar in 1949. Rather than going into legal practice, he established the accounting firm of Haughey and Boland. It was, however, in real estate speculation that he amassed a fortune. In 1951 he married Maureen Lemass, daughter of future taoiseach Sean Lemass (1959-66). The couple had three sons and a daughter.

In 1953, Haughey was elected to a seat on the Dublin City Council representing the Fianna Fáil party, and he served until 1955. In 1957 he was elected as deputy to Dáil Éireann, the lower house of the Irish Parliament, representing the Dublin North-East electoral district. During the ministry of his father-in-law, Sean Lemass, Haughey held the post of parliamentary secretary to the minister for justice (1960-1961) and the cabinet portfolios for justice (1961-1964) and agriculture (1964-1966). Upon Lemass's retirement in 1966. Haughey made a bid for the leadership of the Fianna Fáil. He lost to Jack Lynch, who then became taoiseach. Under Lynch, Haughey headed the Finance Ministry (1966-1970).

Downfall and Comeback

Haughey's political career suffered a setback as a result of his alleged involvement in the Irish arms-smuggling scandal of 1970, when he was compelled to relinquish the finance ministry. Though Haughey, unlike his ministerial colleague Neil Blaney, chose to remain in Fianna Fáil, he was largely relegated to the political back benches for seven years. He then played a major role in his party's return to power as a result of

Charles James Haughey *(Camera Press Ltd./Archive Photos)*

Irish prime minister Charles James Haughey tries on a Russian hat at Moscow's airport in 1989. *(Reuters/Santiago Lyon/Archive Photos)*

the 1977 elections. In Lynch's second ministry, Haughey was returned to cabinet rank to take charge of the Department for Health and Social Welfare (1977-1979). On December 5, 1979, Lynch was pressured into resigning by nationalist hard-liners within his own party. Haughey then became taoiseach by defeating Finance Minister George Colley in an intra-party struggle.

Party Leader

Haughey's first ministry, which lasted until June, 1981, was beset by economic recession and a severe budget deficit as well as by tension between Ireland and Britain over the deaths of IRA hunger strikers in Northern Ireland. Fianna Fáil was defeated in the general elections. Haughey was supplanted as taoiseach by Garrett Fitzgerald until Haughey and his party regained power in March, 1982.

The second Haughey ministry lasted only until November, 1982, but it was during this period that allegations surfaced that Haughey had authorized Justice Minister Sean Doherty to wiretap the telephone conversations of journalist Bruce Arnold of the *Irish Independent* and two gover-

The 1970 Arms-Smuggling Scandal

On May 6, 1970, Irish taoiseach (prime minister) Jack Lynch announced that he would request the resignation of two members of his government, Finance Minister Charles James Haughey and Agriculture Minister Neil Blaney. Both had fallen under suspicion of conspiracy to smuggle arms into Northern Ireland. When they refused to resign, President Eamon de Valera dismissed them from office.

It was alleged that Captain James J. Kelly, an Irish military-intelligence officer, had come into contact with Irish Republican Army (IRA) leaders and then had approached Haughey and Blaney. Haughey, who had the authority to disburse funds for victims of violence in Northern Ireland, was said to have agreed to divert funds to purchase and funnel arms from the Netherlands, through the Irish Republic, into the north. Haughey, Blaney, Kelly, and alleged conspirators John Kelly and Albert Luyxx were indicted and tried on gun-running charges. The first trial ended in no-contest, and the second trial resulted in the acquittal of all defendants on October 6, 1970.

ment ministers, Ray McSharry and Martin O'Donoghue. The taoiseach was able to survive a no-confidence vote. In 1987, Haughey was returned to power and surprised many when he reversed his initially critical attitude toward the Anglo-Irish Hillsborough Accord of 1985 and adopted a less confrontational approach to the situation in Northern Ireland. However, the wiretap scandal broke out once more upon Doherty's confession. On January 30, 1992, Haughey was pushed into resignation as both taoiseach and party leader. He retired from public life.

Bibliography

Allen, Kieran. *Fianna Fail and Irish Labour: 1926 to the Present*. London: Pluto Press, 1997.

Dwyer, T. Ryle. *Charlie: The Political Biography of Charles J. Haughey*. Dublin: Gill & McMillan, 1987.

Feehan, John M. *The Statesman: A Study of the Role of Charles Haughey in the Ireland of the Future*. Dublin: Mercier Press, 1985.

Fitzgerald, Garrett. *All in a Life: Garrett Fitzgerald, an Autobiography*. London: Macmillan, 1991.

Raymond Pierre Hylton

Charles James Haughey in 1997 after testifying in a government inquiry. He confessed that he had lied about a sizable donation he had received while prime minister, and he apologized. (*AP/Wide World Photos*)

Václav Havel

Born: October 5, 1936; Prague, Czechoslovakia

President of Czechoslovakia (1989-1992) and the Czech Republic (took office in 1993)

Václav Havel (VAHT-slahf HAH-vuhl) was born into a prominent business and intellectual family in Prague. Following the communist takeover of Czechoslovakia in 1948, however, his family gradually lost most of their possessions. Havel, a child of the despised bourgeoisie, was not permitted to continue formal schooling. Working as an apprentice in a chemical laboratory, he took night classes to complete his secondary education but could not pursue his dream of a university degree in humanities. Instead, after completing an obligatory two years of military service, he began work as a stage technician. Through that route he moved into the world of drama and literature as well as politics. In 1964 he married Olga Šplíchalová, whom he regarded as a major source of support until her death in January, 1996. A year later Havel married Dagmar Veškrnová, a highly acclaimed Czech actress.

Václav Havel

Havel the Dramatist

As a teenager Havel founded an intellectual group called Thirty-Sixers (all the members had been born in 1936), which met regularly to debate, study Czech history and literature (especially forbidden authors), and publish a typewritten magazine. When Havel subsequently had the opportunity to work in a theater and study drama, he rapidly developed into a major twentieth-century dramatist. The Theater on the Balustrade in Prague produced his first full-length play, *The Garden Party*, in 1963, followed by *The Memorandum* (1965) and *The Increased Difficulty of Communication* (1968). These works, which were published, performed, and acclaimed internationally, satirize the absurdity of life under a totalitarian regime.

Dissident

Although Havel's foremost interest as a writer was in drama, the political milieu in Czechoslovakia and his intense belief in human rights propelled him into political writing. When Alexander Dubček began reforming and liberalizing the Communist Party in Czechoslovakia in 1968 (a movement known as the Prague Spring), Havel responded with commentaries for radio, and he wrote speeches and prepared statements for various liberalization groups.

The crushing defeat of liberalization by Soviet troops in 1968 and the banning of publication of Havel's plays did not silence his voice. In 1975, in an open letter to President Gustav Husák, Havel courageously warned that the citizens of Czechoslovakia were becoming increasingly hostile toward a government that continually deprived them of basic civil rights. Havel then founded a press, Expedition Edition, and began printing the works of forbidden authors, producing more than a hundred volumes between 1975 and 1981.

In 1977 Havel helped write and became a major spokesperson for *Charter 77*, a document that protested the repressive policies of the communist government. Havel's dissident activities led to a series of imprisonments that kept him in jail for nearly five years between 1977 and 1989 and under constant police surveillance the remainder of the time. Yet Havel continued to write and to organize protest groups.

In 1989 Havel, just out of prison, recognized the growing unrest in Czechoslovakia. He helped author a new manifesto, *Just a Few Sentences*, which demanded fundamental changes in the government and quickly gained forty thousand signatures. Under Havel's leadership, dissident groups merged into a loose alliance known as the Civic Forum. This alliance was instrumental in bringing about the "velvet revolution" in 1989-1990, which replaced the communist regime with a parliamentary democracy.

Czech president Václav Havel at a 1990 rally marking the forty-sixth anniversary of the Slovak uprising during World War II. *(Reuters/David Brauchi/Archive Photos)*

President of Czechoslovakia

Under pressure from the Civic Forum, Communist Party leaders resigned on November 21, 1989, and Parliament elected Václav Havel president on December 29. Havel promised free elections, and the first of these occurred in June, 1990. Havel was named president for a two-year term,

---

Charter 77

In early 1977 dissidents in Czechoslovakia spelled out their demands for respect for human rights in a document called *Charter 77*. Of the numerous examples of repression of human rights in the 1970's, the arrest of a musical group called the Plastic People of the Universe attracted the most attention. Their arrest was instrumental in inspiring the writing of *Charter 77*. Following publication in the West in January, 1977, one spokesperson for the movement, Jan Patočka, elderly and in poor health, died from the intensive interrogation. Another leader, Václav Havel, was harassed and then imprisoned. The communist government temporarily prevailed, but the spirit of the *Charter 77* movement persisted. In 1989 it reemerged in the Civic Forum, the dissident group that effected the velvet revolution.

The Velvet Revolution

In 1989 and 1990, the shift of power in Czechoslovakia from a communist to a democratic government occurred so rapidly, peacefully, and smoothly that the transition became known as the velvet revolution. The dissident movement, suppressed but never destroyed following the Prague Spring in 1968 and *Charter 77* in 1977, reemerged even stronger in the late 1980's. The opposition movement was disturbed by a decline in the standard of living in Czechoslovakia and buoyed by democratic reforms being instituted in Russia. Dissident movements were growing in other communist countries as well, and the Czech opposition movement steadily gained momentum.

On November 17, 1989, students staged a peaceful demonstration in Prague. When police reacted violently, more demonstrations and strikes broke out. The Civic Forum, a loosely formed coalition of opposition forces, demanded that Communist Party leaders resign and that the government be democratized. Demonstrations and strikes spread rapidly and on November 24, Czechoslovakian Communist Party leaders resigned. Noncommunists gained control of Parliament and elected Havel president.

During free elections in June, 1990, the Civic Forum and the corresponding Slovak dissident group, Public Against Violence, won a majority and subsequently reelected Havel president. The new government immediately restored the basic civil liberties of freedom of speech, press, and religion and began establishment of a market economy, reformation of the legal system, and restoration of property rights.

Václav Havel just after announcing that he would run for reelection in 1998. To the right is Alexander Dubcek, the chairman of Parliament. *(Reuters/Petr Josek/Archive Photos)*

and under his leadership the government began to move immediately toward democratization and a market economy. Havel also sought to establish friendly relations both with Western nations and the Soviet Union (itself on the verge of disintegration) and to help end the Cold War.

Conflicts between the Czechs and Slovaks, submerged during the communist regime, resurfaced almost immediately. They slowed economic reform and the adoption of a new constitution. Havel desperately wanted to keep the country united but was unable to negotiate an agreement between the Czechs and Slovaks. The Slovak National Council issued a declaration of autonomy on July 17, 1992, and Slovaks opposed Havel's reelection bid. Havel resigned, refusing to preside over the death of Czechoslovakia. The federation was dissolved effective January 1, 1993.

President of the Czech Republic

After a short respite from public life, Havel was elected to a five-year term as president of the newly established Czech Republic on January 26, 1993. During the early years of his term, corruption, scandals, and disagreements with Prime Minister Václav Klaus over economic reform led to diminished accomplishments. By 1997 Havel had prevailed over Klaus. Having reestablished his leadership, Havel was elected to his second term as president in January, 1998.

Although Havel's reputation as a writer has continued to grow, it has been overshadowed by his accomplishments as a political leader. In recognition of his work for human rights, Havel has received many prestigious international awards, including the Erasmus Prize (1996) and the UNESCO Prize for the Teaching of Human Rights (1990). He has also achieved recognition as an effective voice in foreign policy. Critics within his country have decried his failure to prevent the breakup of Czechoslovakia and complained that his leadership has not effectively solved the country's economic problems. Supporters celebrate his success in preparing the Czech Republic for membership in the North Atlantic Treaty Organization (NATO) in 1999 and in moving the country forward in its establishment of a parliamentary democracy and a market economy.

Bibliography

Kriseová, Eda. *Václav Havel: The Authorized Biography*. New York: St. Martin's Press, 1993.

Simmons, Michael. *The Reluctant President: A Political Life of Václav Havel*. London: Metheun, 1991.

Symynkywicz, Jeffrey. *Václav Havel and the Velvet Revolution*. Parsippany, N.J.: Silver Burdett Press, 1995.

Verbie Lovorn Prevost

Robert Hawke

Born: December 9, 1929; Bordertown, South Australia, Australia

Prime minister of Australia (1983-1991)

Robert James Lee Hawke (RO-burt JAYMZ LEE HAWK) was the son of a Congregational minister and was raised in a conservative Christian household. He attended Perth Modern School and the University of Western Australia, completing degrees in Law and Arts. In 1952 he won a Rhodes Scholarship to study at Oxford University in England, where he was awarded a bachelor of letters in December, 1955. On returning to Australia, he married Hazel Masterson in 1956. The Hawkes divorced in 1995, and Hawke married Blanche d'Alpuget, who was writing a biography of him.

Robert Hawke *(Popperfoto/Archive Photos)*

Hawke and the ACTU

Hawke commenced a Ph.D. in Law at the Australian National University, but he took a position as research officer for the Australian Council of Trade Unions (ACTU) in 1958, beginning a distinguished career in Australia's powerful trade union movement. He rapidly established a reputation as a brilliant courtroom advocate in labor relations cases. He was president of the ACTU from 1970 to 1980 and president of the Australian Labor Party (ALP) from 1973 to 1978. As ACTU president, he displayed a fiery personality that initially alienated the public, but he became a popular and charismatic figure, mainly from his successes in resolving a series of damaging labor disputes. In 1980 he became an ALP member of the House of Representatives.

Hawke as Prime Minister

Hawke became the leader of the parliamentary ALP in February, 1983, and was elected as prime minister on March 5 of that year. During his period as prime minister, from 1983 to 1991, the government concentrated on decisive but sound economic restructuring rather than on social reforms. When Hawke came to power, the Australian economy was in a deep recession triggered by a wages explosion that had started in 1980. The policy centerpiece of the new government was the Prices and Incomes Accord, which the ALP had finalized with the trade union movement.

The accord was a formal compact covering most domestic political issues. It was based on wage restraint, including the reintroduction of pay increases indexed in line with inflation. It emphasized the "social wage" benefits provided to workers, such as public education, public health measures, and welfare. Agreement with the accord's broad direction was obtained from the state leaders, employers, and business groups at the National Economic Summit, chaired by Hawke in April, 1983.

Hawke and his federal treasurer, Paul Keating, were instrumental in restructuring the Australian economy, including deregulation of finance and banking, taxation reform, and new approaches to labor relations. The most dramatic single decision was that taken on December 9, 1983, to float the Australian dollar—in other words, its exchange rate would no longer be subject to governmental controls. Most commentators considered the structural changes initiated by Hawke and Keating to be necessary to make Australia competitive in the increasingly globalized world economy. However, some critics condemned the closeness of the government to the unions. Others criticized Hawke and Keating for betraying ALP ideals. Hawke led the ALP to victory in a total of four elections: in 1983, 1984, 1987, and 1990. However, dissatisfaction with his leadership led to his replacement as prime minister by Keating in 1991. Hawke immediately left politics to pursue business and academic interests.

Australian prime minister Bob Hawke playing cricket in 1991. *(Popperfoto/Archive Photos)*

Bibliography

D'Alpuget, Blanche. *Robert J. Hawke: A Biography*. Melbourne, Australia: Penguin, 1984.

Hawke, Bob. *The Hawke Memoirs*. London: Heinemann, 1994; Melbourne: Mandarin, 1996.

Kelly, Paul. *The End of Certainty: Power, Politics and Business in Australia*. Rev. ed. Sydney: Allen & Unwin, 1994.

_____. *The Hawke Ascendancy: A Definitive Account of Its Origins and Climax, 1975-1983*. London: Angus & Robertson, 1984.

Russell Blackford

The Election of 1983

By the second half of 1982, the Australian economy was in deep recession, and there was speculation that the Liberal Party prime minister, Malcolm Fraser, would call an early election. Many observers believed that Bill Hayden, the leader of the Australian Labor Party (ALP), could not win the election despite the economic situation and that the party's best chance was with the charismatic Robert Hawke.

In a dramatic sequence of events on February 3, 1983, Fraser called an election for March 5, but not before Hayden suddenly resigned in favor of Hawke. Hawke campaigned with the slogan "Bob Hawke, Bringing Australia Together." His key idea was the need to build consensus in the Australian community as a way to overcome the country's social and economic problems. He won the election by a comfortable majority, the first of his four election victories as leader of the ALP.

Víctor Raúl Haya de la Torre

Born: February 22, 1895; Trujillo, Peru
Died: August 2, 1979; Lima, Peru

Peruvian political leader, founder of Aprista movement (1924)

Víctor Raúl Haya de la Torre (VEEK-tohr rah-EWL AH-yah thay lah TOH-ray), charismatic Peruvian populist, was born in a northern coastal region of Peru where traditional landowners were being supplanted by foreign business interests. The region also contained ruins of historic Indian cultures, which greatly impressed the young Haya. Although he was from an established family, he suffered from its insecure economic status.

Early Activities

As a student in Lima, Haya became a leader in the university reform movement, which had an agenda of broad educational and social changes. Spearheading demonstrations against the dictatorial government of President Augusto Leguía, Haya was exiled from Peru in 1923.

Going to Mexico, he witnessed the Mexican Revolution and founded the Aprista movement, advocating social and political reforms throughout the Americas. He then spent time in the Soviet Union; he concluded that communism would not be an adequate political system for the reforms he sought. Haya traveled and lived in various countries of Europe, as well as in the United States, and he came to know many of the leading intellectual and cultural figures of his time.

In 1930 Leguía was overthrown by a military uprising led by Luis M. Sánchez Cerro, and the following year Haya returned to Peru. Before his return, his followers organized the *Partido Aprista Peruano* (PAP, the Peruvian Aprista Party). In elections at the end of 1931, he ran as the presidential candidate of his party against Sánchez Cerro. He was defeated.

Peruvian Politics

Followers of Haya believed that he lost the election because of fraud by the opposition. Haya was arrested and sentenced to prison the following year, prompting an Aprista uprising in Trujillo. It culminated in the assassination of Cerro. The new president, General Oscar Benevides, freed Haya and allowed the Apristas to resume po-

Peruvian political leader Víctor Raúl Haya de la Torre in England, at the University of Oxford in 1964. At the time he was considering living in England permanently. *(AP/Wide World Photos)*

644

The Aprista Movement

The *Alianza Popular Revolucionaria Americana* (APRA, the American Revolutionary Popular Alliance) was a political party founded in Mexico City in 1924 by a group of young Latin American reformers led by Víctor Raúl Haya de la Torre. It sought to build an organization in each country of Latin America. APRA believed that the Indian races and the mystical force of their history would be the basis for developing the region, which it referred to as Indo America. The Aprista movement (Aprista is simply the adjective form of APRA) also believed that an alliance of intellectuals, laborers, and peasants was necessary to oppose North American economic imperialism. It supported economic nationalization, unification of Latin America, and solidarity with all oppressed peoples. Only in Peru did the Aprista movement achieve political significance, operating extensive social, cultural, and educational programs. Frequently repressed during Haya's lifetime, it finally obtained power during the presidency of Alan García Pérez (1985-1990). Since then it has declined.

litical activity. He soon reverted to repression of the party, however, causing Haya to go into hiding until 1945. In that year Aprista was crucial in electing President José Luis Bustamante y Rivero. However, the party's manipulation of Bustamante's government prompted him to suppress the party after a military uprising in Callao, the port city of Lima.

Haya went into hiding again, and in 1949 he obtained asylum in the Colombian embassy. He remained there until 1954, when he went again into exile in Mexico and Europe until 1956. In 1962 the Aprista Party, despite military opposition, nominated Haya as its candidate for the presidency. He was defeated. Nonetheless, the armed forces staged a coup to prevent negotiations that might lead to Aprista influence in a new government.

Presidential elections were again conducted in 1963, with Haya a candidate. However, with the electorate assuming that the military would never allow him to assume office, he was defeated by Fernando Belaúnde Terry, who proceeded to carry out significant reforms based on the Aprista program. In 1968 a military coup led by Juan Velasco Alvarado overthrew Belaúnde and inaugurated a regime that, while once again prohibiting the Aprista Party, carried out further parts of its reform program. The last public act of Haya before he died in 1979 was to preside over the constituent assembly that returned Peru to democratic government the following year. Never married, Haya was accompanied throughout his life by his secretary and companion Jorge Idiáquez.

Bibliography

Haya de la Torre, Víctor Raúl. *Aprismo: The Ideas and Doctrines of Víctor Raúl Haya de la Torre.* Edited by Robert J. Alexander. Kent, Ohio: Kent State University Press, 1973.

Klarén, Peter F. *Modernization, Dislocation, and Aprismo: Origins of the Peruvian Aprista Party, 1870-1932.* Austin: University of Texas Press, 1973.

Pike, Frederick B. *The Politics of the Miraculous in Peru: Haya de la Torre and the Spiritualist Tradition.* Lincoln: University of Nebraska Press, 1986.

Edward A. Riedinger

Edward Heath

Born: July 9, 1916; Broadstairs, Kent, England

Prime minister of Great Britain (1970-1974)

Edward (Ted) Richard George Heath (EHD-wurd "TEHD" RIH-churd JOHRJ HEETH) was born to skilled working-class parents. He obtained a scholarship to Chatham House School, Kent, where he showed considerable interest in music, public affairs, and debating. In 1935 he obtained entrance to Balliol College, Oxford, to study philosophy, politics, and economics. He joined the Conservative Party and became a leading member of the Oxford Union, the major debating society of the university. He graduated in 1939.

Edward Heath *(Library of Congress)*

Early Days in Politics

Heath joined the army at the outbreak of World War II. After demobilization in 1945, he decided to seek election as a Conservative member of Parliament (M.P.). After several years working in the civil service, he was chosen as a prospective candidate for Bexley, Kent, a constituency held by the Labour Party by a large majority.

Heath's chance came with the February, 1950, general election. He won and was never to lose his seat in any subsequent election. However, the Labour Party was returned to power, with Heath joining the opposition. He took a firm pro-European stance. He became a member of the One Nation Group; its philosophy remained central to Heath throughout his parliamentary career. Its aim was "improvement in the well-being of the people," with emphasis on education, housing, and the reform of industrial relations. Heath soon attracted attention and when, in October, 1951, the Conservatives gained power, Heath became a member of the government, as lord commissioner of the Treasury. His long ministerial career had begun.

Government Minister

Heath served as chief whip under Sir Anthony Eden and, after Eden's resignation, under Harold Macmillan. After his 1959 election victory, Macmillan gave Heath his first cabinet job, as minister of labor, and his first experience of dealing with the Trades Union Congress. Heath was then made lord privy seal, a post associated with the Foreign Office. In 1961 Macmillan made Britain's first (unsuccessful) proposal to join the European Economic Community (the EEC, the Common Market). Heath took a leading role in the ensuing negotiations. After Macmillan's retirement in 1963, Heath supported Lord Home, who became the new prime minister. Home appointed him president of the Board of Trade. Under him, resale price maintenance was abolished. However, the post was short-lived, as the Conservatives lost the 1964 general election.

The Conservative Party, now the opposition party, needed a new set of policies to gain reelection. Heath was chosen to chair the National Advisory Committee on Policy. Then, in 1965, Home resigned. Heath entered the leadership race and was elected. At forty-nine he was the youngest Conservative leader since Benjamin Disraeli. It would be another five years before he became prime minister. In that time, Conservative policies were reshaped.

British prime minister Edward Heath signing the 1972 agreement to bring Great Britain into the European Community (the Common Market). *(Popperfoto/ Archive Photos)*

Prime Minister

In the June, 1970, general election, Heath campaigned on the so-called Selsdon Programme, as the new Conservative policies were called. He advocated less government, but government of a better quality, firmer industrial relations, and re-

form of local government. The Conservatives were determined not to bail out failing industries, but rather to let free-market forces take their course. On their election, Heath's cabinet set about an expansionist economic policy. This proved to be the first of a long series of U-turns for the Heath administration. Prices rose sharply, and imports grew, but the growth rate did not

---

Heath the Master Gunner

On the outbreak of World War II in September, 1939, Edward Heath volunteered for the army. He was eventually called up into the Royal Artillery in August of 1940 and posted to Merseyside as a second lieutenant in a heavy anti-aircraft regiment.

He was soon promoted to captain, becoming adjutant of his regiment. He was involved in the

invasion of Europe in July, 1944. By the winter he had been promoted to major and assigned to a front-line battery involved in the crossing of the Rhine. After the war he continued in the Territorial Army, becoming lieutenant-colonel commanding the Second Regiment, the Honorable Artillery Company. For three years he was master gunner in the Tower of London.

Great Britain's Entry into the EEC

Edward Heath had been pro-European since his student days. In 1961 Heath led the British negotiating team in the first of Britain's two efforts to join the European Economic Community (the EEC, or European Common Market) that were vetoed by France's President Charles de Gaulle. Then, as prime minister, he determined to make another attempt to take Britain into the EEC. This time he was successful. Britain entered in January, 1973, together with Ireland and Denmark. It was one of the solid achievements of the Heath administration.

Entry into the EEC had long been a divisive issue within Britain's two main political parties.

Heath had critics from within his own party as well as opposition from the Labour Party. For this reason, entry was not fully resolved till 1975, when, under the Labour government of James Callaghan, there was a successful national referendum on the issue. The two main contentious issues were sovereignty and economic benefits. Heath's philosophy was always to view the wider European picture. It could be argued that Britain lost out economically through the EEC's common agricultural policy and by losing Commonwealth preferential rates of trade. To Heath, this was a small price to pay for an extension of the international community.

Edward Heath campaigning in 1974, preparing for Britain's upcoming general election. *(AP/Wide World Photos)*

improve, nor did unemployment drop. Two major "lame duck" failing industries had to be rescued.

The 1971 Industrial Relations Act, which established a series of legal structures, was widely opposed and caused widespread industrial unrest. In January, 1972, the first of two damaging miners' strikes began, soon producing a power shortage and a state of emergency. In November, 1972, the "boom" had to be halted with a statutory freeze on wages. Heath's effort to end the stop-and-go economic cycle of the 1960's had failed. In Northern Ireland, too, affairs went awry after "Bloody Sunday" (in January of 1972). The government had to impose direct rule over the province; then an attempt to provide a new constitution failed after only five months.

Economic Crisis Worsens

In October, 1973, the Arab-Israeli War (the Yom Kippur War) led to the quadrupling of world oil prices. This event compounded the deep economic trouble the country was in. The miners, the most militant of the unions, were demanding that wages rise above the agreed ceiling. Heath decided to confront them this time. By December the country had to move to a five-day working week; in January, 1974, it went to a three-day week. Heath decided to take the matter to the country by declaring an election on the question "Who rules Britain?"

The Conservative Party, although slightly ahead of Labour, was unable to form a minority government and had to concede defeat. Heath continued to lead the Conservatives for another year, but in the 1975 leadership election he was defeated by Margaret Thatcher. He retired from the front benches but continued a long and distinguished parliamentary career as a backbencher. He spoke consistently for pro-European policies and for moderate economic and social policies. Although often fairly isolated in the Thatcher era, he saw much of the Selsdon Programme being implemented. It was left to Thatcher, however, to break the power of the miners. In the end, Heath outlasted her in the House of Commons, becoming its longest-serving member (the "grandfather of the house") after the 1997 election.

A Pragmatic Idealist

Heath was both committed philosophically to an integrated Europe and to moderate social and economic programs that would benefit the whole nation. His failures were often the result of factors outside his control, and ones from which later British leaders learned. His undoubted success was taking Britain into the EEC.

Bibliography

Campbell, J. *Edward Heath: A Biography*. London: Cape, 1993.

Heath, Edward. *The Course of My Life*. London: Hodder & Stoughton, 1998.

Hutchinson, George. *Edward Heath: A Personal and Political Biography*. London: Longmans, 1970.

Laing, M. *Edward Heath: Prime Minister*. London: Sidgwick and Jackson, 1972.

David Barratt

Arthur Henderson

Born: September 13, 1863; Glasgow, Scotland
Died: October 20, 1935; London, England

British politician and diplomat, foreign secretary (1929-1931), winner of 1934 Nobel Peace Prize

Arthur Henderson (AHR-thur HEHN-dur-suhn) was the son of David Henderson, a cotton spinner who died when his son was only nine years old. Arthur's formal education was very limited; at twelve, he left school and became an apprentice in a locomotive foundry. Within six years he had joined the Ironfounders Union and become a union activist. In 1888 he married Eleanor Watson; they had three sons and one daughter.

Arthur Henderson *(The Nobel Foundation)*

Early Political Life

Henderson's union activities were both a liability and an asset to his career. Henderson launched his first political campaigns within the ranks of the Ironfounders Union. In 1892 he was elected to the Newcastle City Council and elected as a union delegate representing northern counties; in 1903, Henderson was elected as mayor of Newcastle. During the 1890's Henderson's political allegiance shifted from the liberalism of William Gladstone to the more radical socialism of the day. In 1899 Henderson participated in the London Conference, which resulted in the formation of the Labour Party in 1900. His talents and his commitment to the working class led the party to nominate him as a candidate for Parliament. In 1903 Henderson was elected to the House of Commons representing Barnard Castle.

Henderson in Parliament

Henderson's parliamentary career extended more than thirty years, with some interruptions. Between 1903 and 1917, his vision of government was national in character and scope; after 1917, with the Russian Revolution and the establishment of the League of Nations, it became increasingly international. Prior to the outbreak of World War I in 1914, Henderson worked with Keir Hardie and Ramsay MacDonald to strengthen the Labour Party; in 1911 Henderson was named secretary of the party. The unity of Labour was challenged by the outbreak of the war: MacDonald refused to support the war effort, while Henderson gave it enthusiastic support. In August, 1914, Henderson replaced MacDonald as the leader of the party in the House of Commons. During the war he would serve in the governments of H. H. Asquith and David Lloyd George as president of the Board of Education, paymaster-general, and cabinet minister without portfolio. Throughout the war Henderson was criticized increasingly by his own Labour colleagues for his collaboration with the Liberals and Conservatives.

After the collapse of the czarist regime in Russia in March, 1917, Henderson traveled to Russia to secure the support of its new provisional government in continuing Russian involvement in the war against Germany. The provisional government endorsed Russia's continuation in the struggle, but the commitment was short-lived. After the Bolshevik Revolution in November, 1917, Russia withdrew from the war.

The trip to Russia transformed Henderson's worldview. He returned to London as an internationalist who urged his government and his party to send representatives to the Stockholm Conference, an international meeting of socialists. The government declined, and Henderson resigned from the cabinet. The Stockholm Conference convinced Henderson of the need to maintain the unity of the British Labour Party and to support the establishment of the League of Nations. Dur-

ing the 1920's he succeeded in achieving both these goals. In the first Labour government in 1924, Prime Minister Ramsay MacDonald appointed Henderson to his cabinet as home secretary. While officially assigned to domestic affairs, Henderson occupied himself with the development of the League of Nations and with the Dawes Plan. The Dawes Plan was a plan to rework the war reparations payments that Germany was required to make after World War I. It was motivated by the Ruhr crisis (1923-1924), in which French and Belgian troops occupied Germany's Ruhr Valley because of Germany's defaulting on its reparation payments.

Before the end of 1924, another general election resulted in the fall of MacDonald's government and the return of the Conservatives to power. Between 1925 and 1929, Henderson devoted himself to strengthening the Labour Party and to expanding the support for its programs and to "internationalizing" both his party and nation. Henderson's support for the League of Nations and the concept of international cooperation was unwavering. In 1928 he assisted in the writing of *Labour and the Nation*, which incorporated his

The Rise of Britain's Labour Party

Arthur Henderson's life paralleled the rise of the Labour Party in Britain. The Labour Party was formed in February, 1900, as a result of a resolution of the Trades Union Council. As the political voice of both organized and unorganized labor, the new Labour Party allied itself with the Liberal Party in its opposition to the Conservatives. By the time of the outbreak of World War I in 1914, however, the leadership of the Labour Party had become disillusioned with the Liberals. This disillusionment was exacerbated by Britain's decision to enter the war. The disastrous impact of the war, and then the success of the Communist Revolution in Russia (1917), bolstered radical Labour

leaders and contributed to the adoption of a new socialist constitution for the Labour Party.

By 1923 the Labour Party had gained 191 seats in the House of Commons. With Liberal support, the first Labour government was formed, under the leadership of Ramsay MacDonald (January-November 1924). In 1929 a second MacDonald Labour government was established; in 1931 the financial collapse caused by the Great Depression resulted in MacDonald forming a coalition national government. After 1935 Labour's influence declined until 1945, when British voters rejected Winston Churchill and the Conservatives in favor of a Labour government led by Clement Attlee.

The 1932 International Disarmament Conference

Arthur Henderson's commitment to peace and to rendering the League of Nations an effective instrument in achieving it was evident during his tenure as Britain's foreign secretary (1929-1931). Henderson believed in the need to regulate disarmament and feared that the crisis caused by the Great Depression would unleash forces that would lead to another war. His French ally, Foreign Minister Aristide Briand, succeeded in May, 1931, in naming Henderson as the presiding officer of the International Disarmament Conference, which was scheduled for 1932.

The conference was held over a period of twenty months. It occurred in an environment dominated by a mounting financial crisis and increasing unemployment that threatened the fiscal integrity of the major powers. Its accomplishments were minimal, and they were overshadowed by the Lausanne Conference of the same year: At Lausanne, direct negotiations between the great powers resulted in the cancellation of reparations from Germany. The world's hope for a prolonged period of peace would soon be shattered. In less than a year, Adolf Hitler would become leader of Germany and the Japanese would extend their war in Manchuria.

basic values. This document was influential in gaining public support for Labour and contributed to the Labour victory in the general elections of 1929.

In the second MacDonald ministry, Henderson reached the zenith of his career when he was appointed foreign secretary; he would serve from 1929 to 1931. During the 1920's, Henderson had developed personal and professional relationships with the two major figures of European diplomacy of the era—France's Aristide Briand and Germany's Gustav Stresemann. All three were committed to making the League of Nations effective, and they worked to stabilize the peace. Stresemann died in 1929, but Briand and Henderson developed a working relationship that gave hope to the internationalists. Henderson achieved a few notable victories as foreign secretary, notably with Britain's agreeing to the General Act of Arbitration in 1930. However, his most ambitious effort, the International Disarmament Conference in 1932, was a failure.

The financial crisis caused by the Great Depression, combined with differences between Henderson and MacDonald, resulted in Henderson's resignation. Between 1932 and 1935 he worked in Geneva as British representative to the League of Nations and to advance the interests of his party. Henderson's principal achievements were to develop the British Labour Party and extend the influence of internationalism among the great powers.

Bibliography

Leventhal, F. M. *Arthur Henderson.* Manchester, England: Manchester University Press, 1989.

Mowat, Charles Loch. *Britain Between the Wars, 1918-1940.* Chicago: University of Chicago Press, 1958.

Wrigley, C. *Arthur Henderson.* London: GPC Books, 1990.

William T. Walker

BIOGRAPHICAL ENCYCLOPEDIA OF
20th-Century
World Leaders

Index

In the following index, volume numbers and those page numbers referring to full articles appear in **bold face** type.

Index

Index

Index

Himmler, Heinrich, **3: 685-687**

Hindenburg, Paul von, **3: 688-691**, 695, 942; **4:** 1190

Hirohito, **1:** 21; **3: 692-694**

Hiroshima and Nagasaki, bombing of, **5:** 1437, 1506-1507

Hiss, Alger, **4:** 1051, 1146

Hitler, Adolf, **2:** 464, 571; **3: 695-698**; Sudetenland and, **1:** 120. *See also* Nazi Party; World War II, Germany and

Hoare, Samuel, **3:** 898

Hoare-Laval Agreement, **3:** 898

Hobby, Oveta Culp, **3: 699-701**

Ho Chi Minh, **3: 702-705**; **5:** 1617

Ho Chi Minh Trail, **5:** 1542

Hoffa, Jimmy, **3:** 824

Hohenzollern Dynasty, **5:** 1578

Holmes, Oliver Wendell, Jr., **3: 706-708**

Holocaust, **3:** 686, 698; **5:** 1571, 1575. *See also* Jews, Nazi genocide against

Holt, Harold, **3: 709-711**

Home, Lord. *See* Douglas-Home, Alexander

Honecker, Erich, **3: 712-714**

Hong Kong, return to China of, **3:** 771

Hoover, Herbert, **3: 715-718**; **5:** 1410

Hoover, J. Edgar, **3: 719-721**

Hoover Commission, **3:** 717

Houphouët-Boigny, Félix, **3: 722-724**

Hourani, Akram, **1:** 60

House Committee on Education and Labor, **4:** 1257

House Committee on Un-American Activities, **4:** 1052

House of Lords, British, **2:** 426

Howard, John, **2:** 428; **3: 725-727**

Hsuan-tung. *See* Pu-yi

Huerta, Adolfo de la, **4:** 1167

Huerta, Victoriano, **1:** 247; **3: 728-729**, 965; **4:** 1165, 1191; **5:** 1537, 1606

Hughes, Charles Evans, **3: 730-732**

Hughes, William Morris, **3: 733-736**

Huk Rebellion, **3:** 967

Hull, Cordell, **3: 737-740**

Hull House, **3:** 892

Humanae Vitae, **4:** 1203

Hume, John, **1:** 12

Humphrey, Hubert H., **3: 741-743**

Hungarian revolt, **4:** 1125, 1127

Hussein I, **3: 744-747**

Hussein, Saddam, **1:** 235; **3: 748-751**; **4:** 1261

Hutus, **2:** 611

Hutu-Tutsi conflict, **2:** 609

Ibn Saud, **2:** 494

Ideology, definition of, **5:** 1633

Ikeda, Hayato, **3: 752-754**; **5:** 1377

Il duce. *See* Mussolini, Benito

Immigration Restriction Act of 1901, Australian, **3:** 710

Imperial Conference of 1926, **3:** 862

Imperial War Cabinet, **1:** 161

Imperialism, **5:** 1638

Imperialism, the Highest Stage of Capitalism (Lenin), **3:** 914

Inchon landing, Korean War, **3:** 951

India, independence of, **2:** 563; **4:** 1097

India, state of emegency in, 1975-1977, **2:** 537

Indian Home Rule Leagues, **5:** 1482

Indian National Congress, **1:** 100; **4:** 1133, 1197

India-Pakistan War, **2:** 537

Indochina War, **3:** 704

Industrial Relations Act, British, **2:** 648

Inkatha Freedom Party, **1:** 238

İnönü, İsmet, **3: 755-757**

Institutional Revolutionary Party (PRI), Mexican, **5:** 1609

Intermediate Range Nuclear Forces Treaty, **4:** 1260

International Arbitration League, **2:** 359

International Atomic Energy Agency, **2:** 475

International Disarmament Conference, **2:** 652

International Olympic Committee, **2:** 356

International Peace Bureau, **1:** 90; **2:** 567

International Peace Conference, **1:** 112

Interparliamentary Union, **1:** 90; **2:** 359, 567; **3:** 890

Intifada, **1:** 48; **4:** 1274

Inukai, Tsuyoshi, **3:** 692

IRA. *See* Irish Republican Army (IRA)

Iran, Islamic revolution in, **3:** 842; **4:** 1275; OPEC and, **5:** 1594

Iran-Contra scandal, **1:** 234; **4:** 1289; **5:** 1424

Iranian hostage crisis, **1:** 263

Iran-Iraq War, **3:** 751, 843; **4:** 1276

Iraq, U.N. sanctions against, **1:** 39

Irgun Z'vai Leumi, **1:** 114

Irish arms-smuggling scandal of 1970, **2:** 635-636

Irish Free State, **2:** 342, 394

Index

Index

Molotov, Vyacheslav Mikhailovich, **4: 1085-1087**
Monarchical absolutism, **5:** 1635
Mondale, Walter F., **2:** 503; **4:** 1289
Mondlane, Eduardo, **3:** 959
Monnet, Jean, **5:** 1427
Montagu-Chelmsford Reforms, **4:** 1198
Montevideo Conference, **3:** 740
Montgomery, Bernard Law, **1:** 179; **4: 1088-1090**, 1201
Montgomery Bus Boycott, **1:** 4; **3:** 856
Morgenthau, Henry, Jr., **4: 1091-1092**
Morgenthau Plan, **4:** 1092
Moro Islamic Liberation Front, **4:** 1280
Moro National Liberation Front (MNLF), **4:** 1031
Mosaddeq, Mohammad. *See* Mossadegh, Mohammad
Moscow Conference of Foreign Ministers, **3:** 740
Mossadegh, Mohammad, **4:** 1081, **1093-1095**
Motherland Party, Turkish, **4:** 1181
Mother Teresa. *See* Teresa, Mother
Mountbatten, Louis, **2:** 563; **4: 1096-1098**
Mubarak, Hosni, **4: 1099-1102**
Mugabe, Robert, **4: 1103-1106**; **5:** 1413
Muhammad V, **4: 1107-1108**
Muhammad, Elijah, **3:** 978
Muldoon, Robert, **4: 1109-1110**
Mulroney, Brian, **1:** 166, 250, 259, 305; **4: 1111-1114**
Munich Agreement, **1:** 120, 282; **2:** 464
Museveni, Yoweri Kaguta, **4: 1115-1117**
Mussolini, Benito, **2:** 380; **3:** 898; **4: 1118-1121**, 1241
Mutesa II, **4:** 1164
Muzorewa, Abel, **4:** 1104; **5:** 1414
Myrdal, Alva, **4: 1122-1123**
Myrdal, Gunnar, **4:** 1122

NAACP. *See* National Association for the Advancement of Colored People (NAACP)
NAFTA. *See* North American Free Trade Agreement (NAFTA)
Naguib, Muhammed, **5:** 1364
Nagy, Imre, **4: 1124-1127**
Nalundasan, Julio, **4:** 1029
Nasser, Gamal Abdel, **1:** 45; **2:** 465; **4: 1128-1131**; **5:** 1363, 1365
Nation of Islam, **3:** 978-979
National Aeronautics and Space Administration (NASA), **1:** 190
National Association for the Advancement of Colored People (NAACP), **2:** 439; **4:** 1036-1037

National Democratic Party (NDP), Rhodesian, **4:** 1103
National Front, French, **3:** 917
National government, British, **1:** 93
National Guard, Nicaraguan, **5:** 1423
National Health Service, British, **1:** 74
National Insurance Act of 1911, British, **1:** 56; **3:** 935
National Insurance Bill, Israeli, **4:** 1060
National Liberation Front (FLN), Algerian, **1:** 169
National Liberation Front (NLF), Vietnamese, **3:** 705
National Party of Australia, **2:** 525
National Party of New Zealand, **4:** 1110
National Resistance Movement (NRM), Ugandan, **4:** 1116
National Security Council (NSC), **2:** 613; **3:** 869; **4:** 1289
National Socialist Party, German. *See* Nazi Party
National Socialists, German. *See* Nazi Party
National union government, French, **4:** 1247
Nationalism, **2:** 516; **5:** 1637
Nationalist Party, Australian, **3:** 735
Nationalist Party, Chinese. *See* Kuomintang (KMT)
NATO. *See* North Atlantic Treaty Organization (NATO)
Nautilus, USS, **4:** 1309
Nazi Party, **2:** 581; **3:** 685, 691, 695; propaganda of, **2:** 571. *See also* Hitler, Adolf
Nazi-Soviet Nonaggression Pact, **4:** 1086, 1306
Négritude, **5:** 1391
Negro World, **2:** 550
Neguib, Muhammad, **4:** 1128
Nehru, Jawaharlal, **4: 1132-1135**
Neoconservative movement, **3:** 863
Netanyahu, Benjamin, **4: 1136-1139**
Netanyahu, Jonathan, **4:** 1136, 1212
New Deal, **3:** 732, 951; **4:** 1091, 1322; **5:** 1460
New Democratic Party, Canadian, **2:** 421
New Economic Policy (NEP), Soviet, **1:** 221; **3:** 913
Newfoundland, **5:** 1407, 1440
New Guinea, **2:** 362; Australia and, **2:** 362
New State, Portuguese, **5:** 1372
Newton, Huey, **3:** 857
Niagara Movement, **2:** 439
Nicholas II, **3:** 831; **4: 1140-1143**
Nigerian Civil War, **1:** 84
Night (Wiesel), **5:** 1571
Nimitz, Chester W., **3:** 854; **4: 1144-1145**

Index

Paul VI, **4: 1202-1204**
Pearce Commission, **5:** 1414
Pearl Harbor, Japanese bombing of, **3:** 738; **4:** 1144;
   5: 1590
Pearson, Lester B., **4: 1205-1207; 5:** 1499
Peng Dehuai, **4: 1208-1210**
P'eng Te-huai. *See* Peng Dehuai
People's Army of Vietnam (PAVN), **5:** 1540
People's Liberation Army (PLA), Chinese, **3:** 922;
   4: 1209; **5:** 1621
People's National Party (PNP) of Jamaica, **4:** 1018
People's Progressive Party (PPP), Guyanan, **3:** 766
People United to Save Humanity (PUSH), **3:** 762
Peres, Shimon, **4: 1211-1214**
Perestroika, **2:** 575; **5:** 1370
Pérez de Cuéllar, Javier, **2:** 531; **4: 1215-1217**
Permanent Court of International Justice, **3:** 886;
   4: 1330
Perón, Eva, **4: 1218-1220**, 1222
Perón, Juan, **4:** 1218, **1221-1224**
Peronism, **4:** 1222
Perot, H. Ross, **2:** 334; **4: 1225-1227**
Pershing, John J., **4: 1228-1230; 5:** 1539
Persian Gulf War, **1:** 235; **2:** 493; **3:** 749, **4:** 1261;
   Britain and, **3:** 972; Morocco and, **2:** 634. *See also*
   Desert Storm
Pétain, Philippe, **3:** 676, 898; **4: 1231-1233**
Petrov affair, **4:** 1066
Petty-Fitzmaurice, Henry, **4: 1234-1235**
Philippine insurgent movements, **4:** 1031
Philippine Insurrection, **1:** 19; **4:** 1228
Philippines, martial law in, **4:** 1030
Ping-pong diplomacy, **3:** 867
Pinochet Ugarte, Augusto, **1:** 32; **4: 1236-1239**
Pius XI, **4: 1240-1242**
Pius XII, **4: 1243-1245**
PLA. *See* People's Liberation Army (PLA), Chinese
PLO. *See* Palestine Liberation Organization (PLO)
Pluralistic government, **5:** 1631
Podgorny, Nikolai, **5:** 1365
Poher, Alain, **4:** 1255
Poincaré, Raymond, **4: 1246-1249**
Poindexter, John, **4:** 1289
Point Four, Truman foreign-policy plank, **1:** 8
Pol Pot, **4: 1250-1252**
Pompidou, Georges, **4: 1253-1255**
Poole, Elijah, **3:** 979
Popular Front, French, **1:** 154

Popular Front for the Liberation of Palestine (PFLP),
   3: 746
Powell, Adam Clayton, Jr., **4: 1256-1258**
Powell, Colin, **4: 1259-1262**
Powers, Gary Francis, **3:** 847
Prague Spring, **2:** 435, 638
Prats, Carlos, **1:** 32
Pratt, Hodgson, **1:** 90
Pravda, **1:** 221; **4:** 1085
Presidential system of government, **5:** 1633
President's Summit for America's Future, **2:** 579
Princeton University, **5:** 1586
Profumo scandal, **3:** 961; **5:** 1583
Progressive Conservative Party, Canadian, in
   Alberta, **3:** 874
Progressive movement, **1:** 214; **3:** 883
Prohibition, **2:** 627; **5:** 1409-1411, 1587
Pure Food and Drug Act, **3:** 937
Pu-yi, **3:** 693; **4: 1263-1265**

Qaddafi, Muammar al-, **4: 1266-1268**
Quebec independence referendum of 1995,
   1: 167; 299
Quebec separatist movement, **1:** 166; **3:** 920; **5:** 1500.
   See also Bloc Québécois; Parti Québécois
Quezon, Manuel, **3:** 951; **4: 1269-1271**
Quiwonkpa, Thomas, **2:** 412
Quotations from Chairman Mao Zedong, **4:** 1026

Rabin, Yitzhak, **4:** 1213, **1272-1274**
Rabuka, Sitiveni, **2:** 429
Raeder, Erich, **2:** 417
Rafsanjani, Hashemi, **4: 1275-1278**
Railroad strike of 1910, French, **1:** 201
Rainbow Coalition, **3:** 763
Rakosi, Matyas, **4:** 1127
Ramos, Fidel, **1:** 43; **4: 1279-1280**
Rankin, Jeannette, **4: 1281-1282**
Rapallo, Treaty of, **3:** 928
Rathenau, Walther, **5:** 1442
Rawlings, Jerry John, **4: 1283-1286**
Reagan, Ronald, **1:** 234; **2:** 612; **4: 1287-1290**
Rebellion of 1914, South African, **1:** 164
Red Army, **5:** 1497
Red Guards, **3:** 767, 931
Red Record, A (Wells-Barnett), **5:** 1564
Re-establishment and Employment Act, **2:** 510
Reform Party, Canadian, **4:** 1023